Contents

AUTO RACING . . . 1

BASEBALL . . . 31

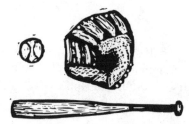

THE
HANDY
SPORTS
ANSWER
BOOK

ALSO FROM
VISIBLE INK PRESS

HANDY TITLES

The Handy Answer Book for Kids (and Parents)

The Handy Bug Answer Book

The Handy Dinosaur Answer Book

The Handy Geography Answer Book

The Handy History Answer Book

The Handy Ocean Answer Book

The Handy Physics Answer Book

The Handy Religion Answer Book

The Handy Space Answer Book

The Handy Weather Answer Book

SPORTS TITLES

The Unauthorized NASCAR® Fan Guide

THE

HANDY
SPORTS
ANSWER
BOOK™

Kevin Hillstrom
Laurie Hillstrom
Roger Matuz

VISIBLE
INK

Detroit

THE HANDY SPORTS ANSWER BOOK™

Visible Ink Press™
43311 Joy Road #414
Canton, MI 48187-2075

Visible Ink Press is a trademark of Visible Ink Press LLC.

Most Visible Ink Press books are available at special quantity discounts when purchased in bulk by corporations, organizations, or groups. Customized printings, special imprints, messages, and excerpts can be produced to meet your needs. For more information, contact Special Markets Director, Visible Ink Press, at www.visibleink.com.

Art Director: Michelle DiMercurio
Typesetting: The Graphix Group

ISBN 0-57859-075-2

HOCKEY . . . 275

HORSE RACING . . . 331

OLYMPICS . . . 349

SOCCER . . . 413

TENNIS . . . 437

Introduction

How do you define sports? Game, business, diversion, obsession, religion, reason for living, waste of time, pastime, economic boon, false hope? From the fan perspective, organized sports is a rich, diversified spectacle, bound historically by tradition, repetitious in its application of rules and order, but astoundingly fresh in drama and outcome. As the games that we watch and play keep expanding and changing, it becomes even more important for fans to understand the tradition, rules, records, and terminology, and be able to extract fun facts from the ever-growing trove of sports trivia. *The Handy Sports Answer Book* digs into this cornucopia of sports information and delivers more than 1,100 questions and answers pertaining to all the major sports.

Just as important as the history and rules, for most sports fans, are the great moments, the spectacular events or odd coincidences that give each sport a unique personality. We've tried to highlight the people, famous games, records, and achievements that have become, in some cases legendary, in others just a good story. *Handy Sports* also reports the little-known fact or interesting detail that goes along with the legend, hoping to make a good story better.

The world of organized sports has grown tremendously in the last few years. Sports, or at least sports programming, is everywhere. On television alone, six major cable networks are devoted to sports 24 hours a day, not to mention the broadcast networks and other cable ventures such as HBO Sports. With ESPN, ESPN 2, ESPNews, Fox Sports, Fox World, The Golf Channel, CNN-SI, Classic Sports, and the like, the television set has become a 24-hour sports telethon. And we haven't even touched on sports talk radio yet. There's probably more people getting paid to write and talk about sports now than people who played professionally 40 years ago.

With all this exposure, the established sports such as football and basketball are reaching wider and more diverse audiences. At the same time, emerging and so-called "minor" sports, such as volleyball and "Extreme" sports are gaining fans in leaps and bounds. Sports previously viewed as regional, such as hockey and NASCAR racing, are going national, as new teams in Nashville and Atlanta and new tracks in Texas and California attest. Soccer, long the favorite sport around the world, is finally gaining steam in the United States, especially at the youth level. Baseball has become global, with Japanese, Korean, and Australian imports joining the already established Latin American contingent in the Major Leagues. This new influx of talent has many observers hoping that Major League Baseball will follow the lead of the NBA and NHL and let its stars participate in the 2000 Summer Olympics in Sydney, Australia.

And with all that growth, what is perhaps the most exciting trend in sports? That's easy—the explosion in women's sports at all levels. Women's sports have blossomed in the last few years—two new professional basketball leagues have debuted, the U.S. women's hockey team won the gold in Nagano in thrilling fashion, the U.S. women's soccer team is the best in the world, and the list goes on and on. After years of being told that they couldn't play as well as the boys and that no one wanted to watch them play, women are asserting themselves all over the world of sports and refusing to take a backseat to anyone. *Handy Sports* covers everything from the WNBA to the LPGA and spends some time on that traditional venue for women athletes, The Olympics.

The Handy Sports Answer Book should deepen the knowledge of both the new and experienced sports fan. It provides answers to those questions you may have thought of while watching a game on TV but didn't have anyone to ask. You may know what a "caddie" or a "bogey" is, but did you ever wonder where those terms originated? Just what is a "nickel defense," and when (or why) should it be used? What is the highest scoring game in World Cup history? Who introduced the jump shot? Who invented the slap shot? How many players have won the Grand Slam in tennis? Many of the questions found in this book are ones we've asked ourselves (or others) at some point. Why *do* they call it a bullpen? How did the game of volleyball come about? Where is the remote?

Acknowledgments

This book is the result of the hard work and talent of three groups of people: Visible Ink Press, Manitou Wordworks, Inc., and Northern Lights Writers Group. At Manitou, Roger Matuz would like to thank Dean Dauphinais, Jay Dooley, Dan Fricker, Peter Gareffa, Allison Jones, Kelly Judsen, Ralph Primo, Mary Ruby, Les Stone, and Bill Szumanski, as well as their respective sports connections, all of whom teamed with him to compile this book. They executed the game plan, challenged each other, and completed what they set out to do; if you find yourself returning to this source time and again, they will have achieved their goal.

Kevin and Laurie Hillstrom of Northern Lights would like to thank contributors Neil Schlager, Matt Trotsky, and Tim Thomas, who provided their time and expertise where it was most needed. They would also like to thank Visible Ink Press editors Jim Craddock and Brad Morgan for their help on this project.

Also at Visible Ink, Christa Brelin provided wise counsel and insight throughout the process. Michelle DiMercurio and Cindy Baldwin contributed their usual outstanding efforts on the page and cover designs. Sarah Chesney handled photo acquisition, and Randy Bassett, Robert Duncan, and Pam Reed tackled the imaging process. And of course, Marco Di Vita at the Graphix Group typeset this tome in record time. We can't forget the people who brought the project into being; Martin Connors, Julia Furtaw, Roger Janecke, and Brian St. Germain.

Photo Credits

Wayne Gretzky and Stanley Cup courtesy of the Hockey Hall of Fame.

Bobby Orr, Satchel Paige. Arnold Palmer, and Pele courtesy of Archive Photos, Inc.

Wilt Chamberlain/Bill Russell, and Julius Erving courtesy of Corbis Corporation.

Joe Dimaggio, Elizabeth I, Vince Lombardi, Babe Ruth, and John L. Sullivan courtesy of the Library of Congress

The early football team courtesy of the National Archives and Records Administration.

The photos of the Chicago White Sox and Patrick Ewing (head shot) are in the public domain.

NASCAR pit stop courtesy W. Dennis Winn.

Lee Petty/Richard Petty courtesy Al Pearce.

All others courtesy of AP/Wide World Photos.

AUTO RACING

HISTORY

What two auto racing "firsts" occurred during the 1895 Paris to Bordeaux race?

The first racing fatality—a dog hit by a Panhard car—and domination by gasoline-powered cars (propelled by Daimler engines) occurred during that 1895 race. Gasoline-powered engines finished in the first four spots, effectively ending the superiority of electric-powered automobile engines.

When was the first long-distance auto race held in the United States, and why was it stopped?

The Automobile Club of America organized the first long distance race—500 miles, from Cleveland to New York—in 1901. News that President William McKinley had been assassinated led to the race being canceled as the leaders reached Buffalo, New York. McKinley, incidentally, had been the first American president to ride in an automobile.

Which legendary auto racer was the first to break the one-minute mile in a gasoline-powered vehicle?

Barney Oldfield reached the speed of 64 mph in 1903 in a car called the 999 built by Henry Ford. The next year, Louis E. Rigolly, a Frenchman driving a Gabron-Brille, became the first to exceed 100 mph when he reached a top speed of 103 in Ostend, Belgium. Back in April 1899, Belgian driver Camille Jenatzy ran an electric car at 65.79 mph.

1

When was the first major organized automobile race in the United States, and what made it important?

The first widely publicized auto race in the United States occurred on Thanksgiving Day in 1895 and was organized by the *Times Herald* newspaper of Chicago. The race was won by an American vehicle made by Charles and Frank Duryea, who in 1896 would be credited as the first American manufacturers of gasoline-powered automobiles. The Duryea car finished ahead of a Benz, the most noted carmaker in the world at the time, further inspiring many American tinkerers, including Henry Ford, Ransom Olds, and others, to continue their experiments with the new-fangled horseless carriage.

The first American race was preceded in early November 1895 by a reliability demonstration that ran from Chicago to Waukegan, Illinois, and back (92 miles). The official race of 52 miles on Thanksgiving Day was won with an average speed of 5.1 miles per hour.

What were the first **American car and driver to win an international auto racing event**?

George Robertson drove a 16.2 liter Locomobile to victory in the 1908 Vanderbilt Cup, held on Long Island, New York. He posted an average speed of 64.3 miles per hour over the 258 mile course.

What was a **Le Mans start**?

In the days before race car drivers were strapped into their machines with a sophisticated system of seatbelts, some automobile races began with a foot race. The cars would be lined up in their qualifying order along one side of the track, and the drivers would be lined up along the other side facing their cars. When the starter's gun sounded, the drivers would sprint across the track to their vehicles, climb in, start the motor, and peel away to begin the race. The Le Mans start was the traditional opening for the classic 24-hour French sports car race at Le Mans from its beginnings in 1923 until safety concerns forced a change in 1969. It was also used in many other auto races around the world.

What is the history of the **Pikes Peak hill-climb event**?

A treacherous dirt road winds through 154 turns in 12.5 miles on its way to the top of 14,110-foot Pikes Peak in Colorado's Rocky Mountains. It was inevitable that men and machines would race to see who could climb the hill the fastest. The first organized event took place in 1916 and was won by Rea Lentz in an aircraft-engined Romano Special. Racing's famous Unser family—who lived at the base of the mountain in Colorado Springs before moving to Albuquerque, New Mexico—claimed more than half of the early Pikes Peak titles.

Why was the **24-hour race at Daytona canceled** in 1974?

Because the oil-producing countries of the Middle East had raised prices dramatically, leading to a national energy crisis. Race officials decided that it wouldn't look good to have a bunch of cars zooming around a track at 100 miles per hour for 24 hours when many Americans were forced to wait in line at the gas pumps. When the race resumed in 1975, five-time winner Hurley Haywood and four-time winner Peter Gregg teamed up to win it for the second time in three years in a Porsche Carrera.

GENERAL

What are the **different kinds of auto racing**?

Auto races are held on three types of courses: the oval track, which can be dirt, asphalt, or concrete, can range in length from .16 to 2.5 miles, and can be banked (high-banked tracks are called superspeedways); road courses, which follow twisting routes on city streets or courses that duplicate conditions of country roads; and the straight-line course—a strip of asphalt or concrete used for drag racing.

Major types of oval track racing include Indy Car, Stock Car, Dirt-Track, Sprint Car, Midget-car, and Sports Car racing; Formula racing (usually called Grand Prix races), Rallying, and Off-Road races are held on road courses; and Drag Racing and other sprint races are held on straight-line courses.

What is the difference between **Formula racing and Indy racing**?

Formula racing is strictly regulated by an international governing body, Fédération International de l'Automobile (FIA; International Automobile Federation), which sets technical regulations for building, maintaining, and racing many different classes of cars. Formula One (F1) vehicles are single-seat racing cars designed to allow the flow of air over and under the car to create a downward force that holds them close to the ground despite high speeds. Slower and less sophisticated single-seat racing cars

3

What is a chicane?

The dictionary would tell you that it's a form of trickery or deceit. In road racing, it's a tight bend or S-curve in an otherwise straight part of the course that can sometimes trick drivers. Chicanes were originally added to racing circuits as a form of handicapping. The turns slowed down larger, faster cars but allowed smaller cars to pass through relatively easily. Chicanes were introduced in some European circuits to favor local, better-handling cars over foreign, better-powered cars. Other tracks added chicanes for the benefit of spectators. A more recent development in racing circuit design has involved using chicanes to improve safety. Chicanes are placed just before difficult or dangerous curves in order to slow the cars down on their approach.

compete in such categories as Formula Two (F2), Formula Three (F3), Formula Atlantic, Formula Renault, and Formula Ford.

These cars are run on Grand Prix circuits, a term that refers to the principal F1 auto race in a nation; in the United States, however, the term is used by several cities hosting annual Formula One races. The World Championship of Drivers was established in 1950 to honor the winner in points from the various F1 races each year.

Indy Car Racing developed with the establishment in 1911 of the Indianapolis 500 and has since become a circuit of races with the winner determined by a points-per-finish system. Indy cars are similar to F1 cars but were originally designed to only turn left since they were raced on oval tracks, while F1 cars could turn in either direction for racing on road courses. F1 cars also required more efficient braking systems because Grand Prix tracks have corners and a variety of turns. F1 designs began influencing Indy cars during the 1960s and 1970s, and since the 1980s, Indy car races have been held on ovals and road courses. Indy car circuit racing is governed by IndyCar, known from its formation in 1979 until 1992 as Championship Auto Racing Teams (CART).

What distinguishes the other kinds of **automobile racing**?

Drag Racing features two cars racing on a straight-line course—the drag strip. Drag racing originated with hot rods, modified for improved acceleration, first built in southern California in the late 1930s. The first drag racing organization, the Southern California Timing Association (SCTA), was formed in 1937. The first paved strips for drag racing were runways at air bases and airports, and the first formal drag strip was opened in Goleta, California, in 1948.

The Rally is a test of endurance and speed over great distances and in tougher conditions than those of a closed course. Professional international rally drivers and teams use racing cars to negotiate routes in deserts and other rough terrain in Africa, Australia, and Europe; the annual Monte Carlo Rally, begun in 1911, is the most famous race of this kind. Each year the Monte Carlo rally begins in a different European city and winds down to Monte Carlo, Monaco. FIA is a major sanctioning body in international rallying.

Rallying in the United States generally features amateur drivers using tuned production vehicles on streets and country road routes. Competitors try to reach checkpoints at specified times while maintaining a speed set by the race's organizers (penalties for arriving early or late help ensure fairness).

Off-Road Racing is run on rudimentary trails, with major events being the Baja 500 and the Mexican 1000. Dirt-track racing, which originally served as a means for Indy car training, has evolved from use of miniature Indy cars to other specific forms.

What do the various **flags** mean in auto racing?

Flags are used to alert race car drivers to different conditions on the course. As all fans know, a green flag is used to start the race. When green is displayed during a race, it simply means that the track is clear and all systems are go. A yellow flag means that some sort of hazardous situation exists—for example, there may have been an accident. When drivers see a yellow flag, they must reduce their speed and are no longer allowed to pass. In most cases, a pace car will pull onto the course to lead the field at a safe speed until the track is cleared. Many drivers will try to schedule their pitstops during yellow flag laps because they do not lose as much ground on the slow-traveling field. A red flag tells drivers that an extreme emergency situation exists and they should stop immediately. This usually occurs when an accident blocks the course or when a race must be stopped due to rain. Pit crews are not allowed to do any work on the cars during a red flag stoppage. Another flag you might see is a black flag. This flag is usually used to alert drivers to possible mechanical problems, but sometimes it is thrown to penalize a driver error, such as passing under a yellow flag. A driver who receives a black flag is required to report to the pits immediately to discuss the situation with race officials. Ignoring a black flag can result in disqualification. A white flag usually means that the leaders are starting the last lap of a race, although it can also mean that the pace car or an emergency vehicle is on the track. A blue flag with a diagonal yellow stripe is typically shown to slow-moving cars to alert them that faster traffic is approaching. The car receiving the flag is supposed to move aside and allow the faster cars to pass. Finally, a checkered flag means that the lead car has completed the required number of laps and the race is over.

Why do they call the service area on racetracks the **pits**?

The first service areas actually *were* pits—two trenches separated by a counter beside the track where crews could quickly service race cars. The first pits were used in a Grand Prix race in Dieppe, France, in 1908.

What is a **spotter**?

In addition to the crew in the paddock and the pits, every racing team has at least one member sitting high in the grandstands to act as a spotter. This person is in constant radio contact with the driver and is able to alert him to accidents, debris, or other situations on the track. The spotter also talks to the crew in the pits to let them know when the driver is coming in for a pitstop.

What sort of **protection** do race car drivers have in the event of a crash or a fire?

All fans are familiar with the terrifying sight of a race car flying through the air, tumbling end over end, and turning into a hunk of scrap metal on the track. The amazing thing is that, in many cases, this happens without causing the driver any major injuries. The first line of protection for drivers in case of a crash is the roll cage—a frame of metal tubing that completely encloses the driver compartment and reinforces the structure of the car. Drivers are secured in a form-fitting aluminum seat by heavy nylon seatbelts that come over their shoulders, around their waist, and between their legs. They also wear helmets to dissipate the force of any impact to the head. There are a number of other precautions that racers take to protect themselves from fire. They wear a full-length drivers' suit made of flame resistant material, along with fire-retardant gloves, shoes, and hood. The fuel on board most race cars these days is contained in a "fuel cell"—a flexible fuel tank constructed with layers of Kevlar, foam, and steel—which is designed to withstand impacts without exploding. Finally, the cars are equipped with an internal fire extinguisher system in case of emergency.

What does it really mean when a race announcer says that cars are **drafting** each other?

When you see two or more cars running nose-to-tail at high speeds, there's a good chance the drivers are taking advantage of an aerodynamic principle known as the slipstream or draft. The first car in line cuts through the air, reducing the wind resistance encountered by the cars behind it. In this way, two or more cars running together are able to travel at faster speeds than a single car running alone. Drafting can also give drivers who are not at the head of the line an advantage over the lead driver. When they pull out from behind their opponent's bumper and break the draft, their own added momentum—coupled with the increased drag on the lead car—can enable them to "slingshot" past the leader. For this reason, many top drivers prefer to be a close second or third—rather than the leader—near the end of a race.

What are **camber and toe**?

Camber and toe both describe the degree of tilt displayed by the wheels on a race car. If you were to look at a car from the front, the tires might be slanted inward from vertical at the top (negative camber) or outward at the top (positive camber). Toe is a similar concept. A car with toe-in would look pigeon-toed from the front, as the tires would point slightly toward each other. Toe-out is the opposite—the tires would splay outwards from each other. Camber and toe can be adjusted to fine tune the handling of a car.

What is the difference between **supercharging and turbocharging**?

A supercharged engine uses a compressor to raise the air pressure inside the cylinders, thus allowing more fuel to be burned in each cycle and increasing the engine's power output. A turbocharged engine uses the same basic technology, except that it makes use of the exhaust gases from the engine to drive the system. The exhaust gases are fed into an impeller turbine, which is then connected to a supercharger. The flow of exhaust drives the turbine, the turbine drives the supercharger, the supercharger increases the rate of combustion in the engine, the engine produces greater power as well as more exhaust gases, and the cycle repeats itself. Both types of systems have been used extensively in auto racing. In fact, technological developments made for racing efforts led to the adoption of the technology on many passenger vehicles.

FORMULA ONE

Who was the **winningest all-time Formula One driver**?

Frenchman Alain Prost claimed 51 victories on the Formula One circuit between 1980 and 1993, as well as 35 second-place and 20 third-place finishes. He also won four world driving championships during that time—in 1985, 1986, 1989, and 1993—second only to Argentinean Juan Manuel Fangio's five world titles.

How many **Americans have won the Formula One World Drivers' Championship**?

Two. Well-known endurance racer Phil Hill claimed the title in a Ferrari in 1961, and Mario Andretti won it in 1978 in a black John Player Special Lotus.

Who was the only **second-generation Formula One world champion**?

Damon Hill, who won the prestigious World Drivers' Championship in 1996. His father, Graham Hill, was a two-time Formula One champion, claiming the title in

7

Alain Prost accumulated 51 career Formula One victories and four world driving championships in his career.

1962 and 1968. The elder Hill also won the technically demanding Grand Prix of Monaco five times.

What problem did **Jackie Stewart** overcome to become a three-time Formula One World Champion?

As a child growing up in Scotland, Stewart was characterized as "thick" by his teachers. Despite his intelligence, he always had trouble in school and earned low marks. It was only years later, when he retired from racing and had a child of his own, that doctors were able to pinpoint the problem—Stewart, like his young son, suffered from dyslexia. This condition interferes with the way images that are seen with the eyes are processed by the brain. Numbers and letters are often transposed or flipped backwards or upside-down, making it very difficult for sufferers without special training to learn to read.

How many drivers have **won both the Formula One World Championship and the Indy Car series championship**?

Just four. Mario Andretti won four Indy Car titles, in 1965, 1966, 1969, and 1984. In between the last two championships, he captured the Formula One title in 1978. Emerson Fittipaldi, affectionately known as "Emmo," took the Formula One driving title in 1972 and 1974, then claimed the Indy Car championship in 1989. Nigel Mansell was the Formula One champion in 1992, then prevailed on the Indy Car circuit the following year. Most recently, 1995 Indy Car champion Jacques Villeneuve squeaked out a Formula One title in 1997. Michael Schumacher, the Formula One world champion in 1994 and 1995, was leading Villeneuve in the standings by one point going into the final race, the European Grand Prix. After the two drivers bumped on lap 48, Schumacher failed to finish and Villeneuve took third, thus scoring enough points to take the championship 81–78.

9

Jackie Stewart overcame dyslexia to become one of the most successful drivers in Formula One racing.

> ## What was notable about
> ## Greg Moore's victory in the 1997 Detroit Grand Prix?
>
> **E**ven Moore would have to admit that he lucked out in this race. The first and second place drivers, teammates Mauricio Gugelmin and Mark Blundell, both ran out of gas on the last lap. This allowed Moore to pass them and claim the victory.

INDY CARS

GENERAL

What was the **closest finish ever in Indy Car racing**?

This very old record belongs to Ralph DePalma, who beat Roscoe Sarles by .02 seconds in the Beverly Hills 25 in April 1921. The tightest 500-mile race was the 1992 Indianapolis 500, in which Al Unser, Jr. beat Scott Goodyear to the line by an amazing .043 seconds. "I knew he didn't get past me when we hit the bricks," Unser recalled. "It was very exciting and exhilarating." Another memorable close finish came during the Portland 200 in June 1986, when Mario Andretti defeated his son Michael by .07 seconds—the smallest margin of victory ever in an Indy Car road race.

Which driver **won an Indianapolis 500, a Daytona 500, the 12 Hours of Sebring, a Formula One World Championship, and four USAC Indy Car championships**?

Mario Andretti, who first began racing competitively during the late-1950s in a 1948 Hudson he and his brother, Aldo, adapted for racing, is among racing's most versatile drivers. His family, which had been interred in a displaced person's camp during World War II in Italy, had emigrated to the United States in 1955. Since their father forbade the brothers to race, Mario and Aldo tinkered and raced secretly but were exposed when Aldo was injured in a crash. Mario kept racing, against his father's wishes; he himself proved a more encouraging father when it came to auto racing, considering the successes of his race driver sons, Michael, Jeff, and John. Mario was USAC Champion and Rookie of the Year in 1965. He finished third at Indy that year but won the race in 1967, and two years later he won at Daytona.

11

Indianapolis 500

What is the **largest sporting venue** in the United States?

The Indianapolis Motor Speedway in Indianapolis, IN, which has room for more than 300,000 fans. For years, the Indianapolis 500 was the main attraction at the track, but in 1994, NASCAR brought its stock cars to the historic site and ran the inaugural Brickyard 400, which was won by Jeff Gordon.

When did Indianapolis Motor Speedway open, and why is it dubbed **"the Brickyard**?"

Indianapolis was opened in 1909 as a testing ground. The oval track surface was laid with 3,200,000 bricks. The first Indianapolis 500 was run in 1911; even though the race is run on one day, testing, practice, and qualifying continue to occur over a three-week period preceding the race.

How come many of my favorite drivers haven't raced in the **Indianapolis 500** the past few years?

In a word, politics. The governing body of Indy Car racing has changed several times since the American Automobile Association (AAA) sponsored the first championship race in 1909. The United States Auto Racing Club (USAC) took over the series in 1956, and then was replaced by Championship Auto Racing Teams (CART) in 1979. CART changed its name to IndyCar in 1992. CART/IndyCar is the governing body of the PPG Indy Car World Series, which features most of the best-known drivers, like Al Unser, Jr., Michael Andretti, and Alex Zanardi. In 1996, the Indy Racing League (IRL) was formed, which suddenly created a second, all-oval Indy Car racing series populated by lesser-known drivers. Tony George—the president of the Indianapolis Motor Speedway, where the Indianapolis 500 is held—was one of the founders of the IRL. As a result, the Indianapolis 500 was made the final event in the IRL series. The qualifying rules for the Indy 500 were changed to favor participants in the IRL series. The former CART responded to this by organizing a boycott of the Indianapolis 500. Most of its drivers joined the protest, preferring to race in the sanctioned events of the PPG Indy Car series. So while the new IRL provides opportunities for more drivers, few of the big-name drivers have appeared in the Indy 500 the past few years. Attendance and fan interest has declined significantly as a result. "What made the Indianapolis 500 so great is what it meant to the fans," Unser noted. "They are the ones who are losing out because the best drivers in the world are not competing in the Indy 500."

What driver won the Indianapolis 500 in his first try, but was nevertheless passed over for Rookie of the Year honors?

Two-time Formula One World Champion (1962 and 1968) Graham Hill won at Indy in his first attempt in 1966. But the Rookie of the Year award, which is voted on by a panel of auto racing journalists, was presented to another Formula One driver from the United Kingdom—Jackie Stewart. Stewart ran a great race and was leading with ten laps to go, but then lost oil pressure and ended up finishing sixth.

How many drivers have **won the Indianapolis 500 two years in a row**?

Just four racers have notched consecutive victories at Indianapolis, beginning with Wilbur Shaw in 1939 and 1940 (he had also appeared in the winners' circle in 1937). Mauri Rose claimed his only two Indianapolis 500 victories in 1947 and 1948, as did Bill Vukovich in 1953 and 1954. Most recently, Al Unser won the race in consecutive years in 1970 and 1971. Unser went on to claim the prize two more times, in 1978 and 1987.

Who was the first **four-time winner** of the Indianapolis 500?

Three drivers have won the race four times: A.J. Foyt, Jr., Al Unser, and Rick Mears, with Foyt the first to win four times. Foyt also won two Daytona 500s, the 24 Hours of LeMans, the 24 Hours of Daytona, and the 12 Hours of Sebring, as well as races on the dirt and midget circuits. Foyt's feats were encouraged by his father, a garage owner and racer of midget cars who gave his son an engine-equipped red racer at about the time young Foyt learned to walk. After years of experience racing around the yard, Foyt, at age five, competed against an established midget car driver in a three lap exhibition and won.

To signal the **start of the Indianapolis 500**, the announcer traditionally says, "Gentlemen, start your engines." How did this change in 1977?

That year, Janet Guthrie became the first woman ever to compete in the race. In recognition of her presence in the field, the owner of the Indianapolis Motor Speedway made the historic call, "In company with the first lady ever to qualify at Indianapolis—gentlemen, start your engines." In subsequent years, whenever a woman was included in the field, the traditional announcement was changed to "Drivers, start your engines." Unfortunately, Guthrie only managed to complete 27 laps in that first race due to mechanical problems, but she came back the following year to finish ninth

13

Janet Guthrie was the first woman to race in the Indianapolis 500. She also raced in a number of NASCAR events.

despite a badly broken wrist. Her appearances in "the greatest spectacle in racing" sparked the interest of many young girls who have since gone on to compete in auto racing at various levels.

What was unusual about the **1992 Indianapolis 500 Rookie of the Year**?

The driver who earned this honor was female. Lyn St. James became the second woman ever to race in the Indianapolis 500 that year, and she finished a respectable 11th. Not surprisingly, St. James owns a number of records for female racers. For example, she was the first woman ever to win a professional road race and the first woman to exceed 200 miles per hour on an oval track.

Who was **Evelyn Cornwall**, and what does she have to do with auto racing?

Evelyn Cornwall was the name given at birth to top woman road racer Lyn St. James. She changed her name in the late 1970s, after achieving some success as an amateur and deciding to become a professional race car driver. Knowing that she would need to attract sponsors for her racing effort, she adopted the last name of actress Susan St. James and shortened her own first name to Lyn in order to sound more professional.

Who was the **first African-American driver** ever to compete in the Indianapolis 500?

Willy T. Ribbs made his way up through the racing ranks to qualify for the big race in 1991, thus becoming the first African-American driver to be included in the field. Unfortunately, he failed to finish the race.

Who is the only driver to run in the **Indianapolis 500 and a Winston Cup stock car race on the same day**?

In May 1994 John Andretti, nephew of racing legend Mario Andretti, finished 10th at the Indianapolis 500. Not content with running just one race that day, Andretti hopped in a waiting helicopter and flew to Charlotte, North Carolina, where he suited up for the Coca-Cola 600. His long day had an early finish when he crashed and ended up 36th at Charlotte.

15

NASCAR

GENERAL

When was the **first NASCAR race** held?

Up until 1948, stock car racing was full of uncertainty: Would the next race be held? Would the track owner be able to afford to pay the winning driver? Would there be enough drivers to hold a race? With no governing body, there was chaos. Into that disorganized scene stepped Bill France, Sr., who founded the organization known as the National Association of Stock Car Auto Racing in late 1947. France had some success running races in 1948 with what were known as Modified cars, but on June 19, 1949, he hit paydirt when he held a race in Charlotte, NC, for fresh-off-the-showroom-floor "stock" cars. Crowds showed up in record numbers to watch Jim Roper claim victory in that race. The Strictly Stock races, as they were known, evolved into the Grand National series and then into today's wildly popular Winston Cup circuit.

What are the **Crown Jewels of NASCAR racing**?

The Daytona 500, Winston Select 500, Coca-Cola 600, and the Mountain Dew Southern 500. Between 1985 and 1997, R.J. Reynold's Winston brand cigarettes offered drivers a shot at the Winston Million—a $1 million bonus that would be paid to any driver who could win three of the big four races in a single year. It didn't take long for someone to claim the prize—Bill Elliott won the Daytona, Winston, and Southern races the very first year. Only Jeff Gordon was able to repeat the feat in 1997 before Winston changed the format of the bonus offer. Before the Winston Million, only two other men had won three of the races in a single year: Lee Roy Yarborough in 1969 and David Pearson in 1976. The Daytona 500 has been run since 1959, with Richard Petty winning seven times and Cale Yarborough four times; the Winston Select 500 has been run since 1970, with four drivers winning the race three times; the Cocal Cola 500 has been run since 1960, with Darrell Waltrip finding Victory Lane five times; and the Southern 500 has been run since 1950, with Cale Yarborough winning five times.

What are some of the **rules** that keep NASCAR racing so competitive?

The tight, bumper-to-bumper racing that makes NASCAR so popular is due in large part to rules that ensure that cars are virtually the same. They all have a maximum wheelbase of 110 inches and a maximum height of 51 inches. In fact, only six body types have been approved for competition—the Chevrolet Monte Carlo, Ford Taurus (which recently replaced the Thunderbird), Pontiac Grand Prix, Oldsmobile Cutlass Supreme, Buick Regal, and Mercury Cougar. The majority of teams use the Monte Carlo, most others use the Taurus, and a few use the Grand Prix. All of the cars feature 358 cubic inch V-8 engines fitted with Holley carburetors. All run on 108-octane Unocal gasoline and use the same size wheels and four-wheel disc brakes. NASCAR rules also limit the use of high technology, such as the computer-controlled devices found in Formula One cars, so that the teams with the most money don't have too big an advantage. As a result, there are probably 20 different teams capable of winning any given race. "NASCAR's rules are so stringent that any of the technology that is out there today is stuff we're not allowed to use," driver Rusty Wallace told Richard Huff in *The Insider's Guide to Stock Car Racing*. "We're being restrained. But if it controls the cost of the cars and the action that NASCAR puts on, I think everybody would have to say it's a step above everything."

Jeff Gordon won ten races in 1996 compared to Terry Labonte's two, but Labonte won the **Winston Cup championship**. How come?

The NASCAR championship is based on a point system that rewards consistency over the entire season more than victories in individual events. The Winston Cup point system, which was developed by Bob Latford and instituted in 1975, has come under some criticism from participants and fans alike. Here's how it works: the winner of a race receives 175 points, the second place finisher receives 170, and so on counting down by five to the sixth place finisher, who receives 150. The sixth through eleventh place finishers are only separated by four points, so that seventh place is worth 146, eighth is worth 142, and so on to eleventh, which receives 130. From eleventh place on down to fortieth, each finisher receives three fewer points than the previous one, ending at 43 points for fortieth place. To complicate matters, drivers also receive five points for every race lap they lead, plus five bonus points for leading more laps in a race than any other competitor. These bonus points were originally intended to provide incentive for drivers to race hard, even if they did not end up winning. Today, the point system affects the strategy of leading teams—which often make a greater effort to lead races and keep cars in races longer—as well as the season standings.

17

A good pitstop requires precision timing from every crew member.

What goes into a **good pitstop**?

In NASCAR, the difference between first and second place is often less than a tenth of a second. With that in mind, a driver's crew must get him in and out of the pit stops as soon as possible. A good pitstop today is one that is completed in less than 20 seconds—this includes a full tank of gas and four fresh tires. A pitstop works something like this:

When the driver pulls in, three men sprint around to the right (passenger) side of the car. One man lifts the car with a pneumatic jack, while the other two loosen the lug nuts, receive fresh tires from the tire carriers, and put the new tires in place. Sprinting, the three men shift to the left side of the car and repeat the procedure. While that is happening, the gas man is responsible for filling the gas tank using two 11-gallon dump cans that use aviation-style refueling nozzles. Finally, one man is responsible for cleaning the windshield and grill, and another crew member makes sure the driver gets a drink of water. Vroom! Less than 20 seconds, and the driver is back on the track.

How much does it **cost** to become involved in Winston Cup racing?

Experts estimate that it takes a minimum of $4 million per year to run among the top 15 teams on the NASCAR circuit. Much of this money goes toward paying employees—the average race mechanic makes $41,000 per year in salary, plus benefits, and many teams have upwards of 40 people on the payroll. It also costs between $80,000 and $150,000 to prepare for, enter, and travel to each event. Each car costs $100,000, and many teams keep ten cars on hand at a time. Tires alone can cost more than half a million dollars per year. On the plus side, NASCAR teams have the potential to make a great deal of money as well. Top sponsors generally pay between $3 and $6 million per year to display their name prominently on a car. Teams also claim a percentage of the prize money earned by drivers, and a percentage of the income from merchandise and collectible sales. It's also worth noting that—thanks to the rules limiting the use of technology—NASCAR is actually a relatively inexpensive form of pro racing. Formula One teams have an average annual budget of about $50 million.

DRIVERS AND OWNERS

Who are some of the **most successful NASCAR team owners**?

If you measure success in terms of money earned, then Rick Hendrick—whose Hendrick Motorsports team features drivers Terry Labonte, Jeff Gordon, and Ricky Craven—tops the field with $35.6 million. Of course, this sum does not seem as large when it is compared to the team's annual operating budget of $29 million. Richard Childress ($27.5 million), Junior Johnson ($22.1 million), Jack Roush ($16 million), and Robert Yates ($13.8 million) round out the top five earning NASCAR owners as of 1996. If you measure success in number of wins, then Richard Petty's Petty Enterprises holds the title with 269 victories. Junior Johnson is a distant second with 139.

Who **won the most races** in a single NASCAR season?

In 1967, Richard Petty was already known as "The King" and was widely considered to be one of the top stock car drivers in the country. That season, however, he made it clear that he was the unquestioned No. 1 driver when he won 27 of the 48 races he started, finishing in the top-five 11 other times and the top-10 once. To top all that off, Petty is also considered to be one of the nicest people in the world of sports. His easygoing manner and great sense of humor made him a fan favorite and helped turn NASCAR into the huge sport that it is today.

Just how many **major NASCAR records does Richard Petty own**?

Just about all of them. Not only did The King have one of the longest careers, but he had the most successful. Among the major career records Petty holds are: career victories (200), races started (1,164), top-5 finishes (555), top-10 finishes (712), poles (126), laps completed (307,836), laps led (52,194), races led (599), consecutive races won (10), consecutive years racing (35), and performance points (3,645). He has also won a record-tying seven Grand National/Winston Cup championships in his career (tied with Dale Earnhardt), and on most of the records, no one else is even close— David Pearson is second in career victories with 105, for example.

When you think of NASCAR, you think of Richard Petty. He owns twelve career records, and he was named NASCAR's most popular driver nine times during his career.

What young NASCAR star racked up **25 wins** the fastest?

This is one of the few records not held by Richard Petty. NASCAR's 1993 Rookie of the Year, Jeff Gordon, won his 25th career race at the Pocono 500 on June 6, 1997—in just his 137th start. The next fastest to reach the 25-win milestone was Darrell Waltrip, who needed 198 starts. Gordon owns many of NASCAR's "youngest" records. In 1997, he became the youngest driver ever to win the Daytona 500 at 25 years, 196 days.

Who had one of the most **impressive comebacks in NASCAR** history?

Among the top contenders for this title would have to be Ernie Irvan. He nearly died from head injuries suffered in a terrible crash at Michigan International Speedway in 1994, then came back to win the Miller 400 there in 1997.

Who is the **youngest man to win the Winston Cup** championship?

Jeff Gordon, the "Rainbow Warrior," was 24 when he claimed his first Winston Cup title in 1995. Gordon, who is loved by many fans and probably hated by just as many, won his second title in 1997.

NASCAR is full of father-son teams and other family connections. Who are some of the most **successful families in stock car racing**?

NASCAR has always seemed to draw its share of fathers and sons, brothers and cousins, nephews and uncles, and so on. One of the earliest families to take the track by storm was the Flocks—brothers Tim, Fonty, and Bob Flock all raced in the 1950s and early '60s. The Flocks were overshadowed, however, by the man who would become the patriarch of the greatest racing family of all-time—Lee Petty. Lee won his first race in 1949 and went on to win 53 more before he called it quits in the 1960s. By that time, he was racing side-by-side with son Richard, who of course went on to set the NASCAR record of 200 career victories. The latest addition to the Petty family album is Richard's son Kyle, who has won eight Winston Cup races and is still going strong today.

Ernie Irvan came back from a horrific 1994 crash at Michigan International Speedway to win the 1997 Miller 400 on that very same track.

Other leading families include the Allisons—brothers Bobby and Donnie, and Bobby's sons Clifford and Davey, both of whom were tragically killed while in their prime; the Jarretts, father Ned and son Dale, who created a special moment in NASCAR history when Ned was the television color commentator at the Daytona 500 in 1993 when Dale took the checkered flag; Ralph Earnhardt and son Dale; Buck Baker and son Buddy; brothers Brett, Todd, and Geoff Bodine; brothers Rusty and Kenny Wallace; brothers Michael and Darrell Waltrip; brothers Bobby and Terry Labonte; Mario Andretti and nephew John; and brothers Jeff, Mark, and David Green.

Lee Petty drapes his arm around his son Richard's shoulder. Together, the two of them won 254 races to form the greatest father-son combination in racing history.

Who was the **first woman ever to win** a major NASCAR race?

Shawna Robinson claimed this honor in 1988, when she won the AC Delco 100 in Asheville, North Carolina, driving in the Dash division. Later that year, she was named Most Popular Driver in her division, and her winning Pontiac Sunbird was placed in the International Motorsports Hall of Fame.

Who was the **first woman ever to qualify for the pole position** in a NASCAR Grand National race?

Shawna Robinson achieved this feat in 1994, when she set a new track record lap speed of 174.330 miles per hour in qualifying for the Busch Light 300 in Atlanta, Georgia. But her hopes of becoming the first woman to win on the Grand National circuit were dashed on the very first lap. Fellow driver Mike Wallace hit her car from the side, causing her to hit another car. Although her car suffered serious damage in the crash, Robinson got back into the race and managed to complete 63 laps before a bad radiator ended her day. Some other racers suggested that Wallace hit her intentionally, but there was no way to know for sure. Still, Robinson was very disappointed with the outcome of the race. "How many fans were taking bets, 'Is the girl going to crash on the first lap?'" she said in *Sports Illustrated*. "By starting on the pole and racing well, I hoped I could have changed those attitudes."

23

Who was the first woman to race in a NASCAR race?

While Janet Guthrie gained fame and notoriety when she competed on the Winston Cup circuit in the late 1970s and early '80s, she was far from the first woman to strap herself behind the wheel of a stock car. In fact, a woman started 13th and finished 14th in the very first NASCAR race ever run on June 19, 1949. Sarah Christian started in the No. 71 car, which was owned by her husband Frank, and drove the first 110 laps before turning the car over to Bob Flock, who drove the final 90 laps. Just three weeks later, Christian was joined by Louise Smith and Ethel Mobley in a 166-mile race at Daytona Beach, FL. Christian finished 6th in that race, Mobley 11th, and Smith 20th after surviving an early roll-over.

Who were the **first husband-and-wife drivers ever to race against each other** on the NASCAR Grand National circuit?

Patty Moise, daughter of veteran stock car racer Milton Moise, ended up racing against her husband, fellow driver Elton Sawyer, during the 1994 season. Since then, Moise has racked up the most career starts by a female driver in the series. In 1996, Moise and Sawyer founded their own Busch Grand National team with the support of the Dial Corporation, and Moise became the team's full-time driver.

DAYTONA 500

What top NASCAR driver *was* known for his **inability to win the Daytona 500**?

Dale Earnhardt has won seven Winston Cup championships during his storied career, but this prize had continued to elude him, until 1998. In 19 tries, he finished second at Daytona four times—in 1984, 1993, 1995, 1996—and in the top five 10 times. In 1990, he led on the last lap but cut a tire before crossing the finish line. Similar bad luck struck in 1994, when he lost the lead on the final lap after bumping with Dale Jarrett. After his 1997 bid was ruined by a spectacular crash—he hit the wall and rolled end over end—he refused to get out of his car and limped it around the track to finish the race. In 1998, on his 20th try, Earnhardt finally took the checkered flag at Dayton.

What was the **fastest Daytona 500** ever? How about the **fastest Indianapolis 500**?

In 1980, Buddy Baker won the fastest Daytona 500 ever, driving his Olds Cutlass to victory at an average speed of 177.602 miles per hour. A decade later, Arie Luyendyk of

Dale Earnhardt waves after winning the 1998 Daytona 500. It was his first victory in the 500 in 20 tries.

the Netherlands chalked up the fastest victory in Indianapolis 500 history, completing the required 200 laps in a Chevy-powered Lola in 2 hours, 41 minutes, for an average speed of 185.981 miles per hour.

Why is the **1979 Daytona 500** considered to be such an important race?

At the time, auto racing was just beginning to gain in popularity on a nationwide basis. The sport was wildly popular in the South, where more than 100,000 people would show up to watch a race, but the people who ran the television networks didn't think that people in the rest of the country would enjoy the sport. CBS decided to gamble on the sport and agreed to televise the Daytona 500 live from start to finish, the first time that had ever been done for a NASCAR race. The results were amazing. With a huge snowstorm forcing many people inside in the Northeast, millions of fans saw one of the most exciting races of all-time. Cale Yarborough and Donnie Allison battled it out side-by-side for much of the race, and on the final lap, second-place Yarborough tried to pass Allison, causing both to crash in the infield. As the nation watched, Richard Petty sped by to claim his sixth Daytona crown while Yarborough and Allison staged a memorable fistfight on the infield grass that was joined by Donnie's brother Bobby. It was great television, and the ratings soared, proving that NASCAR was ready for the big-time.

Why is the 1976 Daytona 500 considered one of the most memorable races ever?

It featured an epic battle between two of the best and most popular racers of their day—Richard Petty (the King) and David Pearson (the Silver Fox). They were the only drivers in contention for the checkered flag with 20 laps to go, and they ran each of those laps with only inches between their cars. Pearson held a slight lead going into the last lap, but Petty made a desperate attempt to pass in the final turn. Unfortunately, he couldn't quite hold his line and tapped Pearson's car, sending both of them careening into the wall. Both cars were nearly destroyed and rolled to a stop just short of the finish line. Pearson, who had managed to keep his engine running, radioed his crew to ask, "Has Richard crossed the line?" When they responded that the King had not yet finished the race, Pearson put his car in gear and agonizingly nursed it across the line for the victory. Petty had to wait for a push-start from his crew and settled for second place.

How many drivers have **won the Daytona 500 two years in a row**?

Only two racers have managed to repeat as Daytona 500 champions—seven-time winner Richard Petty in 1973–74, and four-time winner Cale Yarborough in 1983–84.

Who are the only two men to win the crown jewels of American automobile racing, the Indianapolis 500 and the Daytona 500?

Indy-style cars and NASCAR stock cars have absolutely nothing in common, with the exception that they both travel nearly 200 miles per hour. That being said, there were two legendary drivers who were able to do the improbable and not just race both types of cars, but win in both types of cars. Mario Andretti won at Daytona in 1967 and at Indianapolis in 1969, while A.J. Foyt won at Daytona in 1972 and claimed victory at the Brickyard a record-tying four times.

Mario Andretti is one of only two men who have won the Indianapolis 500 and the Daytona 500. A.J. Foyt is the other.

Shirley Muldowney was the first woman to race a top-fuel car on the NHRA circuit.

DRAG RACING

In drag racing, what's the **difference between Top Fuel dragsters, Pro Stock dragsters, and Funny Cars**?

Top Fuel dragsters are the wedge-shaped, open-wheeled machines most people think of when they hear the word dragster. They're powered by huge 4,000-horse-power, nitromethane-burning engines that are mounted behind the driver. Top Fuel dragsters are the fastest of the bunch, with a record quarter-mile time of 4.592 seconds (recorded by Blaine Johnson in 1996). Funny Cars are similar to Top Fuel dragsters but they have a shorter wheelbase and feature a fiberglass body that looks like a production car. They're called funny because of the exaggerated body features and extremely large tires. Funny Cars are the second-fastest type of dragster, with a record time of 4.889 seconds for the quarter mile (recorded by John Force in 1996). On the surface, Pro Stock dragsters appear similar to the stock cars that you see on oval tracks at NASCAR events, but they're quite different under the hood. Under NHRA rules, Pro Stock dragsters can have a 500 cubic inch engine displacement (NASCAR racers are limited to 358 cubic inches) with extensive modifications. They aren't quite as fast as the other types of dragsters. The fastest time ever recorded for a Pro Stock dragster over a quarter mile was 6.947 seconds by Jim Yates in 1996.

Who was the first woman licensed by the NHRA to drive a top-fuel dragster?

Of course, it was Shirley Muldowney. She achieved this feat in 1965, when most people thought that the drag strip was no place for a lady. In fact, Muldowney was booed regularly in her first few years participating in the sport. But she took the criticism in stride, and even flaunted her femininity by wearing a pink driver's suit and painting her car pink. Muldowney went on to win the NHRA top-fuel championship three times and earned 17 NHRA titles, despite the fact that many of her male rivals made a special effort to beat her. Many people remember the epic battles between Muldowney and "Big Daddy" Don Garlits, another top drag racer of the day. In 1983, a critically acclaimed movie about her life, *Heart Like a Wheel*, was released.

BASEBALL

PLAY BALL!

HISTORY, RULES, AND TERMS

What are the **origins of baseball**?

People have been playing stick and a ball games since the early days of civilization. On that premise, baseball can be traced back to games played in ancient Egypt, China, and Persia. But if we recognize baseball as a game played with four bases in a diamond configuration and a few other definite particulars, the organized sport we recognize as baseball began on June 19, 1846, on the Elysian Fields in Hoboken, New Jersey. Two amateur teams of nine players played a game umpired by Alexander J. Cartwright, a surveyor and athlete, who established guidelines for a game that most closely resembles modern baseball.

Games somewhat similar to baseball were played before that date in North America. The English sport of Cricket was played in the early 1800s, but another game brought over from England called Rounders is even more similar to baseball. In Rounders, a batter strikes a ball and runs around bases. Balls caught on the fly are outs and fielders can put runners out by hitting them with the ball as they run between bases. Clubs began forming to play this game, which they called baseball, based on those rules.

Legend has it that Abner Doubleday invented baseball in Cooperstown, New York, in 1839. However, while several varieties of baseball were played then and prior to 1846, and though Doubleday helped popularize them, there is little evidence that his

When did professional baseball begin?

By the 1850s, baseball parks were rented to clubs and teams would collect donations from fans to cover costs. The National Association of Base Ball Players (NABBP) was formed in 1858. After restricting members from taking payment for playing baseball, even though ballpark owners earned profits by renting the field and by selling food and beverages, the NABBP changed its policy in 1868. The first professional baseball team, the Cincinnati Red Stockings, began play in 1869.

game resembles baseball as we know it, even though a baseball-type game thrived in Cooperstown, which became the home for baseball's Hall of Fame.

Alexander Cartwright is recognized as having founded the first true organized baseball club, the Knickerbocker Base Ball Club, in 1842 in New York City. Cartwright and his Knickerbockers developed a set of 20 rules in 1845: the rules called for nine-player teams and a playing field with a home base and three additional bases set apart at specific distances (42 paces, later standardized to 90 feet); instead of hitting runners with the ball, they introduced the new rule of having fielders tag runners or being able to force runners out by tagging the base a runner has to advance to after a batter puts the ball in play; and they created foul lines that marked a distinct field of play, differing from the Rounders and Cricket format where the ball can be hit anywhere.

The Knickerbocker-styled game (popularly called the New York Game) began spreading. During the Civil War, Union soldiers from New York City introduced the game in places they were stationed, and by 1865 the game with the Knickerbocker rules had become the most popular style of baseball.

What were some of the **first teams and leagues**?

The Cincinnati Red Stockings barnstormed around the country in 1869, winning 60 games without a loss. In 1871, The National Association of Base Ball Players (NABBP) became the National Association of Professional Base Ball Players (NAPBBP), representing players from ten clubs that made up the first professional baseball league. The teams played each other and the best teams met for a championship series. In 1876, the National League of Professional Base Ball Clubs, known as the National League, was created with teams in Boston, Chicago, Cincinnati, Hartford, Louisville, New York, Philadelphia, and St. Louis. The rival American Association was founded in 1882. In 1883, the two leagues formed an agreement that included playing exhibition games between the leagues' best teams following the regular season and adopting the reserve clause, which required players to obtain permission from their club's owner before joining another club. The American Association folded after the 1891 season and its four best teams joined the National League. Before it went defunct, the American Association was considered a Major League.

When were the **Major Leagues** formed?

In 1900, Ban Johnson, president of the minor league Western League, renamed the organization the American League and teams began play the following year. Along with the already-established National League, which had begun play in 1876, they became recognized as the Major Leagues, ushering in the modern era of baseball.

What important **records** predate Major League baseball?

The top four season averages of all time, led by Hugh Duffy's .438 in 1894, and the most runs scored during a season (196 by Billy Hamilton in 1894) are among the enduring season records established before the turn of the century. Pitching records include Amos Rusie's 52 games started, 50 complete games, 482 innings pitched, and 218 walks—all in 1893. Cy Young earned 289 of his 511 career victories (the most ever) before 1900. The great Cap Anson amassed over 3,000 hits in 22 seasons before 1900.

What was the **Federal League**?

The Federal League was created when a minor league elevated itself and attempted to lure star major leaguers to jump ship in the process. The first player to sign a contract with the fledgling league was George Stovall of the St. Louis Browns. Future Hall of Famers Joe Tinker and Walter Johnson also signed with the Feds, although Johnson changed his mind when the owner of the Washington Senators gave him a nice raise and bonus to stay put. The Federal League's history was short-lived, lasting a mere two seasons (1914–1915), but its legacy lives on in Chicago's Wrigley Field, which was originally built for the Windy City's Federal League entry.

When did the **7th inning stretch** originate?

According to baseball legend, the 7th inning stretch originated when President William Howard Taft attended a game in 1910. Between the top and the bottom of the 7th inning, Taft stood up to stretch his legs; the crowd, thinking he was getting up to leave, also stood up as a show of respect. Taft then sat down, and the crowd followed. Since that time, the story goes, the tradition of stretching began, and many teams have taken the opportunity to invite the crowd to sing, "Take Me Out to the Ballgame" during the 7th inning stretch.

How did the bullpen get its name?

The origin of the term bullpen has long been debated. It's the place where relief pitchers and warmup catchers hang out during games. And when they weren't actually preparing for a game, they often could be found gabbing and "shooting the bull" with fans and each other. Manager Casey Stengel once commented that the pen in the outfield often looked like a place to keep cows and bulls, while longtime Yankees pitcher Johnny Murphy claimed it originally came from Bull Durham tobacco advertising signs that used to hang near the spots where relievers warmed up.

Taft was also the first president to throw out the ceremonial first pitch at the beginning of the baseball season. That also happened in 1910. His vice-president, James Sherman, was hit that day by a foul ball off the bat of the Philadelphia Athletics' Frank "Home Run" Baker and knocked unconscious.

What is the **Dead Ball era**?

From roughly 1900 through the end of World War I, home runs were rare, ERAs were minuscule, and the preferred style of play was "scientific" baseball (what today would be called "small ball.") During this era, pitchers were discovering and mastering new trick pitches. Spitballs were not yet illegal, infields were in poor condition, and the ball was not as lively as in later years. Home run titles were won with totals as low as eight, and most of those were probably of the inside-the-park variety. This caused teams to play for one or two runs at a time, instead of playing for the big inning. A premium was placed on contact hitting, moving runners along with sacrifices, bunting, and speed.

Four developments ended the Dead Ball era: The Black Sox scandal of 1919, the rise in popularity of the home run (personified by Babe Ruth), the banishment of the spitball, and the new composition of the baseball. The new, cork-centered ball became the baseball of choice in the 1920s, as Ruth's popularity grew with each home run. The owners needed a popular figure in 1920 to distract the public from the growing scandal of the 1919 World Series, when eight White Sox players were accused of conspiring to "throw" the Series. Pitchers must've felt like there was a conspiracy against *them* when, along with all the other changes, the spitball was outlawed. A few pitchers who were at the end of their careers and relied on the spitter were allowed to throw it until they retired.

Mike Marshall, the first reliever to appear in 100 games in a season (106 in 1974), was the prototypical '70s fireman.

How has **relief pitching** changed or evolved over the years?

In the early years of professional baseball, pitching staffs had no regular relief pitchers. Instead, all pitchers had a spot in the rotation, and anyone who was not starting that day could take over for the regular pitcher in case of emergency. Around the 1920s, teams began adding relievers to their staffs, but except for rare exceptions, they were mostly guys who couldn't crack the starting rotation. Since the mid-50s, relief pitching has become a specialized art. Casey Stengel popularized the use of relief specialists with his great Yankee teams. The "save" became an official stat in 1966, and with that the age of the "closer" was born.

At first, closers were used to get out of a late-inning jam that had been created by another pitcher. They would be called upon in the middle of an inning, usually with men in scoring position, to end the rally (or, "put out the fire," thus earning themselves the nickname "firemen"). In the 1980s, that role began to change. The power-pitching closers started coming in at the beginning of an inning, usually the ninth, to prevent rallies from even starting, thus shortening the game for the opposition's offense. Instead of a tiring starter who they've seen three times, batters face a fresh arm, usually throwing in the mid-90's or higher. This left the rally-killing duties to other relievers. "Middle" relief thus became just as important, and just as specialized, as late relief. Now every team has, or is looking for, a pitcher they consider the "set-up man," someone to bridge the gap between the starter (who nowadays is only counted on for about five or six innings) and the closer. The idea is again to keep hitters off-bal-

35

ance with yet another fresh arm. The specialization doesn't stop there, though. There are situational pitchers, whose job is just to get one batter out. He's usually a left-hander, brought in to face a lone left-handed hitter in the opponent's lineup.

Mike Marshall was the first reliever to appear in 100 games in a season (106 with the Dodgers in 1974). Hoyt Wilhem was the first reliever to appear in 1,000 career games and record 200 saves. Rollie Fingers was the first to record 300 saves. The all-time saves leader is Lee Smith, with 478. Fingers, Sparky Lyle, Willie Hernandez, and Dennis Eckersley were all relievers who won Cy Young Awards, while Hernandez, Eckersley and Jim Konstanty have also won MVP honors.

When did baseball first institute **playoffs**?

The ultimate baseball playoff, the World Series, has been played since 1903 between the winners of the American and National Leagues. Major League Baseball introduced the American and National League Championship Series (ALCS and NLCS, respectively) in 1969. These two playoff series between the first place teams in the American and National League's two (Eastern and Western) divisions determined which teams earned the right to face each other in the World Series. With an increase in teams due to expansion, MLB added a new division (the Central) to each league in 1995. This altered the playoff format, allowing for eight teams (six divisional winners and two wild card teams) to fight it out for spots in the Fall Classic. The first round, the Division Series, is best-of-five. The LCS and World Series are best-of-seven.

How did **World War II** impact baseball?

The recruitment of MLB players into military service during World War II severely affected the game. Many players had precious years shaved off their careers as a result of the war. Stars such as Joe DiMaggio, Ted Williams, Bob Feller, and Hank Greenberg lost some of their most productive years, and possibly some major league records, to the war. The All-Star Game was even canceled in 1945. In 1943, Chicago Cubs owner Philip K. Wrigley formed the All-American Girls Professional Baseball League (AAGP-BL) to fill the void and provide entertainment during this terrible time. The league consisted of four teams in its first year (1943), growing to ten in its final season (1954). In 1988, the National Baseball Hall of Fame and Museum opened the "Women in Baseball" permanent exhibit. It quickly became one of the museum's most popular attractions.

Wartime travel restrictions limited where teams could conduct spring training. Most stayed close to home, where the weather wasn't very conducive to baseball-related activities. Equipment was harder to come by, and the quality of play suffered with the infusion of players not yet ready for the big time or well past their primes. The 1945 World Series was described as "the fat guys vs. the tall guys at the company picnic." Joe Nuxhall made his major league debut at the age of 15, one-armed outfielder Pete Gray patrolled the outfield for part of the 1945 season, and players who had been retired for years came back to fill the void left by those who went to fight. One of the oddest developments of wartime baseball was the ascendence of the perrenial doormat St. Louis Browns, who won their first and only pennant in 1944.

The war also served to change baseball's previous stand about race. While the Armed Forces were still segregated, African-Americans played a major part in the Allied victory. Also, the hypocricy of fighting people who considered themselves the "Master Race" while treating a large number of Americans as second-class citizens began to hit home. Shortly after the war, the Dodgers signed Jackie Robinson to a minor league contract.

What is the **Hot Stove League**?

During the dark winter months between the end of the World Series and Opening Day, there is always a plethora of gossip and rumors regarding player transactions and other baseball activity. This scuttlebutt was nicknamed the "Hot Stove League." Trades involving big name players were high points of such discussion, although these types of trades have become less frequent with the advent of free agency and escalating salaries, and the demise of the annual Winter Meetings in December.

Where do teams go during **spring training**?

Spring training is a period of preparation and exhibition play that teams conduct from late February until a few days before Opening Day. Given the inclement weather typical of the northern parts of the country during these months, baseball teams have long sought warmer climates in which to conduct their pre-season training. The main spring training sites are located in Florida and Arizona, although some teams have trained in other locations over the years (New Orleans, for example). Teams that train in Florida are said to belong to the "Grapefruit League," while Arizona teams are nicknamed the "Cactus League." The first Florida site was established in 1888 by the Washington team.

What makes a **curveball** curve?

To throw a curveball, the pitcher presses his middle finger against the outside seam of the ball and releases the ball with a snap of his wrist (a clockwise twist for righties, counterclockwise for lefties), creating top spin. As the ball moves toward the plate air streams by on either side. The raised seams of a spinning baseball passing through the air disrupts the wake in the air created by the ball's movement. One side of the ball is spinning in the same direction as the streaming air, the other is spinning against the air; the ball curves in the direction of least resistance. A curveball can make as many as 15 revolutions before passing over the plate. A righthander's curveball will move away from a right-handed batter.

Making the ball curve in the opposite direction—the pitch called a screwball— requires the right-handed pitcher to twist his wrist in a counterclockwise manner, the lefty to twist his wrist in a clockwise manner, a maneuver that puts tremendous strain on the forearm and elbow. Compare the difference between throwing a curve and a screwball by lifting your arm and dropping it forward while twisting your wrist toward your body, and then do the same while twisting it away from your body.

While the curve and screwball have topspin, a slider has sidespin. The pitcher grips the ball as he does with a curveball but does not snap his wrist, relying for spin instead on the pressure of his finger against the seam. The slider is faster and curves less, but it begins to curve later—closer to the plate—making it more difficult for the batter to pick up and judge the ball's movement.

Pitchers throwing fastballs and fielders making a play place their index and middle fingers on the seams or across the seams to avoid top or side spin and achieve maximum velocity.

How do speeds in **fast-pitch softball** compare in speed with baseball pitches?

The softball is larger—between 11 7/8 and 12 1/8 inches in diameter—and weighs 6 1/4 to seven ounces. Many leagues use a kapok ball or a solid polyurethane sphere that is anything but soft. But it is fast: Michele Granger, college softball's sultana of strikeouts, has an underhand "riseball" that blasts over home plate somewhere in the mid-70s. The pitching rubber in softball is closer to the plate (46 ft.) than it is in baseball (60 ft. 6 in.); Granger's pitch, adjusted to distance, is somewhere in the neighborhood of a 96-mph major league fastball.

What are baseball **bats** made of?

White Ash. The tree is felled when it reaches a foot in diameter (when it's about 60 years old) and cut into 40-inch cylinders, called "billets." The average 60-year-old White Ash will yield about 60 billets, of which about six or seven are generally considered good enough to make bats. The billets are aged for two years, then dried, sorted by weight, and graded.

Billets have been carved into bats by lathe since about 1884, when a teenager named Bud Hillerich carved a bat for Pete Browning of the Louisville Eclipse—thus, the Louisville Slugger was born. Almost three decades later, Hillerich formed a partnership with Frank Bradsby, a salesman, and the batmakers Hillerich & Bradsby was born.

After the billets have been aged, those that pass inspection are carved by a lathe that has 28 knives and can be adjusted to over 200 different shapes. The process takes 15 seconds. The bat is then branded with the trademark, sanded, and either dipped into one of six finishes or briefly roasted over flame, depending on the specifications of the order.

Speaking of specifications, Ted Williams once returned a shipment of bats because the grip "just didn't feel right." The bats were remeasured and found to be .005 of an inch thinner than Williams had specified.

Where is the **sweet spot** on a baseball bat?

The sweet spot is usually located six to eight inches down from the end. You'll know it when you hit the ball there—your hit will feel as effortless as running a hot knife through a stick of butter, and you'll cream the ball. There is no sting in the sweet spot, "the center of percussion." To find the sweet spot, hold the bat off the ground by the knob and tap it up and down gently with a hammer: when you don't feel a vibration, you've found the sweet spot.

Why is the "ping" of an **aluminum bat** more powerful than the "crack" of a wooden bat?

Aluminum bats are made of a seamless tube: the hollowed bat is lighter than a similarly-sized wooden bat, allowing the batter to swing faster. The weight of aluminum bats is more evenly distributed and the sweet spot is larger, since the quickness of the swing brings the center of gravity closer to the body. Balls fly off aluminum bats as much as four mph faster than they do off of wooden bats, which increases potential distance by as much as 10%. This differential works well enough in little league, and aluminum bats last longer and are cheaper investments. They work equally well in college, but at that level there is concern about the dangerous speeds the ball reaches off the bat, as well as the inflated offensive potential. Some great college players have had trouble adjusting to wooden bats in professional baseball. Considering that a baseball is crushed by up to 8,000 pounds of force by a full swing (which compresses the baseball as much as half of its original diameter upon impact), the concerns of danger and inflated statistics are very real. Besides, few things are as sweet to hear as the crack of wood launching a baseball, at least for the hitter.

What are **baseballs** made of?

From the inside out, a baseball consists of a cork core within a rubber ball that is a little smaller than a golf ball. The rubber is surrounded by woolen yarn topped by a thin layer of cotton string. The cotton and yarn are wound tight—by machine—to precisely 8 1/2 inches in circumference, four and 1/8 ounces before the cover is added. The leather cover—made from cowhide, which replaced horsehide in 1974—is tanned, cut, punctured with holes along the edges, and stamped. The cover is then sewn on with red cotton thread, a process that takes a skilled sewer about 15 minutes.

How did **catcher's** equipment evolve?

Catcher's equipment has been referred to as "the tools of ignorance" (and that by a catcher—Bill Dickey, one of the greats of the position), but think of being a catcher without that protection: so it was in the early days of baseball. It wasn't until 1875 that catchers and the other fielders began wearing padded gloves. The catcher's mitt, with extra padding in the pocket, was designed by Harry Decker in 1889 (for a while catcher's mitts were called deckers). The catcher's mask was invented in 1876 by Frederick Winthrop Thayer, captain of Harvard's baseball team. The chest protector came along in the 1880s, and catcher Roger Bresnahan (a future Hall of Famer whose nickname was The Duke of Tralee) introduced shin guards in the early 1900s. Since then there have been subtle variations—the chest protector today is lighter and no longer has a seam running down the center, changes that have increased mobility and made throwing easier. In the early 1980s, Steve Yeager popularized the neck guard, a flap of metal or hard plastic that hangs from the chin pad of the mask and protects the throat. Yeager, a catcher for the Dodgers who played on four World Series teams, had suffered a serious injury when part of a shattered bat punctured his throat, but the incident occurred while he was in the on deck circle, waiting to bat, not when he was

catching.

When did each of today's **major league ballparks** first open?

With 30 teams in two leagues, Major League Baseball is home to a wide variety of ballparks. From the classics of yesteryear like Tiger Stadium and Fenway Park, to state-of-the-art stadiums like the Skydome and Bank One Park, there's something for everyone. Here's a rundown of when the homes of today's teams opened their turnstiles to fans:

Anaheim Angels	Edison International Field (formerly the Big A)	1966
Arizona Diamondbacks	Bank One Ballpark	1998
Atlanta Braves	Turner Field	1997
Baltimore Orioles	Oriole Park at Camden Yards	1992
Boston Red Sox	Fenway Park	1912
Chicago Cubs	Wrigley Field	1914
Chicago White Sox	New Comiskey Park	1991
Cincinnati Reds	Cinergy Field (formerly Riverfront Stadium)	1970
Cleveland Indians	Jacobs Field	1994
Colorado Rockies	Coors Field	1995
Detroit Tigers	Tiger Stadium	1912
Florida Marlins	Pro Player Stadium (formerly Joe Robbie Stadium)	1987
Houston Astros	Astrodome	1965
Kansas City Royals	Kaufman Stadium	1973
Los Angeles Dodgers	Dodger Stadium	1962
Milwaukee Brewers	County Stadium	1953
Minnesota Twins	The Metrodome	1982
Montreal Expos	Olympic Stadium	1976
New York Mets	Shea Stadium	1964
New York Yankees	Yankee Stadium	1923
	(closed for renovations in 1973, reopened in 1976)	
Oakland Athletics	UMAX Coliseum (formerly Oakland Alameda Coliseum)	1966
Philadelphia Phillies	Veterans Stadium	1971
Pittsburgh Pirates	Three Rivers Stadium	1970
San Diego Padres	Qualcomm Stadium (formerly Jack Murphy Stadium)	1967
San Francisco Giants	3Com Park (Formerly Candlestick Park)	1960
Seattle Mariners	The Kingdome	1976
St. Louis Cardinals	Busch Stadium	1966
Tampa Bay Devil Rays	Tropicana Field (formerly the Thunderdome)	1990
Texas Rangers	The Ballpark in Arlington	1994
Toronto Blue Jays	The Skydome	1989

During a baseball game, when may a **stadium's lights be turned on**?

Before the game or between completed innings. Neither team should gain an advantage because of the lights.

What are the dimensions of the baseball diamond?

The bases are spaced 90 feet apart (someone once said that if first base were 89 or 91 feet away from home plate there would be fewer close plays). The pitcher stands 60 feet, 6 inches away from home plate, a distance standardized in 1893. Home plate (pentagon shaped and resembling a house) is 17 inches wide, 17 inches high (8 1/2 on the side and another 8 1/2 inches tapering to the point at the top). Batters stand in a 6 ft. long batters box (centered in relation to the plate) that is four feet wide. The pitcher's plate, better known as the rubber, is two-feet long and six inches wide. The pitcher must keep one foot on the rubber while delivering a pitch. The distance of the outfield walls varies from ballpark to ballpark, but has become somewhat standardized in recent years.

How can a batter **strike out** against a pitcher he never batted against?

Remember that a pitcher brought into a game must pitch to at least one batter and a hitter cannot be pinch hit for once he has two strikes.

In a minor league game in 1997, a right-handed batter was ejected from the game by the umpire for arguing a strike call. He had two strikes on him. The batter was replaced by a left-handed batter, and the opposing manager changed pitchers, bringing in a lefty. The second pitcher struck out the second batter.

Because the first batter had accumulated two strikes, the out was charged to him. Because the second pitcher was on the mound when the out was made, he gets credit for the strikeout.

How does a **squeeze play** work?

An aggressive attempt to score a runner from third base, the squeeze play occurs when the batter tries to bunt the ball at just the right place in fair territory so the fielder cannot get the runner out as he races to home plate. The suicide squeeze describes the situation when the man at third runs with the pitch while the batter bunts the ball, while the safety squeeze finds him waiting at the base to see if the bunt is effective. Obviously, the squeeze play is only attempted with less than two outs.

What is the **score of a forfeited game**?

The official score of a forfeited game is 9–0. A team gains victory through forfeit when the umpire-in-chief rules that the opposing team acted in an illegal manner. Refusing to take the field, causing unnecessary delays, or failing to leave the field after an ejection are all infractions that could result in a forfeit. Even fan behavior has been known to cause a forfeit. In a game on June 4, 1974, the Cleveland Indians offered fans all the beer they could drink for ten cents a cup. This led to heavy intoxication, unruly patrons, and a forfeited game for the Indians. Another famous forfeit occurred in the second game of a double header on July 12, 1979, when White Sox owner Bill Veeck staged another one of his outrageous promotions: "Disco Demolition Night" was held between games of a doubleheader with the Detroit Tigers. The huge bonfires and burning disco records between the two games caused thousands of fans to storm the field, create a massive disturbance, and give Detroit a 9–0 victory.

What are the penalties for **throwing spitballs or using foreign objects** (such as an emery board) on the mound?

The infamous spitball or "spitter" involves moistening a ball with saliva or another foreign substance, causing it to break more sharply. Pitchers have also been known to use emery boards, sandpaper, and belt buckles to hack up the ball to achieve the same effect. It was once a legal pitch, but was banned from Major League Baseball in 1920 (although 17 pitchers who were already throwing it were permitted to continue). In 1968 a strong anti-spitter rule was added that prohibited the pitcher from bringing his pitching hand in contact with his mouth or lips while in the 18-foot circle surrounding the pitching rubber. For violation of this part of the rule the umpires are supposed to immediately call a ball. However, if the pitch is made and a batter reaches first base on a hit, an error, a hit batsman, or otherwise—and no other runner is put out before advancing at least one base—then the play proceeds without reference to the violation. Repeated offenders are subject to a fine by the league president.

If a pitcher is caught applying a foreign substance of any kind to the ball during a game, he is issued a warning and the umpire calls the pitch a ball. If there is a second offense by the same pitcher in the same game, the pitcher is ejected and subject to further punishment. The last pitcher to legally throw a spitter was Burleigh Grimes, who retired in 1934. Still, others have continued to throw it, including Gaylord Perry, whose 1974 autobiography was entitled "Me and the Spitter." Both pitchers are members of Baseball's Hall of Fame.

What do the rules say about **corking bats**?

They're against it. Throughout the history of MLB, batters have been known to tamper with their bats in order to hit the ball further and harder. Some common practices include hollowing the bat and filling it with cork, flattening the bat, or covering it with a foreign substance such as wax or pine tar. If a batter attempts to use a bat that, in the umpire's judgment, has been altered in this manner, he is immediately called out. No advancement on the bases will be allowed and any outs made during a play

Gaylord Perry, Hall of Famer and 300-game winner, was a well-known proponent of the spitter, at least that's what he wanted the hitters to think.

> ## In what instances can an umpire's ruling be protested?
>
> Any umpire's decision which involves judgment is final. Players, managers, coaches, or other team officials are not supposed to argue any such judgment decisions (balls and strikes, for example). Still, all major league umpires put up with a limited amount of unofficial protesting. An official protest against an umpire can be filed when it is felt that the official rules of baseball were misinterpreted or misapplied. If the protest is upheld, the call is declared invalid and the game may have to be replayed.

stand. In addition to being called out, the hitter is automatically ejected from the game and may be subject to additional penalties (fines or suspensions) as determined by the league president.

What is the **infield fly rule**?

This rule comes into effect when a ball is popped up over the infield in a situation where there are fewer than two outs and runners occupying first and second or all three bases. When an umpire applies the rule, the batter is automatically called out before an infielder makes a play on the ball. Even if the defensive player misses or drops the ball, it is still an out, because the umpire deemed it playable. The rule is used to prevent the defensive player from intentionally misplaying the pop up and forcing a double play.

What is a **balk**? Why is 1988 known as the year of the balk?

One of baseball's least understood rules, the balk is any motion a pitcher makes that an umpire interprets as a direct attempt to deceive a runner into making a move that may get him picked off base. Failure by the pitcher to complete delivery, not coming to a stop after a stretch, and departures from the pitcher's common delivery are common balk infractions. The official rules list 13 specific balk situations, allowing runners to advance one base when they occur. In the early part of the 1988 season, it was decided that the balk rule should be more strictly enforced. This led to more balks (and confusion) than ever before.

What is the **double switch**?

This changing of the lineup only occurs in the National League or other leagues that do not allow the designated hitter. It's used to get a good hitter into a pitcher's place in

Who is the smallest player ever?

Eddie Gaedel, at three feet, six inches, was the smallest player ever to appear in a major league game. He led off a game in 1951 for the St. Louis Browns, who were owned by Bill Veeck, a showman not afraid to bring novel approaches to the game and its marketing. Gaedel walked on four pitches (he was ordered not to swing)—getting on base like a good lead-off man should—and was promptly replaced by a pinch runner. The catcher, crouched on his knees, was taller than Gaedel.

the batting order while bringing in a relief pitcher. While his team is on the defensive and knowing that the pitcher's turn in the batting order is coming up, a manager will change hurlers as well as one player in the field. This allows the new player (most likely a better hitter) to be inserted into the pitcher's spot, while the pitcher takes the spot vacated by the departing defensive player.

What is **pepper**?

To loosen up before games, ballplayers can often be found participating in a game of pepper. During pepper, one player bunts grounders and line drives to a group of fielders standing about 20 feet away. The fielders try to throw it back as quickly as possible, so the batter can hit the return throw. Pepper is banned in some ballparks for fear that it will result in injured spectators.

What is a **fielder's choice**?

A fielder's choice is the act of a fielder who handles a fair grounder and, instead of throwing to first base to put out the batter, throws to another base in an attempt to put out a preceding runner. The term is also used by scorers 1) to account for the advance of the batter who takes one or more extra bases when the fielder who handles his safe hit attempts to put out a preceding runner; 2) to account for the advance of a runner (other than by stolen base or error) while a fielder is attempting to put out another runner; and 3) to account for the advance of a runner made solely because of the defensive team's indifference (undefended steal).

Who is the **youngest player** ever to appear in a Major League baseball game?

Joe Nuxhall was 15 when he made his debut as a pitcher for the Cincinnati Reds in 1944. He pitched in one game, lasting 2/3 of an inning while walking five, allowing two hits, and giving up five runs. He didn't make it back into the majors until 1952. Nuxhall won 17 games in 1955 at the ripe old age of 27, and 15 in 1963. He retired after the 1966 season and became a popular broadcaster of Reds games.

More auspicious debuts were made by Bob Feller (age 17 when he played for Cleveland in 1936), who had over 100 wins by the time he was 23, and Mel Ott (age 17 when he played for the New York Giants in 1926), who went on to play 22 years for the Giants and slugged 511 home runs. Al Kaline was 18 and straight out of high school when he debuted for Detroit in 1953, and he won the batting title two years later with a .340 average. David Clyde was the most recent player to go from the Prom to the Show, pitching for Texas in 1973 at the age of 18. Clyde pitched five years and lost almost twice as many games as he won. With the tutoring and experience available at the college, rookie

Satchel Paige, legend of the Negro Leagues, helped the Cleveland Indians over the top in 1948, and pitched for the Kansas City A's at the age of 59 in 1965.

league, and the minor league levels these days, players are more likely to have to pay their dues before breaking into the Bigs.

Who is the **oldest player** ever to appear in a Major League baseball game?

Satchel Paige. He made his Major League debut in 1948 after he turned 40, delayed only by the color barrier. The legend of the Negro leagues posted an impressive 6-1 record with a 2.48 ERA in 1948 for Cleveland. Paige retired in 1953 at age 47, then returned in 1965 at age 59. He pitched three scoreless innings for the Kansas City A's, giving up one hit and striking out one.

Minnie Minoso was 58 when he got in for two at bats for the Chicago White Sox in 1980, marking the fifth decade in which he played in a Major League game. A native Cuban, Minoso batted over .300 in eight different seasons. Knuckleball pitcher Hoyt Wilhelm was the oldest to play regularly, pitching in 16 games for the Los Angeles Dodgers in 1972 at the age of 49. Wilhelm pitched in more games (1070) and won more games in relief (123) than any other pitcher, and he earned 227 saves before the advent of the closer.

THE WORLD SERIES

What was the **Black Sox scandal**, and who were the eight players implicated?

In 1919, the Chicago White Sox ran away with the American League pennant and were heavily favored to win the World Series against the Cincinnati Reds. The early betting lines reflected the general prediction of a Chicago rout. As the Series was about to get underway, however, the odds started shifting toward the Reds. At the time, the phenomenon was dismissed as optimism on the part of Reds fans. Later on it was viewed as another piece of damning evidence.

Late in the 1920 season, the story broke that eight Chicago players had, indeed, conspired with gamblers to "throw" the Series for $10,000 each. The eight implicated were first baseman Chick Gandil and shortstop Swede Risberg (the supposed ring leaders), ace starting pitchers Eddie Cicotte and Lefty Williams, outfielders "Shoeless" Joe Jackson and Happy Felsch, third baseman Buck Weaver, and backup infielder Fred McMullin.

Amid numerous double-crosses and changes of heart, it is believed that only Cicotte and Jackson ever received anything close to what was promised. Weaver argued his innocence until his death, proclaiming that he was at the meeting where the "fix" was discussed but never participated in the scheme. His Series performance would seem to verify his story. In 34 at-bats he collected 11 hits (four of them doubles) for a .324 average. He also played errorless ball at third. McMullin, a reserve, didn't have much effect on the outcome. He just happened to overhear a conversation and wanted to cash in by promising to keep quiet. The level of participation of Gandil, Risberg, Felsch, Williams, and Cicotte is pretty undeniable. Risberg hit .080 with four errors, Gandil hit .233 with an error, while Felsch contributed two more errors and a .192 average. Williams had a 6.61 ERA to go with two losses, and Cicotte contributed two losses (aided by two errors of his own). Cicotte did win Game 7 (it was a best-of-nine Series that year) after the players had decided to go ahead and try to win after being double-crossed by the gamblers. Jackson's role is a little harder to decipher. He

The 1919 Chicago White Sox. The Sox lost the 1919 World Series to the Cincinnati Reds amid allegations that eight players had conspired with gamblers.

admitted in an affidavit (later stolen) that he was involved, but he led the team with a .367 average, 12 hits, five runs, and six RBI.

All eight players were indicted and tried in court. The key evidence, signed confessions of the players, turned up missing during the trial. Without these documents, the prosecution's case collapsed and the eight players were acquitted. It has been hypothesized that the disappearance of the confessions was the work of Arnold Rothstein (the gambler who had financed the fix) and Charles Comiskey, the tightwad owner of the White Sox, who didn't want to lose his team.

After the acquittal, Judge Kenesaw Mountain Landis, who had been appointed Commissioner of Baseball in the wake of the scandal, disregarded the verdict and banned all eight players from baseball for life.

To learn more about the Black Sox, read Eliot Asinof's excellent book, *Eight Men Out*. The book was faithfully adapted into a movie by John Sayles in 1988.

What teams have made the **most World Series appearances**?

The Yankees lead by far with 34 and are the only franchise to have won more than nine times, sporting a 23–11 record. The Dodgers rank second with 18 (6–12 overall, 3–8 vs. the Yankees), followed by the Giants (16, 5–11), the Cardinals (15, 9–6), and

What is the rule on force outs?

Force outs occur when a runner must leave a base about to be occupied by the batter or by another runner. A runner on first must run for second, for example, after a batter puts the ball in play and the ball will not be caught in the air. If there are runners on first and third, the runner on third is not being forced to move because there is no runner on second.

A runner is no longer forced to leave a base if the runner behind him is retired. For example, a runner is on first and the batter hits a grounder to the first baseman, who touches first and retires the batter. The runner who had occupied first must then be tagged out to be retired, since he is no longer being forced.

the A's (14, 9–5). The Cubs haven't won a Series since 1908, but they've been to the Fall Classic 10 times, ranking sixth in appearances while sporting a 2–8 record.

What teams have won the **most World Series titles**?

The New York Yankees have the most World Championships with 23. The A's franchise—counting the Philadelphia and Kansas City incarnations—has nine, for second place in the AL.

The St. Louis Cardinals lead the National League in World Championships with nine. The Los Angeles/Brooklyn Dodgers have tallied six World titles.

How many **World Series** have been canceled?

The World Series has been played during World Wars, the Great Depression, and an earthquake, but on two occasions baseball officials have allowed their concerns to become bigger than the game.

The 1904 Series was canceled because New York Giants owner John T. Brush refused to allow his team to play against a representative of the upstart American League. The American and National Leagues had joined to form the Major Leagues in 1901, and the first World Series was held in 1903. The agreement between the leagues placed a franchise in New York—the Highlanders, later to become the Yankees—which competed for fans with Brush's Giants. Brush had other grudges, including the fact that the American League had consistently raided players from the National League.

As early as August of the 1904 season Brush announced that his team would not participate in the World Series. The Highlanders were likely to win the American League pennant, especially after a mid-season deal that brought them outfielder Patsy

Doughtery from the defending champion Boston Pilgrims (later the Red Sox). The deal was pushed along by American league president Ban Johnson, who wanted a strong presence in the country's largest market.

Even though Boston won the American League pennant (the pennant-clinching run scored on a wild pitch by the Highlanders' great Jack Chesbro, who had 41 wins that season), Brush stuck to his guns, and the series was canceled. A New York newspaper cartoon depicted him as a rat scurrying down a hole. Brush later apologized and even helped formalize the seven-game World Series format, which was put in place in 1905. That Series was won by his Giants.

Labor/management problems led to the cancellation of the 1994 Series. The Players Association had gone on strike in August, and with no agreement in sight, the Series was canceled on September 14.

How many **World Series have ended on a home run**?

The two most famous World Championship-winning hits were home runs. Bill Mazeroski led off the bottom of the ninth of Game 7 for Pittsburgh in the 1960 World Series with the score tied 9–9: he hit the second pitch delivered by the Yankees' Ralph Terry over the left-field fence for a game winning homer, finishing one of baseball's great games. The Pirates had scored two runs in the first and second innings, but the Yankees rallied back and led 5–4 after six innings. They scored two more in the top of the eighth to make it 7–4, but a bad hop in the bottom of the eighth on a sure double-play grounder kept a Pirate rally alive and they ended up scoring five runs, for a 9–7 lead. The Yankees didn't die: they scored twice more in the top of the ninth, saved by an alert base running move by Mickey Mantle. Mantle was on first when the batter hit a grounder to the first baseman, who touched first and threw to second base to complete a double play: but Mantle stopped running and returned to first safely to keep the rally alive. Then Maz ended it all.

Another wild ending occurred in 1993. The Toronto Blue Jays led the Series three games to two and had a 5–1 lead in Game Six after six innings. But the Philadelphia Phillies rallied for five runs in the top of the seventh and held the 6–5 lead going into the bottom of the ninth. Rickey Henderson led off the bottom of the ninth with a walk, Paul Molitor followed with a single, and Joe Carter then sent a low slider into the leftfield seats for a Series-winning three run homer.

There have been several subway series, but has **one ballpark ever hosted all the games of a single World Series**?

Before the completion of Yankee Stadium, the New York Yankees and the New York Giants both played in the Polo Grounds. They met in the 1921 World Series and took turns being the home team.

Gene Tenace is one of only two players to hit a home run in each of his first two World Series at-bats.

Reggie Jackson connects for the first of his three homers in Game 6 of the 1977 World Series.

In 1944, The St. Louis Cardinals and the St. Louis Browns played all six of their World Series games in Sportsman's Park. It was the Cardinals's third straight Series appearance and the Browns' first (and only) one before moving to Baltimore in 1954 to become the Orioles.

Who are the only two players to hit **home runs in their first two World Series at-bats**?

In 1972, Oakland's Gene Tenace homered in his first two World Series at-bats. He went on to hit two more homers and become the World Series MVP.

Andruw Jones went deep in his first two World Series at-bats in 1996, becoming an instant celebrity in the process. Jones' feat wasn't enough to bring the Braves a title, however, as the Yankees overcame a two games to none deficit to beat Atlanta in six games.

Which two players have hit **three homers in a World Series game**?

Reggie Jackson did it in 1977, on three consecutive pitches off three different Dodger pitchers (Burt Hooten, Elias Sosa, and Charlie Hough). Babe Ruth did it twice, in the 1926 Series, which the Yankees lost to the Cardinals, and in 1928, when the Yankees defeated the Cardinals. In the 1926 Classic, Ruth also made headlines by making the last out of the Series while attempting to steal second base.

What team has **gone the longest** since their last World Series title?

That would be the Cubbies, who haven't celebrated a championship since 1908, when the words "Cubs" and "dynasty" could actually be used in the same sentence without a hint of sarcasm.

This legacy of futility, now entering its 90th year, is the longest championship drought in the majors. The Chicago White Sox, who haven't won since 1917, are in the middle of the longest title drought in the American League, followed closely by the Boston Red Sox, who last hoisted the championship banner in 1918.

Who is the only player to complete an **unassisted triple play in the World Series**?

Cleveland Indian Bill Wambsganss turned an unassisted triple play in a World Series game against the Brooklyn Robins on October 10, 1920. The feat occurred in the fifth inning of Game 5. Although still a rare play, unassisted triple plays have occurred several times during regular season games.

Has there ever been a **World Series no-hitter**?

Yes. Don Larsen not only threw the only World Series no-hitter, he threw a perfect game: 27 batters up, 27 batters down, and not one reached base in Game 5 of the 1956 Series. The first hit of the game didn't happen until the bottom of the fourth, when Mickey Mantle hit a homer off the Brooklyn Dodgers' Sal Maglie.

Larsen had developed a no-windup pitching style during that 1956 season, in which he won a career-high 11 games (against 5 losses). Larsen's perfect game put the Yankees ahead three games to two in a Series they went on to win 4–3. In Game 2 of that Series, the Yanks staked Larsen to a six-run lead (one in the top of the first, five runs in the second inning), but he couldn't hold it and was knocked from the game after walking four batters during a six-run Dodger rally in the second inning. Considering his Game 2 performance, the fact that Larsen had lost 21 games (winning 3) two years earlier, and sported a lifetime record of 81–91, his perfect achievement is all the more remarkable. The image of Yogi Berra running up and jumping into Larsen's arms after the final out is one of the great shots in sports history. That last pitch, Larsen's 97th of the game, was a called strike on the Dodgers' Dale Mitchell. "I thought it was outside, but what's the difference," said Mitchell. "I couldn't hit the strikes he threw me anyhow."

What pitcher recorded the **most strikeouts in a single World Series**?

In 1968, Bob Gibson of the St. Louis Cardinals struck out 35 batters in a seven game series with the Detroit Tigers. In Game 1, he set the single-game Series record with 17 K's.

Bob Gibson was always a fierce competitor, but he turned it up another notch at World Series time. In three World Series, Gibson struck out 92 batters and had a 7–2 record.

When was the designated hitter first used in the World Series?

1976. The Cincinnati Reds, with Dan Driessen as the National League's first-ever designated hitter, swept the Yankees for their second straight World Championship. Driessen contributed a .357 average in the Series.

Starting with the 1976 Series, the DH was used in even-numbered years. In the 1990s the format changed to allow the DH in every World Series, but only in the home park of the American League champ. Pitchers still bat when the NL team hosts a Series game.

In his three World Series (1964, 1967, 1968), totalling 81 innings pitched, Gibson struck out 92 batters.

Who was the last **player-manager** to participate in a World Series?

Lou Boudreau was the Cleveland Indians' everyday shortstop and manager in 1948. That year, his club met—and beat—the Boston Braves in the World Series. Boudreau, who had four doubles in the Series, had been the Tribe's manager since 1942.

Who is the only manager to win World Series titles in his **first year with two different teams**?

Bucky Harris took over the Washington Senators (and played second base) at the age of 27 in 1924. The Senators beat the New York Giants four games to three in the World Series for their first World Championship.

In 1947, Harris, now retired as a player, led the Yankees to a Series title by beating the Brooklyn Dodgers four games to three in his first season as Yankee skipper.

Approximately how much higher is the **players' share** of a seven-game World Series than a four-game World Series?

There is no difference: the players' share is frozen to prevent foul play.

Who was the only **president** ever booed while participating in a World Series ceremony?

Herbert Hoover was booed because of his support of Prohibition.

What was baseball's **"Shot Heard 'Round the World?"**

On October 3, 1951 the New York Giants' Bobby Thomson hit a three-run home run in the bottom of the ninth inning of the third playoff game to decide the National League pennant.

In an era before the League Championship Series, the Brooklyn Dodgers and New York Giants needed a three-game playoff to decide the pennant after a furious race in the last weeks of the regular season. Brooklyn had led most of the year before a late-season collapse.

After splitting the first two games, the two teams returned to the Polo Grounds to finish the series. Don Newcombe of the Dodgers took a 4–1 lead into the ninth but tired. Giants' shortstop Alvin Dark opened the ninth with an infield single, followed by Don Mueller's single. After Monte Irvin popped out, Whitey Lockman doubled Dark home. Mueller went to third, breaking his ankle on the slide (Clint Hartung ran for him). Charlie Dressen, the Brooklyn manager, brought in Ralph Branca to pitch to Thomson. On Branca's 2–1 pitch, Thomson deposited the ball into the Polo Grounds' cozy (256 ft.) left-field corner stands.

The World Series, which that year seemed a bit anti-climactic, wasn't as kind to the Giants. They were beaten by the powerhouse Yankees. That Series did mark the World Series debuts of Willie Mays (who was on deck when Thomson hit his blast) and Mickey Mantle, however.

Branca was also the losing pitcher in the first playoff game ever. In 1946, the Dodgers and St. Louis Cardinals ended the season deadlocked. Branca started and lost Game 1, 4–2.

What **expansion team** was the quickest to win a world championship?

By winning the World Series in their fifth season of existence (1997), the Florida Marlins became the youngest expansion team to accomplish this great feat. They beat the Cleveland Indians in an exciting, seven-game series which saw the final game go to extra innings. The Marlins rise to greatness was marked by steady improvement in each of their first five seasons, progressing from sixth place in 1993 to fifth in 1994, fourth in 1995, third in 1996, and second in 1997 (they made the playoffs as the National League wild card winner). They were also the first team to improve its winning percentage in each of its first five years.

But the championship came at a price. In an effort to cut down costs and make the team more attractive to prospective buyers, owner H. Wayne Huizenga drastically cut the payroll and purged the team of veterans shortly after winning it all. Huizenga claims the team lost $34 million in its World Championship year, which is perhaps not surprising since he spent an estimated $89 million to acquire the collection of top free agents that made the World Series victory possible.

As of June, 1998 only two starting position players remained from Game 7: Second baseman Craig Counsell and shortstop Edgar Renteria. Series MVP Livan Hernandez inherited the No. 1 role in the starting rotation when the other starters were traded (Kevin Brown to San Diego, Al Leiter to the Mets), injured (Alex Fernandez), or left unprotected in the expansion draft (Tony Saunders).

THE HALL OF FAME

When was the **Hall of Fame** established?

The Baseball Hall of Fame was established in 1936 for two purposes: to honor the greatest players of the past, and as part of the celebration of baseball's upcoming "centennial." The first induction class of Ty Cobb, Christy Mathewson, Honus Wagner, Babe Ruth, and Walter Johnson was elected in 1936, none unanimously. The 1937 class consisted of Cy Young, Tris Speaker, and Nap Lajoie. The Hall itself didn't open formally until 1939.

Why is baseball's Hall of Fame in **Cooperstown**?

Cooperstown was chosen as the site for the Baseball Hall of Fame because that is where Abner Doubleday, according to the officially sanctioned myth, "invented" baseball in 1839.

In the early part of the century, a patriotic nation needed American origins for its National Pastime. A.G. Spalding, a former player and owner of the White Sox, as well as owner of a rather famous sporting goods company, formed a blue-ribbon panel to find baseball's American origins. Based on the barest of circumstantial evidence, the panel rubber-stamped the story of Abner Doubleday laying out the diamond and setting out the rules of baseball in a cow pasture near Cooperstown, N.Y.

The debate raged on, however, as historians persisted in pointing out baseball's origins in the English games of Cricket and Rounders. The Doubleday myth was finally put to rest for good in the 1960s.

Doubleday had been a Union officer in the Civil War—he was present at Fort Sumter when the first shots were fired. But he could not count inventing baseball among his accomplishments. He was a cadet at West Point in 1839. The only connection he could claim is that, as a participant in the Civil War, he probably played baseball and helped spread its popularity at his various posts.

Why isn't baseball's leader in hits, at bats, and games in the Hall of Fame?

With a probe involving his gambling habits looming, Pete Rose accepted a lifetime ban from baseball in 1989. This put his future in Cooperstown in serious jeopardy. A conviction for income tax evasion and a prison sentence didn't help matters any. The only hope for Rose is reinstatement, but despite numerous appeals on his part, this does not appear forthcoming. The only person who can reinstate Rose is baseball's Commissioner, currently Bud Selig. Pete Rose retired in 1986 with 4,256 hits in 14,053 at bats while playing in 3,562 games.

Cooperstown, already known as the birthplace of James Fenimore Cooper, is a picturesque setting, and is representative of the area where baseball evolved and gained its popularity in America.

What does it take to get elected into the **Baseball Hall of Fame**?

An outstanding career and a little help from the baseball writers. The members of the Baseball Writers Association of America (BBWAA) elect the Hall of Famers. To be eligible for the Hall of Fame, a player must have played at least ten years in the Major Leagues and be retired for five years. Once he is on the ballot, he needs to be named on 75% of the ballots cast to be elected. If he falls below that, he remains on the ballot unless he recieved less than 5% of the ballots cast. A player can remain on the ballot for 15 years as long as he stays above 5%. After 15 years, players are taken off the ballot and can no longer be considered for enshrinement by the BBWAA. The Veterans Committee can then consider them. The 15-member Veterans Committee is made up of five Hall of Famers, five members of the baseball media, and five members who have been involved in the game in a capacity other than playing or covering it (such as managers, team executives, etc). The Veterans Committee can consider anyone who appeared on at least 60% of the BBWAA ballots cast when he was eligible. As with the writers' voting, a candidate must receive support from 75% of the Veterans Committee to be enshrined.

Who entered the Baseball Hall of Fame the **soonest after playing his last game**?

Roberto Clemente was killed in a plane crash after the 1972 season, while on a humaitarian mission of bringing supplies to earthquake-ravaged Nicaragua. Clemente was a cinch for the Hall, having compiled 3,000 hits and leading the Pittsburgh Pirates to the 1971 World Championship. The standard five-year wait after a player's retirement was waived. The annual Roberto Clemente Award honors players for community service.

What is the only **father-son tandem in the Hall of Fame**?

Larry and Lee MacPhail. Larry MacPhail served as President of the New York Yankees and Brooklyn Dodgers where he introduced night-time baseball in 1939. Lee MacPhail was general manager of the Yankees, where he developed the talent that provided nine pennants and seven World Championships in ten years, and Baltimore Orioles. In Baltimore, Lee MacPhail put together the team that would win the franchise's first World Championship in 1966. For this he was named 1966 Executive of the Year. He worked in the Commissioner's office as chief administrative assistant to William Eckert after leaving Baltimore. From 1974–1983, Lee MacPhail served as American League President, where he preserved the Designated Hitter, helped settle the 1981 strike, and presided over the first expansion of the AL since 1969.

Lee's son Andy is president of the Chicago Cubs, and his grandson, Lee, is the scouting director for the Cleveland Indians.

OUTSTANDING INDIVIDUAL FEATS

PITCHING

Who pitched the only **back-to-back no-hitters**?

Several pitchers have hurled two no-hitters during a single season, but Johnny Vander Meer of the Cincinnati Reds is the only pitcher to throw no hitters back-to-back. They came on June 11 (winning 3–0 against the Boston Braves) and June 15, 1938 (winning 6–0 against the Brooklyn Dodgers). Vander Meer was 23 at the time and only in his second big league season. Some feel his accomplishment is the one baseball record that will never be broken, considering it will take three consecutive no-hitters to beat it.

Who are the two most recent pitchers to hurl **two no-hitters during a single season**?

Nolan Ryan pitched two no-hitters in 1973 for the California Angels and Jim Maloney tossed two in 1965. Maloney's no-hitters were excruciating: he lost the first one 1–0

Who is the only pitcher to throw a perfect game and lose?

Technically this is impossible, but on May 26, 1959, Harvey Haddix of the Pirates retired the first 36 Braves he faced. He thus pitched 12 perfect innings—or a game and a third, if you look at it that way. Unfortunately, Haddix lost the game in the thirteenth inning. The Braves' leadoff hitter, Felix Mantilla, reached first base on a throwing error by Pirates third baseman Don Hoak. Then Eddie Mathews hit a sacrifice fly to move the runner to second. After walking Hank Aaron intentionally, Haddix gave up a hit to Joe Adcock, and the Braves won by a score of 1-0. So, one of the greatest pitching performances ever was entered into the "L" column of the record books (which don't count it as an "official" perfect game).

---

and gave up a hit in the tenth inning (which reflects the fact that a no-hitter covers nine innings), and he won the other game 1–0 in ten innings. Sandy Koufax pitched a perfect game that year and he, too, won a 1–0 battle.

Has anyone ever pitched a **no-hitter on Opening Day**?

Yes. Bob Feller blanked the White Sox 1–0 in Chicago on April 16, 1940.

Mike Witt of the California Angels pitched a perfect game on the last day of the season in 1984.

Who threw a **no-hitter to clinch a division title**?

Mike Scott clinched the NL West Division Championship for the Houston Astros on September 25, 1986. Scott's 2–0 mastery of the San Francisco Giants included 13 strikeouts and eliminated the Cincinnati Reds.

Cy Young won the most games (511), but which pitcher **lost the most games** in baseball history?

None other than Denton True (Cy) Young, who lost 316. At 511–316, though, his winning percentage was still over .600. Pud Galvin was the second biggest loser, but he, too, posted a winning record (361–308). Same with Nolan Ryan, who ranks third with 292 losses. In fact, only one pitcher in the top 15 in career losses sported a career losing record—Jack Powell at 245–256—proving you have to be darn good to lose so often.

61

What active major league baseball player was the first to **win the Cy Young Award four times in a row**?

Atlanta Braves pitcher Greg Maddux. His first came in 1992 with the Chicago Cubs. After joining the Braves via free agency, Maddux continued his dominance of the National League in 1993 and the strike-shortened seasons of 1994 and 1995. Twice during that span his ERA was under 2.00 (1.56 in 1994 and 1.63 in 1995). His record for the four years was an amazing 75–30.

Who is the only pitcher to have both a **20-win season and a 20-save season**?

Dennis Eckersley, who broke in with the Cleveland Indians in 1975 and was recognized as one of the hottest young starting pitchers around. He tossed a 1–0 no-hit victory against the California Angels on May 30, 1977, and posted a 20–8 record in 1978 while with Boston Red Sox. Eckersley rejuvenated his career in the late 1980s when he switched to the bullpen upon joining the Oakland A's. He went on to become the most dominant relief pitcher in baseball history, winning the American League Most Valuable Player and Cy Young awards in 1992. While pitching for the A's, Eckersley recorded 323 saves—setting the American League career record—including 45 in 1988, 33 in 1989, 48 in 1990, 43 in 1991, 51 in 1992, 36 in 1993, and 29 in 1995. In 1996, Eck was traded to the St. Louis Cardinals of the National League. He continued his fine performance, recording 30 saves that year and another 36 in 1997. He re-signed with Boston for the 1998 season, agreeing to serve as the set-up man for closer Tom Gordon in his final season.

Who was the last **switch-hitter to win the A.L. MVP**?

Vida Blue, 1971. The Oakland A's pitcher, who won 24 games that year for the Western Division champions, batted from both sides of the plate.

The last non-pitching switch-hitter to win the MVP was Mickey Mantle in 1956.

How many pitchers were used by both sides combined in the **longest major league game** ever played, 26 innings, in 1920?

Two: Leon Cadore pitched for Brooklyn, Joe Oeschger for Boston.

Has a player ever won the Triple Crown and not been named the league's Most Valuable Player?

Ted Williams won the triple crown twice, in 1942 and 1947, but was not voted the MVP for either season. In 1942, the Baseball Writers Association of America voted the Yankees' Joe Gordon MVP. Gordon's statistics pale against Williams' (he hit .322, with 18 homers and 103 RBI, compared to Williams' .356, 36, 137), but Gordon was a key member of the pennant winning team that year. In 1947 Williams' .343 average, 32 home runs, and 114 RBI were not enough to sway voters from Joe DiMaggio's stats (.315, 20, 97) for a pennant winner. Williams did win the MVP twice, though, in 1946 (.342, 38, and a league-leading 142 RBI) and 1949 (.343 average, and league leader in homers with 43 and RBI with 159; for good measure, he also led the league in 1949 in runs with 150, doubles with 39, and walks with 162).

HITTING

What is the **Triple Crown**?

The Triple Crown—one player leading his league in home runs, batting average, and runs batted in—has been accomplished 14 times. Paul Hines (Providence, 1878) and Hugh Duffy (Boston, 1894) accomplished it before the turn of the century. The last player to do it was Boston's Carl Yastrzemski in 1967. St. Louis' Joe Medwick was the last National Leaguer to turn the trick, in 1937.

Pitchers have a less-recognized but equally impressive Triple Crown to shoot for—leading the league in wins, earned run average and strikeouts. Roger Clemens of the Toronto Blue Jays was the last to accomplish this feat, in 1997. Winning this Triple Crown usually adds up to a Cy Young Award, as it did for Clemens.

How many players are in the **30/30 club**?

The 30/30 club is made up of players who have stolen 30 bases and hit 30 home runs in a single season. There are 36 members through 1997. Ken Williams of the St. Louis Browns was the first to do it, slugging 39 homers and stealing 37 bases in 1922. No one else did it until Willie Mays hit 36 homers and stole 40 bases in 1956, then the Say Hey Kid did it again in 1957 (35 HR, 38 SB). Jose Canseco was the last American Leaguer to do it, in 1988. The 30/30 club was expanded 23 times in the National League during the 1990s. 28 National Leaguers and eight American Leaguers have reached the 30/30 plateau. In 1997, four players joined (or renewed membership in) the club: Raul Mondesi of the Los Angeles Dodgers, NL MVP Larry Walker of the Colorado Rockies, Jeff Bagwell of the Houston Astros, and Barry Bonds of the San Francisco Giants. Bonds joined his father Bobby Bonds as the only five-time members.

Has anyone ever gone **40/40**?

Jose Canseco did it in 1988 (42 HR, 40 SB) and Barry Bonds in 1996 (42 HR, 40 SB): they are the only two members of the 40/40 club.

Cal Ripken broke Lou Gehrig's streak of consecutive games, but whose **streak did Gehrig break**?

The Iron Horse passed Everett Scott, a shortstop who played for Boston and New York in 1,307 straight games from 1916 through 1925; interestingly, his streak stopped on May 5, 1925, and Gehrig's started a few weeks later on June 1, 1925. Scott was traded from the Yankees to the Senators on June 17th. Joe Sewell, of Cleveland, had a streak of 1,103 games from 1922 to 1930, running ahead of Gehrig for five years, but Gehrig went on to play through to 1939.

Even though Cal Ripken's streak continues on into 1998 from May 30, 1982 and has passed 2,500 games, he still hasn't reached the top 20 all-time in games played. Gehrig isn't in the top 20, either. In fact, no player who appeared in over 1,000 straight games (there are six) is in the top 20 in career games played, which shows the value of an occasional day off. George Brett is 20th, by the way, at 2,707 games played, and Pete Rose is first at 3,562.

Who is **Wally Pipp**?

When a player contemplates taking himself out of the lineup due to illness or injury, he should always pause for a moment and remember Wally Pipp. Then he should consider the severity of the problem and wonder if it's really worth missing a game. Pipp was the Yankees first baseman who took a day off (because of a headache or to go to the track, depending on whose story you believe) and was replaced by Lou Gehrig. Gehrig went on to play in 2,130 consecutive games (a streak that stood for over 50 years until it was broken recently by Cal Ripken, Jr.) while Pipp went on to play in Cincinnati.

How many people have **hit safely in at least 40 consecutive games**?

Only six players have had 40-game hit streaks, led by Joe DiMaggio at 56 in 1941. He broke Willie Keeler's 44-game hit streak of 1897, and Pete Rose tied Keeler at 44 in

Joe Dimaggio has the longest hitting streak in Major League history. He hit in 56 straight games in 1941. After the streak was ended in Cleveland, he promptly started a 17-game streak.

1978. Bill Dahlen of the 1894 Cubs (42), George Sisler of the 1922 Cardinals (41), and
Ty Cobb of the 1911 Tigers (40) are others with hit streaks of 40 games or more. Paul
Molitor had a streak of 39 in 1987.

Who won a major league **batting title** in 1972 without hitting a single home run during the season?

Rod Carew won the first of his six batting titles with a .318 average in '72. Of his 170
hits, none were home runs, and only 27 of them were for extra bases.

That season wasn't out of the ordinary for Carew. His highest single-season home
run total was 14 (in 1975 and 1977), and of his 3,053 career hits, only 92 were dingers.

Who is the only **rookie to win a batting title** in baseball's "modern era" (since 1900)?

Tony Oliva of the Minnesota Twins hit .323 to lead the American League in 1964. He
also led the league in hits (217), doubles (43), and runs (109) that year. Throw in 32
home runs, 94 RBI and 161 games played, and he was a shoo-in for AL Rookie of the
Year.

Has a player on a **first-year expansion** team ever won a batting title?

Yes. In 1993, first baseman Andres Galarraga hit .370 to win the NL batting crown
while playing for the Colorado Rockies.

The only other first-year expansion team member to lead the league in a positive
stat was the Washington Senators' Dick Donovan, who led the American League in
ERA with a 2.40 mark in 1961.

Who is the only player to be named **Most Valuable Player in both leagues**?

Frank Robinson. In 1961, Robinson took NL MVP honors by hitting .323 with 37 home runs and 124 RBI, scoring 117 runs, and leading the Cincinnati Reds' charge to the National League pennant.

After the Reds, considering him "old" at 30, traded him to Baltimore after the 1965 season, Robinson had a career year in 1966. That year he hit .316, with 49 home runs and 122 RBI to win the Triple Crown. He also led the league with 122 runs scored and a .637 slugging percentage. He again led his team to a pennant (and a World Championship) and was the easy choice for AL MVP.

Who was the only **rookie to be named Most Valuable Player**?

Fred Lynn of the Boston Red Sox hit .331 with 21 homers and 105 RBI, led the league in doubles (47), runs (103), and slugging percentage (.566), and stole ten bases to lead Boston to the pennant and earn AL Rookie of the Year and MVP honors in 1975.

Who was the first player to collect **500 hits with four different teams**?

Rusty Staub had started with the Houston Colt .45s/Astros, where he collected 792 hits. He then went to Montreal, where, in the first of two tours with the Expos, he had 508 hits. New York was another two-time destination (1972–1975 and closing out his career from 1981–1985), where he tallied 709 hits. In Detroit from 1976–1978, he added 524 more safeties. Staub ended up with a career total of 2,716 major league hits.

What baseball great holds the record for **most career walks**?

Babe Ruth holds the career record at 2,056. He led the league in walks 11 times during his career, with a high of 170 in 1923.

How many **at-bats** did it take Pete Rose to set the record for most career hits?

It took Rose 14,053 at-bats (number one all-time) to compile 4,256 career hits. He compiled a .303 career batting average, had ten 200-hit seasons, and led his league in hits seven times.

Rose added 35 post-season hits in 130 at-bats for a .269 average in October.

What player hit **the most grand slams in one season**?

In 1987, Don Mattingly of the New York Yankees hit six grand slams to set the single-season mark.

What National Leaguer holds the record for the most **home runs hit after his fortieth birthday**?

Stan Musial, who hit 46 dingers from 1961 to 1963.

Who are the only two players to have **back-to-back 50-homer seasons**?

Babe Ruth and Mark McGwire. Ruth smashed 54 home runs in 1920, then followed that up with a 59 homer season in 1921. He also had 54 homers in 1928, the season after he set the record with 60.

McGwire posted 52 round-trippers in 1996, followed by his 58-homer performance for the A's and Cardinals in 1997.

How many players **homered on the first pitch in their first major league at bat**?

72 players have hit a home run in their first at bat through 1997, eleven on the first pitch. Chuck Tanner (1955), Bert Campaneris (1964), and Jay Bell (1986) are the best-known, and Jay Gainer in a 1993 game for Colorado was the last to do it.

THE ALL-STAR GAME

When was the **first All-Star Game**?

The first All-Star Game was part of Chicago's Century of Progress Exposition in 1933. It was founded by Chicago Tribune sports editor Arch Ward as the featured sports event for the celebration. Comiskey Park was the host park.

> ### Did baseball ever have more than one All-Star game in a single season?
>
> **B**etween 1959 and 1963, MLB decided to stage two All-Star games. This idea was quickly abandoned, as it became apparent that the thrill and novelty of seeing all the game's best players on one field wore thin when it happened more than once a year. The only time the All-Star game was not held was in 1945, when World War II travel restrictions made it impossible.

Ward went on to create the Chicago College All-Star Football Game in 1934, and the All-American Football Conference (AAFC) in 1946.

What are the only days of the year on which none of the four major sports leagues (NBA, NHL, NFL, and Major League Baseball) have any games scheduled?

There are no regular-season or playoff games for any of the four major sports on the day before (Monday) and the day after (Wednesday) Major League Baseball's All-Star Game. Baseball is the only one of the four that's in season in July.

Who hit the first All-Star Game grand slam?

In the third inning of the 1983 All-Star Game at Chicago's Comiskey Park, Fred Lynn of the California Angels came to the plate with the bases loaded and a 5–1 lead. Lynn drilled Atlee Hammaker's 2–2 delivery into the right field seats, scoring Cleveland's Manny Trillo, Angel teammate Rod Carew, and Milwaukee's Robin Yount ahead of him. The AL went on to win 13–3, breaking the NL's 11-game winning streak.

Who is the only manager to suffer All-Star Game losses in both leagues?

Cincinnati's Sparky Anderson was the NL manager in the 1971 classic at Detroit's Tiger Stadium for the NL's only loss of the decade. Five future Hall of Famers homered (and 11 future Hall members played) in the 6–4 AL victory.

Anderson's other All-Star loss came in 1985, 6–1. Anderson, now Detroit's skipper, faced Dick Williams, who had three previous All-Star losses as an AL manager.

69

What is an **Eephus pitch**?

Pronounced "eee-fuss," this unorthodox pitch is a ball thrown overhand and aimed up into the air in hopes that it will confuse batters as it drops across the strike zone from the top to the bottom. Eephus pitches often reach a high point of 25 feet as they travel from the mound to home plate. Pitcher Truett "Rip" Sewell once threw three straight Eephus pitches to Ted Williams in the 1946 All-Star game. On the third pitch, Williams stepped a few feet towards the mound and blasted the ball over the right-field fence. It is not a widely practiced pitch in the big leagues, although Bob Tewksbury used it on Mark McGwire (successfully) in a 1998 game.

CHANGE, INNOVATION, AND MONEY

BASEBALL AND RACE

Who were the first players to break the **color line**?

In 1884, African-American brothers Welday and Moses Fleetwood Walker played for Toledo of the American Association, which was at the time considered a major league. No African-American played Major League Baseball again until 1947.

In 1947, Jackie Robinson became the first African-American to play Major League Baseball. Playing for the Brooklyn Dodgers, Robinson debuted in April of 1947. Larry Doby broke the American League color line with the Cleveland Indians on July 5th of that year.

After Jackie Robinson broke the color barrier, how long did the **Negro Leagues** survive? Did they produce any additional major leaguers?

The integration of Major League Baseball in 1947 took its toll on the Negro Leagues quickly. By the early 1950s, the Negro Leagues were little more than a stopover on the way to the majors. By the early 1960s, they were gone completely.

Many of Robinson's contemporaries followed quickly after he opened the gate. On the Dodgers alone, he was quickly joined by Joe Black, Roy Campanella, and Don Newcombe. Larry Doby's debut in Cleveland later in 1947 made him the first African-American to play in the American League, where he suffered many of the same hardships as Robinson in relative anonymity. Early in 1998, Doby joined Robinson in the Hall of Fame, elected by the Veterans Committee. Stars such as Monte Irvin of the New York Giants and Luke Easter of the Indians came later in the decade.

Jackie Robinson broke the color barrier in 1947 with the Brooklyn Dodgers. He led the Dodgers to the NL pennant and was named the first Rookie of the Year.

Who was the first black manager in the Major Leagues?

Frank Robinson made history when he was named player-manager of the Cleveland Indians for the 1975 season.

Robinson again made history when he became the first black manager in the National League by taking over the San Francisco Giants in 1981.

Larry Doby, the second African-American *player* in the majors, was also the second African-American to manage in the bigs, taking the helm of the Chicago White Sox in 1977.

Some of the biggest stars of the 50s and 60s served brief apprenticeships with the fading Negro Leagues in the late 40s and early 50s. Hank Aaron, Ernie Banks, and Willie Mays were all signed out of the Negro Leagues.

Satchel Paige, legendary for his skill and showmanship in the old days, arrived in Cleveland in time to help the Indians to a pennant in 1948, though he was way past his prime. He made another appearance for Charlie Finley's attention-starved Kansas City A's in 1965.

Who was baseball's first **Rookie of the Year**?

Jackie Robinson batted .297 and led the league in stolen bases during his rookie year of 1947, helping lead the Dodgers to the World Series and becoming the first Rookie of the Year. The first two Rookie of the Year awards were given to one major league player; in 1949, awards went to the best rookie in their respective leagues, as voted by the Baseball Writers Association of America. Two years later, Robinson won the MVP award. The Rookie of the Year Award now bears the name of its first recipient.

Who were some of the finest players in the **Negro Leagues**?

Some of the finest players in baseball history never made it to the major leagues, and many others only made it when they were well past their prime. These players were denied a chance to compete simply because of the color of their skin, during a time when racial prejudice would not allow them to play with the white players. Instead, they became legends of the Negro Leagues.

Josh Gibson was known as "the Black Babe Ruth." A catcher and powerful hitter, he and one-time battery mate Satchel Paige were the star attractions in the Negro Leagues. Gibson played for the Homestead Grays and Pittsburgh Crawfords before dying of a brain tumor at the young age of 35. It's said that he once hit a ball com-

Josh Gibson was one of the greatest players of the Negro Leagues. Unfortunately, he died before the Major Leagues' color line was crossed.

pletely out of Yankee Stadium. Since recorded stats and recaps are rare, there's no documentation, but there are plenty of eye witness accounts that bear out the veracity of the claim. Satchel Paige won hundreds of games during his 22-year Negro League career. On his 42nd birthday he was sold by the Kansas City Monarchs to Bill Veeck's Cleveland Indians, becoming the majors' oldest rookie. Paige also played for the Browns and—in 1965 at the age of 59—pitched three innings for the A's. James "Cool Papa" Bell was considered the fastest Negro Leaguer by his contemporaries. The switch-hitting center fielder played for the St. Louis Stars, the Pittsburgh Crawfords, the Homestead Grays, and the Kansas City Stars between 1922 and 1950. If Josh Gibson was black baseball's Babe Ruth, then Buck Leonard was its Lou Gehrig. From 1937 to 1946, Leonard and Gibson were the most feared combination in Negro baseball, helping the Homestead Grays to nine straight pennants between 1937 and 1945. Consistently a .300 hitter, Leonard was also a spectacular fielder.

Other prominent Negro Leaguers in Baseball's Hall of Fame include infielders Buck O'Neil, Mule Suttles, Ray Dandridge, Toni Stone, Lorenzo Davis, Jackie Robinson, Pop Lloyd, Artie Wilson, Willie Wells, and Judy Johnson; outfielders Willard Brown, Larry Doby, Oscar Charleston, Monte Irvin, Henry Thompson, Turkey Stearnes, Wild Bill Wright, and Gene Benson; pitchers Joe Black, Chet Brewer, Ray Brown, Max Manning, Leon Day, Martin Dihigo, Willie Foster, Bullet Rogan, Hilton Smith, Smokey Joe Williams, and Dan Bankhead; catchers Ted Radcliffe and Biz Mackey; and manager Rube Foster.

What **number is retired** by every Major League team?

The number 42. In 1997, every team in the Major Leagues retired the number in honor of the 50th anniversary of Jackie Robinson's breaking the color barrier. In that magical 1947 season, Robinson batted .297 and led the National League in stolen bases while playing for the Brooklyn Dodgers. He went on to play for them until 1956. Robinson was elected to the Hall of Fame in 1962. Players who were wearing the number at the time of the retirement were allowed to keep it until *they* retire. After that, the number will never again be worn. Players who decided to keep it include Mo Vaughn of the Boston Red Sox and Butch Huskey of the New York Mets, both chose the number in honor of Robinson.

CHANGING THE RULES

When was the first **night game** played?

Although suggested as early as the 1880s, night baseball didn't make its Major League debut until May 24, 1935 at Crosley Field. The Cincinnati Reds hosted the first night baseball game in major league history, defeating the Philadelphia Phillies.

What is the "ten and five rule"?

The clause is part of the Basic Agreement between the players' union and the owners which stipulates that a player with ten or more seasons in the majors and five consecutive years of service with one team has the right to refuse to be traded. This clause was part of the contract signed between the owners and players in February of 1973. On December 5, 1973, Ron Santo, a lifelong Chicago Cub, was the first to exercise his veto right when he refused to be traded to the California Angels. A week later, Santo approved a trade to the Chicago White Sox.

In March of 1973, Jim Perry, who had been in the majors since 1959, and had been a member of the Minnesota Twins since 1963, accepted a trade to the Detroit Tigers, waiving his veto right.

Falling attendance due to the Great Depression was one of the main reasons for night baseball. Owners figured that the novelty, plus the fact that people who *were* working would be able to attend more games at night would make the experiment a success. Eventually they were proven correct and now a weekday (or even Saturday) afternoon game is a rarity.

The first night-time World Series game was Game 4 of the 1971 Classic. Many purists took this as a sign of the coming apocalypse

When were the first **radio and television broadcasts** of baseball games?

The first radio broadcast of a baseball game was during the 1922 World Series. Post-season games were broadcast regularly after that, but it wasn't until the 30s that owners (who feared that radio would affect gate reciepts) finally realized that radio could be a revenue producer and allowed regular-season contests to be aired.

The first televised baseball game came in 1939. The Brooklyn Dodgers hosted the Reds, as well as over 33,000 paying customers. At the time, New York City had about 500 TV sets.

When was **interleague play** introduced in baseball?

The owners voted to bring interleague play to baseball in 1997, in hopes of creating new regional rivalries to generate fan interest. Baseball purists were quick to denounce the concept, claiming it would cause confusion (the designated hitter rule, for example) and dilute the World Series. Ultimately, it was up to the fans to decide.

Judging by some attendance figures, interleague play appears to be a success, particularly in the case of intercity rivals like the Yankees and Mets or Cubs and White Sox.

Who was the first **Designated Hitter**?

Ron Blomberg of the New York Yankees. On April 6, 1973 Blomberg came to bat in the first inning with the bases loaded and walked.

The idea of the designated hitter had been around for a while—early proponents included Connie Mack—but it wasn't until the American League (in a quest for more offense) decided to give it a three-year trial, that it actually reached the majors. The "experiment" stuck, and now the National League is the only league in organized baseball that still lets the pitcher bat.

How did baseball's **free agency** develop?

In 1970, outfielder Curt Flood was traded from the Cardinals to the Phillies, much to his displeasure. Flood refused to report to his new team and instead tested a reserve clause in his contract. The reserve clause was a standard part of every contract at the time that stated that the ball club retained a player's rights from the time he signed his first contract until the team no longer required his services. This marked the first time a player had challenged his team in this manner, and it was a catalyst for free agency. Flood took his case to the Supreme Court, and lost. But his case served to open the door to other challenges to the reserve clause. In 1975 arbitrator Pete Dietz granted free agency to pitchers Andy Messersmith and Dave McNally, after they played all season without contracts. This further modification of the reserve clause shifted even more power to the players from the owners. Messersmith, after winning 19 games for the Dodgers that year, went on to win only 18 more games in his entire career, earning him the dubious distinction as the first free agent bust. The first star player to be granted free agency was Catfish Hunter. He sued owner Charlie Finley for breach of contract over an unfulfilled clause in his contract and was given his freedom by the court. The former Oakland Athletic and future Hall-of-Fame pitcher was involved in a bidding war for his services and signed a free agent contract with the New York Yankees in 1975.

The cumulative effect of these cases was the fall of the reserve clause. The now-powerful players' union negotiated it out of existence in the 1970s, setting up the lucrative free agent era. Union head Marvin Miller, who knew that universal free agency would be just as bad as having no free agency, negotiated a system based on service time for potential free agents.

Free agency became a hot topic in baseball again in the mid-1980s. At that time, several big-name players decided to test the waters as free agents, only to encounter a curious lack of interest among other major-league clubs. *Sports Illustrated* even ran a

Jim "Catfish" Hunter's courtroom win against Charlie Finley helped open the door for free agency in the 1970s.

cover story about Kirk Gibson, a speedy outfielder and power hitter for the Detroit Tigers, and his lack of success in the free agent market. At the end of the 1987 season, a federal arbitrator determined that major-league baseball owners had illegally agreed among themselves not to pursue free agent players from other teams. This collusion had enabled the owners to save money, but it had also unfairly prevented some big-name free agents—such as Gibson—from using competitive bids for their services to gain lucrative contracts. To address the past unfair treatment, the arbitrator declared all affected players to be immediate free agents and ordered the owners to pay compensatory damages.

Nolan Ryan's $1,000,000 per year contract shocked baseball in 1980, now it's well below the league average. During the winter of 1997, Mike Piazza turned down an offer from the Dodgers worth $11,000,000 a season, prompting Los Angeles to trade him to the bargain basement Marlins, who turned around and swapped him to the New York Mets for prospects. Most trades made today are prompted by such off-the-field concerns as salary and signability rather than by things like ability and positional need.

FINANCIAL CONCERNS

Who formed the **$100,000 infield**?

Connie Mack's Philadelphia A's of the 1910s boasted a veritable All-Star team, especially in the infield. The "$100,000 infield," so named because their combined salaries added up to that sum, consisted of "Stuffy" McInnis at first base, Eddie Collins at second, Jack Barry at shortstop, and Frank "Home Run" Baker at third.

By 1915, spiraling salaries caused by the Federal League forced Mack to break up his dynasty, and the A's sank to the second division until the late 1920s.

How much did the Red Sox get for **Babe Ruth**?

In 1920, Harry Frazee, cash-strapped owner of the Boston Red Sox, sold Babe Ruth to the New York Yankees for the then-unheard-of sum of $125,000. Frazee needed the money to finance a theatrical venture. The play closed shortly after it opened. Ruth led the Yankees to seven AL pennants and four World Championships.

What is the **Curse of the Bambino**?

By selling Babe Ruth to the New York Yankees in 1920, some believe that Boston Red Sox owner Harry Frazee put a curse on the franchise. The team's knack for losing the

The Yankees' acquisition of Babe Ruth from the Red Sox drastically changed the fortunes of the two storied franchises.

What is the most valuable baseball card and why?

The T206 card of Honus Wagner is the Holy Grail of sports cards, commanding prices upwards of $25,000 for one in mint condition. Issued in 1909 by the Sweet Caporal cigarette company, this card became scarce when anti-smoker Wagner demanded that his image be discontinued in the promotion because he did not want to set a bad example for children. The eight-time National League batting champion (between 1900 and 1911) also lead the league in RBIs four times and in stolen bases five times during his impressive career with Pittsburgh. The combination of the card's scarcity, and the fact that it pictures a Hall of Famer contributes to its high value.

seventh game of the World Series (1946, 1967, 1975 and 1986) gives some credence to this theory. Bill Buckner's crucial 10th inning error in Game 6 of the 1986 Series with the Mets—who were one strike from elimination—was particularly painful. The Red Sox have not won a World Series since the Babe packed his bags for the Big Apple.

Who was the first player to earn **$1,000,000** for a single season?

In 1980, Nolan Ryan left the California Angels for the home cookin' of his native Texas and the $1,000,000 per season that the Houston Astros offered him.

ODDS AND ENDS

What player was **drafted out of college** by the Utah Stars (ABA), the Minnesota Vikings (NFL), and the San Diego Padres (NL)?

Dave Winfield. He chose the Padres, which turned out to be a good choice. Winfield had a Hall of Fame career with the Padres, Yankees, Angels, Blue Jays, Twins, and Indians.

Who holds the record for the **most strikeouts in the College World Series**?

Carl Thomas struck out 64 batters over the course of three years (1954–56) while playing for the University of Arizona.

Hank Aaron connects for one of his 755 home runs. He and brother Tommie lead all Major League brother acts in homers with 768.

Which teams have won **multiple college baseball championships**?

Through 1997, the University of Southern California has won the College World Series 11 times. Arizona State (five) and Texas (four) are next; Arizona, Cal State Fullerton, Louisiana State, and Minnesota have won three, California, Miami of Florida, Michigan, Oklahoma, and Stanford have won twice. Florida Southern has been the Division II champion eight times.

What **father-son tandem** is the first to be drafted in the first round of the free-agent draft?

Tom and Ben Grieve. Tom was the Washington Senators' first round pick in 1966. Ben, chosen second overall, was the first choice of the Oakland A's in 1994.

After a nine-year career, Tom Grieve served as the Texas Rangers' general manager. Ben Grieve impressed many in his brief stay with the A's in 1997, and is being counted on as a major part of Oakland's rebuilding project.

What **brother combination** has hit the most home runs?

Between them, Hank and Tommie Aaron smacked 768 homers. Hank, of course, is the all-time leader with 755. Tommie, who played on the same Milwaukee and Atlanta Braves teams as Hank from 1962 to 1971, contributed 13 dingers to the total.

81

Who made his major league debut by **pitching against his brother**?

Pat Underwood beat the Toronto Blue Jays—and brother Tom—1–0 in his first major league start. Pat went 8 1/3 innings and gave up only three hits. Older brother Tom went the distance, allowing six hits, one of which was a Jerry Morales home run.

Who are the only two major leaguers to **play each of the nine positions in a single game**?

Bert Campaneris and Cesar Tovar. Playing for the Kansas City A's against the California Angels on September 8, 1965, Campaneris played all nine positions before leaving the game after a home plate collision in the ninth inning. Campaneris started the game at shortstop (his natural position), moved to second base, then third, then proceeded around the outfield—moving from left field to right—to first base before taking the mound in the eighth. Campaneris finished up behind the plate, where the aforementioned collision ended his night. Jose Cardenal, Campaneris' second cousin, played in the game for California.

Tovar matched Campaneris' feat, ironically against Campaneris' A's, on September 22, 1968. Tovar started the game on the mound, where he faced—and retired—leadoff man Campaneris. Tovar's Twins won the game 2–1.

What were some of the **promotions and gimmicks** that **Bill Veeck** put on? How about **Charley Finley**?

Above anything, baseball maverick Bill Veeck (1914–1986) thought a day (or night) at the ballpark should be fun. As owner of the Indians, Browns, and White Sox, Veeck broke attendance records with winning teams and promoted the heck out of losing ones in a never-ending quest for attendance. He used bizarre gimmicks like letting the fans manage games, cow-milking contests, exploding scoreboards, and the infamous

"Disco Demolition Night." One of his most famous stunts involved hiring Eddie Gaedel—a midget who stood three feet seven inches tall and weighed a mere 67 pounds—as a pinch hitter. Veeck also signed Larry Doby, the American League's first black player, in 1947, and hired the league's oldest rookie, 42-year-old Satchel Paige, in 1948. In 1960, he became the first owner to put players' names on the backs of uniforms. Veeck was elected to baseball's Hall of Fame in 1991.

Another one of baseball's most colorful personalties was A's owner Charley Finley. Like Veeck, he often resorted to wacky stunts (orange baseballs, mechanical ballboys, having the players enter the field on the backs of mules and from the backs of limos) to keep things interesting, but proved to be a knowledgeable baseball man as well. He introduced nighttime World Series games and had an uncanny knack for evaluating talent. His Oakland teams won five straight divisional titles (1971–75) and three straight World Championships (1972–74). In 1972 Finley encouraged his players to wear mustaches as an intimidation factor, giving them a $300 bonus to do so. Several players—including Rollie Fingers, Catfish Hunter, Reggie Jackson, and Gene Tenace—took him up on the offer and became part of the notorious "Mustache Gang." He also offered Vida Blue a bonus to change his first name to "True." Blue passed on that one.

What franchise has had the **most Rookies of the Year**?

The Brooklyn/Los Angeles Dodgers have had 16 Rookie of the Year winners, beginning with the first-ever Rookie of the Year recipient: Jackie Robinson in 1947. Dodger rookies have had four- and five-year winning streaks: From 1979–82, pitchers Rick Sutcliffe, Steve Howe, and Fernando Valenzuela, as well as second baseman Steve Sax, brought the award back to Los Angeles. Dodger kids also dominated from 1992–96, when Eric Karros, Mike Piazza, Raul Mondesi, Hideo Nomo, and Todd Hollandsworth took the hardware.

Other Dodger rookie winners are Don Newcombe (1949), Joe Black (1952), Jim Gilliam (1953), Frank Howard (1960), Jim Lefebvre (1965), and Ted Sizemore (1969).

The only other franchise to have more than two consecutive winners is the Oakland A's, who had Jose Canseco, Mark McGwire, and Walt Weiss win from 1986–1988.

The New York Yankees lead the AL with eight winners.

What was **Murderer's Row**?

Arguably the most feared lineup ever, the 1927 New York Yankees were nicknamed Murderer's Row for their hitting prowess. The lineup included Lou Gehrig (47 homers and 175 RBIs) at first, Tony Lazzeri at second, Mark Koenig at shortstop, and Joe Dugan at the hot corner. The outfield of Babe Ruth, Bob Meusel, and Earle Combs combined for 597 hits and a .350 average. Ruth also hit 60 homers and drove in 164 runs. In fact, his home run output surpassed the entire Philadelphia Athletics team

(which hit 56). The Yankees won 110 games that year, taking the American League
pennant and sweeping the Pittsburgh Pirates in the World Series.

Have **non-playing managers ever been traded**?

Yes. On August 3, 1960, the Detroit Tigers and Cleveland Indians traded managers.
Tigers skipper Jimmy Dykes jumped two places in the standings when he took over
the fourth-place Indians. Joe Gordon moved from Cleveland to Detroit, and settled in
at sixth place.

Who is the only player to play for both the **Seattle Pilots and the Seattle Mariners**?

Pitcher Diego Segui helped usher in both Major League Baseball eras in Seattle. In
1969 (the Pilots' only year of existence before moving to Milwaukee to become the
Brewers), Segui went 12–6 with a 3.35 ERA. In the Mariners' debut season of 1977,
Segui, at the end of his career, compiled an 0–7 record with a 5.68 ERA. He is the
father of first baseman David Segui, who, in 1998, signed as a free agent with...Seattle.

Lou Piniella was an original member of the Pilots, but was traded to fellow expan-
sionists Kansas City during spring training of 1969. He is currently the Mariners'
manager, and led them to their first post-season appearance ever in 1995.

What was the **Pine Tar incident**?

Hitters have been known to rub pine tar on their bat handles in order to obtain a better grip. League rules state that the tar cannot extend beyond 18 inches from the bottom of the bat, although it is unknown what further advantage a batter would have if

George Brett applying pine tar to his bat. In 1983, that got him in trouble.

he extended the pine tar further up the handle. This strange rule led to one of the game's most controversial incidents. In the infamous game at Yankee Stadium in 1983, George Brett of the Kansas City Royals hit a home run with two outs in the ninth inning to give his team the lead. But the umpires voided the round-tripper, stating that the pine tar on Brett's extended past the legal limit, after Yankees manager Billy Martin brought it to their attention. This ended the game and allowed the Yankees to win. Kansas City filed a protest to the American League's highest office, eventually getting the home run restored and forcing the game to be resumed at a later date. At the time, Brett was not amused, although there were some humorous moments. After the out call was made, Brett went ballistic and charged at the umpires in a rage. While he was being restrained and order was being restored, Gaylord Perry (known for allegedly throwing a spit ball and not really ever denying it) tried to spirit the offending bat away to the Royals' clubhouse but was caught.

What is the **Mendoza Line**?

The "Mendoza Line" signifies a batting average at or around .200 (a mark that usually sends a player to the bench or back to the minors). It's named after Mario Mendoza, an infielder for the Pittsburgh Pirates, Texas Rangers, and Seattle Mariners in the 70s and early 80s. Mendoza's career average was .215 and only four times in his nine-year career did he surpass the barrier that bears his name. George Brett is said to have coined the phrase.

Rumor has it that Mendoza's not too pleased with his unique celebrity, and a case could be made in his defense. He had a good glove, and there were plenty of players before him who didn't measure up with the bat. One such player was Bob Uecker, a backup catcher in the 60s with the St. Louis Cardinals, Milwaukee Braves, and Philadelphia Phillies who finished his career with a lifetime batting average of exactly .200. Uecker later became a broadcaster and actor, and used his self-effacing humor to turn his on-field inadequacies and clubhouse clowning into a career as a professional celebrity. Maybe they should call it the Uecker Line.

What are **Blue Darters**?

Blue Darters was a term Shoeless Joe Jackson used to refer to hard hit line drives that fall in safely for hits. They are more impressive than Texas Leaguers—lazy fly balls that fall in between infielders and outfielders.

What ballplayer **wore his birthdate** on the back of his uniform?

The back of Carlos May's White Sox uniform read "May 17," the date of his birth. May played in the All-Star game as a rookie in 1969, and his brother Lee was also a major leaguer.

Who was the first player to have a candy bar named after him?

Reggie Jackson—the Reg-Gie Bar. The Baby Ruth was not named for Babe Ruth but rather for President Grover Cleveland's granddaughter. In a self-fulfilling prophesy he made while playing for Oakland, Jackson had predicted that if he ever played in New York, they would name a candy bar after him.

What **NFL players** also made noteworthy appearances in Major League Baseball?

There have been many athletes who have been fortunate and talented enough to grace both the diamond and the gridiron, including Pro Football Hall of Famers Jim Thorpe, George Halas, Paddy Driscoll, Greasy Neale, Ernie Nevers, Ace Parker, and Red Bargo. None came close to matching their football success, however. Vic Janowicz and Bo Jackson are the only Heisman Trophy winners to play both sports professionally, and Deion Sanders is the only player to participate in both a World Series and Super Bowl. Brian Jordan, a standout defensive back for the Atlanta Falcons, left football to play the outfield for the St. Louis Cardinals.

Many of the outstanding amateur athletes in the 1998 baseball draft are two-sport stars who must eventually decide between football and baseball. The most ballyhooed of these prospects, Drew Henson, is the University of Michigan's prized quarterback recruit and projected starter, and was drafted in the third round by the New York Yankees.

The name of what slugger is on the **bat Jack Nicholson wields menacingly** at Shelley Duvall in *The Shining*?

That would be Yaz—Carl Yastrzemski, the Red Sox slugger who was the American League MVP in 1967.

What is **Rotisserie League** baseball?

This popular pastime allows fans to pick imaginary teams with real players and chart their progress using actual statistics and performance. Leagues can be informal ventures between friends or complicated affairs involving the Internet or some other outside organization. Type of play can vary as well. Leagues may use cumulative stats in a variety of categories, attaching point values to a player's standing in each category, or use a head to head weekly format, where players' point totals are tracked weekly and owners can change lineups based on matchups. It is said to have been invented by a group of baseball enthusiasts at a New York restaurant called La Rotisserie Francaise.

BASKETBALL

ORIGINS AND HISTORY

Who invented **basketball**?

Basketball was created by Canadian James Naismith in early December 1891 during his tenure as an instructor at the School for Christian Workers, which trained leaders for the Young Men's Christian Association (YMCA). Luther Gulick, chairman of the physical education department at the School (now Springfield College) in Springfield, Massachusetts, suggested to Naismith that he devise a game to keep the school's athletes active and entertained during the winter. Naismith had peach buckets nailed to balcony railings at each end of the school's gym, found a soccer ball, divided his class of 18 young men into two nine-player teams, and introduced them to the game of Basket Ball. The two teams competed by trying to toss the soccer ball into one of the crates (each team defending one of the crates, scoring in the other). The ball could only be advanced by passing, and players had to stop once they caught the ball.

At first any number of players could participate and a team scored a point only by making three consecutive field goals (baskets). Naismith soon limited teams to nine players on each side, awarded two points for a basket, introduced fouls (but only for particularly violent actions) and foul shots. The early game was rough and slow: since the peach baskets were closed at the bottom, someone had to climb on a ladder to retrieve the ball after each basket.

Improvements to the game came quickly over the next two decades as basketball spread in popularity. The peach basket was replaced by a metal rim with a net, and in 1906 the netting was opened to allow the ball to fall through. The ball was improved: basketballs were made from strips of leather stitched over an air-filled rubber bladder;

a cloth lining was added for support and uniformity, then in the early 1940s a molded, factory-made basketball standardized the size and shape.

In Naismith's original 13 rules, the ball could be batted in any direction with one or both hands. Since players could not advance with the ball, dribbling was unnecessary. Ball handlers were allowed to move and dribble beginning around 1910, but a dribbler was not allowed to shoot the ball until 1916.

What are Naismith's **original 13 rules**?

Naismith's thirteen "Basket Ball" rules were originally printed in the *Triangle*, a YMCA School for Christian Workers newspaper, on January 15, 1892. They read as follows:

1. The ball may be thrown in any direction with one or both hands.
2. The ball may be batted in any direction with one or both hands (never with the fist).
3. A player cannot run with the ball. The player must throw it from the spot on which he catches it; allowance to be made for a man who catches the ball when running at a good speed.
4. The ball must be held in or between the hands; the arms or body must not be used for holding it.
5. No shouldering, holding, pushing, tripping or striking, in any way the person of an opponent shall be allowed; the first infringement of this rule by any person shall count as a foul, the second shall disqualify him until the next goal is made; or, if there was evident intent to injure the person for the whole game, no substitute shall be allowed.
6. A foul is striking at the ball with the fist, violation of Rules Three, Four, and such as described in Rule Five.
7. If either side makes three consecutive fouls, it shall count a goal for the opponents. (Consecutive means without the opponents in the meantime making a foul.)
8. A goal shall be made when the ball is thrown or batted from the ground into the basket and stays there, providing those defending the goal do not touch or disturb the goal. If the ball rests on the edge and the opponent moves the basket, it shall count as a goal.
9. When the ball goes out of bounds, it shall be thrown into the field and played by the person first touching it. In case of a dispute, the umpire shall throw it straight into the field. The thrower-in is allowed five seconds. If he holds it longer, it shall go to the opponent. If any side persists in delaying the game, the umpire shall call a foul on them.
10. The umpire shall be the judge of the men and shall note the fouls and notify the referee when three consecutive fouls have been made. He shall have power to disqualify men according to Rule Five.

Why are basketball players called "cagers?"

The Trenton Basketball Team, which originally competed in the YMCA league, introduced a fence, or cage, around the court to keep the ball in constant play. In addition, the fence protected fans from loose balls and charging players. Trenton players were thus called "cagers."

11. The referee shall be the judge of the ball and shall decide when the ball is in play, in bounds, to which side it belongs, and shall keep the time. He shall decide when a goal has been made, and keep account of the goals, with any other duties that are usually performed by a referee.

12. The time shall be two fifteen minute halves, with five minutes rest between.

13. The side making the most goals in that time shall be declared the winners. In case of a draw, the game may, by agreement of the captains, be continued until another goal is made.

Why do professional basketball players have **low digits** on their jerseys?

So the referee can signal with his fingers the number of the player who committed a foul.

Was there a **color barrier** in basketball?

Yes. The NBA became integrated in the 1950s, but there were incidents where all-white college teams refused to play integrated or all-black teams as late as the 1960s.

An all-African American team—the New York Renaissance—was dominant in pro ball during the 1930s, when teams were not yet integrated. The Rens won 88 consecutive games during one stretch. In 1963 the Rens as a team were enshrined in the Basketball Hall of Fame, one of only four teams so honored.

The Harlem Globetrotters were founded in 1927 as a competitive team, but through the years they became better known for their displays of individual skills (ball-handling, trick shooting), acrobatics and humorous routines.

When did professional basketball **break the color barrier**?

Chuck Cooper and Earl Lloyd were drafted by the Celtics and Capitals, respectively, in 1950. The color barrier was broken when Lloyd became the first African American to play in an NBA game. The Knicks obtained Sweetwater Clifton from the Harlem Globetrotters, and he also played during the 1950–51 season.

How are inductees elected into basketball's **Hall of Fame**?

The Naismith Memorial Basketball Hall of Fame, located in Springfield, Massachusetts, was established in 1949 by the National Association of Basketball Coaches. Players and referees can be nominated five years after they retire, coaches must have coached for 25 years or have been retired for five, and contributors must have already completed their service. Nominees are voted on by a 24-member panel comprised of media professionals, Hall of Fame members, and trustees. If a nominee is not voted in after five years, he/she can be considered after another five year wait by the Veteran's Committee.

TECHNIQUES, RULES, AND EQUIPMENT

What are the **dimensions** of basketball courts and three-point lines?

NBA courts are 94 feet in length by 50 feet in width. A playing area of 84 ft by 50 ft is used in recreational, high school, and intercollegiate competition. The three-point line in high school and college games is 19 ft 9 inches from the basket, while in international play it is 21 ft 6 inches and in professional play it is 22 ft.

What is **over and back**?

Once a team has advanced the basketball beyond the half-court line, they may not pass or otherwise let the ball go back on the other side of the half-court line. A team that does so, either because of an errant pass or a mental lapse, is guilty of "over and back" and has to give up the ball to the opposition. There is an important exception to this rule, however. If the basketball ends up going back across the half-court line because of a deflection by a defensive player, the ball may be recovered by a member of either team. If an offensive player is able to retrieve the ball, then the offense can advance the ball across half-court once again.

What is **three seconds**?

An offensive player commits a three-second violation when he or she spends more than three continuous seconds in the area of the court between the free throw line, the free throw lanes, and the end line underneath the opposing team's basket when

What is the ten-second rule?

This rule requires a team to advance the basketball beyond half-court before 10 seconds have elapsed. A team may accomplish this either by dribbling the ball over half-court or passing it to a teammate who is past the half-court line. It is worth noting, however, that the team must be *in possession* of the ball and past half court by the time that 10 seconds have elapsed; if the 10-second count elapses while the passed ball is still in the air, a violation will be called. Full court presses are designed to take maximum use of this rule, by either preventing the opposition from advancing the ball beyond the half-court line in the allotted 10 seconds or creating a situation in which the offense is in such a hurry to get the ball across half-court that it makes a turnover.

the player's team is in possession of the ball. A three-second violation may also be called if the player is in possession of the ball himself but spends more than three continuous seconds in the above-mentioned rectangle of space, which is commonly referred to as "the paint." An exception is made, however, if the player makes an attempt to score as the allotted three seconds are expiring. In addition, if the offensive team's possession of the ball is temporarily halted by an interrupted dribble, the three-second count starts all over again at the point at which the offense regains possession.

How do the NCAA's rules of **alternating possession** work?

Every year, countless college basketball tilts seem to hinge on a last-second flash of the scorekeeper's sideline possession arrow. To many casual fans, the underpinnings of the rules of alternating possession seem hazy, but in reality, it's a pretty simple set-up. Each game begins with a jump ball (overtime periods begin with a jump ball as well). The team that does not obtain control of the initial jump ball will start the alternating possession process by being awarded the ball out of bounds at the spot nearest to where the next jump-ball situation occurs. The alternating possession rule comes into effect in instances in which the officials are uncertain which team last touched the ball before it went out of bounds, or in situations in which a player from each team has partial possession of the ball.

Were **fouls** always part of the game?

Originally, fouls were only called for particularly violent acts. Three fouls committed by the same team was punishable by awarding the other team with a point. A player's second foul led to removal from the game until the next field goal was made.

93

Beginning in 1894 players were given a free throw when fouled, and beginning in 1908 players who committed five fouls were disqualified from the game. Rules were amended to award players either two shots or one shot plus a bonus shot (attempted only if the first shot was made), based on the severity of the foul.

What are the five basketball **positions** and what types of skills do they require?

Guards: Two guards—the point guard (or 1-guard) and the shooting guard (or 2-guard) form the backcourt. The point guard is generally the leader of the team on the court, doing most of the ball-handling and setting up plays through superb passing skills. The shooting guard is generally a good ball handler with excellent shooting skills.

Forwards: The small forward (3-player) is usually a strong scorer near and away from the basket. He is called on to rebound, handle the ball, and pass. Players like Larry Bird, Scottie Pippin, and Grant Hill combine these talents and have often served as a second point guard on the floor. The power forward (4-player) is big and strong, concentrating primarily on defense and rebounding. Though he is smaller than most power forwards, Dennis Rodman combines the defensive and rebounding skills of the ideal power forward.

The Center (5-player) is usually the tallest player on the team and serves as the cornerstone of most set plays. Centers use their height advantage to score over other players and rebound.

These are general characteristics, with some players specializing in a particular facet of the game and others transcending expectations of their position.

What is a **"back door"** play?

The "back door" is an offensive maneuver that is sometimes used against aggressive defensive players who tend to overplay passing lanes. With a back door play, an offensive player who's trying to shake a defender who is playing him very closely to keep him from receiving a pass will run away from the basket toward an open area of the floor. But just as the defensive player catches up, the offensive player will abruptly stop and break back towards the basket to receive a pass and lay the basketball in for an easy two points.

What is a **"triple-double?"**

The fairly rare triple-double refers to a player reaching double figures in points, assists, and rebounds in a single game.

What are the different kinds of passes?

There are five types of passes: bounce—in which the ball is bounced on the ground from one teammate to another; chest—where the ball is passed from chest high; overhead—where the ball is thrown with both hands extended over the head; baseball-style—thrown like a baseball, usually featured in a long pass; and behind-the-back—when a player whips the ball around his back, waist high, sometimes for sheer showmanship, sometimes to avoid a defensive player who comes between onrushing teammates.

What are differences between **NBA and Olympic/International rules**?

Time: A 30-second time clock (rather than 24-second) is used in international competition. International games, like college games, have two 20-minute periods, and, similarly, each have five-minute overtimes in case of a tie. In international play, each team receives two one-minute timeouts per half and one time-out during an overtime period.

Fouling: The eighth team foul in each half, and all succeeding ones, result in two free throws for the other team in international play. The individual foul limit is five. No shots are awarded on offensive fouls.

Substitution: Substitution rules are somewhat different from the pro and college game. On a possession after a violation, the offense may substitute, and the defense may substitute only if the offense substitutes. After successful free throws, the shooter may be replaced if requested prior to the first free throw. The opponent is allowed one substitute if requested before the last free throw.

Lanes: The lanes on an international court flare out as opposed to the rectangular lanes in the NBA and NCAA; there are more three-second violations and driving lay-ups in international play.

Three-point play: The Olympic distance is roughly midway between those of the college and professional sports. The three-point distance in the international game is a little over 20.5 feet, or 6.25 meters, compared to 22 feet in the NBA, and the NCAA's 19 feet, nine inches.

What are the rules and organization of **international professional basketball**?

The shot clock is 30 seconds in international play, as opposed to the 24-second clock in American professional play and the 35-second clock in men's collegiate play; the three-point line is set at a distance between the collegiate and professional distances; and the "key" area is a wider, trapezoidal shape.

The Fédération International de Basketball Association (FIBA, Federation of International Basketball) governs international basketball and its more than 200 leagues. FIBA divides the world into five sections—Africa, Asia, the Americas, Europe, and Oceania—called zone commissions, and the zone commissions conduct regional championships. National federations are subdivided into leagues comprised of club teams. Most international leagues allow two foreign players on their rosters, and the game itself is similar to American basketball. International tournaments include the world championships, played every four years; the European championships, held annually; the championships at the Pan American Games, played every four years; and the Jones Cup, held annually.

When did some of the **basic techniques,** such as the jump shot, come into practice?

Nat Holman, who played with the original Boston Celtics (1920) and coached City College of New York to both NIT and NCAA tournament championships in 1950, is generally credited with having invented the pivot play; Dutch Dehnert (elected to the Hall of Fame in 1968) helped introduce the give and go; and Joe Fulks (the NBA's first season scoring leader and a Hall of Fame member) popularized the jump shot.

PROFESSIONAL

How did **professional basketball** develop?

The first professional basketball association of teams was the National Basketball League (NBL), formed in 1898 principally as a way to organize competition against the Trenton Basketball Team, the finest organized team of the day in the YMCA League. The NBL didn't last long, but by 1920 there were at least twenty leagues in the east and midwest.

The American Basketball League (ABL) began play in 1925 and lasted into the 1930s, when college basketball became increasingly popular. The Basketball Association of America (BAA) was comprised of teams in eastern cities when it began in 1946. Meanwhile, another National Basketball League was founded with teams spreading into the midwest. The BAA and NBL teams competed for players and fans. In 1948, four NBL teams joined the BAA and six more joined the following year, banding with seven remaining BAA teams to form a 17-team league renamed the National Basketball Association (NBA).

How did **NBA teams** enter the league?

Three teams survive from the original BAA: the Boston Celtics, New York Knicks, and Golden State Warriors (known as the Philadelphia Warriors before moving to San Francisco in 1962).

Five franchises survive from the original NBL: the Detroit Pistons (moved from Fort Wayne, Indiana, in 1957); the Los Angeles Lakers (moved from Minneapolis in 1960); the Philadelphia 76ers (moved from Syracuse in 1963); the Atlanta Hawks (originally called the TriCity Hawks until 1951, relocated to Milwaukee from 1951–55, and to St. Louis from 1955–68); and the Sacramento Kings (originally the Rochester Royals before moving to Cincinnati in 1957; known as the Kansas City-Omaha Kings, 1972–75, and the Kansas City Kings from 1975–85).

The remaining teams came through expansion in the following years:

1961: Washington Wizards—Began as the Chicago Packers (1961), became the Baltimore Bullets (1963), the Capitol Bullets (1973) and then the Washington Bullets (1974); renamed the Wizards in 1997.

1966: Chicago Bulls.

1967: San Diego Rockets (moved to Houston in 1971) and Seattle Supersonics.

1968: Milwaukee Bucks and Phoenix Suns.

1970: Buffalo Braves (became the San Diego Clippers in 1978, became the Los Angeles Clippers in 1984), Cleveland Cavaliers, Portland Trailblazers.

1974: New Orleans Jazz (became the Utah Jazz in 1979).

1976: From the ABA merger into the NBA—Denver Nuggets, Indiana Pacers, New York Nets (became the New Jersey Nets in 1977), and San Antonio Spurs.

1980: Dallas Mavericks.

1988: Charlotte Hornets and Miami Heat.

1989: Minnesota Timberwolves and Orlando Magic.

1995: Toronto Raptors and Vancouver Grizzlies.

Who was voted the **top 50 NBA players**?

A league-approved panel of former players and coaches, current and former general managers, team executives, and media people voted on the 50 greatest players to coincide with the league's 50th anniversary in 1996. The players are listed here, with some career highlights:

Kareem Abdul-Jabbar: see question below.

Nate Archibald: 6-foot-1 "Tiny" Archibald was a fearless penetrator, an excellent passer, and had great range as a shooter. In 1972 he averaged 34 points and 11.4 assists per game for the Kansas City Kings, becoming the only player in NBA history to lead the league in those two categories in the same season. Archibald led the NBA in free throws made three times and the Boston Celtics to the 1981 NBA title and the NBA's best record from 1980 through 1982.

Paul Arizin: "Pitchin' Paul" Arizin was a Philly phenom of the '50s, beginning with his college days at Villanova, where he set a single-game scoring record of 85 points as a sophomore and led the nation in scoring (25.3 points per game) as a senior in 1950, when he was named College Player of the Year. Arizin played with the Philadelphia Warriors for ten seasons (1950–52, 1954–62), interrupted by two seasons of military service. He was the NBA scoring champ twice and led the Warriors to the 1956 NBA championship over the Fort Wayne Pistons.

Charles Barkley: Called "Sir Charles" for his commanding court presence, Barkley is a great all-around player and fierce competitor. He was the league MVP during the 1992–93 season, when he led the Phoenix Suns to the championship finals before bowing to the Chicago Bulls.

Rick Barry: Barry was Rookie of the Year in 1966 and led the league in scoring (35.6 points per game) the following season. In 1975, Barry was named MVP of the NBA championship series, leading the San Francisco Warriors to a four-game sweep of the Washington Bullets. His 89.3 percent career foul-shooting, performed with an underhand technique, is second best in NBA/ABA history.

Elgin Baylor: In 1957–58, Baylor led Seattle University to the NCAA championship game and was the tournament MVP. He was the 1959 NBA Rookie of the Year (24.9 points per game) for the Minneapolis Lakers, who moved to Los Angeles in 1960. Baylor averaged 30 points or more three times during his career and became the first player in NBA history to score over 70 points in a game.

Dave Bing: Bing was the NBA's Rookie of the Year in 1967 for his playmaking and scoring. The following year he led the NBA in scoring with a 27.1 per game average for the Detroit Pistons. Bing was a smooth and skillful player who excelled in all aspects of the game.

Larry Bird: see question below.

Wilt Chamberlain: see question below.

Bob Cousey: The "Houdini of the Hardwood," Cousey was the NBA's first great and flashy playmaker, spearheading the Celtic dynasty and winning six championships. Cousey led the NBA in assists eight consecutive years (1953–60). He coached the Cincinnati/Kansas City Royals from 1969–74 and played at age 41 during the 1969-70 season, making him the oldest player in NBA history.

Dave Cowens: During his rookie year Cowens averaged 17 points and 15 rebounds a game and shared the NBA Rookie of the Year Award with Portland's Geoff Petrie. Small for a center at 6-9, Cowens was a deft outside shooter and fearless player who could mix it up inside and hit long jumpers from the perimeter. Cowens was MVP of the 1972–73 season.

Billy Cunningham: The intense Cunningham teamed with fellow Hall of Famers Wilt Chamberlain and Hal Greer to win the NBA title for the Philadelphia 76ers in 1966–67, his second season. He was an athletic forward who could score on the run or from the outside. He later coached the 76ers to the 1983 NBA title.

Dave DeBusschere: DeBusschere was an all-around great player—a defensive specialist, floor leader, and potent offensive force inside and out. He played professional basketball for the Detroit Pistons and pitched for the Chicago White Sox in 1962 and 1963. At 24 he served as player/coach of the Pistons, making him the youngest NBA coach in history. He was traded to the Knicks after the 1967 season and helped them to championships in 1970 and 1973. DeBusschere served as vice-president and general manager of the New York Nets and as the ABA commissioner in its final season in 1976.

Clyde Drexler: "The Glide" is an agile master of the fast break and possessor of an excellent outside shot. After a great 11 years with Portland, in which he twice led the Blazers to the championship finals, the Glide returned to his native Houston, where he had starred as a forward on the University of Houston's "Phi Slamma Jamma" teams of the early 1980s. In 1991–92 with Portland he averaged 25 points per game and finished second to Michael Jordan in MVP balloting. A 1995 trade to Houston reunited him with college teammate Hakeem Olajuwon, and they propelled the Rockets to the their second straight NBA Championship.

Julius Erving: Dr. J became only the sixth player in NCAA history to average more than 20 points and 20 rebounds a game; he did it at the University of Massachusetts, where he also earned the nickname Dr. J. He redefined the forward position in pro basketball, becoming one of the first great jumpers to play the game above the rim with his long, loping slam dunks. He is one of only three players in pro basketball history to score over 30,000 career points, accumulating them over five years in the ABA and 11 in the NBA. He was the ABA's MVP in 1974 and 1976 and co-MVP in 1975 and led the ABA in scoring in 1973, 1974, and 1976. In 1981, Erving was named the NBA's MVP as he helped lead the 76ers to the NBA championship in 1983.

Patrick Ewing: Ewing led the Knicks resurgence in the 1980s and holds many franchise records, including games and minutes played, points, rebounds, steals and blocked shots. He led the Knicks to the NBA Finals in 1994, played in 11 All-Star games, was the NBA Rookie of the Year in 1986 and played on gold-medal-winning Olympic basketball teams as a collegian (1984) and pro (1992). He played college ball at Georgetown, leading the Hoyas to the NCAA Championship Game three times and winning the 1983–84 championship, when he was named the Final Four Most Out-standing Player. He won the Naismith Award as a senior.

Walt Frazier: "Clyde" had style on and off the court as the smooth floor leader of great Knicks teams of the 1960s and 1970s, winning the NBA championship in 1970 and 1973. Along with being a great passer and inside/outside scorer, Clyde was named to the NBA's All-Defense First Team seven times (1969–75). Frazier averaged 20.7 points over 93 playoff games.

George Gervin: The "Iceman" could score and score and score with his smooth jump shot and finger rolls. He is one of three players in NBA history to win four or more league scoring titles (1978–80, 1982). He was an All-Star in 12 of 14 seasons (three ABA, nine NBA) and is second behind Oscar Robertson in scoring among guards. Gervin is one of seven players to score 2,000 points in six consecutive NBA seasons (1977–78 to 1982–83).

Hal Greer: Greer was an all-out and all around performer, playing in more games—1,122—than anyone in NBA history until John Havlicek broke the record in the 1970s. He ranked among the top ten all-time in points scored (21,586), field goals attempted (18,811), field goals made (8,504), minutes played (39,788) and personal fouls (3,825). Greer teamed with Wilt Chamberlain and Billy Cunningham to lead the 76ers to the NBA championship in 1967, ending Boston's string of eight consecutive titles. As a collegian at Marshall University, Greer was the first African-American play-er for a major college team in West Virginia.

John Havlicek: "Hondo" was in perpetual motion on offense and defense, described by Celtics coach Red Auerbach as the "guts of the team." He started as a sixth man—in college at Ohio State, where he teamed with fellow Hall of Famers Jerry Lucas and Bobby Knight to lead the Buckeyes to the 1960 NCAA championship, and in helping Boston win four straight NBA titles from 1963 to 1966. Havlicek would win eight championships in Boston and he became the first player to score 1,000 points in 16 consecutive seasons. Havlicek was MVP of the 1974 NBA Finals and averaged 22 points in 172 career playoff games.

Elvin Hayes: The Big E was master of the turnaround jumper. He was a three-time All-American in college, leading Houston to an 81–12 record, two Final Four appear-ances, and he starred in the historic January 20, 1968, game when his University of Houston Cougars ended UCLA's 47-game win streak in the "Game of the Century," the first-ever nationally televised college game, which was played before over 52,000 fans. Hayes averaged 28.4 points per game and led the NBA in scoring as a rookie. He teamed with Hall of Famer Wes Unseld to form a dominating frontcourt that led the Baltimore Bullets to three NBA Finals and the title over Seattle in 1978. Hayes played in 12 consecutive All-Star Games.

100   Magic Johnson: see question below.

Patrick Ewing holds many of the New York Knicks' team records, has won two Olympic gold medals, and was a member of the National Champion 1983–84 Georgetown team.

Sam Jones: One of the Celtics' "Jones Boys," Sam teamed with K.C. Jones in the Celtics' backcourt. He played on 10 NBA championship teams, was a five-time All-Star, and was known for his speed and graceful shooting. Jones led the Celtics in scoring three times, averaging a career-high 25.9 points in 1965.

Michael Jordan: see question below.

Jerry Lucas: Lucas was a pure shooter with his over-the-shoulder style, including a league-leading 52.7 percent during his Rookie of the Year season in 1962. He was named to seven NBA All-Star teams and chosen MVP of the 1965 game. Lucas helped lead the New York Knicks to the 1973 NBA championship.

Karl Malone: One of the game's great power forwards, "The Mailman" was the NBA's Most Valuable Player for the 1996–97 season. He can run the floor and hit with deadly accuracy from the outside, averaging over 21 points and 9.5 rebounds in each season since his rookie year. Through the 1996–97 season he appeared in 980 of a possible 984 games over 12 seasons. He is in the top 10 all-time in scoring, field goals, and free throws.

Moses Malone: Malone became the first player to move from high school ball to a professional league, joining the Utah Stars of the ABA and immediately becoming a dominant force beneath the basket—scoring, rebounding, and drawing fouls. Teamed with Julius Erving, Maurice Cheeks, and Bobby Jones, Malone helped lead the Philadelphia 76ers to a 65–17 regular-season record and NBA championship in 1983, the year in which Malone won the regular season and playoff MVP awards. He was also the NBA MVP in 1979 and 1982.

Pete Maravich: "Pistol Pete" scored more points in college than any other player in history, averaging 44.2 points in 83 games and leading the NCAA in scoring three times. He led the NBA in scoring in 1977 with a 31.1 average and averaged 24.2 points per game during his career.

Kevin McHale: McHale was known for his low-post moves, including pump fakes, baby jump hooks, shovel shots and fadeaways. As a sixth man he was a key contributor to the Celtics teams that won three championships (1981, 1984, 1986). He won the NBA Sixth Man Award in 1984 and 1985.

George Mikan: see question below.

Earl Monroe: Earl "The Pearl" Monroe was a dazzling guard for the Baltimore Bullets and New York Knicks. In 1967 he was the NBA Rookie of the Year for the Bullets, teaming with Wes Unseld to form a spectacular fast break offense. He was traded to New York in 1971 and teamed with Walt Frazier in a celebrated backcourt that helped the Knicks to the 1973 NBA championship.

Hakeem Olajuwon: Hakeem "The Dream" Olajuwon led the Houston Rockets to back-to-back NBA championships. In 1993–94 he became the first player to be named NBA MVP, NBA Defensive Player of the Year and NBA Finals MVP in the same season, and the following year he rallied the Rockets from a sixth seed in the playoffs to their second straight NBA crown. Olajuwon and Ralph Sampson—the Twin Towers—took the Rockets to the NBA Finals in 1986. He began playing basketball at age 15 in his native Nigeria, then enrolled at the University of Houston, playing three seasons for the "Phi Slamma Jamma" squad that reached the Final Four each year. In his rookie year, 1984–85, Olajuwon averaged 20.6 points and 11.9 rebounds while shooting .538 from the field, finishing second to Michael Jordan in Rookie of the Year balloting. With his height, agility, and creativeness, Olajuwon is virtually unstoppable around the basket. He won rebounding titles in 1989 and 1990, and in 1989 he became the first player to finish among the league's top 10 in scoring, rebounding, steals, and blocked shots for two straight seasons.

Shaquille O'Neal: The 7-1, 300-pound O'Neal has won a scoring title, led the expansion Orlando Magic into the NBA Finals, and revived the Los Angeles Lakers—all during his first five years in the NBA. As a 20-year-old rookie, O'Neal won NBA Player of the Week honors for his first week in the league and was named 1993 NBA Rookie of the Year. His .599 field goal percentage led the NBA in 1993–94, and he won his first scoring title in 1994–95, averaging 29.3 points.

Robert Parrish: "The Chief"—named by fellow Celtic Cedric "Cornbread" Maxwell after Chief Bromden in *One Flew Over the Cookoo's Nest*—was a great rebounder, shot-blocker, and consistent scorer. A member of the 1981, 1984 and 1986 Boston Celtics NBA championship teams and the 1997 champion Chicago Bulls, he holds the career NBA playoff record for offensive rebounds (571) and averaged 15.3 points, 9.6 rebounds, and 1.7 blocked shots over 184 playoff games.

Bob Pettit: Like Michael Jordan, Pettit was cut from his high school basketball team and it only made him practice more and become more determined as he developed a never-quit attitude that became his trademark. He was NBA Rookie of the Year in 1954– 55 for the Milwaukee Hawks. Pettit was the league's MVP in 1956 (25.7 points per game) and 1959 (29.2 points per game). He played in 11 straight All-Star Games and at the time of his retirement in 1965 he was the NBA's all time leading scorer (20,880) and second highest rebounder (12,849).

Scottie Pippin: A multiple threat on the floor, Pippen is an excellent passer, rebounder, shooter, and fast-break finisher. A key to the Chicago Bulls' six NBA championships of the 1990s, Pippin was selected to the NBA All-Defensive First Team six consecutive times. He averaged 21 points, 7.7 rebounds and 7.0 assists per game in 1991–92. Pippen had another great all around season in 1995–96, helping Chicago set an NBA record with 72 victories and leading the team in assists.

Willis Reed: Reed became legendary for hobbling onto the floor for Game 7 of the 1970 championship series between the New York Knicks and Los Angeles Lakers and inspiring the Knicks to victory. He played 27 minutes in that game after being felled by a severe knee injury in Game 5. A second-round choice by the Knicks after having starred at Grambling, Reed was the NBA's Rookie of the Year for 1963–64 and an All-Star his first seven seasons. Reed is the only player named MVP of the All-Star Game, regular season and playoffs in the same year (1970). He won another championship with the Knicks in 1973.

Oscar Robertson: see question below.

David Robinson: "The Admiral" has won a Rookie of the Year Award, a rebounding title, a scoring crown, a Most Valuable Player Award, and a Defensive Player of the Year Award, was selected an All-Star seven times, to the All-NBA First Team four times, and to the NBA All-Defensive First Team four times—all in his first seven seasons. A 1987 graduate with a mathematics degree from the U.S. Naval Academy, Robinson served two years in the Navy before joining the NBA. As a junior, he averaged 22.7 points per game, led the nation in rebounding (13.0 per game), and set an NCAA Division I record by averaging 5.91 blocks (including 14 in a single game and 207 for the season—both NCAA records). San Antonio had posted a 21–61 record in 1988–89, but in Robinson's rookie year the Spurs went 56-26 and captured the Midwest Division title. The 35-game improvement marked the greatest single-season turnaround in NBA history. Robinson scored 71 points against the Los Angeles Clippers on the last day of the 1993–94 season to win the NBA scoring title at 29.8 points per game. His career blocked shot average of 3.60 per game is the highest in NBA history among players with 400 or more games played.

Bill Russell: see question below.

Dolph Schayes: Schayes was always there—scoring, rebounding, and playing in more NBA games than anyone at the time of his retirement in 1964, including a string of 706 consecutive games. He led the NBA in free throw shooting three times (1958, 1960, 1962) and shot 84% from the line in his career. He was the 1949 NBL Rookie of the Year, and after the merger of the NBL and BAA formed the NBA, Schayes led the league in rebounding in 1951. Schayes led his team into the playoffs 15 times, losing in the NBA championship finals in 1950 and 1954 to the George Mikan-led Minneapolis Lakers and winning it all in 1955. He played in 12 consecutive All-Star games.

Bill Sharman: Sharman teamed with Bob Cousey to form one of the NBA's greatest backcourt duos, winning four NBA championships (1957, 1959-61). He played in eight All-Star games. Sharman was also a renowned coach, leading the Los Angeles Lakers to their first NBA title in 1972, when they compiled a 69–13 regular season record that included 33 straight victories. He is the only basketball coach to win titles in three different leagues—the ABL (Cleveland Pipers, 1962), ABA (Utah Stars, 1971), and NBA (Los Angeles Lakers, 1972).

John Stockton: Stockton is the NBA's all time career assist leader and holds assist average records for a season (14.5 per game) and career (11.5 per game). Stockton has made the NBA All-Defensive Team three times, and through 1996–97 he missed only four games in 13 NBA seasons. Stockton and forward Karl Malone have led the Utah

Jazz to the playoffs in each of the seasons they played together, and they shared MVP honors at the 1993 All-Star Game at Salt Lake City. From 1993 to 96 he recorded the highest field goal percentage among guards.

Isiah Thomas: "Zeke" was one of the best small men in NBA history (defining "small" as 6-1 or less). He was a fearless guard, slashing inside to challenge the big men for lay-ups or to dish to the open man, shooting rainbows from outside, and running the show for the two-time champion Detroit Pistons. He made 12 All-Star appearances and won two All-Star Game MVP awards. Thomas averaged 19.2 points and 9.3 assists per game for his career and is one of only four players to amass more than 9,000 assists.

Nate Thurmond: A consummate team player, Thurmond was a smooth shooter, relentless rebounder, and tough shot-blocker. He played 14 seasons with San Francisco/Golden State, Chicago and Cleveland, and appeared in seven All-Star games. He once collected 18 rebounds in one quarter and was the first player to ever record a quadruple double—22 points, 14 rebounds, 13 assists and 12 blocked shots in one game.

Wes Unseld: Short for a center (6-7) but big and strong at 245 pounds, Unseld played a physical brand of basketball coupled with an intelligent court presence (he chose basketball over teaching coming out of college, but the teacher in him persisted on the court, as a coach, and as an executive). In 1969–70, Unseld became only the second NBA player after Wilt Chamberlain to be named Rookie of the Year and MVP in the same season. He finished his career as one of 20 players to score more than 10,000 points (10,624) and grab more than 10,000 rebounds. He was MVP of the NBA championship series in 1978, when his Bullets defeated Seattle for the crown. In 1975, Unseld received the NBA Walter Kennedy Citizenship Award for his community contributions.

Bill Walton: Walton was an excellent shooter, rebounder and outlet passer on the fast break. From the storied UCLA championship teams (he made 21 of 22 shots, scored 44 points, and collected 13 rebounds in the championship game to lead UCLA to the NCAA title in 1973, and the Bruins went 86–4 during his days there) to NBA championships with the Portland Trail Blazers (1977) and Boston Celtics (1987), Walton was a ferocious competitor and team leader. He was named league MVP in 1978 and won the Sixth Man Award during the Celtics championship season of 1986–87.

Jerry West: Always cool and calm, "Mr. Clutch" was one of the best pure shooters in NBA history. After an outstanding collegiate career at West Virginia (in his junior year, West led the Mountaineers to the 1959 NCAA Finals and won the tournament's Most Outstanding Player award) and playing for the fabled 1960 U.S. Olympic gold medal team, West played his entire career with the Lakers alongside Hall of Famers Elgin Baylor and Wilt Chamberlain. He retired third in scoring, second in free throws, and fifth in assists, was named to the NBA All-Defensive First Team four times, and played in 14 All-Star games. West was the NBA Finals MVP in 1969 and played on the 1972 Laker championship team.

Lenny Wilkens: see question below.

James Worthy: Worthy was one of the finest small forwards, featuring one-handed swoop dunks and playing a speed game that made the Lakers a major team of the 1980s. Worthy was MVP of the 1988 NBA Finals, when his late heroics on offense and defense completed an incredible Game 7 performance in which he recorded 36 points, 16 rebounds and 10 assists. The Lakers also won championships in 1985 and 1987 with Worthy.

What was the **Mikan Era**?

The Mikan Era extended from 1949, the NBA's first season, to 1954: during this time the Minnesota Lakers were led by six-foot-ten-inch center George Mikan. The Lakers won five titles during that span, including three in a row from 1952 to 1954. Mikan was previously a star in the National Basketball League and quickly established himself as the NBA's dominant player. He sported a deadly hook shoot and was a tough rebounder and defender. Mikan led the league in scoring from 1949–51 and in rebounding in 1953. He retired after the Lakers won the 1954 title, became the Lakers general manager, coached briefly in 1957, and in 1967 he became the ABA's first commissioner.

Who took over Bill Russell's title as the next **Big Man**?

In his rookie year of 1960, Wilt Chamberlain averaged 27 rebounds and 37.6 points a game. He had seven games with 50 or more points and won both Rookie of the Year and Most Valuable Player (MVP). Of the 25 highest point totals by an individual in a single game, Chamberlain holds 20 of them, including a 100-point performance in 1962. He also holds the record for rebounds in a game (55) and in a career.

Wilt Chamberlain (right, shooting) and Bill Russell (left) battle in Game 2 of the 1964 NBA Championship.

What are some of **Kareem Abdul-Jabbar's** acheivements?

Some of the records Kareem holds include: Most Games Played, 1,560; Most Field Goals Made, 15,837; Most Field Goals Attempted, 28,307; Most Minutes Played, 57,446; Most Blocked shots, 3,189; Most Personal Fouls, 4,657. Abdul-Jabbar, the NBA's all-time leading scorer, won three NCAA championships with UCLA, and six NBA championships, one with the Milwaukee Bucks and five with the Los Angeles Lakers. Bob Cousey, the first great passing guard who had played with Bill Russell during the Celtic glory years, said of Abdul-Jabbar, "he pretty much combines what Bill Russell and Wilt Chamberlain have individually specialized in."

What are some of the all-time NBA **individual game** performances?

Most Points Scored: 100, by Wilt Chamberlain (Philadelphia), March 2, 1962, versus New York Knicks in a regular-season game played in Hershey, Pennsylvania.

Most Rebounds: 55, by Wilt Chamberlain (Philadelphia), November 24, 1960, versus Boston Celtics.

Most Assists: 30, by Scott Skiles (Orlando), December 30, 1990, versus Denver Nuggets.

Most Steals: 11, by Larry Kenon (San Antonio), December 26, 1976 versus Kansas City Royals.

Most Blocked Shots: 17, Elmore Smith (Los Angeles), October 28, 1973 versus Portland Trail Blazers.

Most 3-point Field Goals: 11, Dennis Scott (Orlando), April 18, 1996, versus Atlanta.

What was the **American Basketball Association**?

The ABA was a professional league that began play with ten teams in 1967, featured a red-white-and-blue ball and introduced the three-point shot. The ABA lasted nine seasons before folding in 1976: four teams—the Denver Nuggets, Indiana Pacers, New York Nets, and San Antonio Spurs—joined the NBA. ABA innovations like the three-point shot and an All-Star break slam dunk contest were eventually adopted by the NBA. During its existence, the ABA competed with the NBA for professional and college players, leading to salary increases. Julius Erving of the Nets was the most famous ABA player. Rick Barry (who switched leagues), the flamboyant Connie Hawkins (who was exonerated from a college betting scandal that originally led the NBA to ban him), Spencer Haywood (who left college before finishing his eligibility), and Dan Issel (a highly sought-after graduate) were among the other stars to give the ABA credibility.

Wilt Chamberlain holds single-game records for points (100), and rebounds (55).

Who were some of the **ABA's major stars**?

The ABA had many great players, but the most important was probably Julius Erving, the gravity-defying forward who led the league in scoring on three occasions. Erving, like many other ABA stars, would prove equally formidable in the NBA. If three-time MVP Erving was the league's greatest player at the end, Connie Hawkins, masterful one-on-one attacker, was probably the ABA's strongest player in its debut year. Hawkins led the league with a 26.8 scoring average and was named MVP. Other dominating players in ABA history are Indiana center and two-time MVP Mel Daniels; masterful shooter Rick Barry, who later won an NBA title with Golden State; aggressive scorer George McGinnis; and such future NBA stars as Dan Issel and Artis Gilmore, two powerful centers. The league's last rookie-of-the-year was high-flying sensation David Thompson, who also starred in the NBA, once scoring 73 points in a game.

Who scored the very **first field goal in ABA** history?

Willie Porter of the Oakland Oaks was the first player to score a basket in American Basketball Association competition. The game, which took place on October 13, 1967, pitted the Oaks against the Anaheim Amigos, and Porter's basket took place one minute and four seconds into the game.

What teammates are the **top tandems in winning percentage** in NBA history?

Through the 1996–97 season, Michael Jordan and Scottie Pippin have won 73.9% of all games in which they both played, followed by Magic Johnson/Kareem Abdul-Jabbar at 73.9% (Jordan/Pippin are higher factoring 1997–98), Larry Bird/Kevin McHale (73.5%), and Karl Malone/John Stockton at 63.8%.

Julius Erving helped popularize one league (the ABA) and revitalize another (the NBA) with his fantastic above-the-rim style and slam-dunk prowess.

What hoopster played the **most playoff games without getting a ring**?

Elgin Baylor with 134; coming up from behind through 1996–97 are John Stockton (127), Charles Oakley (119), and Karl Malone (117). Caldwell Jones (119) and Sam Perkins (118) are others who played long and hard but never won the last playoff game.

Michael Jordan has been called the greatest basketball player ever. What are some of his on-court accomplishments?

Michael Jordan was college basketball's Player of the Year in 1984, two years after having helped lead North Carolina to the NCAA championship as a freshman in 1982; he led the U.S. Olympic team in scoring in 1984 en route to their gold medal triumph (he later medaled gold as a pro); he is the only player to win the NBA's MVP and Defensive Player of the Year awards for a single season (1988); he led the league in scoring nine times through the 1996–97 season, led in steals three times, and is the only player to ever lead the NBA in scoring and steals in a single season; he is the only player to have 200 steals and 100 blocked shots in a season, and he did it twice; he is the only player in any sport to win six MVPs and be on six Championship teams (Joe Montana is second with three).

Was there ever a player who **averaged a triple-double for a whole season**?

Incredibly, yes. Oscar Robertson scored 2,432 points, dished out 899 assists, and pulled down 985 rebounds in 79 games during the 1961–62 season, his second in the NBA. Robertson was a member of two high school championship teams in Indiana, led the nation in scoring three times for the University of Cincinnati, led the Olympic gold-medal-winning 1960 U.S. basketball team, and won an NBA championship with the Milwaukee Bucks.

What effect did the **Magic Johnson-Larry Bird rivalry** have on the NBA?

They deserve their own individual chapters, but as contemporaries who met in the 1979 NCAA Final (Magic's Michigan State Spartans defeated Bird's Indiana State Sycamores, and Magic was the MVP), Earvin "Magic" Johnson and Larry Bird helped restore to glory the two most successful NBA franchises (Lakers and Celtics, respectively), and brought unprecedented national exposure to professional basketball.

As a rookie, Magic helped lead the Lakers to the 1980 NBA championship; in an amazing finale, he played center in the Championship's final game when Kareem Abdul-Jabbar couldn't play because of a knee injury. Magic scored 42 points and was the playoff MVP, an award he won again in 1982 and 1987. He led the league in assists four times and held the career record until the 1996–97 season, when John Stockton surpassed it. He played on five championship teams for the Lakers.

Michael Jordan has teamed with Scottie Pippen for the highest all-time winning percentage for teammates and five championships. He's also a pretty good player in his own right.

Who ranks among the game's greatest small players?

Nate "Tiny" Archibald was a great player, but he was 6'1, despite the nickname. Tiny led the league in assists during the 1973-74 season and later starred with the champion Celtics. Calvin Murphy, a 5'9 guard with the Houston Rockets for thirteen seasons, must surely be considered the league's most proficient short player. Murphy scored nearly 18,000 points in his career. He twice led the league in free-throw percentage, and on eight other occasions he finished second. In 1981, he made seventy-eight consecutive tosses from the foul line! He had his greatest game in the 1981 playoffs when he scored forty-two points and led the Rockets to a 105–100 victory in game seven of the Western Conference semi-final against the San Antonio Spurs.

Bird made an immediate and lasting impact, too. As Rookie of the Year during the 1979–80 season, he ignited the greatest season-to-season team turnaround in NBA history: Boston was 29–53 the year before he was drafted by the Celtics, 61–21 during his first year. Bird led the Celtics to three championships (1981, 1984, 1986), was a two-time playoff MVP (1984, 1986), and was the league regular-season MVP three times, 1984–86.

What was the **Celtic Dynasty**?

The Celtic Dynasty extended from 1957 to 1969, a thirteen-year period that coincided with Hall of Famer Bill Russell's career. During those thirteen years the Celtics won an astounding eleven titles! Cigar-chomping mastermind Red Auerbach coached for nine of those titles, when the team featured a host of all-time greats. The 1957 team featured such stars as Bob Cousey and Bill Sharman, in addition to Russell, and succeeding teams would include such notables as Sam Jones, K.C. Jones, Tommy Heinsohn, Don Nelson, and prominent sixth-man John Havlicek. The team's greatest player, though, was center Bill Russell, a skillful defender and rebounder who assumed the dual role of player-coach after Auerbach withdrew to the front office. Russell led the Celtics to two more titles before retiring after winning the 1969 playoffs.

What are the famous "**Three Steals**" of Celtic lore?

1965 Division Final vs. Philadelphia:

In the seventh game of a rough series, Boston clung to a one-point lead with just seconds remaining in the contest. The problem: Philadelphia had the ball. Sixer Hal

Larry Bird helps Magic Johnson off the floor during their epic battle in the 1979 NCAA final. Their rivalry would help revitalize the NBA in the 1980s.

Which Super Bowl head coach played in the NBA?

Stone'faced Minnesota Viking Coach Bud Grant first made a name for himself in professional sports as a member of the Minneapolis Lakers from 1949 to 1951. After that, however, he tossed aside his basketball sneakers and devoted his attention to football. He eventually became the head man of the Vikings and led them to four Super Bowls in the late 1960s and 1970s. In each contest, however, Minnesota came up short, and since Grant's departure from the Vikings for a life of hunting and fishing in Minnesota's north country, the team has yet to return to the big game.

Greer prepared to inbound a pass to Chet Walker with plenty of time for a two-point shot. Greer passed; John Havlicek reached out and stole the ball, preserving a Boston victory. Boston earned the right to meet the Los Angeles Lakers and went on to win championship number eight.

1984 Championship Finals versus Los Angeles:

Los Angeles had won the first game of the series and seemed poised to win the second as they led by two points with twenty seconds to go in the game. The Lakers had possession of the ball. Magic Johnson inbounded it to James Worthy, who tried to pass it to a fellow Laker but instead delivered it to Celtic Gerald Henderson, who singlehandedly converted a field goal to tie the game. Boston won in overtime, 124–121, and went on to take championship number fifteen.

1987 Eastern Conference Finals versus Detroit

The series offered perhaps the quintessential grudge match between an aging Celtics team and a young, hungry group of Pistons. Detroit held a one-point lead in Game Five with just five seconds to go. Piston Isiah Thomas did not hear his coach's frantic calls for a time-out but instead inbounded the ball toward Bill Laimbeer. Larry Bird leaped in front of Laimbeer, grabbed the ball, and passed it to Dennis Johnson, who scored the go-ahead points at the buzzer. The Celtics went on to win the series in seven games.

What **player was involved with more successful teams** than any other?

Bill Russell of Boston Celtics's fame is widely recognized as one of the greatest players in NBA history. Beyond that, though, he is perhaps the winningest player in basketball history, experiencing unprecedented success at the college, Olympic, and professional level. In 1956, Russell led his University of San Francisco team to its second straight NCAA championship. Not only that, but the team won the last 56 games they played

Bill Russell was a winner at every level, leading teams at the college, Olympic, and professional levels to championships.

with Russell as its starting center. Shortly after the end of the tournament, he led the U.S. to an undefeated record and the Olympic gold medal in Melbourne, Australia. He then joined the Celtics in the middle of the team's season and finished off his spectacular year by helping the Celtics win the NBA championship. It was the fastest that anyone had ever pulled off the college-Olympic-NBA trifecta.

Russell went on to have an 13-year career with the Celtics, and in that time period, he led his team to the NBA title 11 times and to the championship finals one other time. In all, the Celtic teams that Russell was a part of had a regular-season winning percentage of .705 and playoff mark of .693.

What team has played in the **most NBA finals**?

The Lakers, originally based in Minneapolis, later in Los Angeles, have appeared in 24 finals, winning 11. The Celtics rank next with 19 appearances, of which they won 16. The Philadelphia 76ers have won three of eight finals, the New York Knicks two of seven, the Warriors (Philadelphia, San Francisco, Golden State) three of eight, and the Chicago Bulls six of six.

Which NBA star won a **H-O-R-S-E** contest among the league's best players?

Back in the 1970s, the NBA launched a season-long H-O-R-S-E competition in which top players from around the league faced off against one another in the playground game. The competition, which lasted for only one season, became a regular feature of NBA half-time shows. The shot selection in the matches themselves ranged from flurries of long-range jumpers to trick shots, and when the dust had settled at the end of the year, All-Star shooting guard Paul Westphal of the Phoenix Suns emerged victorious.

Which **jersey numbers have been retired** by individual teams more than any other?

Through the 1996–97 regular season, both number 15 and number 32 had been retired by seven clubs in recognition of performances by individual players who wore those uniforms. Jersey number 32 has been retired by the Seattle Supersonics (to honor "Downtown" Freddy Brown), Philadelphia 76ers (Billy Cunningham), New Jersey Nets (Julius Erving), Los Angeles Lakers (Magic Johnson), Portland Trail Blazers (Bill Walton), Boston Celtics (Kevin McHale), and Milwaukee Bucks (Brian Winters).

Jersey number 15, meanwhile, has been retired by the New York Knicks (to honor both Dick McGuire and Earl Monroe), Trail Blazers (Larry Steele), the Dallas Mavericks (Brad Davis), the Philadelphia 76ers (Hal Greer), the Celtics (Tom Heinsohn), and the Detroit Pistons (Vinnie Johnson).

Other jerseys numbers that have been retired by at least four teams include number one, six, 23, 33, and 44.

Who were the **"Bad Boys"**?

In the late 1980s the Detroit Pistons put together one of the toughest squads in the history of the NBA. The club's signature style evolved into one of hard fouls, intimidation, and fierce defense, and their physical play became an essential ingredient in their title runs in 1989–90 and 1990–91. Indeed, the team from the Motor City came to embrace their "Bad Boys" persona, even going so far as to take the NFL Oakland Raiders' skull and crossbones insignia and black colors and appropriate them for their own use. The baddest of the Bad Boys were undoubtedly center Bill Laimbeer and forward Rick Mahorn, both of whom became known for their hard—some would say dirty—style of play. Other key members of the Pistons' hard-nosed squad included John Salley and Dennis Rodman, who at that early point in his career had yet to develop his fascination with cosmetics, tattoos, and multi-colored hair styles.

But the true heart of the Pistons teams of the "Bad Boys" era was their three-guard rotation, which was regarded as the best in the NBA at the time. The unquestioned leader of this group was Isiah Thomas, an exciting superstar who personified the Bad Boys' take no prisoners attitude out on the floor. His backcourt mate was Joe Dumars, a quiet star whose reputation as a defensive stopper sometimes obscured a silky smooth offensive game. And off the bench came Vinnie Johnson, a fireplug of a guard who had acquired the nickname "the Microwave" for his ability to supply instant offense when needed.

This unique mix of bravado and talent held the league hostage for two solid years. During the 1988–89 season, the Pistons—who a year earlier had lost the NBA Championship in a seven-game spellbinder against the Los Angeles Lakers—turned into a juggernaut. The team marched to a 63–19 mark, led by Thomas (18.2 points a game), Dumars (17.2 ppg), and Laimbeer (13.7 points, 9.6 rebounds). They rolled through the postseason as well, winning 15 out of 17 games to claim the NBA Championship. Dumars led the way in the NBA Finals rematch against the Lakers, posting a 27.3 point-average in the four-game sweep.

A year later, Detroit successfully defended its title despite the loss of Mahorn in the NBA expansion draft. But the departure of Mahorn marked the beginning of the end of the "Bad Boys" era. In fact, Thomas announced at a June 1989 White House ceremony attended by President George Bush that the loss of the burly power forward meant that Detroit's Bad Boys days were over. Still, Detroit's roster maintained its aggressive edge, and buoyed by a 25–1 midseason streak, the club finished with a 59–23 regular season record. After dispatching its Eastern Conference foes, Detroit rolled over Portland in five games to win its second consecutive NBA Championship, as Thomas burned the Trailblazers for nearly 28 points a game.

But that championship proved to be the last hurrah for the Pistons. In the early 1990s Michael Jordan and the Bulls took center stage, and the other Detroit players most closely associated with the "Bad Boys" era either retired (Laimbeer, Thomas) or were traded (Rodman, Salley). By 1995 Dumars was the only player left from the Bad Boy regime in a Piston uniform. But NBA observers point out that even though the Bad Boys roamed the courts of the league for only a few short seasons, their impact continues to be felt today. Indeed, the current emphasis on defense in NBA locker rooms can be directly traced to the Pistons' defense-fueled championship runs.

Who is the only non-center to win the NBA's Defensive Player of the Year Award since 1992?

Since the early 1990s, shotblocking centers have received the lion's share of recognition for defensive prowess. In 1992 San Antonio center David Robinson won the award, and in 1993 and 1994 the trophy went to Houston's Hakeem Olajuwon. Since then, the finger-wagging Dikembe Mutombo has won three Defensive Player of the Year Awards (with Denver in 1995, and with Atlanta in 1997 and 1998). But in 1996, Seattle point guard Gary Payton—nicknamed "the Glove" in recognition of his ability to smother opposing point guards—won the award to the delight of ballhawks everywhere.

How many times has the NBA All-Star Game Most Valuable Player Award been shared by two players?

Twice, in 1959 and 1993. In the 1959 All-Star Game, which the West won by a 124–108 score, St. Louis legend Bob Pettit and Minneapolis star Elgin Baylor shared the honor. In 1993, Utah Jazz teammates John Stockton and Karl Malone shared the award after leading the West over the East in overtime by a 135–132 score.

Who was the first player to score 2,000 points in a single season?

Detroit's George Yardley pumped in 2,001 points during the 1957–58 season, breaking George Mikan's record of 1,932 points in a single season.

Who are the Top 10 Greatest NBA coaches, according to the 1996 50th anniversary voting in 1996?

The ten with their win and title totals through the 1996–97 season:

Red Auerbach (1037 wins, 9 titles)
Chuck Daly (638 wins, 2 titles)
Bill Fitch (982 wins, 1 title)

> ## Where did Red Auerbach first establish his reputation?
>
> **A**uerbach coached the Washington Capitols in the NBA's inaugural season, leading them to a league-best record, 49–11, that remained the highest winning percentage for many years. He won over 1,000 games and 9 championships. The NBA's Coach of the Year trophy is named for him.

Red Holzman (754 wins, 2 titles)
Phil Jackson (579 wins, 5 titles)
John Kundla (485 wins, 5 titles)
Don Nelson (902 wins, 0 titles)
Jack Ramsay (908 wins, 1 title)
Pat Riley (1002 wins, 4 titles)
Lenny Wilkins (1138 wins, 1 title)

Who is the NBA's **all-time winningest coach, was voted one of the Top 50 NBA Players of all-time, and was an All-Star Game and NIT MVP**?

Lenny Wilkins won the NIT MVP in 1960 as a guard for Providence, ranks sixth all-time in assists in the NBA, coached Seattle to an NBA championship in 1979, and was named Coach of the Year in 1994 for his work with the Atlanta Hawks.

Who was the **first African American head coach** in the NBA?

Bill Russell became the first African American head coach in any major professional sport in 1966 and proceeded to lead the Celtics to two more championships.

Who is the **only coach to win the league championship in the NBA, the ABA, and the ABL**?

Bill Sharman, who had a great playing career with the Boston Celtics, was even better as a coach. In 1962, his first year as a professional coach, he led the Cleveland Pipers of the fledgling American Basketball League (ABL) to the league title—the only league title there would ever be, as it turned out, since the league folded after only one season. Moving on to the ABA, Sharman coached the Utah Stars for three seasons before leading that team to the league title in 1971. He was named ABA Coach of the Year for his efforts. The Los Angeles Lakers wasted no time in hiring Sharman as head coach for the 1971–72 season. It was a good move. The team ended up being one of the best

121

in NBA history, winning a record 33 games in a row on its way to a then-record 69 wins in the regular season (since eclipsed by the Chicago Bulls). In the playoffs, the Lakers capped off a record-setting season by winning the championship and earning Sharman yet another Coach of the Year honor.

Who are the only three NBA players to **total 20,000 points, 6,000 assists, and 6,000 rebounds** during their careers?

Oscar Robertson, John Havlicek, and Clyde "the Glide" Drexler.

Why is it that a player who totals the **most points** during an NBA season won't necessarily win the scoring crown?

The scoring crown goes to the player with the highest points-per-game average. Say player A scores 2400 points and plays in all of his teams' 82 games: his scoring average is 29.2. Player B scores 2350 points but plays in only 80 games for a 29.3 average. Player B wins the title.

How many times has **one team's final score doubled the loser's score** in an NBA game?

Only once has that igniminious feat occurred, on February 27, 1998, when the Indiana Pacers defeated Portland 124–59. Needless to say, the Pacers were hot—making 64% of their shots—and the Trailblazers NOT—making 33% of theirs. Along with doubling the score, the Pacers made twice as many field goals, three-pointers, and free throws than the Blazers, and Pacers players passed around twice as many assists as well.

What was the **biggest blowout** in NBA history?

The 1998 score-doubling drubbing of the Trailblazers by the Pacers, 124–59, is only the second largest margin of victory in NBA history: Cleveland's 148–80 scorching of the Miami Heat ranks as the worst.

What are the **highest and lowest total scores** in an NBA game?

1955 and 1996 were good years for bricks. The lowest scoring game ever occurred in 1955 when Boston defeated Milwaukee 62–57 (119 total), erasing the record set earlier that year when Ft. Wayne defeated Syracuse 69–66 (135 total). Miami defeated Philadelphia 66–57 (123 total) in February of 1996 for the second lowest total.

A triple overtime game between Detroit and Denver, which the Pistons won 186–184, on December 13, 1983, produced 370 points, and another three-OT game ranks second: San Antonio defeated Milwaukee 171–166 (337 total) in March of 1982. The most points in a game that ended in regulation time occurred in 1990, when Golden State beat Denver 162–158 (320 total), which eclipsed the previous record of 318 set in 1984 when Denver beat San Antonio, 163–155 (118).

What team posted the **worst regular season record** in NBA history?

For much of the 1997–98 campaign, it appeared that the woeful Denver Nuggets might claim this unwanted distinction. But a late-season "surge" enabled them to round out the season with a merely awful 11–71 record, two games better than the pathetic 9–73 mark that was registered by the 1972–73 Philadelphia 76ers. Denver's 11–71 mark tied them for the second-worst record in NBA history with the Dallas Mavericks, who did it in 1992–93.

Rounding out the worst half-dozen teams in league history are the 1986–87 Los Angeles Clippers, who finished 12–70; the 1982–83 Houston Rockets (14–68), and the 1996–97 Vancouver Grizzlies (14–68). Interestingly, none of the above teams were first-year expansion clubs in the years in which they finished with these poor records.

Who are the only three NBA players to **average 20 rebounds and 20 points per game for an entire season,** and what was unique about one of them?

Two of the men who accomplished the feat are names that you would expect—giants Wilt Chamberlain and Bob Pettit, both of whom played center. Chamberlain pulled off the feat many times, while Pettit accomplished it once while playing for the old St. Louis Hawks.

The third man to pull off the feat might surprise some basketball fans. Jerry Lucas was generously listed as 6 foot, 8 inches in many media guides, but in reality he was just

> **In any sport, the Most Valuable Player award in the playoffs almost always goes to a player on the winning team. Who is the only NBA player to be named MVP of the finals despite losing?**
>
> The current general manager of the Los Angeles Lakers, Jerry West. In the 1969 finals, West averaged 40 points per game against the Lakers' hated rivals, the Boston Celtics, but it wasn't enough—the Celtics still won the series and the league championship, four games to three.

a shade over 6 foot, 7 inches. Lucas made his living shooting from the outside, but he had the quickness and the hands to dart inside and pull down rebounds. During the 1965–66 season for the Cincinnati Royals, Lucas averaged 21.5 points and 21.1 rebounds per game during 79 regular season games, then also averaged 20–20 in the playoffs.

Who are the **tallest and smallest players** in NBA history?

Manute Bol and Gheorge Muresan at 7-7 are the tallest, followed by Shawn Bradley (7-6) and Mark Eaton, Priest Lauderdale, and Rik Smits at 7-4.

Muggsy Bogues at 5-3 is the smallest, followed by 5-7 players Greg Grant, Keith Jennings, Louis Klotz, and Spud Webb.

What is the **name of the trophy** given to the NBA champion?

The Larry O' Brien Trophy.

What is the **longest shot** ever made in professional basketball?

A regulation basketball court is 94 feet in length, and the record-breaking shot made by Jerry Harkness of the Indiana Pacers was nearly that long. In an American Basketball Association game between the Pacers and the Dallas Chapparals on November 13, 1967, Harkness took an inbounds pass from teammate Oliver Darden with one second left on the clock and heaved the ball 92 feet and watched in amazement as it went in. Since the shot was beyond the ABA's 25-foot three-point line, the shot counted as a three and gave the Pacers an amazing 119–118 victory. Interestingly enough, Indiana coach Larry Staverman didn't even see the winning shot drop in because he had already started for the Pacers' locker room, convinced his team had lost the game.

Who is the only player to **lead the NCAA, NBA, and ABA in season scoring**?

Rick Barry: NCAA, 1965, Miami of Florida; NBA, 1967, San Francisco; ABA, 1969, Oakland.

Who was the first rookie signed to a million dollar contract?

Ralph Sampson, Houston Rockets, 1983.

COLLEGE AND AMATEUR

How did **college basketball** evolve?

The first intercollegiate game was held in 1897. In May 1901 several schools—Yale, Harvard, Trinity, Holy Cross, Amherst, and Williams—formed the New England Intercollegiate Basketball League. The development of collegiate leagues and conferences brought organization, scheduling, and rivalries. By 1905 more than 80 schools had organized teams. Colleges competed mostly in their regions until 1936, when a Stanford University team traveled to New York City to challenge top eastern squads. This tour helped bring variety to the game: eastern teams generally favored the two-hand, stationary shot, while western teams had turned to one-handed jump shots. The jump shot soon became popular in the east as well, and scores rose.

When did the **major tournaments** develop?

In 1937 the first national collegiate tournament was organized by the NAIA (National Association of Intercollegiate Athletics). The following year the Metropolitan Basketball Writer's Association, a group of New York City sportswriters, organized the National Invitational Tournament to conclude the 1937–38 season. The National Association of Basketball Coaches (NABC) founded the NCAA tournament the following year. Oregon defeated Ohio State 46–33 to win the first NCAA championship.

The NIT and NCAA tournaments were originally played at the same time: as a general rule, independent schools played in the NIT and conference-affiliated schools played in the NCAA. For the first 12 years, the NCAA tournament divided the country into eight districts, each with a regional selection committee sending a team to the eight-team tournament. As the tournament gained importance, the field gradually enlarged to 16, then 32 teams, and in 1985 to its present size of 64.

Who makes up the **NCAA's Selection Committee** which determines the 64-team NCAA Men's Basketball Tournament field?

The Selection Committee is made up of NCAA officials, conference commissioners, and university athletic directors. Each year on the last weekend of the college basket-

As the end of the college basketball season nears, teams that have had good, but not great, seasons are said to be "on the bubble." That means that when the 64-team field is announced for the NCAA tournament, any team that has had a so-so season, say roughly a record of 19–11, is busy praying that it makes the field. Each year, several deserving teams are left out because there are more good teams than there are open slots in the tournament. Twenty wins used to almost guarantee that a team would get in, but no more. Parity has leveled the playing field and created more good teams from the smaller athletic conferences. To get off the bubble, teams need to either win their conference championship, thereby earning an automatic berth in the tournament, or win as many games as possible against highly ranked opponents.

ball season, these orchestrators of "March Madness" gather together behind closed doors and determine which teams get a spot in the tournament (conference champions earn an automatic berth), how high each team will be seeded, and what region each team will play in.

What is the **RPI**?

RPI, or Ratings Percentage Index is one of the factors the NCAA's Selection Committee uses to choose the field for the NCAA Tournament. RPI measures strength of schedule and how a team fared against that schedule. Unlike football, RPI does not take into account margin of victory, only wins and losses. Bubble teams are more likely to be affected by RPI than the perennial powers.

What is the **National Invitational Tournament**?

The NIT is a competition that commenced play in 1938 as a means of determining a national collegiate champion. In the first NIT final, Temple defeated Colorado 60–36. The next year, however, the NCAA decided to conduct its own tournament to determine a national champion. The NIT then began inviting teams that were out of the NCAA's competition. In 1950, however, City College of New York won both the NIT and NCAA tournaments. The NIT has always been held at Madison Square Garden in New York City. St. John's University has won five NIT tournaments and Bradley University has won four.

Who was the **first African-American All-American** basketball player?

George Gregory of Columbia in 1931 was the first African-American named All-American. Don Barksdale of UCLA in 1948 became the first African-American Olympic basketball player, and he was also the first African-American NBA All-Star (1952).

What is the **longest winning streak** in basketball history?

While the Los Angeles Lakers NBA winning streak of 33 straight games and UCLA's college winning streak of 88 straight wins are impressive, they fall far short of the amazing 159–game winning streak put together by Passaic High School in Passaic, New Jersey between December 1919 and February 1925. During the string of victories, it outscored opponents by an average of 59.5 to 20.2, topping 100 points on several occasions, including a 145–5 drubbing of a Stamford, Connecticut prep school. Those point totals don't sound like much, but scoring averages were very low in that era. The streak began with a 44–11 win over Newark Junior College and ended with a 39–35 defeat to nearby Hackensack High. During the 1922–23 season, a Passaic game was broadcast live over the radio, which was possibly the first basketball game at any level ever broadcast.

The record winning streak in women's basketball also belongs to a high school team. Beginning in 1947 and ending in 1853, Baskins High School in Louisiana won 218 straight games, winning by an average margin of 31 points. The streak ended when the girls lost 33–27 to Winnsboro High School.

What are some of the greatest **scoring achievements by college players**?

When it came to scoring, nobody matched Louisiana State University's gunning guard Pete Maravich, who nailed 1,381 points in 1970 for a game average of 44.5. Maravich owns the NCAA's top three season averages, all around forty-four points, and three of the top five season point totals. Another phenomenal scorer was Notre Dame's Austin Carr, who averaged 34.6 points during his three school years. In 1970, Carr set an NCAA tournament record when he tallied sixty-one points against Ohio University. Still another great college player was Oscar Robertson, who joins Maravich as the only two players to lead the nation in scoring for three seasons. Robertson ended his college career with a 33.8 scoring average. His University of Cincinnati squad finished third in both the 1959 and 1960 NCAA championships.

Who is **Bevo Francis,** and why does he have a special place in college basketball history?

Clarence "Bevo" Francis is a true All-American story. Born in 1932, and an only child, Bevo was nicknamed after a popular softdrink at the time. He attended Wellsville High School in Wellsville, Ohio and averaged 31 points a game in leading his team to a 19–1 record—all pretty routine stuff to that point. He was recruited by more than 60 colleges, but he followed his high school coach down the road to tiny Rio Grande College (pronounced "Rye-o Grand"). With the school in danger of closing due to lack of money, Bevo and coach Newt Oliver teamed up to literally save the school. Playing against oher colleges, military bases, and any other takers, Bevo led Rio Grande to a 39–0 record in 1953. More amazingly, Francis became the first player to ever average more than 50 points per game for an entire season, highlighted by a 116-point performance against Ashland Junior College in Kentucky, which was also a record.

Newpaper and magazine reporters from around America took note of the Ohio scoring whiz and made him a national hero. That didn't set well with some of the big colleges that were used to getting all the attention, so the national coaches association voted to strip Bevo of most of his records, including his 116-point game, because they didn't occur against four-year colleges. Francis and Oliver were unfazed. With interest in Rio Grande at an all-time high, Oliver scheduled all 25 of the team's games in 1954 on the road, all against four-year colleges, and some against some of the best teams in the country. His efforts payed off. Rio Grande did lose a few games that year, but every game was in front of a packed house, including more than 13,000 at Madison Square Garden. Francis picked up right where he left off the previous season, scoring points in buckets. He failed to average 50 points per game, finishing at a still-record 46.5, but he did manage to break the 100-point plateau, hitting for 113 against four-year Hillsdale College of Michigan. Rio Grande won the game 134–91. His 113 points still stands as the college record for most points in a game, and he also still holds the mark for most field goals attempted in a game (71), most field goals made in a game (38), most free throws made and attempted in a game (37 and 45, respectively), most free throws attempted in a season (510), most 50-point games in a season (8), and most 50-point games in a career (14).

Who is the only other man to **score 100 points in a college game,** and has a woman ever pulled off the feat?

Just 11 days after Bevo Francis poured in 113 points against Ashland, another prolific scorer managed to break the century mark. Frank Selvy, who was averaging nearly 40 points per game for Furman University in Greenville, South Carolina, scored exactly 100 points against Newberry College, a small Lutheran school. His last two points came on a desperation heave from just inside the half-court line as time expired—the ball swished through the net for the last of his 41 field goals. Furman won the game 149–95.

No woman has managed to break the 100-point plateau at the major college level, but two very well-known stars of the women's game pulled off the feat in high school. Cheryl Miller, who went on to become one of the best female players of all-time before switching into sportscasting, scored 105 for her Riverside, California high school in 1982. In 1990, current WNBA poster girl and model Lisa Leslie scored 101 points in a

Lisa Leslie poured in 101 points in one half of a high school basketball game. The score was 102–24 when the opposing coach took his team off the floor at halftime and didn't return.

Who is the oldest player to ever earn All-American honors at the college level?

Thanks to six years in the United States Air Force and a later tour of duty during the Korean War, Doug Williams was in his late-20s by the time he finally got to go to college at St. Mary's University, which competed at the small-college level. Williams was 6 foot, 9 inches tall, and had always wanted to play college basketball. Not letting his age get in the way, Williams tried out for the St. Mary's team as a freshman and made the team, launching his four-year career there. He was a solid scorer who also played excellent defense and rebounded well. Balancing his school, basketball, a part-time job, and his home life with his wife and kids, Williams was rewarded for his efforts on the court his senior year when he was named a first-team selection on the National Association of Intercollegiate Athletics All-American team. Williams was 31 at the time.

single *half* for Morningside High School in Inglewood, California in a game against South Torrance High. Leslie would have shattered the record if the South Torrance coach hadn't pulled his team off the court at halftime trailing 102–24, forfeiting the game because he felt Morningside was making a mockery of his team.

Who is the **winningest coach** in basketball history?

John Wooden at UCLA and Red Auerbach of the Boston Celtics might be the most well-known coaches in basketball history, but not even they can match the feats of a man named Bob Douglas.

"Bob, who?" you ask. Douglas coached an all-African American touring team from the 1920s until the 1940s. The team barnstormed around the country, taking on all-comers and playing up to 140 games a year. And they didn't face lousy competition either—they challenged all the top teams of the time period, defeating the original Boston Celtics on many occasions and winning six professional tournaments, at least one of which was considered to be the world championship. In his 26 years of coaching, Douglas compiled a record of 2,318 victories against only 381 defeats. That's more than twice as many victories as Auerbach posted. It is almost certainly a record that will stand forever.

Have any coaches **won the NCAA Championship game as their final game**?

Three times: John Wooden, appropriately, retired a champion in 1975; Al McGuire retired from Marquette after their 1977 win, and Larry Brown went to the NBA after winning it all with Kansas in 1988.

130

John Wooden, shown here with Lew Alcindor (Kareem Abdul-Jabbar), coached the UCLA Bruins to 10 national championships.

What teams have won the **most NCAA championships**?

The University of California at Los Angeles dominated college basketball from 1963 to 1975. Coached by John Wooden, UCLA won 10 national championships during this time (1964, 1965, 1967–1973, 1975), including seven consecutively. From 1971 to 1974, UCLA also won 88 consecutive games, an NCAA record. UCLA has won 11 championships, Kentucky six, Indiana five, and North Carolina three.

How many teams have gone **undefeated in the regular season** en route to the NCAA title, and what was the last school to do it?

Seven, with Indiana being the most recent, in 1975–76. UCLA did it in 1963–64, 1966–67, 1973–74, and 1974–75; North Carolina did it in 1957 and San Francisco in 1956.

Who is the all-time **winningest college coach**?

Dean Smith of North Carolina retired in 1997 after compiling 879 victories, passing Adolph Rupp, who amassed 876 for Kentucky.

Who were the marquee players on the University of Houston's **"Phi Slamma Jamma"** squad?

During the early 1980s, Clyde "the Glide" Drexler, Akeem "the Dream" Olajuwon, Larry Micheaux and the rest of the Houston Cougars squad unleashed a devastating basketball high-wire act on the rest of college basketball. The high-flying Cougars routinely buried opponents with flurries of spectacular dunks and other acrobatics, and their exciting brand of play eventually led Houston fans to dub the team "Phi Slamma Jamma," America's first dunking fraternity. But while Drexler's gravity-defying flights to the basket and Olajuwon's thunderous dunks carried the Cougars to the Final Four in both 1982 and 1983, the talented Cougars were unable to secure an NCAA title.

In 1982 Coach Guy Lewis's young Houston squad surprised everyone by advancing to the Final Four before succumbing to a North Carolina squad that featured Michael Jordan, James Worthy, and Sam Perkins. But during the 1982–83 campaign, the Cougars did not sneak up on anybody. In fact, they spent a good portion of the season as the nation's top-ranked team, thanks to their 27–2 regular season record. "We can go all the way this time," said Drexler. "You've never seen such a confident team as this one." By the time the 1983 NCAA Tournament started, the publicity machine surrounding Phi Slamma Jamma was in overdrive, and as the tournament progressed the Cougars' aura of invincibility increased as they dunked every opponent they faced into submission. But in the 1983 title game, the men of Phi Slamma Jamma lost to the underdog North Carolina State Wolfpack in a game that ranks as one of college bas-

Dean Smith passed Adolph Rupp in 1997 to become the all-time leader in wins by a college basketball coach.

ketball's biggest and most dramatic upsets. Clinging to a tie game in the final seconds, the Cougars could only watch helplessly as NC State's Lorenzo Charles caught a last-second airball and jammed it in the basket at the buzzer to give the Wolfpack the victory.

That stunning conclusion marked the end of the line for Phi Slamma Jamma, for both Olajuwon and Drexler moved on to the NBA the following season.

Who were the players that made up the **University of Michigan's famed "Fab Five"**?

In the fall of 1991 five highly recruited high school players from around the country came together in Ann Arbor to form what came to be known as the "Fab Five." These five players—Chris Webber, Juwan Howard, Jalen Rose, Ray Jackson, and Jimmy King—comprised the most celebrated recruiting class to hit a single basketball program in many years, and as the beginning of the 1991–92 season drew near, many college basketball observers kept one eye on the Wolverines to see how long it would take Coach Steve Fisher to get the freshman ready for big college action.

As it turned out, the Fab Five showed that they were ready for the college stage far sooner than anyone anticipated. Webber, Rose, and Howard all cracked the starting lineup by the first game of the season, and by midseason, Fisher had added Jackson and King to the starting five as well. The Michigan squad attracted huge amounts of publicity as the season progressed, not only because of their all-freshman starting lineup, but also because of the team's appetite for trash talking, off the cuff interviews, and long baggy shorts. The freshmen were unpredictable—they often looked great against top-ranked opponents and terrible against lesser teams—but as the NCAA Tournament approached, they seemed to share an amazing confidence that they would make some major noise. Sure enough, Michigan stunned the world of college basketball by advancing all the way to the Finals before succumbing to the Duke Blue Devils.

A year later, the Fab Five fueled another run to the NCAA Championship Game. Led by Webber, Howard, and Rose, the squad slamdunked their way to a showdown with the North Carolina Tar Heels. But the Wolverines fell short once again. With the seconds ticking away in a very close game, Webber mistakenly called time after Michigan had used all their time outs up. The blunder, which gave NC the basketball and a couple of insurance technical foul free throws, allowed the Tar Heels to salt the game away.

The 1993 Finals marked the last game in which the Fab Five played together. Webber left for the NBA the following year, where he has had a checkered career. Howard and Rose both left for the NBA after their junior seasons, and both have established themselves in the league. King and Jackson were the last of the Fab Five to leave. After completing their senior seasons, both players made brief appearances in the NBA before joining CBA teams.

Hakeem Olajuwan was a founding member of the University of Houston's "Phi Slamma Jamma" fraternity.

Why will Oregon guard Bobby Anet always be associated with the first-ever NCAA tournament?

Anet made a name for himself in a couple of ways at the tournament. Most importantly, he was a member of the Fighting Ducks squad that claimed the tournament's very first crown with a 46–33 victory over the Ohio State Buckeyes. But he is also remembered as the player who broke the championship trophy when his efforts to save a loose ball during the title game carried him headlong into the sideline trophy table. The expense of fixing the trophy contributed to the NCAA's overall loss of $2,531 on the tournament. That loss remains the only deficit that the event has ever posted.

Which school **did not win an NCAA Tournament or NIT Championship** until the 1970s despite tallying more victories than any other team in the 1950s?

Even though the North Carolina State Wolfpack won more games than any other program in the 1950s, the team did not win an NCAA or NIT crown until 1974, when the Wolfpack defeated Marquette 76–64 in the NCAA Final.

Which eventual NBA great continues to hold the record for **best field goal shooting percentage by a freshman** for an entire season?

As a freshman for the Arkansas Razorbacks, guard Sidney Moncrief posted an amazing 66.5 field goal percentage for the season.

Which college player **scored 25 points in a game without attempting a single field goal**?

On January 30, 1971, Birmingham Southern College's Russell Thompson hit 25 free throws to lead his team over Florence State University of Alabama by a 54–46 score. Birmingham Southern, which had been spanked by Florence State in a game earlier that season, utilized a slowdown game that was choreographed by Thompson, the team's starting point guard. Since the rules did not include a shot clock at that time, Birmingham Southern decided to hold on to the ball until they had a perfect shot. At halftime Birmingham Southern had only attempted eight field goals, but they also had a slim three-point lead thanks to free throws.

As the second half unfolded, Florence State University was unable to take the lead. Instead, the team fell further behind, and they watched helplessly as Thompson and his Birmingham Southern teammates passed the ball among themselves in an effort to drain the clock. Florence State was forced to foul their opponents to stop the clock and get the ball back, and since Thompson was Birmingham Southern's primary ball-handler, it was he who most often went to the free throw line. He went to the line a total of 28 times in the game, converting 25 of his attempts. Florence State, meanwhile, saw five of their players foul out in the latter stages of the contest.

Birmingham Southern's strategy worked to perfection, as Thompson's parade to the free throw line boosted the team to a 54–46 victory. But this game and similar contests scattered around the country ultimately led college basketball to adopt a shot clock to put an end to such shenanigans.

When was the **NCAA men's tournament first televised** on a major network?

The first NCAA Tournament to be nationally televised was the one in 1962 in which Cincinnati defeated Ohio State for the championship. But the telecast bore no resemblance to the current circus, in which the major networks, ESPN, and CNN-SI all provide exhaustive coverage of the event. Back in 1962, all that was shown was a condensed taped version of the championship contest that was crammed into a 90-minute slot on ABC's *Wide World of Sports*. Even the semifinals were left on the cutting room floor, for ABC Sports executives were leery of devoting any more time to what was then regarded as a tournament of questionable attractiveness to viewers.

Who was the first player to be named **NCAA Tournament Most Valuable Player two years in a row**?

Oklahoma A&M center Bob Kurland was the first to accomplish this feat. Kurland was the anchor of the Oklahoma A&M (later to become Oklahoma State) Aggies squad in the mid-1940s. He was the cornerstone of the offense, but it was his defense for which he is best remembered. Kurland used to hang out just in front of the basket that he was defending, where he took full advantage of college basketball's lax goaltending rules. Until Kurland came along, defenders had the option of blocking the ball even when it was on its downward flight. The 6'10 Aggie center took full advantage of this loophole, swatting away shots left and right. In fact, his shotblocking ability was so demoralizing to opponents that after the 1943–44 season—Kurland's sophomore year—the NCAA changed its goaltending rule so that players could no longer block shots when the basketball was on its downward arc to the basket (the rules committee also increased the number of personal fouls allowed for individual players from four to five to partially compensate for the change in goaltending).

As America's college basketball teams prepared for the 1944–45 season, many observers speculated that Kurland would not be nearly as effective. But the big center continued to dominate on both ends of the floor, and he led the Aggies to their first

Oklahoma A&M's Bob Kurland (right, with ball) was the first back-to-back winner of the NCAA Tournament's MVP award.

> ## What team sailed to a 27–3 record and a national championship without playing a single game at its own gymnasium?
>
> In 1946–47 the Crusaders of Holy Cross put together a dominating season, culminated by the NCAA Tournament title. They did so despite the fact that they had to play all their games either on the road or at Boston Garden, since the school did not even have a home gym at the time.

NCAA title in the 1945 tournament by scoring 22 points in a 49–45 victory over New York University. A year later, Kurland once again was named MVP on the strength of his 23-point performance in a title game victory over North Carolina.

Since Kurland's back-to-back MVP awards, five other college players have repeated as tournament MVPs. San Francisco's Bill Russell was honored in both 1955 and 1956. UCLA center Lew Alcindor (who later changed his name to Kareem Abdul-Jabbar) won the award an amazing three times in a row, from 1967 to 1969. He was quickly followed by two other UCLA Bruins, as guard Sidney Wicks took home the MVP trophy in both 1970 and 1971, and center Bill Walton received the award in 1972 and 1973. Since then, the only player to receive back-to-back MVP awards for the NCAA Tournament is Christian Laettner, who paced the Duke Blue Devils to tournament victories in both 1991 and 1992.

What event led the NCAA to move their season-ending tournament from New York's **Madison Square Garden**?

Prior to 1951, all NCAA tournaments had been played in the Garden, but that year a gambling scandal of enormous proportions rocked college basketball. An investigation into point shaving revealed that between 1946 and 1950, more than 80 games in nearly two dozen cities had been fixed by at least 37 players (many more players were suspected of wrongdoing) from 22 schools. The scandal hit some of college basketball's proudest programs, including Adolph Rupp's Kentucky Wildcats, whose 1948 and 1949 championships became tarnished with the revelation that three mainstays of those teams—Ralph Beard, Alex Groza, and Wallace Jones—had participated in point shaving.

News of the scandal triggered a torrent of criticism from the media and a lot of soul-searching by the NCAA and the many programs that were implicated. Critics quickly zeroed in on the NCAA Tournament's traditional location as an element in the scandal, arguing that the big-money atmosphere at Madison Square Garden contributed to the whole mess. NCAA officials decided to move the 1951 tournament to

Minneapolis, and in subsequent years the site of the NCAA championship game was moved on an annual basis.

What were the **Red Cross Benefit Games**?

For three years during World War II, the NCAA and NIT champions faced off in a benefit game at Madison Square Garden to raise money for the Red Cross. The NCAA champions won all three games, increasing the tournament's prestige considerably. In the first clash, which took place in 1943, Wyoming knocked off St. John's by a 52–47 score. A year later, NCAA champ Utah defeated defending NIT victor St. John's 46–36. And in 1945, Oklahoma A&M vanquished George Mikan and DePaul by a 52–44 score.

Which **no-name squad** beat Final Four teams led by Oscar Robertson and Jerry West to win the NCAA Championship?

In 1959 Coach Pete Newell guided the California Bears into the Final Four, where they were joined by Louisville, West Virginia, and Cincinnati. Much of the spotlight that year fell on West Virginia and Cincinnati, for the teams were led by two superstars—West for West Virginia and Robertson for Cincinnati—who had yet to win an NCAA championship despite their individual brilliance. As the semifinal games approached, most observers felt that one star or the other would finally claim that title. But as it turned out, Newell's no-name Bears stole the spotlight from both of them.

California's first opponent in the Final Four that year was the Cincinnati Bearcats. Newell knew his team was in for a tough contest. As he said years later, "Oscar was *the* player in college basketball. He was in every magazine that had anything to do with sports, and he had set all kinds of records and was truly one of our all-time great players." But the California coach devised a defense that bottled Robertson up. "We made Oscar work like the dickens for the ball," he remembered. "We made him bring the ball up, and we did really a good job of defensive rotation. We tried to deny Oscar the ball. If we were going to get beat, we wanted those other guys to beat us." Newell's plan worked. The Bears held Robertson to 19 points on their way to a 64–58 victory.

But looming ahead in the title game was a confrontation with West Virginia's Jerry West, college basketball's other big star at the time. West had been incredible throughout the tournament, scorching every foe that the Mountaineers faced. As the game unfolded, California's poise and steady play enabled them to move out to a comfortable double-digit lead. But as the clock ticked away, the Mountaineers mounted a furious comeback with West (28 points) leading the charge. California's lead dwindled away to one point, but they managed to hold on for a narrow 71–70 victory. Both Robertson and West (who was named tournament MVP) had done their best, but when the final gun sounded to mark the end of another college basketball season, it was the California Bears who wore the mantle of NCAA champs.

Why did the NCAA outlaw dunking in the late 1960s?

By 1968 UCLA center Lew Alcindor had become so unstoppable that the NCAA outlawed dunking in an attempt to make him a little less dominant. But according to many observers, the rule change made Alcindor even more of a force. The towering center continued to post 30- and 40-point games with dizzying regularity, and the rule change gave him the opportunity to block many more shots since opponents had to shoot the ball from short range rather than dunk it. It was not until the 1977 season that the NCAA finally realized the error of its ways and restored the dunk to college ball.

How many coaches have led four different teams into the NCAA Tournament?

Only Eddie Sutton has managed to guide squads from four different universities into the tournament. Over the years he has led Creighton, Arkansas, Kentucky, and Oklahoma State into the "Field of 64."

Which member of the UCLA Bruins scored 70 points in two Final Four games to lead his team to an NCAA title, only to see the tournament MVP award go to a member of a team that did not even make the championship game?

In the 1965 tournament, Bruin playmaker Gail Goodrich shot the lights out to help UCLA to their second consecutive NCAA title. In the team's 93–76 semifinal victory over Princeton, Goodrich tallied 28 points, and in the title game against Cazzie Russell and the Michigan Wolverines, he blitzed U-M for 42 points to lead the Bruins to a 91–80 win. But after the tournament was over, it was learned that Princeton's Bill Bradley had been awarded the MVP trophy in recognition of his role in carrying the underdog Tigers to the Final Four for the first time in the program's history.

Which Division I-A team defeated their opponents by an *average* of more than 30 points a game during an entire season?

The 1971–72 UCLA Bruins set an NCAA record by destroying their foes by an average margin of victory of 30.3 points. The squad, which featured the formidable starting five of Keith Wilkes, Larry Farmer, Greg Lee, Henry Bibby, and Bill Walton, had entered the season as the overwhelming preseason favorite, and they immediately proved that the pre-season hype was legitimate. The Bruins tallied more than 100 points in their first seven games against solid Division I programs such as Iowa, Iowa

Lew Alcindor's dominance of the college game prompted the NCAA to outlaw the dunk in 1968.

State, Notre Dame, and Texas. From there they cruised all the way to the NCAA Tournament title game, where they edged the Florida State Seminoles by an 81–76 score. The victory marked the culmination of an undefeated 30–0 championship season, and a year later John Wooden's Bruins would duplicate the feat, defeating Memphis State in the NCAA title game to finish 30–0 once again.

What is the **lowest-seeded team to ever win the NCAA tournament,** and what team had the most losses—11—when it won the title?

Villanova was seeded eighth in the Southeast region in 1985 after finishing the regular season with a record of 19–10. That didn't stop the Wildcats. In the final, 'Nova defeated Big East conference rival Georgetown 64–63 in one of the biggest upsets in tournament history.

The University of Kansas did Villanova one better in the loss department in 1988, having lost 11 regular season games. Led by All-American Danny Manning however, the Jayhawks, or "Danny and the Miracles" as they became known, defeated Big Eight foe Oklahoma 83–79 to cap an amazing tournament run.

Who is the only player to play in the college national championship game for **two different teams**?

Bob Bender, currently the head coach of the University of Washington, pulled off the double in the late 1970s. In 1976, as a freshman at Indiana University, Bender was a guard on the Hoosier's legendary undefeated national championship squad. After transferring to Duke University, Bender returned to the title game in 1978 when the Blue Devils fell in the finals to the University of Kentucky. Bender has had NCAA success as a coach, also, leading Washington to the Sweet 16 of the tournament in 1998.

What is the **fewest amount of free throws** made by a team in a Final Four game?

University of Nevada, Las Vegas set a record for least free throws made in an NCAA Final Four against North Carolina in 1977. They made one in five attempts. UNLV lost the game 84–83.

What teams have the **best records in NCAA Tournament competition**, having played at least 25 tournament games through 1997?

Duke	57–19	.750
UCLA	77–26	.748
UNLV	30–11	.732
Indiana	50–21	.704

143

North Carolina	72–31	.699
Michigan	40–18	.690
Kentucky	77–35	.688
Kansas	56–26	.683
Ohio State	31–17	.646

Which NCAA final saw the winning team score its **first eight points off goaltending calls**?

The 1982 NCAA Tournament Championship game between the Georgetown Hoyas and the North Carolina Tar Heels ranks as one of the most dramatic in college basketball history. It pitted two coaches—NC's Dean Smith and Georgetown's John Thompson— who rank among the greatest coaches in modern college hoops, and the rosters of the two clubs were dotted with names that would go on to leave huge footprints in the pro game, such as Georgetown's Patrick Ewing and North Carolina's James Worthy and Michael Jordan.

As game time approached, the crowd that packed the New Orleans Superdome seemed to sense that the contest could be a memorable one. Sure enough, even the game's opening moments were spectacular, as Ewing swatted away four Tar Heel shots as stragglers in the record crowd rushed to find their seats. All four blocks were called for goaltending, however, thus providing North Carolina with their first eight points of the game. As the game unfolded, it became a bitterly contested battle in which both squads made spectacular offensive and defensive plays. With 15 seconds left in the game, Jordan gave the Tar Heels a one-point lead on a sideline jumper. The Hoyas promptly moved the ball past midcourt in an effort to launch a final shot to win the game. But then, in one of the craziest endings ever to a title tilt, Georgetown guard Fred Brown passed the basketball directly to Tar Heel James Worthy in the final seconds. A stunned Worthy turned direction and dribbled downcourt to try to ice the game with a final basket. He was fouled before he could make the basket, but even though he missed two free throws he had run out all but two seconds of the clock. The Hoyas did not have enough time to get off a shot, enabling North Carolina to escape with a victory. As tournament MVP Worthy, Jordan, and the other Tar Heel players celebrated, Georgetown Coach John Thompson walked over to the devastated Brown and put his arm around his young player to comfort him. Thompson's gesture was the last memorable moment in a contest that was littered with memorable moments.

Who is the only coach to lead his teams to **championships in the NCAA tournament, the NIT tournament, the Olympics, and the Pan American Games**?

Indiana Head Coach Bobby Knight is the only coach who has managed this feat.

Georgetown's Patrick Ewing (33) swatted away the Tar Heels' first four shots of the 1982 NCAA Final, only to be called for goaltending all four times.

Has anyone ever been a member of NCAA, Olympic, and professional basketball championship teams?

Eight players have:

Clyde Lovelette Kansas 1952	U.S. 1952	Minneapolis and Boston (twice)
K. C. Jones San Francisco 1955	U.S. 1956	Boston (8 times)
Bill Russell San Francisco 1955 &1956	U.S. 1956	Boston (11 times)
Jerry Lucas Ohio State 1960	U.S. 1960	New York
Quinn Buckner Indiana 1976	U.S. 1976	Boston 1984
Magic Johnson Michigan State 1979	U.S. 1992	Los Angeles (5 times)
Michael Jordan North Carolina 1982	U.S. 1984 &1992	Chicago (6 times)
Sheryl Swoopes Texas Tech 1973	U.S. 1996	Houston

What's the history of **Olympic basketball**?

Men's Olympic basketball was introduced as a demonstration sport (with no medal awarded) at the 1904 games in St. Louis, and the first official Olympic basketball was played at the 1936 games in Berlin, Germany. The United States won the gold medal by defeating Canada 19–8 in the final round. The low score reflected the conditions of play: games were held outdoors on clay and sand tennis courts, which were wet from rain in the final, making running and dribbling another kind of Olympic challenge.

The United States dominated Olympic basketball, winning the first seven gold medals and running up a 62-game win streak. The Soviet team ended the streak in 1972, however, in a controversial game where the final seconds were replayed and a seemingly slim U.S. win turned into an agonizing last-second loss. The U.S. team won in 1976 and 1984 (the U.S. boycotted the 1980 games held in Moscow), Yugoslavia won in 1980 and finished second in 1976 and 1988, and the USSR team won in 1988.

Sheryl Swoopes in one of only eight basketball players (and the only woman) to win an Olympic gold medal, NCAA tournament, and a professional championship.

Professional players were first allowed to compete in the 1992 Olympics. USA Basketball, the governing body of Olympic basketball in the United States, assembled a group of NBA All-Stars called the Dream Team, which overwhelmed the other teams.

Women's Olympic basketball competition began at the 1976 games in Montreal, with the Soviet team winning. The U.S. team captured its first gold medal at the 1984 games in Los Angeles.

Which Big Ten head coach was **childhood pals** with San Francisco 49er head coach Steve Mariucci?

Both Mariucci and Michigan State Spartan head coach Tom Izzo grew up in Iron Mountain, Michigan, a remote town in the state's Upper Peninsula. The two sports nuts became close childhood chums, and they continue to see and talk to one another on a regular basis.

WOMEN

How did **women's basketball** develop?

One year after the 1891 invention of basketball, Senda Berenson Abbott, a Lithuanian-born physical education teacher, introduced the game to women at Smith College in Northampton, Massachusetts. Berenson Abbott introduced variations of rules for the women's game: the court was divided into three equal sections and players were required to stay in an assigned area; players were prohibited from stealing the ball from another player, from holding the ball for longer than three seconds, and from dribbling the ball more than three times.

Rules were refined through the years with major changes occurring during the 1960s, when unlimited dribbling became legal and the five-player, full-court game was played. Except for playing with a smaller basketball and using a 30-second shot clock, women's basketball is now played with the same rules, regulations, and styles as men's basketball.

When did **women's college tournaments** begin?

In 1971 the Association for Intercollegiate Athletics for Women (AIAW) was founded and established a national tournament. In 1982 the NCAA held its first national championship for women. Louisiana Tech won the first championship, finished runner-up (to USC) in 1983, and finished third (USC repeated) in 1984. Through 1997,

Louisiana Tech, USC, and Stanford have each won two championships, while Tennessee has won six championships and has made the Final Four 10 times.

What are the **major awards** that are bestowed upon NCAA women basketball players?

Several prestigious awards have come into being since the early 1970s, when passage of Title IX and other developments launched women's basketball on its current course of ever-greater prosperity. These include:

Broderick Award: Several hoopsters have won this Honda-sponsored award, which recognizes the collegiate woman athlete of the year, since its inception in 1977.

Wade Trophy: Named after legendary Delta State women's basketball coach Margaret Wade, this trophy is awarded to women who combine exceptional athletic performance, academics, and community service. Presented by the National Association for Girls and Women in Sport (NAGWS), the Wade Trophy has been in existence since 1978.

Naismith Trophy: Named after basketball's inventory, this trophy was first presented in 1983 by the Atlanta Tip-Off Club.

Frances Pomeroy Naismith Award: This award, which is bestowed by the Basketball Hall of Fame, is given to the outstanding female senior collegian under 5'6" in height. It was first presented in 1984.

Carol Eckman Award: This award was originated in 1983 to recognize coaches who have shown courage, spirit, and integrity in coaching women's basketball.

Which women's Division I basketball team has **won the most NCAA Championships**?

Since 1982, when women athletes were finally admitted into the NCAA, Tennessee's Lady Volunteers have captured six NCAA women's basketball championships. Their first title came in 1987, and since then the Lady Vols have nabbed championship banners in 1989, 1991, 1996, 1997, and 1998. The Lady Volunteers' 1998 title—the team's third straight—was perhaps the most impressive of all of these title runs, for their championship game victory marked the culmination of a 39–0 season in which they routed nearly every opponent they faced. Their perfect season was made all the more impressive by the fact that the Lady Vols had only one senior on the squad, and she played relatively few minutes. Instead, the club relied on superstar sophomore Chamique Holdsclaw and other underclassmen like point guard Kellie Jolly, center LaShonda Stephens, and a freshman class that was touted as the finest in women's collegiate basketball history. Armed with this awesome array of basketball weaponry, Tennessee will enter the 1998–99 season as the prohibitive favorite to add to their growing dynasty with a fourth straight NCAA title.

149

Which nation has won the most World Basketball Championships for women?

The former Soviet Union won six championships (in 1959, 1964, 1967, 1971, 1975, and 1983) before its dissolution. Their hold on the mark, however, is slowly slipping away. Fast closing in on that mark is the United States, which has won the crown on five occasions (in 1953, 1957, 1979, 1986, and 1990). In 1994 the U.S. women's team had an opportunity to tie the Soviet mark, but Brazil's team took the crown, forcing the Americans to look ahead to the 1998 games (the World Basketball Championships have been held approximately every four years since their inception in 1953).

Who coached the U.S. women's team to their first every **Olympic gold medal** in basketball?

Patricia Head Summit, architect of the Tennessee Lady Volunteers dynasty, led the 1984 Olympic team to Olympic gold.

Who is the only American basketball player ever to play on **four U.S. Olympic teams**?

Two-time All-American Teresa Edwards, who played college ball at the University of Georgia, is the only American man or woman to play on four Olympic teams. In 1984, 1988, and 1996, she and her teammates secured Olympic gold, and in 1992 the women's team won the bronze medal.

Who was the first woman in history to wear the uniform of the **Harlem Globetrotters**?

In 1985 Lynette Woodard became the first female member of the Globetrotters, and she went on to wear the Globetrotters' trademark uniform until 1987, when she returned to college ball as a coach. The 'Trotters interest in Woodward was understandable, because she was the most dominant player in women's college basketball in the late 1970s. As a member of the University of Kansas team from 1977–78 to 1980–81, she led the nation in rebounding as a freshman and in steals in her sophomore, junior, and senior seasons. Moreover, she was a seemingly unstoppable scoring machine and eventually became the nation's career scoring leader with 3,649 points, an average of better than 26 points a game.

Which players were singled out for individual honors after the WNBA's first season?

The recipient of the WNBA's first ever Most Valuable Player Award was Houston's Cynthia Cooper. The league's first Sportsmanship Award, meanwhile, went to Haixia Zheng of Los Angeles. New York's Teresa Weatherspoon was named Defensive Player of the Year, while Houston head coach Van Chancellor was named the league's first Coach of the Year.

The All-WNBA First Team, meanwhile, consisted of guards Cynthia Cooper, who was the leading vote-getter, and Ruthie Bolton-Holifield (Sacramento); forwards Eva Nemcova (Cleveland) and Tina Thompson (Houston); and center Lisa Leslie (Los Angeles).

Which women's team went **undefeated** in Division I conference play **for an incredible 12 straight seasons**?

From 1978 to 1990 Coach Jody Conradt's University of Texas Lady Longhorns won an amazing 183 straight games against their Southwest Conference opponents. "To think we took care of business for 12 years," Conradt later marveled. "If I had to name one thing, I think that is a record that is going to be there for a while."

Who was the **first woman to become head coach of a men's college basketball team**?

In 1995 Kerri-Ann McTiernan took the head coaching reins at Brooklyn's Kingsborough Community College.

Who was **Lady Magic**?

Nancy Leiberman-Cline, who is perhaps the most famous woman player in U.S. basketball history. A talented player and dogged competitor, she honed her game as a youngster in playground tilts against bigger and older boys from her Queens, New York, neighborhood. In 1976 Leiberman (who married former pro basketball player Tim Cline several years ago) became the youngest member of the 1976 U.S. Women's Olympic basketball team, which earned a silver medal that year. Leiberman went on to play college ball for Old Dominion from 1976 to 1980. She was a three-time All-American at Old Dominion and led them to NCAA National Championships in both 1979 and 1980 (she also swept the Wade Trophies, Broderick Awards, and Broderick Cups both of these years).

151

Houston Comets' guard Cynthia Cooper was the WNBA's first MVP. Not surprisingly, she was also the league's leading vote-getter for All-WNBA First Team honors.

After finishing college, Leiberman emerged as a major force in efforts to establish women's professional basketball in the United States. She starred for both the Women's Basketball League (WBL) and the Women's American Basketball Association (WABA) in the 1980s before joining a previously all-male professional league in 1986. She spent the next two years as a member of the Springfield Fame of the United States Basketball League, becoming the first woman to play regularly in a men's professional basketball league. "I was good enough to play with the guys and start for the team," she recalled. "No other woman had ever done that. I think my playing in the men's league stretched the horizons for women in the future."

Today, Leiberman-Cline remains a highly visible figure in women's basketball. In 1998, after spending one season as a player in the league, Leiberman-Cline assumed the head coaching reins of the WNBA's expansion Detroit Shock, where she hopes to build a championship tradition.

Who was the **first woman to receive a full athletic scholarship at UCLA**?

One of women basketball's first superstars, Ann Meyers became the first-ever female recipient of a full athletic scholarship to UCLA in 1973. She repaid the university by earning All-American honors each of the next four years, and in 1978 she led the Bruins to a national championship. In recognition of her leadership and performance on the court, Meyers was awarded the 1978 Broderick Award. Meyers also distinguished herself in international competition during her college days, emerging as a key member of the U.S. Women's Basketball silver medal-winning squad at the 1976 Olympics.

After graduating, Meyers made history once again by signing a one-year contract with the NBA Indiana Pacers. She never played for the Pacers, but she did become the first woman player ever to receive a paycheck from an NBA team. In 1993 she was inducted into the Basketball Hall of Fame.

Who were the first women to be inducted into the **Naismith Memorial Hall of Fame**?

In 1992 the Basketball Hall of Fame inducted its first two women members, Lusia Harris and Nera White. Harris was a three-time All-American center for Delta State University in Mississippi and a member of the 1976 Women's Olympic basketball team. White was a legendary figure from the 1950s and 1960s who was named to the AAU All-American team 15 straight years. As a member of the U.S.'s 1957 World Championship team, White was named best female basketball player in the world that year. After retiring from basketball, White went on to become an All-American softball pitcher.

153

What are the only three undefeated NCAA women's basketball national championship teams?

Texas went 34–0 in 1986, Connecticut cruised to 35–0 in 1995, and Tennessee crushed all comers on their way to their 39–0 record in 1998.

Who are some of the stars of NCAA women's play?

Stars of six-time NCAA champion Tennessee include Tonya Edwards, named outstanding player of the 1987 competition, and Bridgette Gordon, leading player in the 1989 tournament. Gordon holds the record for most points, 388, in tournament play. Cheryl Miller led the University of Southern California to titles in 1983 and 1984 and was named player of the tournament on both occasions. She holds the record for most rebounds, 170, in tournament play. The all-time scorer for a season in women's play is Patricia Hoskins, who scored 3122 points for a 28.4 average during her four years at Mississippi State University. She also holds the highest single-season average with 33.6 in 1989. The greatest female rebounder is Wanda Ford, who tallied 1887 for a 16.1 per game average at Drake University.

Who was the first woman to dunk in an NCAA basketball game?

Georgeann Wells of West Virginia became the first on December 21, 1984 against Charleston.

What was the highest scoring women's NCAA basketball game?

Virginia defeated North Carolina 123–120 in a triple-overtime game.

What five-medal Olympic track and field star was a four-year college basketball starter before becoming an Olympic champion?

Jackie Joyner-Kersey started for UCLA for four years, from 1980-81 through 1984–85. She went on to Olympic fame in the heptathlon and long jump

BOXING

RULES, SCORING, AND CLASSIFICATION

What are the **Queensberry Rules**?

Devised in 1867 by Englishman John Graham Chambers and named after his friend John Sholto Douglas, the eighth Marquess of Queensberry, they are a set of 12 rules on which the modern sport of boxing is based. Among other things, the Queensberry Rules established three-minute rounds with one-minute rest periods in-between, the ten-count for a knockout, and the mandatory use of gloves. Chambers was inducted into the Boxing Hall of Fame for his contribution to the sport.

How are boxing matches **scored**?

Judges sitting ringside use a point system to score boxing matches. There are usually five judges in amateur boxing, and three in professional boxing. Each judge keeps track of the number of legal blows landed by each boxer in each round. To score, a boxer must land the knuckle portion of his closed glove on the front or side of his opponent's body (above the waist) or head, without the blow being blocked. Blows that land on the arms do not count, nor do blows that connect without any force. Blows with the side of the glove or an open glove do not count toward a boxer's score either. In amateur boxing, the better boxer in each round receives 20 points, and the opponent receives a lesser number. Both contestants receive 20 points if they scored evenly in a round. In professional boxing, the better boxer receives a maximum of 10 points per round. At the end of the fight—barring a knockout—the boxer with the higher score is declared the winner.

What does a boxing referee do?

Ensuring the safety of the boxers is the main concern of the referee. He checks equipment before the fight and gives instructions to the fighters. During the fight, he uses three commands to control the actions of the fighters: stop, which tells them to cease boxing; box, which tells them it is okay to restart the action; and break, which tells them to separate and each take one step back. The referee is also empowered to give cautions, which inform a boxer about an improper action without stopping the fight, and warnings, which stop the action to inform both the boxer and the judges that a rule has been broken. Three cautions for the same infraction leads to a warning, and three warnings leads to automatic disqualification. Boxers can receive cautions and warnings from the referee for fouls including: hitting below the belt; kidney punching; holding; tripping; heat butts; elbowing; hitting with an open glove; and hitting an opponent who is down.

What happens if, at the end of a fight, the **two boxers are tied** in points received?

When judges have scored two fighters equally at the conclusion of a match, they must make a decision as to who is the winner. The decision is based upon: 1) which boxer was more aggressive during the fight; 2) which boxer demonstrated the better defense; and 3) which boxer fought with more style.

What happens if both fighters go **down at the same time**?

In this situation, the referee begins the count as usual for a knockdown. If both fighters return to their feet before the count of 10, the bout may be allowed to continue. If only one fighter manages to stand up before the count of 10, he is declared the winner. If both fighters are unable to get up before the count of 10, then the bout is stopped and the one who was ahead on points prior to the knockdowns is declared the winner.

When did the rule come into effect that requires a fighter who scores a knockdown to go to a **neutral corner** while his opponent is down?

In 1923, after a brutal match between heavyweight champion Jack Dempsey and Luis Firpo, known as "the wild bull of the Pampas." There were nine knockdowns in the first round alone—the first and last by Firpo, and the rest by Dempsey. During the second round, Dempsey knocked his opponent down again. Then he proceeded to stand over Firpo as he lay on the canvas, knocking Firpo down again and again whenever he attempted to stand up. The new rule requiring fighters to go to a neutral corner was instituted soon afterward.

What is the regulation **size of a boxing ring**?

The minimum size for an amateur ring is 16 feet square, and the maximum size is 20 feet square. Professionals usually fight in a ring that is 18 feet square, though the maximum allowable size is 22 feet square. In the corners are padded posts that stand 58 inches high. Connecting the posts and enclosing the ring are four horizontal ropes per side. The floor of the ring is padded and covered with canvas, and must extend at least two feet beyond the ropes and be less than four feet above the ground.

What are boxing's **seventeen weight divisions**?

Class	Weight limit
Heaveyweight	over 190 lbs
Cruiserweight	up to 190 lbs
Light Heavyweight	up to 175 lbs
Super Middlewight	up to 168 lbs
Middleweight	up to 160 lbs
Junior Middleweight	up to 154 lbs
Welterweight	up to 147 lbs
Junior Welterweight	up to 140 lbs
Lightweight	up to 135 lbs
Junior Lightweight	up to 130 lbs
Featherweight	up to 126 lbs
Bantamweight	up to 118 lbs
Junior Bantamweight	up to 115 lbs
Flyweight	up to 112 lbs
Junior Flyweight	up to 108 lbs
Minimumweight	up to 105 lbs

Who is the only **father-son combination** enshrined in the Boxing Hall of Fame?

In 1998, Prof. Mike Donovan was inducted into the Hall in the Pioneer category (the Pioneer category is for bare-knuckle fighters whose last fight was held before 1892), joining his son, referee Arthur Donovan. Mike's grandson, Art Donovan Jr., played football for the Baltimore Colts and is enshrined in the Football Hall of Fame.

How come there are sometimes **two or three different title-holders** for a single boxing division?

There is no longer a simple answer to the question of which boxer is the champion of his weight class because there are so many different organizations that govern boxing. Today, the four dominant governing organizations are: the World Boxing Association (WBA); the World Boxing Council (WBC); the International Boxing Federation (IBF); and the World Boxing Organization (WBO). Each of these organizations offers its own title in each of the different weight classifications, and there are several smaller organizations that confer titles as well. Boxing was legalized in New York State in 1920, and shortly thereafter groups started to spring up to organize the sport. One of the earliest groups was the National Boxing Association, which became the WBA in 1962. Because the championship voting in the WBA was weighted toward Americans, promoter George Parnassus formed the WBC in 1963. This organization consisted of 11 countries that each received two championship votes. Predictably, the two organizations named different fighters as champions of the same weight classes through most of the 1960s and 1970s. Another organization emerged in 1983, when the former United States Boxing Association split off from the WBA to form the IBF. Finally, the WBO was formed a few years later when another disgruntled group split off from the WBA. Some people criticize the multiple title system because they feel it is impossible to know which boxer is truly the best. But other people like the system because it offers more boxers an opportunity to compete for titles and thus increases the excitement of the sport. In any case, it appears that the system will remain in place for some time to come.

Just how **dangerous** is boxing?

While other sports—like auto racing, football, or skiing—can be dangerous and sometimes involve injuries and even death, boxing is the only sport in which the whole point is to inflict injuries upon an opponent. One study estimated that 400 fighters died as a result of injuries suffered in the ring between 1918 and 1981. Another study found that boxing caused 21 deaths per year between 1970 and 1978, making it by far the most dangerous sport. For many fighters, the glory of the ring is short-lived, only to be followed by a lifetime of dealing with resulting health problems. Some of the common problems experienced by former boxers include blindness, hearing loss, mental impairments, speech difficulties, respiratory problems, and paralysis. Muhammad Ali, whose Parkinson's syndrome was most likely caused by the repeated blows to the head he took during his career, is probably the best-known example of the dangers of boxing.

One of the most recent sad stories involved super middleweight Gerald McClellan, who received life-threatening injuries during a title fight against Nigel Benn in 1995. Immediately after the fight, McClellan had emergency surgery to remove a six-inch

The Hall is located in the small town of Canastota, New York. Eligible candidates must have been a professional boxer (he need not have been a champion) and must be retired from boxing for at least five years prior to election. Nonparticipants will be chosen from among the following catagories: promoters, managers, trainers, journalists, announcers, commentators, rulemakers, executives, officals, patrons, and anyone else who was not a boxer. There is no retirement requirement for nonparticipants. The number of inductees is established each year by the International Boxing Hall of Fame Museum when ballots are sent out to members of the Boxing Writers Association of America and other select individuals.

blood clot from his brain. Today, at the age of 30, he is unable to walk or care for himself, and is nearly blind and deaf. Each time something like this happens, there are calls for the abolition of boxing or at least the institution of reforms (such as frequent medical examinations of fighters and mandatory headgear). But—thanks to the money involved and continued fan interest—boxing still has plenty of participants willing to accept the risks.

FIGHTERS

Who was the **first officially recognized heavyweight champion**?

On August 29, 1885, John L. Sullivan knocked out Dominick McAffrey in six rounds to claim the world championship. The International Boxing Hall of Fame considers Sullivan to be the first heavyweight champion. Sullivan held the title until 1892 when he lost the title to Gentleman James Corbett in an epic 21-round bare-knuckle bout. Corbett and Sullivan were the last of the great bare-knuckle fighters.

What late **nineteenth-century boxer** has been called "America's first great sports personality"?

John L. Sullivan, a bare-knuckled brawler known as "the Boston Strong Boy," was one of the first athletes to play the media game to his advantage, and was probably

John L. Sullivan, the first recognized heavyweight boxing champion.

Who is the only boxer to win titles in five different weight classes?

When the sport of boxing expanded during the 1980s—up to 17 weight classes from four different sanctioning bodies—the number of champions who won titles in multiple weight classes soared. Despite the fact that it became easier, only Sugar Ray Leonard has been able to pull off the feat in five different classes spanning 28 pounds. The five classes and the year he won the title in each: light heavyweight (1988), super middleweight (1988), middleweight (1987), junior middleweight (1981), and welterweight (1979). He actually won two of the titles on the same night in 1988 when the WBC allowed his fight against Donny Lalonde to count towards both the light heavyweight and the super middleweight titles.

the first ever to be paid to endorse products. "As the finest fistfighter in the world, he was America's first athletic super hero but he also was an arch-villain," Wells Twombly wrote in *200 Years of Sport in America*. "Early in the game he learned that acclaim and notoriety went hand-in-hand for a man in his position, and he encouraged both." Sullivan was known for the many conflicting stories that emerged about his background and exploits, many of which he told himself in four autobiographies. For example, he almost certainly quit school before the fifth grade, but he often presented himself as a college graduate. His larger-than-life image was also formed by Richard Kyle Fox, one of the most powerful sports journalists in America at the time. Fox made a secret deal with Sullivan to promote the fighter, then proceeded to do so by publishing stories that called him a cocky, hard-drinking womanizer. Prior to an important match against Jake Kilrain in 1889, Fox claimed that Sullivan was drinking heavily and in terrible shape. In reality, he was working out hard and drinking nothing but water. Sullivan outlasted Kilrain to win the fight in 76 rounds. Unfortunately, Fox's statements about the fighter came true a few years later. Overweight and out of shape, he lost his final match to Gentleman Jim Corbett in 1892. By 1905, however, Sullivan's personality had changed yet again. He spent the rest of his life as a temperance lecturer, crusading about the evils of alcohol consumption.

Who are the **oldest and youngest prizefight champions**?

Wilfred Benitez was 17 years, six months old when he became junior welterweight champion in 1976. George Foreman was 45 years, 10 months old when he became heavyweight champion in 1994.

George Foreman is one of only two men to win an Olympic gold medal in the heavyweight division and a World Heavyweight Championship.

Who is the only boxer to **hold the title in three weight classes at the same time**?

"Hammerin' Hank" Armstrong owned the featherweight, lightweight, and welter-weight titles—which ranged from 126 to 147 pounds—at the same time in 1938.

Only two men have won **both an Olympic gold medal and a world championship** in the heavywieght division. Who are they?

Joe Frazier and George Foreman. Frazier won his gold medal at the Tokyo Olympics in 1964, while Foreman won his four years later in Mexico City. Four other men have won an Olympic gold medal outside the heavyweight division and then gone on to win the heavyweight world title—Floyd Patterson and Michael Spinks turned the trick in the middleweight division, while Cassius Clay (Muhammad Ali) and Leon Spinks earned medals as light heavyweights. It was Leon Spinks, of course, whom Ali defeated when he won the heavyweight title for an unprecedented third time in 1978.

What fighters were **named "Fighter of the Year" the most times** by the Boxing Writers Association of America?

Three fighters each won the award three times: Muhammad Ali, in 1965, 1974, and 1975; Joe Frazier, in 1969, 1971, and 1975 (tied for the award with Ali); and Sugar Ray Leonard, in 1976, 1979, and 1981. Leonard's award in 1976 was part of a joint award to the five U.S. boxers who won gold medals at the Summer Olympics in Montreal—Leonard, Howard Davis, Leo Randolph, Michael Spinks, and Larry Spinks.

What strange twist of fate **led Muhammad Ali (Cassius Clay at the time) to take up boxing**?

When Ali was 12 years old and living in a poverty-ridden section of Louisville, Kentucky, his brand new bicycle was stolen. He was told to report the incident to Joe Martin, a policeman who was teaching youth boxing in the basement of Louisville's Columbia Auditorium. But when Ali went inside to find Martin, he recalled that "The sights and sounds and the smell of the boxing gym excited me so much that I almost forgot about the bike." He returned the following week to begin training as a boxer. Ali went on to become possibly the greatest fighter of all time, winning 100 of 108 fights as an amateur, an Olympic gold medal, and three world heavyweight championships.

Why was Muhammad Ali **stripped of his first heavyweight boxing title**?

In 1967, at the peak of his boxing career, Ali was drafted by the U.S. Army to fight in the war in Vietnam. He tried to avoid military service by applying for conscientious objector status based on his Islamic beliefs. "How can I kill somebody when I pray five times a day for peace?" he asked. But his application was denied, and he was called up for service by the Army in April 1967. Ali then formally refused to be inducted into the military, in violation of the law. Shortly after Ali refused his induction, the World Boxing Association stripped him of his title and his boxing license. In June, he was found guilty of violating the Selective Service Act, fined $10,000, and sentenced to five years in jail, but he remained free until his case could be appealed. Throughout the war years, Ali appeared on college campuses and at peace rallies around the country to speak out against injustice and for social change. The U.S. Supreme Court reversed Ali's conviction in June 1970, clearing the way for him to regain his boxing license.

What pair of boxers engaged in what has been called "the **greatest individual rivalry** in sports history"?

Muhammad Ali and Joe Frazier fought three brutal matches, two of them with the heavyweight title on the line. The animosity between them was so great that they also fought an ongoing war of words that lasted well beyond their retirement from boxing. The irony is that they started out as friends. Frazier even helped Ali regain his boxing license after it was stripped from him during the Vietnam era. Their first fight was scheduled for March 1971 at Madison Square Garden. Despite their previously friendly relationship, Ali launched into his familiar pre-fight antics with a vengeance. He humiliated Frazier by characterizing him as ugly, ignorant, and controlled by the interests of whites. The fight itself—which has been called the greatest single sporting

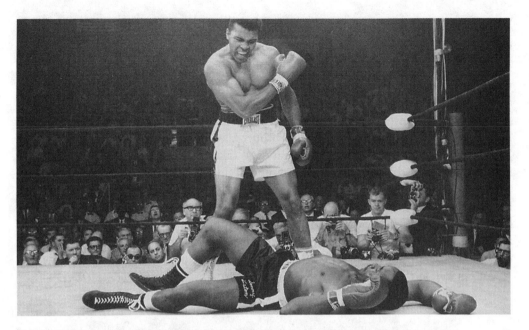

Muhammad Ali became World Heavyweight Champion three different times against three different opponents.

event of the past 50 years—was a dramatic see-saw battle of wills. The deciding moment came in the 15th round, when Frazier floored Ali with a sweeping left hook. But after appearing to be knocked out, Ali climbed to his feet by the count of four. Frazier ended up winning the hard-fought battle by unanimous decision to retain his heavyweight title.

In January 1974, Ali and Frazier faced off for a second time. Tensions between the two fighters still ran high. In fact, a pre-match press conference turned into a wrestling match. But the fight itself was something of a letdown. Ali was in top form, while Frazier's punches lacked the power they had had before. Ali won an easy 12-round decision. The third match between the two rivals took place in Manila, the Philippines, in September 1975. Defending champ Ali was relentless in his pre-fight hype, calling his opponent a gorilla and beating on a small rubber gorilla that he carried around in his pocket. In the actual fight, Ali won the early rounds, but then Frazier seemed to wake up. By the 11th round, it looked like Frazier would win easily. But Ali reached down inside himself and found the energy to land repeated blows to Frazier's face, causing his opponent's eyes to swell shut. Ali was declared the winner of the "Thrilla in Manila" when Frazier couldn't answer the bell for the 15th round.

Many years later, Frazier aroused controversy by publishing derogatory comments about Ali—whose health was failing by then—in his autobiography. He eventually apologized.

165

What is the "rope-a-dope" and where did it come from?

The "rope-a-dope" is a boxing strategy that a fighter can use against a stronger, but presumably less intelligent, opponent. It involves laying back against the ropes and waiting for the opponent to tire himself out, and then taking advantage of the opponent's exhaustion to come back and win the fight. The strategy originated with Muhammad Ali—commonly viewed as one of the most intelligent fighters of all time—who used it to defeat George Foreman in their highly touted "Rumble in the Jungle" in Kinshasa, Zaire, in 1974. Few people gave Ali a chance to take the heavyweight title from Foreman, a huge man who packed a powerful punch. Sure enough, it looked as if Foreman would dominate in the early rounds of the fight. Ali spent most of his time leaning far back on the ropes and absorbing all the punishment that his opponent could dish out. But eventually Foreman began to tire, and then Ali came to life, circling around him and landing flurries of punches. Ali finally knocked out the champ in the eighth round to claim his second heavyweight title. This fight became an enduring part of boxing legend, as well as the subject of a 1997 documentary film, *When We Were Kings*.

What former boxing champion enthralled a worldwide television audience estimated at 3.5 billion when he lit the flame to open the 1996 Olympic Games in Atlanta, Georgia?

Three-time world heavyweight champion Muhammad Ali—by then a shadow of his former self due to the crippling effects of Parkinson's syndrome—made a breathtaking surprise appearance in the opening ceremonies of the Atlanta Games. The identity of the final torch bearer is traditionally kept secret, so it brought tears to the eyes of many observers when they saw Ali holding the torch with trembling hands and slowly ascending the stairs to light the flame. Even NBC commentator Bob Costas got choked up at the sight. "Here's a guy who was once the most alive of men—the most dynamic and beautiful athlete we'd ever known—and now, to an extent, he was imprisoned by Parkinson's," Costas stated. "His lighting that torch said something about the human spirit." Before Ali left the stadium, he was stopped by President Bill Clinton, who placed his hands on the champ's shoulders and said, "They didn't tell me who would light the flame, but when I saw it was you, I cried."

Who are the only boxers to be inducted into the International Boxing Hall of Fame in their first year of eligibility?

In 1998, Matthew Saad Muhammad became the ninth fighter to gain entry in his first year of eligibility. The others are Sugar Ray Leonard, Alexis Arguello, Marvin Hagler, Michael Spinks, Carlos Zarate, Wilfredo Gomez, Wilfred Benitez, and Aaron Pryor.

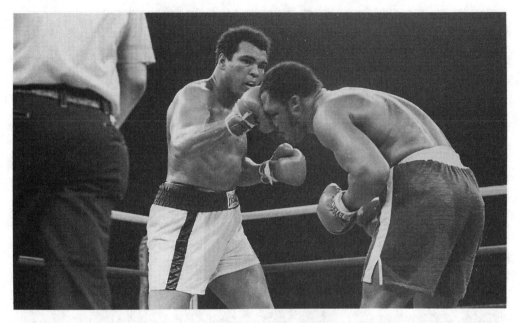

Muhammed Ali connects with Joe Frazier's head during the "Thrilla in Manila," which definitely lived up to the pre-fight hype.

Who was the only world heavyweight champion to retire **without losing a fight**?

Rocky Marciano retired in 1955 with a record of 49–0, including six successful title defenses. He took the title with a 13-round knockout of Jersey Joe Walcott in September 1952, then defended it against Walcott, Roland LaStarza, Ezzard Charles (twice), Don Cockell, and Archie Moore before retiring at the age of 32. Of course, several other champions could have matched this accomplishment if only they had avoided the temptation to come out of retirement. For example, James J. Jeffries ruined his perfect record when he returned to the ring after a six-year layoff and was knocked out by the first black heavyweight champion, Jack Johnson, in 1910. The only loss on Michael Spinks's career record came after a retirement that lasted nearly two years. His weight was at an all-time high when he got knocked out in the first round by Mike Tyson in 1988.

How many heavyweights have **lost the title only to win it back again**?

Only seven in over a century of bouts. The first was Floyd Patterson, who lost the heavyweight title to Ingemar Johannsson in 1959 only to regain it from the same opponent the following year. Muhammad Ali accomplished the feat twice: he lost the title to Joe Frazier in 1970, won it back from George Foreman in 1974, lost it again to Leon Spinks in 1978, then reclaimed it from Spinks in a rematch later that year. Evan-

Rocky Marciano (left) battles "Jersey" Joe Walcott for the heavyweight championship in 1952. He would win the title in the 13th round, and go on to successfully defend it six times before retiring with a perfect record.

Which boxers fought the most bouts in their careers, and which ones scored the most knockouts?

Len Wickwar, who fought as a light heavyweight between 1928 and 1947, holds the record with 463 career bouts. Welterweight Jack Britton (1905–1930) and featherweight Johnny Dundee (1910–1932) are next with 350 and 333 bouts, respectively. Archie Moore recorded the most knockouts—130—during a career as a light heavyweight that lasted from 1936–1963. Heavyweight Young Stribling (1921–1933) is next with 126, and welterweight Billy Bird (1920–1948) is third with 125.

der Holyfield has also reclaimed his heavyweight championship twice: he lost it to Riddick Bowe in 1992 and took it back from the same opponent the following year, then lost it to Michael Moorer in 1994 and won it back from Mike Tyson in 1996. Foreman reclaimed his title from Moorer in 1994 after losing it to Ali 20 years earlier. Moorer went on to win the then-vacant title in a 1996 bout with Axel Schulz. Tyson is the final heavyweight to lose a title and reclaim it later. After being upset by Buster Douglas in 1990, he rebounded to beat Frank Bruno in a championship bout in 1996.

Who held the **heavyweight boxing title** for the longest time?

The great Joe Louis was the heavyweight champion of the world for 11 years, 252 days. He knocked out James J. Braddock to claim the title on June 22, 1937, and then defended it a record 25 times before announcing his retirement from boxing on March 1, 1949. In fact, Louis's record is the longest anyone has ever held a boxing title in any division.

Who explained his loss of the heavyweight title to his wife by saying, **"Honey, I just forgot to duck"**?

Jack Dempsey—"the Manassa Mauler"—supposedly spoke this line to his wife, the former movie star Estelle Taylor, after losing a 10-round decision to Gene Tunney in 1926. Dempsey had been a 5–2 favorite going into the match, but Tunney surprised him with a hard right hand in the first round and controlled the fight from that point forward.

Who is known as **"the greatest fighter, pound for pound**, who ever lived"?

Sugar Ray Robinson, who fought 202 professional bouts between 1940 and 1965 and failed to go the distance only one time. He claimed his first championship in 1946, **169**

Joe Louis held the heavyweight title for over 11 1/2 years, defending it an incredible 25 times.

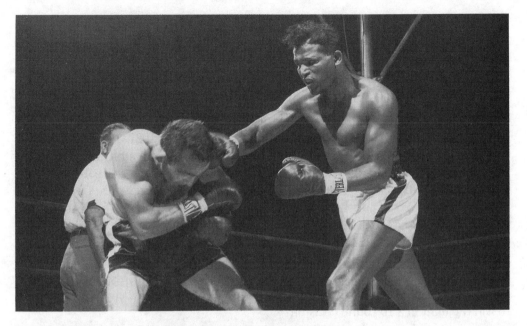

Sugar Ray Robinson (right) was considered the greatest pound-for-pound fighter ever.

when he defeated Tommy Bell in a 15-round decision for the welterweight title. He defended that title successfully for four years, and then added the middleweight title in 1951 by scoring a technical knockout in the thirteenth round over "Raging Bull" Jake LaMotta. He ended up losing the middleweight title six times and winning it back five over the next decade, and also making an unsuccessful challenge for the light heavyweight title in 1952. In one memorable match, against Britain's Randy Turpin, Robinson demonstrated his amazing quickness by throwing 31 punches in 25 seconds.

What boxer has won the greatest number of fights **by decision**?

Maxie Rosenbloom, the light heavyweight champ from 1930 to 1934, won 186 of his 299 career bouts on the scorers' cards. He was a weak puncher, which earned him the nickname "Slapsie Maxie," but a consummate defensive fighter. Willie Pep, the featherweight champion from 1942 to 1948 and from 1949 to 1950, is second on the list. A graceful, dancing fighter who kept his opponents off-balance and threw only enough punches to win, Pep scored 165 victories by decision in 242 career contests.

FAMOUS AND INFAMOUS BOUTS

What championship fight is remembered for **"the long count"**?

The highly publicized rematch between Jack Dempsey and Gene Tunney that took place in front of 140,000 fans at Soldier Field in Chicago in 1927. Prior to the fight, both boxers were notified that in the event of a knockdown, the count would not begin until the man still standing went to a neutral corner. It was a see-saw battle between two powerful punchers for the first six rounds. Then, in the seventh, Dempsey hit Tunney with a flurry of punches that sent him to the canvas. Dempsey retreated to the near corner, and the timekeeper began the count. But then referee Dave Barry noticed that Dempsey was not in the farthest neutral corner, as the rules required, and rushed over to shove the challenger across the ring to the appropriate spot. By the time the referee returned to Tunney and started the count over again at one, the timekeeper had already reached five. Tunney rose to his feet at nine of the new count and went on to win the fight in a 10-round decision.

What **pre-World War II heavyweight championship bout** attracted the attention of Franklin Roosevelt and Adolf Hitler?

The American president and German fuhrer were very interested when Joe Louis, known as "the Brown Bomber," faced off against Max Schmeling of Germany in June 1938. Nazi troops were preparing to roll through Europe at that time, and Hitler wanted a victory by Schmeling to demonstrate the superiority of the Aryan race. At a White House meeting prior to the fight, Roosevelt squeezed Louis's biceps and told him, "We need muscles like yours to beat Germany." The two fighters had met for the first time two years earlier. The up-and-coming Louis was a heavy favorite in that match, but Schmeling scored a surprise knockout with a right cross in the twelfth round. When they met for a second time, Louis was the newly crowned heavyweight champ and desperately wanted to avenge his only professional loss. A crowd of 70,000 gathered for the rematch at Yankee Stadium. Louis, who usually began fights cautiously, pummeled Schmeling from the opening bell and knocked the challenger down three times in the first round. The American was declared the winner after just two minutes, four seconds. Unfortunately, it would take much longer for American troops to defeat the Germans in World War II.

What are some of the most famous **fixed fights**?

Suspicions involving the fixing of fights have been around as long as boxing itself. Basically, this is because boxing—which only involves two participants, each of whom has

What was the shortest boxing match of all time?

It was all over in four seconds flat. At a Golden Gloves tournament in Minneapolis in November 1947, Mike Collins knocked out Pat Brownson with the first punch, and the match was stopped without a count after four seconds had elapsed. The shortest professional bout took place between junior middleweights in Australia in June 1991. Spectators certainly didn't get their money's worth in this one, as Paul Rees scored a TKO on Charlie Hansen in five seconds. The shortest title fight was for the WBC middleweight championship in Puerto Rico in August 1993. It took Gerald McClellan only 20 seconds to beat Jay Bell. In contrast, the longest boxing match (with gloves) on record lasted 7 hours, 19 minutes—that's 110 rounds! It took place in New Orleans in 1893 between Andy Bowen and Jack Burke. And when it was all over, the fight was declared a draw.

direct control over the outcome of the match—is relatively easy to fix. But although charges of fixing have been made many times, only a few instances have been admitted or proven. One of the earliest known fixes took place in 1822, when Jem Ward threw a fight against Bill Abbott. Another took place in 1947, when Jake LaMotta took a dive against Billy Fox in exchange for a later shot at a title. One of the top fights in the fix-suspected-but-not-proven category came when Jack Sharkey lost the heavyweight championship to Primo Carnera. Sharkey denied the charges, but Carnera had under-world connections that had arranged the outcomes of some of his other fights.

The year after ownership of the Panama Canal passed to Panama, the **world welterweight title** followed. Who was the fighter that took it?

Roberto Duran took the title from American Sugar Ray Leonard in a close, 15-round decision in June 1980. It was the fight of the year, witnessed by over 46,000 fans in Montreal, Canada. Leonard was a 1976 Olympic gold medalist and media darling, known for his quickness and dancing style in the ring. He had also won 27 straight professional fights. Duran was a hard-hitting bull of a fighter, known as "Hands of Stone." He brought with him a professional record of 70–1 with 55 knockouts, including 18 in the first round. For some reason, Leonard decided to change his usual tactics for this match. Instead of moving and jabbing, he went toe-to-toe with Duran, landing punches underneath while his opponent repeatedly pushed him into the ropes. When the final bell sounded, Leonard extended his hand but Duran walked right past him. Duran took the decision by one point on

Roberto Duran (left) walks away after uttering his famous "No Mas" line in the 1980 rematch with Sugar Ray Leonard (right).

two of the judges' cards, and by two points on the other. The three officials had scored a combined 19 rounds as draws.

What Spanish-speaking fighter is remembered for throwing up his hands in the ring and pleading, "No mas, no mas" (no more)?

Duran struck this pose five months later during his celebrated rematch against Leonard. It was in the eighth round, and he was losing and growing increasingly frustrated at the time. Leonard was declared the winner by knockout.

What fighter, upon winning the middleweight title, uttered the famous phrase "Somebody up there likes me"?

Rocky Graziano, known as "The Dead End Kid," used the line after defeating his nemesis, "Man of Steel" Tony Zale, in 1947. It was the second of their three legendary battles for the middleweight championship. Their first match, which took place in 1946, was voted the fourth-best fight of all time by *The Ring*. In that one, the two fighters traded explosive punches—each scoring what appeared to be the deciding blow on several occasions—before Zale knocked Graziano out with a left hook in the sixth round. Graziano prevailed with a sixth round knockout in their first rematch, despite the fact that he was nearly blinded from a cut over his left eye for two rounds. The

> ## What fighter won the light heavyweight title in 1997 despite the fact that his opponent knocked him out?
>
> In the first fight between Roy Jones Jr. and Montell Griffin, Jones knocked Griffin out. But then Jones was disqualified for continuing to punch his opponent when Griffin was down. Griffin was awarded the light heavyweight championship even though he was lying on the canvas at the conclusion of the fight. But Jones regained the title five months later by knocking Griffin out in the first round of their rematch.

rubber match came less than a year later. Zale dominated that one, knocking Graziano out in the third round to reclaim his middleweight championship.

What three Don King-promoted heavyweight fighters were **disqualified** in 1997 title fights, and why?

Of course, the most infamous of these incidents occurred when Mike Tyson was disqualified in the third round for biting Evander Holyfield's ear. But King's stable produced two other embarrassing moments in 1997. In February, Oliver McCall was disqualified for "reluctance" in the fifth round of a fight against Lennox Lewis. In his first match after emerging from drug rehab, McCall apparently had a nervous breakdown in the ring, crying openly and refusing to fight. Henry Akinwande was the third of King's fighters to be disqualified in 1997. Also facing Lewis, Akinwande chose to embrace his opponent rather than punch him. He was disqualified in the fifth round for excessive holding. These three fighters have the dubious distinction of helping make 1997 one of the worst years in boxing history.

What was the **biggest upset** in heavyweight boxing history?

As far as oddsmakers were concerned, the biggest upset occurred when Buster Douglas scored a tenth-round knockout against previously undefeated champion Mike Tyson in February 1990. Douglas was a 50–1 underdog at the time. But boxing has seen a number of other unexpected results over the years. For example, most people were shocked when relative unknown Cassius Clay (who later changed his name to Muhammad Ali) defeated big hitter Sonny Liston for the heavyweight title in 1964. Another big surprise came when Leon Spinks took that title away from Ali on a split decision in 1978. No one expected a 45-year-old George Foreman to knock out Michael Moorer in 10 rounds in 1994, and Evander Holyfield was a heavy underdog when he beat Mike Tyson on an eleventh-round technical knockout in 1996.

Commentator Howard Cosell (left, with microphone) went from being the "voice of boxing" to becoming one of the biggest advocates of the sport's abolition.

ODDS AND ENDS

Who played **Rocky Graziano in the film version** of his autobiography?

Paul Newman portrayed the colorful fighter on screen in the movie *Somebody Up There Likes Me*. Tony Zale, who fought three memorable middleweight title bouts against Graziano in the late 1940s, made a brief return to the ring to play himself in the film.

Who was Joe Louis talking about when he said, **"He calls 'em like he sees 'em"**?

The famous boxing referee Ruby Goldstein. A former boxer, Goldstein started to referee while serving in the army during World War II. He first met Louis when he refereed some of the exhibition matches Louis fought at military installations. Louis made his famous comment after Goldstein officiated at his 1947 heavyweight title match against Jersey Joe Walcott. The two judges scored the 15-round fight in Louis's favor, allowing him to keep his heavyweight championship. But Goldstein—as well as many other observers—had Walcott as the winner. When reporters asked Louis about Goldstein's scoring of the bout, he expressed his respect for the referee's opinion. This gave a boost to Goldstein's reputation, and he went on to officiate at many other important fights. He retired in 1962, shortly after refereeing the Emile Griffith-Benny "Kid" Paret welterweight championship match in which Paret was killed in the ring.

Howard Cosell went from being "the voice of boxing" on television to one of the most vocal opponents of the sport. How come?

Cosell was always a man of strong opinions, and he was never shy about expressing them. His connection with boxing—and his rise to national prominence—began in the early 1960s, when he became the color commentator on ABC boxing broadcasts. He became the unofficial "voice of boxing" in 1966, when he called the heavyweight title bout between Muhammad Ali and Karl Middleberger from Frankfurt, Germany. Cosell's rapport with Ali, which was apparent in the many bantering interviews between the two, helped solidify his connection with boxing. He continued calling fights for ABC until 1982, when he became disgusted with the sport after calling a particularly brutal match between Larry Holmes and Randall "Tex" Cobb. Cobb took a terrible beating from Holmes, as the referee failed to stop the fight even when Cobb appeared defenseless. Cosell then emerged as one of the most outspoken opponents of boxing and crusaded for the abolition of the sport for many years.

FOOTBALL

KICKOFF

THE ORIGINS OF FOOTBALL

When did **football begin**?

The ancient Greeks played a game in which the object was to move a ball across a goal line by throwing, kicking, or running with it. Several modern games derived from this, including English rugby and soccer, from which American football directly evolved. Soccer, of course, allows players to advance the ball only with their feet, but watch a game of rugby and you'll see what look like "downs" as well as laterals and scoring by carrying the ball over a goal line and by kicking it.

Football historians generally agree that the first game of American football was played on November 6, 1869, in New Brunswick, New Jersey, between teams from Rutgers and Princeton universities. They played on a field 120 yards long and 75 yards wide and used a round, soccer-style ball. Rutgers won the contest, 6–4; but in a rematch the next week, Princeton got revenge, 8–0. Other eastern schools, including Columbia, Yale, and Harvard, soon added the rough sport to their athletic programs. A set of rules was compiled in 1876, making the whole thing official.

At this point, however, the game still looked more like the English sports than the game we know as American football. But in the early 1880s, Yale player Walter Camp revised the rules. He limited teams to 11 players, established the scrimmage system for putting the ball into play, invented the concept of requiring a team to advance the ball a certain number of yards within a given number of "downs," and came up with the idea of marking off the field with yard lines, which led to the term "grid iron."

An early football team circa 1915.

How did the **modern scoring system** evolve?

Scoring was fairly informal at first. One point was usually awarded for advancing the ball past the goal line, either by kicking or carrying it over. In 1883 the first real scoring system was put in place, with five points being awarded for field goals, two points for touchdowns, and four points for kicking the point-after through the uprights; obviously, the emphasis was still on kicking.

The next year, touchdowns were changed to four points, the point-after conversion to two points, while field goals remained five points. As the game moved farther away from its English roots, the rules reflected the new emphasis on carrying the ball, not kicking it. In 1898 the value of a touchdown was raised to five points and the point-after was reduced to one. The field goal stayed at five points until 1904 when it was lowered to four points; and in 1909 it was reduced again to its current three points. The touchdown was finally raised to its present value of six points in 1912.

When was the **forward pass** legalized?

As in rugby and similar games, advancing the ball by throwing it forward was illegal in the early days of American football. The emphasis on the running game (with minimal protective equipment) made it a very brutal sport, and, in fact, football was banned by some colleges (including Columbia) by 1905. As controversy brewed and football began to get a somewhat unsavory reputation, a number of changes were implemented to make it more of a finesse game than a show of brute strength. Among these was a 1906 rule allowing the forward pass.

Amid growing concern about the future of football, the organization that would eventually be known as the National Collegiate Athletic Association (NCAA) was founded in 1910. This group embarked on a reform movement to keep the game both safe and interesting. Among other things, in 1910 and 1912 it further revised the passing rules to allow even more latitude in forward passes.

In 1912, Virginia Wesleyan College enjoyed its first undefeated season, becoming the first team to succeed while depending on the forward pass. The following year, Notre Dame, a very good but little-known team from Indiana, also went undefeated and brought national attention to the forward pass by staggering the mighty Army team 35–13 at West Point.

EQUIPMENT AND UNIFORMS

When did players **start wearing helmets**?

In the 1890s many players began wearing leather helmets, which became common by World War I. But protective headgear—although widely worn—was not mandated by the NCAA until 1939. With advancements in plastics during World War II, plastic helmets came into use in the late 1940s. Face masks were actually illegal until 1951, and mouthpieces became mandatory in 1971.

Have the **goalposts** always been stationed at the back of the end zone?

No. For many years the goalposts were planted squarely in the middle of the end zone. This location made for some spectacular collisions, as countless wide receivers and defensive backs who lost track of their whereabouts in the end zone could attest. The old location of the goalposts also disrupted the passing game in other ways. For example, otherwise well-aimed passes directed at streaking receivers all too often caromed against the arms or crossbar of the goalpost to flutter harmlessly to the ground, to the delight of beaten cornerbacks and safeties.

The old goalpost placement played a particularly notorious part in the outcome of the 1945 NFC championship game between the Washington Redskins and the Cleveland Rams. The Redskins were quarterbacked at that time by Slingin' Sammy Baugh, a Hall of Fame quarterback who led the 'Skins to two NFL titles. But in that game against the Rams, he was victimized by the goalpost in bizarre fashion. In first quarter action, he dropped back in his own end zone to throw a pass, but his toss was carried by the wind so that it touched the goalpost. Cleveland was subsequently awarded a safety, and those two points proved to be the difference in their 15–14 victory.

When did numbers get added to uniforms?

In the 1890s, officiating crews increased from one to three, but the officials were still having a hard time keeping the players straight and fans were complaining that they found it difficult to keep an eye on their favorite grid iron heroes. Finally, in 1915, the rules were changed to allow the addition of numbers to the players' uniforms. But numbers were not required until 1937, when a rule was instituted mandating numerals on both the front and back of football jerseys.

In 1961 the University of Maryland became the first college team to add players' names to the back of their jerseys. In 1967, a numbering system was devised according to player position, with those offensive players ineligible to receive forward passes being assigned numbers in the 50–79 range.

RULES AND TERMS

What is a **nickel back**?

The terms "nickel back" and "nickel defense" refer to the defensive practice of adding a fifth defensive back to the secondary in situations where the defense expects the offense to try a pass. The nickel defense was popularized by coach George Allen, who made it a staple of his Chicago, Los Angeles, and Washington defensive schemes in the 1960s and 1970s. Whenever he thought that the opposition was going to attempt a pass, Allen would replace one of his linebackers with a fifth defensive back to help with pass coverage. With the extra defensive back, Allen's defenses could double cover both wide receivers and still have a safety who would be free to cover the tight end or a running back going into a receiving pattern out of the backfield.

As other teams copied the nickel package, however, offensive coordinators around the league countered the move by adding a third receiver or a second tight end to their offensive packages. This marked the beginning of a tremendous acceleration in defensive and offensive strategy innovations, as NFL coaching staffs embraced and discarded various packages designed to give them an edge over the opposition's newest schematic wrinkle. Today, the nickel package remains a staple of every team's defensive repertoire, although its exact character differs somewhat from team to team.

What are the primary rules that govern a **fair catch**?

Returners receiving a punt or kick-off have the option of waving one arm above their head while the ball is in flight to signal a "fair catch." By doing so, the player receiving the ball is entitled to catch the ball without being touched or interfered with by any members of the kicking team (fair catch interference will cost the kicking team 15 yards from the spot of the foul). In exchange, use of the fair catch makes it illegal for the returner to advance the football after the catch. However, any receiver is allowed to recover and advance the ball after a fair catch signal if the kick either: 1) touches the ground, or 2) touches one of the members of the kicking team in flight. A returner who advances the ball after a fair catch may be called for a five-yard delay of game penalty.

A player who signals for a fair catch is not obligated to catch the ball. But if a returner signals for a fair catch, he may not block or otherwise initiate contact with a member of the kicking team until the ball touches a player. The penalty for this infraction is a steep 15 yards.

Finally, if time expires while the ball is in the air and a fair catch is called, the receiving team has the option of extending the quarter with one fair catch kick down. However, the placekicker is not allowed to use a tee in this situation.

What is **clipping**?

Clipping is the act of throwing the body across the back of the leg of an opponent or charging or falling into the back of an opponent below the waist after approaching him from behind, provided the opponent is not a runner or the situation is not categorized as "close line play." It is almost always called on offensive linemen, running backs, or wide receivers engaged in blocking activity.

What is **hang time**?

"Hang time" refers to the amount of time that a football stays in the air after it's punted. In other words, hang time starts from the instant the ball leaves the punter's foot to the instant that it either is caught by the punt returner or hits the field. Hang time is regarded as one of the most important qualities that a punter can have. A punter that gets good hang time on his punts gives his teammates more time to get downfield and cover the punt returner than does a punter who kicks line drive punts that can be easily caught and carried upfield by the returner.

What is the **waiver** system?

The waiver system is a procedure by which player contracts or rights to a player are made available by one team to the other teams in the NFL. When a player is "waived," the other 29 clubs either file a claim to obtain the player or waive the opportunity to do so. If two or more teams want the same player who has been waived, then the team with the worst record (either in the current season or in the previous year) gets first

183

crack. The claiming period is usually 10 days long during the offseason and 24 hours long from early July through December, but in some cases, the original club may be given an addition 24 hours to rescind its waiver action—an action known as a recall of waiver request. If a player passes all the way through waivers without a single club claiming him and he's not recalled by his original team, he becomes a free agent.

Many penalties that are called on the defense, such as pass interference, personal fouls, roughing the passer, etc., result in automatic first downs for the offense. Which eight penalties will **not necessarily give the offense an automatic first down**?

>Offside
>Encroachment
>Delay of game
>Illegal substitution
>Excessive time out(s)
>Incidental grasp of facemask
>Neutral zone infraction
>Running into the kicker

What are the various **field officials responsible for** besides positioning themselves to enforce rules?

The referee supervises the other officials. He decides matters not under the other officials' specific jurisdiction, he enforces penalties, and he identifies them (through hand signals and over a loud speaker) to teams and fans. The referee indicates when the ball is out of play and when it can be put into play again. The umpire makes decisions on questions concerning the players' equipment, their conduct, and their positioning. The head linesman marks the position of the ball at the end of each play and has assistants who mark the spot of the ball on the sideline and who man the yard markers.

The linesman also watches for violations of the rule requiring players to remain in certain positions before the ball is put into play. The field judge times the game with a stopwatch to coincide with a stadium's scoreboard clock.

PROFESSIONAL FOOTBALL

Who was the **first professional football player**?

American football began as an amateur sport, played primarily between college teams or athletic clubs. The inevitable move to professionalism took place in 1892, when Yale All-America guard William "Pudge" Heffelfinger received a $500 "performance bonus" from the Allegheny Athletic Association to join their team for a crucial game with the Pittsburgh Athletic Club. Heffelfinger proved to be worth every penny, as he returned a Pittsburgh fumble 35 yards for a touchdown to give the AAA a 4–0 win (touchdowns were worth four points at the time). Heffelfinger thus became the first professional football player on record.

Not to be outdone, the Pittsburgh Athletic Club hired triple-threat back Grant Dibert for the entire 1893 schedule. This was the first professional football contract. From that point, things began happening quickly, with other teams scrambling to buy players. Professional football was off and running.

When did the **first professional football game** take place?

The game that is generally considered to be the first professional American football contest took place in 1895 in Latrobe, Pennsylvania, between the Latrobe YMCA and the Jeannetee (PA) Athletic Club. But, even in this game not all of the players were paid.

The first team to field an all-professional lineup was the Allegheny Athletic Club, for two games in 1896. The following year, for the first time, the Latrobe Athletic Association used paid personnel for its entire season.

What is the **early history of professional football leagues** in the United States?

In 1902, two Philadelphia baseball clubs, the Athletics and the Phillies, established pro football teams and joined the Pittsburgh Stars to form the National Football League, the first such professional league.

At the end of the first season, a World Series of Professional Football was conducted, featuring players from more than a dozen teams. The second, and last, football

185

World Series took place in December of 1903. After that season, several Ohio teams were founded and recruited most of the top Pennsylvania players. By the 1904 season, seven of the game's top professional teams were located in Ohio.

In 1920, representatives of teams from a four-state area met in Canton, Ohio, to form a new, better organized league called the American Professional Football Association (APFA). A prime mover in this alliance was George Halas, manager and head coach of the Decatur (IL) Staleys. By 1921, the APFA was comprised of 22 clubs.

In 1922, the APFA changed its name to the National Football League (NFL), which is the league we know today. Halas renamed his team and moved them to a larger city: they became the Chicago Bears.

How did the NFL fare against the college game?

Despite the efforts of the NFL leadership, the professional game ran a poor second in popularity to the college version. On Saturdays, the major university stadiums were packed with cheering throngs, while the pros played before a relative handful of people on Sundays. Halas recognized the need to legitimize the NFL in the public's view or the league would not survive. Halas kept an eye out for a college star who might lend credibility to the professional game and to draw crowds on Sundays. He concentrated on a halfback from the University of Illinois named Harold "Red" Grange. The "Galloping Ghost" was a national sports hero: as soon as he could, Halas signed him to a pro contract. Using the services of an agent, C.C. ("Cash and Carry") Pyle, Grange leveraged Halas for a share of the gate receipts.

Grange made his pro debut at Wrigley Field on Thanksgiving Day, 1925, in front of 36,000 Bears fans, the largest crowd ever assembled for a professional football game at that time. At the end of the day, Grange was $12,500 richer. When the Bears went on the road, fans around the country flocked to see Grange work his magic. At New

York's Polo Grounds, a record 73,000 spectators watched the Galloping Ghost lead the Bears to a 14–7 win over the Giants. The National Football League had arrived.

When was the **AFL** formed?

The first American Football League was founded in 1926. Red Grange, the highest-paid player in professional football (he earned almost $100,000 in his three months with the Chicago Bears in 1925), quit the Bears in a salary dispute. The new AFL was hastily concocted by his agent, C.C. Pyle. This league folded after the 1926 season, but Grange's team, the New York Yankees, was absorbed into the NFL for 1927.

Then there was the All-America Football Conference (AAFC), which was formed in 1945 and fielded eight teams, including the Yankees, the Brooklyn Tigers, the Cleveland Browns, and the Buffalo Bills. This league folded in 1949, and three of its teams were taken into the NFL: the Browns, the San Francisco 49ers, and the Baltimore club. The Browns made an immediate impact, playing in the NFL Championship game its first six years, winning the league title in 1950, 1954, and 1955, losing in 1951 through 1953.

The modern American Football League (AFL) was founded by Lamar Hunt of Dallas and a consortium of other monied sportsman, who put together eight teams to begin play in the fall of 1960. On January 26, 1960, Hunt was named the new commissioner of the AFL, and on that same day Pete Rozelle became commissioner of the NFL. Thus began a battle—for players, for television contracts, and for status—that continued throughout the 1960s.

When and how did the **NFL and the AFL merge**?

During the spring of 1966, a series of secret meetings between the NFL and AFL led to a merger of the two leagues. The decision was made to maintain separate schedules through 1969, with a World Championship game (the Super Bowl) between the two leagues' champions set to begin in 1967, along with a common college draft. Then, the leagues would come together officially in 1970. Congress approved the merger, exempting it from antitrust legislation.

Famous Games

What is the history of **crowning professional football's champion**?

From 1920 to 1931 the league champion was the team with the best regular season record. That period covers the American Professional Football Association (1920–21), which changed its name to the National Football League in 1922, and the early NFL. In 1932, the NFL held its first postseason game to break a tie between the Chicago Bears and the Portsmouth (Ohio) Spartans, each of whom won six games. Beginning in 1933, the NFL created two divisions and held a championship games between the division winners. Following the 1966 season, the NFL champion played the American Football League champion (which held championship games from its inception in 1960) in what has become known as the Super Bowl. When the NFL and AFL merged in 1970, the Super Bowl began pitting the National Football Conference and American Football Conference Champions.

When was the **first NFL Championship to be played indoors**?

Surprisingly, it was in 1932, in Chicago—the first NFL Championship game. The Bears finished the season 6–1–6, having beaten the three-time champion Green Bay Packers in the last game of the season to finish tied in wins with the Portsmouth Spartans, who had a record of 6–1–4. Up until then the league champion was simply the team with the best season record. No one wanted the 1932 season to end in a tie, so they came up with the idea of a playoff game.

The NFL Championship game was scheduled to be played at Wrigley Field on December 18, 1932. But as the date approached, Chicago was snowed in, and there was no way to make the field playable. A couple of years earlier, an indoor exhibition football game had taken place at Chicago Stadium, home of the Blackhawks hockey team. Bears owner George Halas proposed moving the 1932 playoff game there.

The field was only 80 yards long, it was 15 feet narrower than normal, the end zones were not regulation size, and the stadium had a cement floor. On the plus side, a circus had just left town, so there was already a layer of dirt in place (further cushioning being provided by leftover elephant droppings), and the stadium looked a lot better to the players than the outside sub-zero temperature and driving snowstorm.

A few special rules were needed for the unusual circumstances: there were no field goals (the field was too short) and all kickoffs were spotted at the ten-yard line. Each time a team crossed the mid-field point, it was automatically penalized 20 yards, thus making the field 100 yards long. And inbounds lines—or hashmarks— were created: when the ball went out of bounds it could be spotted on one of those lines, rather than being placed next to a wall.

The Bears won the game, 9–0. More importantly, the concept of an NFL Championship game was born. The fans loved it, and the owners saw the potential for generating extra income. The next year, the NFL was split in half, with the two division winners playing a final championship game.

What game could be called **the original "Ice Bowl"**?

While many football games, both college and professional, have been played under brutally frigid conditions, one that stands out is an NFL championship game that took place on December 16, 1945, between the Cleveland Rams and the Washington Redskins. An hour before game time, the temperature on the field in Cleveland stood at three degrees below zero, Fahrenheit. By kickoff, the needle barely nudged six above. A week earlier, the groundskeepers had covered the turf with hay to keep the ground from freezing, but even this measure, requiring the help of 275 men to spread 9,000 bales of hay into a four-foot thick blanket of insulation, had failed to keep the field in playable shape: the hay was cleared, but the ground was frozen solid.

Snow began sticking to the field, and the wind whipping off Lake Erie further added to the players' misery. Both veteran Washington quarterback Sammy Baugh and Cleveland rookie Bob Waterfield had trouble gripping the ball and reported that passing it felt like throwing rocks—which didn't matter much, since the receivers could barely hold on to it, anyway.

Late in the third quarter, a water main broke at the south end of the stands. The concrete steps were first a waterfall, then a solid sheet of ice. The stands were like a walk-in freezer, and the field was as hard as a concrete parking lot. When the game ended, with Cleveland on top 15–14, players and spectators alike fled the stadium for warmer environs.

A month later, the entire Cleveland team headed for a warmer climate, as owner Daniel F. Reeves announced that they were moving west to become the Los Angeles Rams.

What game is **best known as the "Ice Bowl"**?

On December 31, 1967, Vince Lombardi's Green Bay Packers won their fifth NFL title in seven years, defeating the Dallas Cowboys 21–17 on what NFL Films has immortalized as "the frozen tundra of Lambeau Field." At game time the temperature was 13 below. But Lambeau Field sported a new heating system that was supposed to keep the top six inches of ground from freezing. It might be cold, but at least the field would be playable. Unfortunately, the heating system worked only as long as a tarp covered the field. Once it was removed, the ground froze solid in minutes, leaving the turf slick on the coldest New Year's Eve in Green Bay history.

With 16 seconds left to play, and Dallas ahead by three points, Lombardi conferred on the sidelines with his quarterback, Bart Starr, during the Packers' last time out. The ball rested two feet outside the Dallas end zone. A field goal would send the game into overtime, but Lombardi worried that, at this point, the kicker might not be able to feel his foot. And on their last two running plays, Green Bay's Donny Anderson had

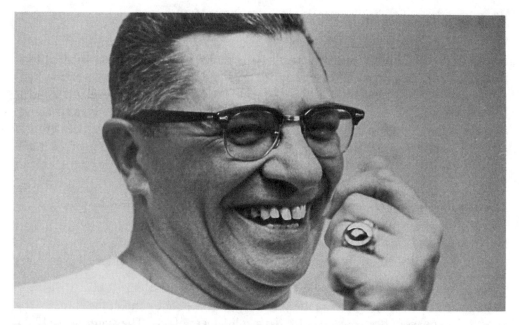

Vince Lombardi coached the Green Bay Packers to victory in the first two Super Bowls. The championship trophy (as well as an award for college linemen) is named for him.

slipped on the icy ground, barely avoiding fumbling. "I can sneak it in," Starr told his coach. Lombardi replied, "Then do it, and let's get the hell out of here."

Following an outstanding block by guard Jerry Kramer, Starr sneaked the final yard for the game-winning touchdown. Asked later about his decision to go for the TD rather than a field goal, Lombardi said, "I wanted the touchdown so everyone could go home and get warm." Two weeks later, in considerably warmer conditions at Miami, Green Bay defeated the AFL champion Oakland Raiders in Super Bowl II. And two weeks after that, Lombardi resigned as head coach of the Packers.

When was the **first Super Bowl**?

On January 15, 1967. The Green Bay Packers of the NFL defeated the AFL's Kansas City Chiefs, 35–10, at Los Angeles Memorial Coliseum. The Packers were favored by 13 points, but head coach Vince Lombardi was careful not to allow his team to become complacent in the California sun. Kansas City was not to be taken lightly, in his opinion. Chiefs quarterback Len Dawson was a seasoned veteran with NFL experience. Wide receiver Otis Taylor was capable of breaking a game wide open. The KC defense featured huge linemen and an outstanding linebacker in Bobby Bell. And, finally, they were coached by the experienced and innovative Hank Stram.

Two networks, CBS and NBC, televised Super Bowl I, and each paid an unprece-dented $1 million for the privilege. With daily televised interviews and insults flying back and forth between the two teams, the pregame hoopla rose to a fever pitch. Kansas City cornerback Fred "The Hammer" Williamson told reporters, "I have bro-ken thirty helmets with my forearm . . . I can't wait to add to my total against the Packers." Meanwhile, Lombardi professed in an interview to being so blase about the upstart league that he had never even seen one AFL game, live or on television.

To everyone's surprise, the Packers struggled on their opening series, but they established their running game on their second possession. Still, Kansas City refused to roll over. At halftime, the score was 14–10, Green Bay.

The Packers defense came on strong on the first series of the second half. Willie Wood intercepted a Dawson pass and ran the ball to the KC five-yard line. Running back Elijah Pitts carried it in on the next play and Green Bay increased their lead to 21–10. Kansas City would not score in the second half: in fact, they never got inside the Green Bay 40, as the Packers went on to score two more touchdowns. In the fourth quarter, the Packers ran a sweep to Williamson's side of the field. Following a huge collision with Donny Anderson, "The Hammer" failed to get up. He was carried off the field with a broken arm. After the game, Lombardi summed up the game: "The Chiefs are a good team. But they don't compare with the top teams of the NFL."

Which Super Bowl made the game truly Super and ensured that it would become one of **America's premier sporting events**?

In 1969, Super Bowl III was assumed to be a done deal: The mighty Baltimore Colts were favored by 18 points over the New York Jets, the upstart team from the Mickey Mouse league with the quarterback who wore fur coats and white shoes. CBS person-nel had already marked out camera positions in the Colts' locker room for the postgame celebration.

But, absurdly, the Jets' "Broadway" Joe Namath had guaranteed a victory to the press. Moreover, Namath told reporters there were at least four quarterbacks in the AFL who were better than league MVP Earl Morrall of the NFL champion Colts— including Namath! And it wasn't all talk. The Jets had spent hours poring over Balti-more game films, and they spotted a few holes. They felt the Colts had no big running threat and there were some weaknesses in the secondary that Namath could exploit. Baltimore had a great team, but they weren't unbeatable.

New York was forced to punt on its first series of the game, and Baltimore imme-diately drove to the Jets' 19-yard line. But on the next play, wide receiver Willie Richardson fumbled on his way into the end zone. Then Morrall overthrew an open receiver on second down and was tackled at the line of scrimmage on third down. Lou Michaels' 27-yard field goal attempt went wide. Namath came back with a long pass, proving that Baltimore could be beaten deep. The Colts continued their series of miscues by failing to score on a fumble. But, with 9:03 left in the first half, Randy Beverly of the Jets intercepted a pass by Morrall, spawning a 12-play, 80-yard touchdown drive.

Behind by seven at the half, Baltimore coach Don Shula wondered if he should replace Morrall with Johnny Unitas, who had been out with an elbow injury. He stuck with Morrall, but the Colts fumbled on the first play of the second half, and the Jets recovered and drove for a field goal, putting them up 10–0. When the Jets kicked another field goal, Shula turned to Unitas. But the great Unitas, too, looked flat, and the Colts failed to move the ball. Namath, on two nice pass plays, led the Jets to the Baltimore 10-yard line, and another field goal made it 16–0.

But suddenly Unitas kicked into gear. Within seconds the Colts were at the 25 of the Jets, and the crowd of 75,000 began to roar. Unfortunately, Unitas threw short to a receiver in the end zone, and the pass was intercepted. Later, Baltimore was able to take advantage of three Jets penalties and score from the New York 1-yard line. They recovered an on-side kick and got to the Jets' 19 but failed in their touchdown attempt. Final score: 16–7, Jets.

The closing moments of television coverage on the field saw Namath jogging out of the Orange Bowl with his index finger extended, indicating his team's status in the world of football. It was the first championship for the AFL and remains the biggest upset in Super Bowl history. The game legitimized the AFL, which was about to become the American Football Conference under the merger and cemented the importance of the Super Bowl.

What was **the *Heidi* game**?

It was November 17, 1968, and the New York Jets were playing their perennial rivals, the Oakland Raiders. Recent meetings of the two AFL teams were pockmarked with brawls and trash talk by colorful personalities on both sides, and this game had the makings of great television. NBC was broadcasting the game, and the network's executives expected both an exciting match and high ratings from the national audience.

The game turned out to be even better than anticipated. On the opening kickoff, the Jets were penalized for a personal foul; and after that it seemed that every play resulted in players getting angrier and angrier. They went after each other, verbally and physically, and yellow flags filled the air.

In between penalties, the teams played an incredible football game. Both Jets quarterback Joe Namath and the Raiders' Daryle Lamonica ran exciting offenses, and the lead bounced back and forth repeatedly. With 1:05 remaining in the game, and the score tied at 29, Namath had taken the Jets down the field and the team prepared for a 26-yard field goal.

Joe Namath (throwing) played in two of the most famous games in football history—winning Super Bowl III, and losing the "Heidi" game.

By this point—undoubtedly due to the unusual number of penalties—the game had used up the three-hour time slot NBC allotted for it. Someone at the network dutifully threw a switch, and the national broadcast switched over to the next scheduled program: the children's movie *Heidi*. As the national audience stared at a little Swiss girl on their screens, Lamonica connected for two quick passes following the Jets' field goal. On the second one, rookie Charlie Smith ran 43 yards for a touchdown, putting the Raiders ahead 36–32, with 42 seconds to play. The Raiders' kickoff was fielded by the Jets' Earl Christy at the 15-yard line, but Christy was hit by several Raiders and fumbled the ball. It was picked up at the two by fullback Preston Ridlehuber of the Raiders and carried in for Oakland's second touchdown in nine seconds. Final score: Raiders 43, Jets 32.

Needless to say, NBC received tens of thousands of complaints. The next day, network president Julian Goodman issued a public apology. The damage was done, and the *Heidi* Game was in the record books, but—in light of the national furor caused by enraged sports fans—it's unlikely that any television network will ever make that mistake again, which is why "60 Minutes" used to come on late (7:15 or 7:30) on Sunday nights in the fall, even while it was the highest-rated show on television.

What was the **NFL's longest game** ever?

A grueling playoff game between the Miami Dolphins and the Kansas City Chiefs, on Christmas day, 1971, lasted an incredible 82 minutes and 40 seconds (a regulation game is 60 minutes). Heavily favored Kansas City had won Super Bowl IV the previous year and, according to Miami coach Don Shula, still had the best personnel in the AFL. Miami had never beaten the Chiefs.

The Dolphins had a well-rounded offense, with quarterback Bob Griese's passing ability balanced by a running attack that featured the great Larry Csonka, Jim Kiick, and a speedy array of linemen. But Kansas City coach Hank Stram had an outstanding bunch of linebackers ready to control the Miami offense, while the Chiefs' potent offense was led by quarterback Len Dawson.

The teams turned out to be well matched. The score was tied at 10 at the half. Kansas City marched 75 yards for a touchdown in the third quarter, then Miami came right back to tie it again. The Chiefs scored in the fourth following an interception, making it 24–17, but the Dolphins tied the game once more on an outstanding series of passes by Griese. KC's Ed Podolak ran the kickoff back to the Miami 22-yard line and, with 35 seconds remaining in the game, kicker Jan Stenerud trotted confidently onto the field for the chip-shot field goal. But, amazingly, the reliable Stenerud missed by inches, and the game went into overtime.

Miami placekicker Garo Yepremian had the chance to end it in the first overtime with a 52-yard field goal, but his effort sailed wide to the left. The game went into double-overtime. Miami's running game had been thwarted all day by the Kansas City linebackers, but Griese and Csonka were confident they could come up with a play that would surprise the Chiefs. Finally, on a roll-right, trap-left play, Csonka found some running room. At 7:40 into the second overtime he ran 29 yards to the Kansas City 36. A couple of plays later, Yepremian kicked a 37-yard field goal to end the game, 27–24, Miami.

What was the **Immaculate Reception**?

It was December 23, 1972, at Three Rivers Stadium in Pittsburgh. The Steelers, after years of failing to make the playoffs (since 1947), had finally put together a respectable team, going 11–3 in the regular season and taking the AFC Central Division championship under the leadership of quarterback Terry Bradshaw. Now they had to get past coach John Madden's Oakland Raiders to keep their season alive.

The game was a defensive battle, which Pittsburgh led most of the way on the strength of two field goals by Roy Gerela. Then, with 1:13 to go, Oakland backup quarterback Ken Stabler (playing for Daryle Lamonica, out with the flu) ran 30 yards for a touchdown. After the kickoff, the Steelers, down 7–6, were on their own 40-yard line with 22 seconds left in the game. Three straight Bradshaw passes had gone incomplete; only one play left.

Bradshaw took the snap and dropped back seven steps. He was flushed out of the pocket and was scrambling to his right when he saw running back John "Frenchy"

Fuqua burst into the open 20 yards downfield, followed closely by Oakland's All-Pro safety Jack Tatum. With a crash, the ball and Tatum arrived at the same time.

The next few seconds have been analyzed thousands of times—with little assistance from video replays that gives different stories from different angles. Bradshaw's pass was deflected backwards 15 yards, having hit either Tatum or Fuqua, and it was grabbed at shoe level by Steelers rookie running back Franco Harris, who ran it all the way into the end zone.

Madden accosted the nearest official screaming, "No good. No good." At the time, an NFL rule stated that a pass deflected by one offensive player to another was not legal—it was an incomplete pass and a dead ball. But who touched the ball last, Fuqua or Tatum? The officials weren't immediately sure; no touchdown had been signaled. After conferring with other officials and calling the league's supervisor of officials from the field telephone, referee Fred Swearingen finally raised his arms: Touchdown.

The entire Oakland bench went berserk, screaming at the call. Tatum was incensed. He grabbed Fuqua, shouting, "Tell them you touched it." But Fuqua, a joker who was always willing to stir up controversy, merely erupted with laughter. Ever since, he has reportedly refused to tell even his teammates what happened, at one point even alleging that the Immaculate Reception was a planned play that he and Harris had cooked up. Unlikely, but proof once again that in football anything can happen.

What game featured **"The Catch"**?

It was January 10, 1982, at Candlestick Park in San Francisco. The 49ers were playing the Dallas Cowboys for the NFC Conference championship. San Francisco had scored first in the game when Freddie Solomon caught an eight-yard touchdown pass from quarterback Joe Montana. Dallas replied with a 44-yard Rafael Septien field goal and a touchdown pass from Danny White. Each team scored again, making the halftime score 17–14, Dallas.

Johnny Davis put San Francisco ahead 21–17 with a two-yard run in the third quarter. Then, following a field goal and a touchdown after a fumble recovery, Dallas went ahead in the fourth quarter, 27–21. That's where the score stood with a minute to play in the game, Niners' ball at the Cowboy 6, third down and three.

Montana took the snap and rolled right. Almost immediately his blocking coverage broke down, and he was forced to scramble with Dallas's Ed "Too Tall" Jones and Larry Bethea bearing down on him. He was close to the sidelines: he could step out and try again on fourth down. With a split second to make a decision, Montana couldn't even see his receivers, just Too Tall Jones. He jumped as high as he could and heaved the ball to an area where he knew receiver Dwight Clark should be.

Clark was not the primary receiver on the play. He expected to be serving mainly as a decoy so that Solomon, the primary target, could get open. Montana's blind pass had been thrown high, and Clark was not particularly known for his jumping ability. But on this play he leapt into the air and came down with the ball, his feet just inches from the back line of the end-zone. Touchdown!

With 51 seconds left in the game, Dallas came close to scoring again, but the San Francisco defense held. Final score: 28–27. Looking at tape of The Catch later, Montana said: "Dwight must have jumped three feet to get that. I don't know how he got it. He can't jump that high!"

What game featured **"The Drive"**?

First down and 98 yards to go. The Denver Broncos had botched a kickoff from the Browns on January 11, 1987, in the NFC Championship game at Municipal Stadium in Cleveland. The Broncos were down, 20–13, with five minutes left in the game, maybe the season.

Denver quarterback John Elway called a short pass to running back Sammy Winder, who took it for a five-yard gain. Winder's next run was almost stopped by Browns defensive end Reggie Camp, but he still squeezed out three yards. With two yards to go, Winder got the ball again and just barely made the first down.

Winder again, for three more. Then, on second down, Elway called a pass play but couldn't find an open receiver. With the Browns closing in, he was forced to scramble, still looking for someone to throw to. Finally, he tucked the ball in and ran for 11 yards, sliding safely to the 26-yard line.

The next play was a 22-yard pass to Steve Sewell, one of the fastest Denver receivers, taking the Broncos to their own 48. Elway next passed to Steve Watson: another 12 yards and a first down, with 1:59 to play. After the two-minute warning, Elway was caught behind the line of scrimmage and was forced to throw the ball away. It was almost intercepted by Cleveland safety Ray Ellis, but Ellis just barely failed to hold on. Then, on the next play, Elway was sacked by nose tackle Dave Puzzuoli. With his already sprained left ankle re-injured on the play, Elway called time out. The Cleveland fans were rejuvenated. They began dancing in the stands as Elway conferred with Coach Dan Reeves.

Ball at the Cleveland 48, third down and 18, 1:47 to go in the game. Denver lined up in the shotgun formation. On the snap, the ball grazed Watson, who was in motion, and bounced off the ground. Elway grabbed it and passed to Mark Johnson for 20 yards. On the next play, Elway was forced to throw the ball away when no receivers could get open. Next, a screen pass to Sewell went for 14 yards, then a pass to Watson near the goal line was ruled out of bounds. Second down at the 14-yard line. Reeves called a quarterback draw play: when the hole failed to develop, Elway ran

Joe Montana led the San Francisco 49ers to their first Super Bowl with the help of Dwight Clark's miraculous leaping catch in the end zone. The play came to be known simply as "The Catch."

John Elway engineered one of the most thrilling (and heartbreaking, if you're a Browns' fan) comebacks in history on January 11, 1987.

When was the first televised football game?

On October 22, 1939, New York fans huddled around the City's 1,000 television sets to see the Philadelphia Eagles play the Brooklyn Dodgers at Ebbets Field. For the first time, they would be able see the action as it was described by the announcer. The broadcast wasn't exactly a rousing success, however. TV cameras then weren't what they are now: they needed a lot of light. Every time a cloud passed over the field, the television picture grew dark, and as the day got cloudier, fans were reduced to listening without pictures, just as they had with radio.

to the outside and made it to the five. Third and one, with 39 seconds left. The blitz was on, and Elway had to throw the ball while he was still backpedalling. It was a classic Elway pass, something like a smoking fastball, but Mark Jackson hung on for the touchdown. The extra point was good.

Cleveland received the kickoff in overtime, but the Broncos defense, charged up by The Drive, did its job. Elway immediately connected on two passes for 50 yards. Winder drove up the middle three times, and kicker Rich Karlis won the game for Denver with a 33-yard field goal. Final score: 23–20.

What was the **worst defeat** in professional football?

On December 8, 1940, the Chicago Bears beat the Washington Redskins, 73–0, in the NFL Championship game at Griffith Stadium. Several weeks earlier, in the regular season, the Redskins had beaten the Bears, 7–3, on a close call by the officials. After that game, Washington owner George Marshall called the Bears "cry babies" for protesting the call and referred to them as "quitters." Before the rematch in the championship game, Chicago coach George Halas read Marshall's remarks to his team for inspiration. The enraged Bears scored 21 points in the first 13 minutes of the game, and the score at halftime stood at 28–0. And they didn't let up in the second half, scoring another 45 points. In all, the Bears gained 501 total yards and intercepted Washington eight times, with three returned for touchdowns.

When the Bears scored their tenth touchdown, officials asked Halas if he could please not kick for the extra point; so many balls had been kicked into the stands and kept by fans that they were down to their last football. So, with a 66-point lead, Halas had his team pass for the two-point conversion. At the final gun, a reporter in the press box remarked, "Marshall just shot himself."

What is the **highest scoring game in** NFL history

The Washington Redskins and New York Giants kept the scoreboard operators hopping on November 27, 1966 when the Giants blitzed the 'Skins 72–41, a total of 113 points. Only one other game topped 100 points, when the Oakland Raiders defeated Houston 52–49 in an AFL game on December 22, 1963.

Who won the NFL's first **regular season overtime** game?

Nobody. After the NFL decided to institute overtime in its regular season contests for the 1974 season, many fans rejoiced, reasoning that the change would finally get rid of those dissatisfying ties. Yet the very first regular season overtime game ended in a tie as well. The game took place on September 22, 1974, and pitted the Denver Broncos against the Pittsburgh Steelers at Denver's Mile High Stadium. All day long the offenses went wild, and when the regulation period ended in a 35–35 tie, fans prepared themselves for a wild overtime. But both offenses floundered in the extra session. Pittsburgh was unable to get untracked, and Denver missed a 41-yard field goal early. The game ended with the Steelers sitting on the ball on their own 26-yard line.

Later that season, on November 10, the NFL finally got its first overtime victory when Joe Namath hit Emerson Boozer for a five-yard touchdown pass to lift the New York Jets over the New York Giants 26–20 in a game at New Haven, Connecticut.

Which team won the **first Monday Night game** in NFL history?

On a September evening in 1970, the Cleveland Browns defeated the New York Jets 31–21, marking the beginning of a long and fruitful arrangement for both the NFL and ABC Sports.

Has there ever been a **perfect season in the NFL**?

One. It was put together by the Miami Dolphins in 1972. Miami coach Don Shula had been hired away from Baltimore, where his Colts had gone 73–26–4 between 1963 and 1969. In 1970 he took the Dolphins to second place in the AFC East, and, following an outstanding 1971 season, the team made it to the Super Bowl, where they were humbled by the Dallas Cowboys, 24–3.

The Dolphins of 1972 featured such standouts as quarterback Bob Griese; running backs Larry Csonka, Jim Kiick, and Mercury Morris; and receivers Paul Warfield and Howard Twilley—not to mention the legendary No-Name Defense, a group of players little-known at the beginning of the season but famous by its conclusion: Nick Buoniconti, Mike Kolen, Doug Swift, Manny Fernandez, Bill Stanfill, Bob Heinz, Dick Anderson, and Jake Scott.

Miami shut out the Baltimore Colts 16–0 in the last game on their schedule, making them the only team in NFL history to have a 14–0–0 regular season. The No-Namers had allowed the fewest points in the league, and backs Csonka and Morris had each rushed for 1,000 yards or more, the first time one team ever had two 1,000-yard rushers.

The Dolphins defeated the Cincinnati Bengals 34–16 in the AFC Conference play-off game and went on to a 27–17 victory over the Pittsburgh Steelers for the AFC title. They lined up against the Washington Redskins on January 14, 1973, in the Super Bowl at Los Angeles. Surprisingly, Washington was favored. The word was that Miami had enjoyed an easy schedule; they had been lucky in several games; Griese was coming back from a broken ankle; and Washington had a veteran defense, strong at stopping the run, Miami's major strength.

The Dolphins dominated early, leading 14–0 throughout most of the contest. Late in the game, Washington scored on a botched Miami field-goal attempt. The kick was blocked and little Garo Yepremian, the Miami placekicker, picked up the ball, ran, and then tried to throw it. The ball slipped from his hands, he batted it, and a Redskins' defensive back caught it and ran in for a touchdown. Miami held the 14–7 lead, and the Dolphins emerged as the first team in NFL history to go undefeated through the regular season and all the playoffs.

PLAYERS

Who was named to the **NFL's 75th Anniversary All-Time Team**?

In 1997, in recognition of the game's illustrious history and incredible talents, the NFL unveiled a grand all-star team that included players from throughout its history. The team was selected by a committee of distinguished media and league personnel.

Offense:

QB	Sammy Baugh	Washington Redskins 1937–52
QB	Otto Graham	Cleveland Browns 1946–55
QB	Joe Montana	San Francisco 49ers 1979–92, Kansas City Chiefs 1993–94
QB	Johnny Unitas	Baltimore Colts 1956–72, San Diego Chargers 1973
RB	Jim Brown	Cleveland Browns 1957–65
RB	Marion Motley	Cleveland Browns 1946–53, Pittsburgh Steelers 1955
RB	Bronko Nagurski	Chicago Bears 1930–37, 1943
RB	Walter Payton	Chicago Bears 1975–87

201

RB	Gale Sayers	Chicago Bears 1965–71
RB	O.J. Simpson	Buffalo Bills 1969–77, San Francisco 49ers 1978–79
RB	Steve Van Buren	Philadelphia Eagles 1944–51
WR	Lance Alworth	San Diego Chargers 1962–70, Dallas Cowboys 1971–72
WR	Raymond Berry	Baltimore Colts 1955–67
WR	Don Hutson	Green Bay Packers 1935–45
WR	Jerry Rice	San Francisco 49ers 1985-present
TE	Mike Ditka	Chicago Bears 1961–66, Philadelphia Eagles 1967–68, Dallas Cowboys 1969–72
TE	Kellen Winslow	San Diego Chargers 1979–87
T	Roosvelt Brown	New York Giants 1953–65
T	Forrest Gregg	Green Bay Packers 1956, 1958–70
T	Anthony Munoz	Cincinnati Bengals 1980–92
G	John Hannah	New England Patriots 1973–85
G	Jim Parker	Baltimore Colts 1957–67
G	Gene Upshaw	Oakland Raiders 1967–81
C	Mel Hein	New York Giants 1931–45
C	Mike Webster	Pittsburgh Steelers 1974–88, Kansas City Chiefs 1989–90

Defense:

DE	David "Deacon" Jones	L.A. Rams 1961–71, San Diego Chargers 1972–73, Washington Redskins 1974
DE	Gino Marchetti	Dallas Texans 1952, Baltimore Colts 1963–64, 1966
DE	Reggie White	Philadelphia Eagles 1985–95, Green Bay Packers 1996-present
DT	Joe Greene	Pittsburgh Steelers 1969–81
DT	Bob Lilly	Dallas Cowboys 1961–74
DT	Merlin Olsen	Los Angeles Rams 1962–76
LB	Dick Butkus	Chicago Bears 1965–73
LB	Jack Ham	Pittsburgh Steelers 1971–82
LB	Ted Hendricks	Baltimore Colts 1969–73, Green Bay Packers 1974, Oak./L.A. Raiders 1975–83
LB	Jack Lambert	Pittsburgh Steelers 1974–84
LB	Willie Lanier	Kansas City Chiefs 1967–77
LB	Ray Nitschke	Green Bay Packers 1958–72
LB	Lawrence Taylor	New York Giants 1981–93
CB	Mel Blount	Pittsburgh Steelers 1970–83
CB	Mike Haynes	New England Patriot 1976–82, Los Angeles Raiders 1983–89

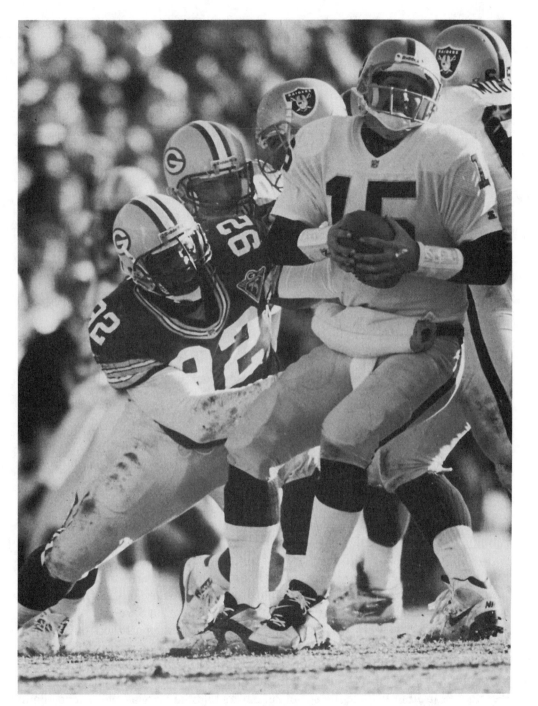

Reggie White, the NFL's all-time sack leader, was named to the league's 75th Anniversary All-Time Team at defensive end.

CB	Dick "Night Train" Lane	L.A. Rams 1952–53, Chicago Cardinals 1954–59, Detroit Lions 1960–65
CB	Rod Woodson	Pittsburgh Steelers 1987–96, San Francisco 49ers 1997-present
S	Ken Houston	Houston Oilers 1967–72, Washington Redskins 1973–80
S	Ronnie Lott	S.F. 49ers 1981–90, L.A. Raiders 1991–92, N.Y. Jets 1993–94
S	Larry Wilson	St. Louis Cardinals 1960–72

Special Teams:

P	Ray Guy	Oakland/L.A. Raiders 1973–86
K	Jan Stenerud	K.C. Chiefs 1967–79, G.B. Packers 1980–83, Minnesota Vikings 1984–85
KR	Gale Sayers	Chicago Bears 1965–71
PR	Billy "White Shoes" Johnson	Houston Oilers 1974–80, Atlanta Falcons 1982–87, Washington Redskins 1988

Who owns the record for the **longest fumble return** in NFL history?

On September 24, 1972, Oakland Raider defensive back Jack Tatum returned a Green Bay fumble 104 yards for a touchdown.

What **interracial friendship** between two NFL players helped many fans change the way they thought about people who were different from themselves?

In 1967, during the height of the Civil Rights Movement, Chicago Bears head coach George Halas decided to assign rooms on road trips by position. This decision meant that star running back Gale Sayers, who was black, became roommates with backup running back Brian Piccolo, who was white. At that time, it was unusual for a black person and a white person to hang around together, let along share a room. Though the two athletes viewed their living arrangements somewhat warily in the beginning, they soon became close friends. They laughed about it when prejudiced fans or members of the media attacked their friendship. Piccolo supported Sayers in his recovery from a knee injury in 1969, and then it was Sayers' turn to support Piccolo when doctors found a cancerous tumor on his lung. When Sayers was presented with the George Halas Award as the most courageous player in the NFL that year, he accepted the honor in Piccolo's name and asked the audience to pray for his friend. Sadly, Brian Piccolo died in June 1970, at the age of 26. Sayers told the story of their friendship in his autobiography, *I Am Third*. It was made into an award-winning television movie called *Brian's Song* that was watched by nearly 50 million people when it was first broadcast in 1971.

Which NFL quarterback not only threw a record-tying seven touchdown passes in one game, but also officiated a game in which another player tied that same record?

Adrian Burk was a quarterback with the Philadelphia Eagles when he tossed seven touchdown strikes against the Washington Redskins on October 17, 1954. Fifteen years later, on September 28, 1969, he watched from his back judge position as Minnesota Viking quarterback Joe Kapp strafed the Baltimore Colts in similar fashion, becoming the last player to throw seven touchdown passes in a single game.

Only three other NFL players have thrown for seven touchdowns in a single game. The first was Sid Luckman, who blitzed the New York Giants as a member of the Chicago Bears on November 14, 1943. Burk became the second player to accomplish the feat. Seven years later, on November 19, 1961, young Houston Oiler quarterback George Blanda smoked the New York Titans for seven scores. The last player to strike for seven TD passes prior to Kapp was Hall of Famer Y.A. Tittle, who tied the record by tossing for seven scores for the New York Giants against the Redskins on October 28, 1962.

What is a **"Slash"**?

"Slash" is the name Pittsburgh Steelers Coach Bill Cowher gave to the position he created for Kordell Stewart in order to make use of the young quarterback's incredible athletic skills. When Stewart was drafted in 1995, he was the fastest runner on the Steelers, could throw the football 70 yards, had the soft hands of a wide receiver, and could even punt. "For now, his position for us is quarterback-slash-wide receiver-slash-running back-slash-punter," the coach explained. Cowher began using Stewart in each of these various positions in the seventh game of his rookie season, when the Steelers' record was a disappointing 3–4. With Stewart adding excitement and unpredictability to the offense, the Steelers won their next eight games in a row. Then "Slash" put in the best performance of his professional career (to that point) to help the Steelers beat the Indianapolis Colts in the AFC Championship game. During one critical Steelers drive, he made two first downs as quarterback and one as a running back, and then caught a touchdown pass as a wide receiver. Although Stewart put in another solid performance in the Super Bowl—running twice as a quarterback and twice as a running back for three first downs—the Steelers lost to the Dallas Cowboys 27–17. He finished his rookie season having completed 5 of 7 passes for 60 yards and a touchdown, caught 14 passes for 235 yards and a touchdown, and rushed 15 times for 86 yards and a touchdown.

What player **misplaced his helmet** prior to Super Bowl XXVI, causing him to miss the first two plays of the game?

Running back Thurman Thomas—who led the league in total yards for the third straight year in 1991 (with 2,038) and was named the NFL's most valuable player—was nevertheless unable to help the Buffalo Bills claim their first Super Bowl championship. The Bills were making their second of four straight appearances in the big game that year; unfortunately, they were destined to become the only team ever to lose four consecutive Super Bowls. For Thomas, who had starred in the previous year's contest, Super Bowl XXVI was a disaster. As the players took the field to start the game, he was unable to locate his helmet. "For some reason, somebody moved it," he recalled. "I don't know why. It was just one of those situations where everybody was running around. I was very upset." He ended up missing the first two plays while he searched for his helmet and never managed to get back on track, finishing with 10 carries for just 13 yards. The Bills lost to the Washington Redskins, 37–24. After the game, Thomas was subjected to endless questions about his missing helmet and his poor performance. To make matters worse, reporters kept bringing up these issues the following year, especially when the Bills made it to Super Bowl XXVII. Although Thomas was hurt by all the attention that had been given to the missing helmet incident, he eventually managed to show a sense of humor about it. He brought a huge bag of miniature Bills helmets to a pre-Super Bowl press conference and handed them out to reporters, challenging everyone who attended to keep from losing their helmets before the big game.

What NFL lineman will be remembered equally for his work toward securing **unrestricted free agency** for players and for his tendency to remind quarterbacks he had just sacked that "Jesus loves you"?

Reggie White, the NFL's career sack leader, is an ordained minister who also helped revolutionize free agency in professional football. He was the lead plaintiff in a 1992 class-action lawsuit brought by the players against the NFL for antitrust law violations. The players wanted an unrestricted free agency system, which would give them greater freedom to offer their services to other teams in the league, but the team owners feared that such a system would lead to a bidding war for top players that could bankrupt the sport. In early 1993, facing the threat of a court-ordered settlement, the owners and the players' union worked out an agreement that instituted free agency with a cap on players' salaries.

Everyone knows that **Deion Sanders** has played both football and baseball professionally. Which was his best sport in high school?

Neither. Strangely enough, considering his future careers in professional sports, all of Sanders's friends and teachers agree that his best sport in high school was basketball.

What NFL Hall of Famer was also inducted into the Lacrosse Hall of Fame?

The multi-talented Jim Brown—who set a number of NFL rushing records during his nine-year pro career and later broke through other barriers as an actor (his love scene with Raquel Welch in the movie *One Hundred Rifles* was the first on-screen love scene between a white actress and an African-American actor)—is considered by many to have been the greatest lacrosse player of all time. During his three years at Syracuse University, Brown spent the football off-season playing lacrosse for the Orangemen. If anything, he was even more dominant in lacrosse than he was in football. He was a terror as a midfielder, barreling over opponents and scoring at will. In his senior season, the lacrosse team went undefeated and Brown was named All-American in his second sport. He was later inducted into the Lacrosse Hall of Fame.

"He was incredible at basketball, just incredible," recalled one faculty member at North Fort Myers High School in Florida. "Just before games, to entertain people, he'd stand flat-footed under the basket with a ball in each hand, then leap up into the air and dunk both balls, one right after the other, like he was hanging in the air, defying gravity. The fans would just go nuts when he did that."

Who was the number one pick in the NFL draft in 1961, earned Rookie of the Year honors that year, and went on to **win the Super Bowl as both a player and a coach**?

These were some of the highlights in the storied football career of Mike Ditka. Ditka was actually the top pick in both the NFL (by the Chicago Bears) and AFL (by the Houston Oilers) drafts in 1961. He signed with the Bears and had a tremendous rookie season. Playing tight end, he quickly became known around the league for his pass-catching ability and his tough blocking. He narrowly beat out quarterback Fran Tarkenton for Rookie of the Year honors. After bouncing from the Bears to the Philadelphia Eagles and suffering a number of injuries, Ditka joined the Dallas Cowboys in 1969 and rejuvenated his playing career. He even scored a touchdown to help the Cowboys defeat the Miami Dolphins in Super Bowl VI. Ditka retired as a player following the 1972 season, having caught 427 passes and scored 43 touchdowns during his career. He then became the Cowboys' wide receiver coach under Tom Landry for the next 10 years. In 1982, Ditka got the opportunity to become the head coach of his first NFL team—the Bears. Within three years he had established himself as one of the

207

top coaches in the game. The Bears posted a 15-1 record in 1985 and easily advanced to Super Bowl XX, where they dismantled the New England Patriots and earned Ditka his second ring.

Who was the **first black player** to play professional football?

In 1902 a six-foot, 200-pound halfback named Charles W. Follis joined the Shelby, Ohio, team in the Ohio League. Prior to joining the Shelby team, Follis had been a star player with the Wooster Athletic Association. After playing against Follis's Wooster squad in 1901, the management of Shelby's team pursued the young athlete with zeal. He agreed to play for Shelby the following season, and the team's ownership made employment arrangements for him at a local hardware store. Historians remain uncertain about whether or not Follis received a salary to play for Shelby, but it is certain that the hardware store job, which gave the young halfback flexible hours so that he could play ball, was designed as compensation for his participation on Shelby's team.

From 1902 to 1906 Follis was one of the stars of the Ohio League. Dubbed the "Black Cyclone from Wooster," Follis led his teammates to victories over nearly all of their opponents, leading fellow Shelby player Branch Rickey—who would play an instrumental role in integrating Major League Baseball more than 40 years later—to describe him as a "wonder." By 1904 it was clear that Follis was indeed employed to play football, for he signed a contract that made the arrangement explicit. By 1906, however, lingering injuries led Follis to turn to the less violent sport of baseball. He was talented on the diamond as well, advancing to the black professional leagues in Cleveland before being felled by pneumonia in 1909 at the age of 31.

How many times has a **defensive player been named Super Bowl MVP**?

Six defensive players have been so honored. The first was Dallas Cowboy linebacker Chuck Howley, who was named MVP of Super Bowl V even though his team lost to the Baltimore Colts 16–13 on a last-second field goal by Jim O'Brien. Howley remains the only player on a losing team ever to be named most valuable player. Two years later, Miami Dolphin safety Jake Scott was named most valuable player of Super Bowl VII, in which Miami knocked off Washington by a 14–7 score. In Super Bowl XII, Dallas Cowboy defensive linemen Randy White and Harvey Martin were named co-MVPs of the contest, in which Dallas delivered a 27–10 pasting of the Broncos. Super Bowl XX marked the fifth time that a defensive player was named MVP, as Chicago Bear defensive lineman Richard Dent won the honor after the Bears trounced the New England Patriots by a 46–10 score. Dallas cornerback Larry Brown was named MVP of Super Bowl XXX on the strength of two interceptions that helped the Cowboys over the Steelers.

Who was the first college player ever drafted by the **Dallas Cowboys**?

In 1960 the expansion Cowboys made Texas Christian University defensive lineman Bob Lilly their very first draft selection. Lilly turned out to be a pick for the ages. After wasting Lilly's rookie season with a boneheaded attempt to convert him to defensive end, the Cowboys returned him to his natural spot at defensive tackle. Over the next dozen years, he wreaked havoc from his position in the interior, using his cat-like quickness and game smarts to terrorize opposing backfields. Big number 74 became the anchor of Dallas's "Doomsday Defense" of the 1970s, and in the 1972 Super Bowl he tackled Dolphin quarterback Bob Griese for a 29-yard loss, a sack that continues to stand as the biggest in Super Bowl history. A perennial All-Pro who has been called one of the top two or three defensive tackles in the history of the game, Lilly became the first player to be inducted into the Cowboys' famed Ring of Honor, and he was also the first Dallas player to be selected for induction into the Pro Football Hall of Fame.

Who holds the NFL single-season record for **most points** scored?

In 1960 Green Bay Packer Paul Hornung parlayed his dual ballcarrying and kicking abilities into a 176-point season. A former Heisman Trophy winner from Notre Dame, Hornung arrived in Green Bay with blonde good looks and a playboy reputation. Luckily for Packer fans, the "Golden Boy," as Hornung was often called, also had talent. He combined with fullback Jim Taylor to form one of football's best backfields as the Pack rode roughshod over opposing teams. Hornung enjoyed several top-notch seasons, but his best year was undoubtedly 1960, when he scored 15 touchdowns, kicked 41 extra points, and booted 15 field goals despite a pinched nerve in his neck that bedeviled him most of the campaign. Hornung led the NFL in scoring in 1961 as well, but his impact on the game tapered off dramatically after that, as injuries and a suspension for gambling on football kept him out of uniform for long stretches of time. He retired in 1966, and in 1981 he was named to the Pro Football Hall of Fame.

Which Hall of Fame great is credited with **revolutionizing the position of wide receiver**?

Green Bay Packer wide-out Don Hutson is regarded as the game's first great wide receiver. A star on the gridiron from Alabama's Crimson Tide, he had a tremendous impact on the developing game. On his very first play as a pro, he struck for an 83-yard touchdown against the Bears, providing Packer fans with a glimpse of the future. From 1935 to 1945 Hutson routinely led the league in pass receiving. The speedy flanker scored a total of 99 touchdowns, a record that stood for more than 40 years, and he still holds the records for most seasons leading all receivers in receptions

Has an NFL quarterback ever rushed for more than 1,000 yards in a single season?

Given the number of scrambling quarterbacks who've made their mark in the NFL over the years—Fran Tarkenton, Steve Young, Randall Cunningham, etc.—one might reasonably think that the 1,000-yard mark might have been broken by some young signal caller during the league's long history. But in fact, no quarterback has been able to accomplish this feat. The quarterback who came closest was Bobby Douglass, who in 1972 rushed for 968 yards for the Chicago Bears.

(eight), most consecutive seasons leading the league in catches (five), and most seasons leading the league in touchdowns (eight). His productivity was even more amazing when you consider that passing wasn't nearly as sophisticated or commonplace as it is in today's game.

Hutson's dominance could be traced to two factors: speed and smarts. He could run the 100 yard dash in 9.8 seconds in an era when such speed was practically unheard of. But coaches and teammates often pointed to his intelligence as an even bigger factor in his success. In fact, he was the first receiver to utilize fakes, feints, and sharp cuts as an essential part of his pass route repertoire to get open in coverage. Hutson was also a tricky fellow, as opposing defensive backs could attest. After a 1942 game between the Packers and the Bears, *Pittsburgh Press* sportswriter Pat Livingston recounted a particularly memorable example of Hutson's ingenuity: "Lining up as a flanker, harassed by three Bears, the cagy old Alabaman ran a simple post pattern, diagonally in on the twin-poled uprights [which at that time were located in the center of the end zone], Bears convoying him, stride by stride. As the four men raced under the bar, Hutson hooked his elbow around the upright, stopping abruptly, flung his body sharply left, and left the red-faced Bears scrambling around in their cleats. He stood alone in the end zone as he casually gathered [Green Bay quarterback Cecil] Isbell's throw to his chest."

Who won the NFL rushing title in 1940 and later went on **to become a U.S. Supreme Court justice?**

Byron "Whizzer" White was an outstanding athlete who excelled on the football field and in the classroom. As a running back for the University of Colorado in 1938, White finished second in the Heisman Trophy voting and then moved on to the NFL. He only

San Francisco 49ers' quarterback Steve Young is known for his scrambling ability.

played for three years before quitting to begin his law career and was appointed to the Supreme Court in 1962 by John F. Kennedy.

Who is the only player to **rush for more than 200 yards in the Super Bowl**?

Timmie Smith was hardly a household name at the start of Super Bowl XXII, but he was by the end of the game. After rushing for only 126 yards during the entire regular season for the Washington Redskins, Smith broke loose for 204 yards in the 'Skins 42–10 rout of the Denver Broncos. Unfortunately for Smith, his success didn't last. He played only two more seasons in the NFL and ran for only 612 more yards in his entire career.

What NFL receiver holds the Super Bowl records for **most receptions and most yards receiving**?

It's not exactly a shock to find that perennial All-Pro Jerry Rice, who holds practically every meaningful regular season receiving mark, also holds a number of Super Bowl records. The long-time 49er has pulled in 28 receptions in his three Super Bowl appearances (all of which were San Francisco victories), one more than Buffalo's Andre Reed. Those receptions were good for 512 yards and seven touchdowns, both of which are records as well. Finally, Rice holds the Super Bowl record for most career points scored, with 42.

211

Jim Brown dominated his era, leading the league in rushing eight times in a nine-year career.

Barry Sanders has a 2,000-yard and four straight 1,500-yard rushing seasons under his belt.

Who is the only running back to **win the league rushing title five years in a row**?

Jim Brown led the league in rushing eight times during his nine-year career, from 1957–61 and 1963–65. Brown is also the only back in the top 10 in career rushing to average more than five yards per carry. Barry Sanders is next at 4.9 through 1997.

Who are the only three backs to **rush for 2,000 yards** in a season?

Eric Dickerson, 2,105 yards in 1984; Barry Sanders, 2,053 in 1997; and O. J. Simpson, 2,003 in 1973.

Who is the only back to **rush for 1,500 yards or more for four straight seasons**?

Barry Sanders, 1994–97.

What's the record for **most yards rushing in a single game**?

Walter Payton ran for 275 yards in a 1977 game against Minnesota. O. J. Simpson had the next two best games, 273 yards against Detroit in 1976, and 259 yards against New England in 1973.

Brett Favre, who led the Green Bay Packers to the 1997 Super Bowl championship, only became a quarterback because he was such a bad wide receiver.

What legendary quarterback threw the **most career interceptions**?

George Blanda threw 277 career interceptions. Rounding out the top five are John Hadl (268), Fran Tarkenton (266), and Norm Snead and Johnny Unitas with 253 each. Blanda—who is also the oldest player (48) to ever appear in a professional football game—was the AFL MVP in 1970 and still holds the record for regular season and playoff scoring among place kickers. He was 43 during that legendary MVP season, in which he was also named AP Male Athlete of the Year. During one amazing five-week stretch in 1970, Blanda replaced injured starting QB Darryl Lamonica and led a comeback by throwing three touchdown passes in a 31–14 victory; he kicked a 48-yard field goal with three seconds left the next week to tie the game (which ended 17–17); he came into the next game with his team down late and threw a tying touchdown with 1:14 left, then won the game with a 52-yard field goal with three seconds left; the next week he came in with four minutes left and Oakland down 19–17, led the Raiders on an 80-yard drive and tossed a game-winning TD; and the fifth week he booted a 16-yard field goal with four seconds left for a 20–17 victory.

What defensive back has the **most career interceptions,** and who had the most in a single season?

Paul Krause of the Minnesota Vikings is the career leader with 81. Rounding out the top five are Emlen Tunnell with 79, Dick "Night Train" Lane with 68, Ken Riley with

> ## Which famous running back (a movie was made based on a book he wrote) is the all-time leader in kickoff return yardage (based on at least 75 returns)?
>
> Gale Sayers returned 91 kicks for 2,781 yards—an astounding 30.6 yard average—and six touchdowns. Sayers also shares the record with four others for longest run from scrimmage in a college football game—99 yards—which he ran in a 1963 game for Kansas against Nebraska.

65, and Ronnie Lott with 63. Lane has the record for most in a season, snatching 14 in 1952.

What is the record for **longest punt** in an NFL game?

Steve O'Neal of the New York Jets got a great roll when he booted a 98-yarder against the Denver Broncos on September 21, 1969.

What number is the **most popular retired jersey number** in the NFL

The number 14, which was worn by five players whose teams have retired their jerseys: Dan Fouts of the San Diego Chargers, Otto Graham of the Cleveland Browns, Steve Grogan of the New England Patriots, Don Hutson of the Green Bay Packers, and Y.A. Tittle of the New York Giants. Three other numbers—7, 12, and 40—have been retired by four teams each.

The **Heisman Trophy has often been the kiss of death** for college players when they moved on to the NFL. In fact, only six winners of college football's top award have made it to the Pro Football Hall of Fame. Who are they?

Doak Walker, half back; Paul Hornung, running back; Roger Staubach, quarterback; O.J. Simpson, running back; Tony Dorsett, running back; and Earl Campbell, running back. Campbell and Dorsett pulled off a bit of a trifecta by also being named NFL Rookie of the Year, Dorsett in 1977 and Campbell in 1978.

What Super Bowl winner and NFL **Most Valuable Player** became a quarterback because he was such a miserable failure as a wide receiver?

Brett Favre, star signal caller for the Green Bay Packers, adopted the quarterback position in the fifth grade after trying the wide receiver position—once. "I caught a pass,

215

fell on the football and had the wind knocked out of me," Favre recalled. "I'm laying there on the field, crying, and my dad comes out and says, 'Get up, you baby.' I told him I didn't want to play wide receiver no more. So he put me at quarterback, and that day I threw for two touchdowns and ran for two. I knew this was the position for me. The cheerleaders were cheering and the fans were yelling, and afterwards I felt like, man, I'm really good." He was good enough to win the NFL's Most Valuable Player award three times (in 1995, 1996, and 1997—when he shared the award with running back Barry Sanders of the Detroit Lions) and lead his team to the Super Bowl championship in 1997.

ODDS AND ENDS

Which are the only two **wild-card teams to have won Super Bowls**?

Along with divisional champions, teams with outstanding records can also qualify for the playoffs as wild card teams. Only two nondivision winners have won Super Bowls, though, Oakland in 1981 and Denver in 1998.

Which former NFL head coach used to leave game tickets for **Elvis Presley** at the gate for each home contest?

During the mid-1980s Atlanta Falcons Head Coach Jerry Glanville got in the habit of leaving tickets for the King at every Falcons home game. Apparently Presley felt that Glanville was nothin' but a hound dog, though, because he never did swing by to pick the tickets up.

What NFL head coach was the first to **win over 100 games** in 10 years with the same team, and why did he retire shortly afterwards?

John Madden, the legendary coach of the Oakland Raiders turned demonstrative television commentator, never had a losing season in a decade on the sidelines. The culmination of his career came in 1976, when the Raiders posted a 13-1 record and earned a trip to the Super Bowl, where they dominated the Minnesota Vikings. Madden continued coaching the Raiders through the 1977 and 1978 seasons, despite suffering from a painful stomach ulcer, partly because he hoped to become the first coach to win 100 games in 10 years with the same NFL team. But something happened during a Raiders exhibition game in August 1978 that cinched his decision to quit. Darryl Stingley, a wide receiver for the visiting New England Patriots, broke his neck in a collision with Raiders free safety Jack Tatum. The injury caused Stingley to be permanently paralyzed from the neck down. "In my decision to stop coach-

Running back Terrell Davis helped Denver become the second wild card team to win the Super Bowl when the Broncos defeated the Green Bay Packers in 1998.

ing, Darryl's situation was a factor. Not the only factor, but a factor," Madden explained. "Not many people seemed to care enough. That's when I started wondering if football people really care about a player, or if football people just care about what a player does." Madden announced his retirement as head coach of the Raiders in January 1979, shortly after surpassing his personal goal by posting 103 career regular-season wins.

How come you always see television personality John Madden in the parking lots outside of NFL stadiums with his **"Maddencruiser"**?

Madden gradually developed an acute fear of flying over many years of extensive travel as an NFL coach and broadcaster. He never did like cramming his large body into tiny airplane seats, but his discomfort increased considerably after the California Polytechnic tragedy of 1960. Just two years after Madden had ended his college football playing career at the school, a plane carrying the Cal Poly football team crashed, killing 22 of the 44 people on board, including 16 players. Madden experienced more and more anxiety each time he had to travel by plane, until one day he decided that he couldn't take it anymore. He then began taking trains back and forth across the country. Later, he began traveling in the familiar "Maddencruiser," a specially-equipped Greyhound bus, so that he could set his own schedule.

Which two coaching legends led their teams into the most playoff games?

Long-time Dallas Cowboys coach Tom Landry and Miami Dolphins coach Don Shula each roamed the sidelines as head coach in 36 playoff games. Landry made all of his playoff appearances with Dallas, but Shula's three dozen appearances came at the helm of two clubs, the Baltimore Colts and the Dolphins. Shula and Landry also top the list of Super Bowl appearances by a head coach. Shula led his teams to six Super Bowl appearances, where he posted a 2–4 record (0–1 with Baltimore, 2–3 with Miami). Landry, meanwhile, has five Super Bowl appearances on his resume (he posted a 2–3 record).

What top college and current NFL coach had originally planned to become a **psychologist**, and fell into coaching by accident?

Jimmy Johnson—who won the NCAA championship as coach of the University of Miami Hurricanes and the Super Bowl as coach of the Dallas Cowboys—never intended to become a football coach at all. He was an undersized but smart defensive nose-guard for the Arkansas Razorbacks when the team went undefeated and claimed the national championship in 1964. He graduated with a degree in psychology that year and planned to continue on for a master's degree. But that summer Arkansas held a coaching clinic, and several members of the coaching staff from Louisiana Tech University attended. Johnson had such a strong grasp of the Razorbacks' overall defensive scheme—and such a confident, well-spoken manner—that his coaches sent him to the chalkboard to lecture. When the Louisiana Tech defensive line coach was forced to take the season off after suffering a heart attack, the Tech coaches remembered the bright senior from Arkansas and asked him to fill in during the 1965 season. Johnson leaped at the opportunity, and the rest is history.

What two coaches coached in the **Super Bowl and the Canadian Football League's Grey Cup** championship game?

Bud Grant (Minnesota and Winnipeg) and Marv Levy (Buffalo and Montreal). Bud Grant was 4–1 in Grey Cups, Levy was 2–1. They share another distinction: both were 0–4 in Super Bowls.

What teams have been the **winningest** squads of the last several decades?

Several teams have constructed enduring dynasties that have lasted for stretches of 10 or even 20 years. During the 1930s, the Chicago Bears and the Green Bay Packers

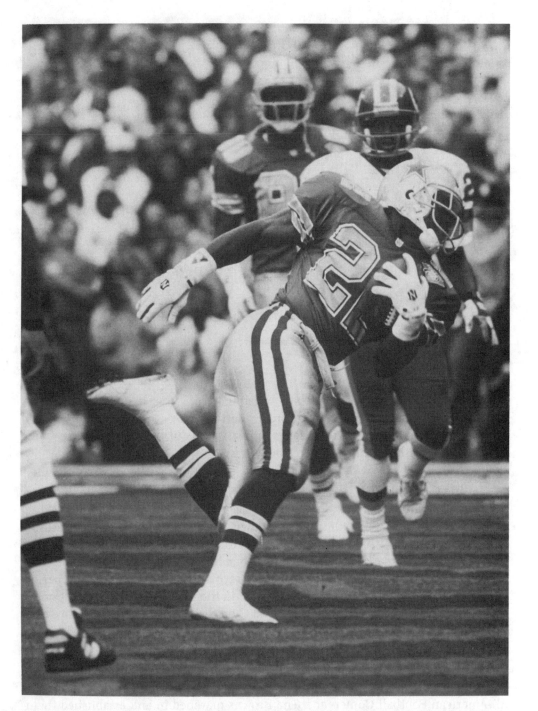

Running back Emmitt Smith is one big reason the Dallas Cowboys were one of the best teams in the NFL in the 1990s.

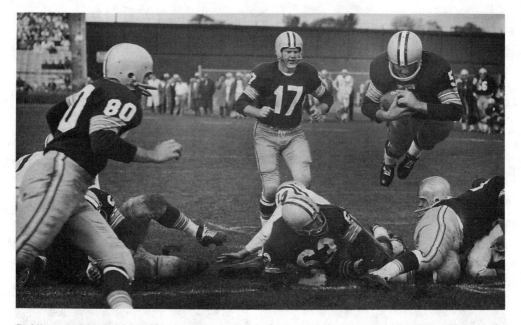

Paul Hornung, shown here leaping for a touchdown against the San Francisco 49ers, helped the Green Bay Packers to a 96-37-5 record in the 1960s.

duked it out for supremacy. The Bears posted the best regular season winning percentage, compiling an 85–28–11 record while the Packers mustered an 86–35–4 record. But the Pack garnered twice as many NFL titles during that period, marching to four championships while Chicago managed to win two.

During the 1940s, the Bears and Packers were once again the elite teams, but they were joined by the Washington Redskins. Once again the Bears compiled the best regular season mark (81–26–3), but this time they also dominated the NFL postseason, winning four titles over the course of the decade. The Redskins, meanwhile, put together a 65–41–4 mark for the decade, with one NFL championship, while the Packers tallied one championship and a 62–44–4 record. The most dominating performance of the decade, however, took place over in the All-American Football Conference, where the Cleveland Browns went 47–4–3 on their way to four consecutive titles from 1946–49.

The Browns proved that their late-1940s performance was no fluke in the 1950s. In 1949 both Cleveland and San Francisco entered the NFL after the collapse of the All-American Football Conference. The Browns marched in and established themselves as the elder league's best club, going 88–33–2 and winning three titles during the '50s. They were followed by the New York Giants (76–41–3, one title), the Bears (70–48–1, no titles), and the Detroit Lions (68–48–4, three titles).

In the 1960s the Packers reestablished themselves as the league's preeminent team. Led by legendary figures like Vince Lombardi, Bart Starr, and Paul Hornung, the Pack posted a 96–37–5 record for the decade, winning the first two Super Bowls in the process. Other tough teams of the 1960s included the Browns, the Baltimore Colts, the Kansas City Chiefs, and the Dallas Cowboys, who went from expansion doormat in 1960 to dangerous contender by the mid-1960s.

In the 1970s it was "America's Team" that led the way. Dallas posted a sparkling 105–39–0 record during the decade, winning Super Bowls VI (1972) and XII (1978) along the way. But two teams from the rival American Football Conference were arguably even more dominant. The Miami Dolphins went 104–39–1 during the 1970s and matched the Cowboys' title total by winning Super Bowls VII (1973) and VIII (1974). And the Pittsburgh Steelers, while only the sixth-best team of the decade as measured by regular season winning percentage (99–44–1), won four Super Bowls during the decade, VIX (1975), X (1976), XIII (1979), and XIV (1980).

The 1980s, meanwhile, were the decade of the 49ers. San Francisco put together a 104–47–1 record during the decade on their way to four Super Bowl wins; XVI (1982), XIX (1985), XXIII (1989), and XXIV (1990). Other top teams of the 1980s included the Washington Redskins (97–55–0, two Super Bowl wins), the Miami Dolphins (94–57–1, no titles), the Denver Broncos (93–58–1, no titles), and the Chicago Bears (92–60–0, one Super Bowl victory).

Thus far in the 1990s, the top teams have been the San Francisco 49ers (one Super Bowl win), the Dallas Cowboys (three Super Bowl victories), the Buffalo Bills, the Kansas City Chiefs, and the Pittsburgh Steelers.

What are the longest **field goals** of all time?

Tom Dempsey's 63-yard game winning field goal against Detroit in 1967 in the closing seconds still stands as the longest of all time. Tulane Stadium went wild. Alex Karras, the great Lions defensive tackle, later joked that players were so sure Dempsey wouldn't make it that they battled on the line of scrimmage for the best view of watching the ball fall back to Earth. Steve Cox kicked a 60-yarder in 1984 for Cleveland, and Morten Anderson booted a 60-yarder in 1991 for New Orleans.

Eleven teams have **never played in the Super Bowl.** Who are they?

Arizona Cardinals, Atlanta Falcons, Baltimore Ravens, Carolina Panthers, Cleveland Browns, Detroit Lions, Jacksonville Jaguars, New Orleans Saints, Seattle Seahawks, Tampa Bay Buccaneers, and Tennessee Oilers.

What are the longest plays in NFL history?

There have been eight touchdown passes of 99 yards. In 1983, Tony Dorsett ran 99 yards from scrimmage against the Minnesota Vikings. Robert Bailey of the Rams returned a punt 104 yards in a 1994 game against New Orleans, and three players have returned kickoffs for 106 yards. James Willis of Philadelphia intercepted a pass four yards deep in the endzone, ran out to the 10, and lateralled to Troy Vincent, who took it the remaining 90 yards to complete the longest interception return—104 yards—in NFL history in 1994.

Which NFL team has **never won a post-season game**?

Oddly enough, it's not one of the four most recent franchises to enter the NFL—Tampa Bay, Seattle, Jacksonville, and Carolina all have won at least one playoff game. The Ain'ts of New Orleans ain't never won a post season game since entering the league in 1967. They've made the playoff four times during those years. The City of New Orleans has hosted five Super Bowls, though, and could qualify as a permanent neutral field site.

What is the **largest stadium** in the NFL? The smallest?

The Detroit Lions have the distinction of owning the largest stadium in the league, the Pontiac Silverdome, which seats 80,365. The Silverdome has the distinction of being the only cold-weather stadium to host the Super Bowl. The smallest stadium is an outdoor multipurpose park—Three Rivers Stadium, home to the Pittsburgh Steelers, seats 59,600.

Where is the **Pro Football Hall of Fame,** and how is one elected to it?

The Pro Football Hall of Fame was established in 1963 in Canton, Ohio. To be eligible, players must be retired for five years, coaches must be retired, and other contributors to the game can still be active. Voting on entry is done by a 36-member panel, composed of 30 media representatives (one from each NFL city), one representative from the Hall of Fame, and five electors-at-large.

What was the **largest trade** in NFL history?

The NFL has seen plenty of blockbuster trades in its history, but the single largest, based on number of players or draft choices involved, was the October 13, 1989 trade in which the Cowboys traded Herschel Walker to the Minnesota Vikings for a truck-

> ## Where did the term "taxi squad" originate?
>
> The taxi squad referred to players under contract to an NFL team, but who didn't suit up for games because of 40-man roster limit. At one time, the Cleveland Browns couldn't put all their players on the roster, so they employed some as part-time taxicab drivers.

load of players and draft choices. This trade, which was a vital component in replenishing the Cowboys' then-depleted stock of talent and launching them to three Super Bowl wins in the 1990s, broke down as follows: Dallas traded Walker, its 1990 third-round draft pick, its 1990 tenth-round pick, and its 1991 third-round choice to Minnesota. In exchange, the Vikings packed off linebacker Jesse Solomon, linebacker David Howard, cornerback Isaac Holt, defensive end Alex Stewart, its first- and sixth-round choices in 1990, its first- and second-round choices in 1991, its first-, second-, and third-round choices in 1992. Minnesota also traded halfback Darrin Nelson to Dallas, but he was quickly moved on to the Chargers for San Diego's fifth-round pick in the 1990 draft, which the Cowboys passed along to the Vikings to seal the deal.

Other major NFL trades in history include the March 26, 1953, trade between the Baltimore Colts and the Cleveland Browns. On that day, the teams exchanged a whopping 15 players. Eighteen years later, on January 28, 1971, another trade of similar dimensions took place, as the Los Angeles Rams and the Washington Redskins made a trade involving seven players and eight draft choices.

Who were the "Steagles"?

During the mid-1940s. NFL players were in short supply since so many were off fighting in World War II. A few teams, such as the Cleveland Rams, suspended operations altogether, while others came up with more unique solutions. The Pittsburgh Steelers and Philadelphia Eagles decided to merge and share a roster, playing home games in both cities—hence, the "Steagles" were born. The experiment lasted for only the 1943 season—in 1944 the Eagles resumed as a separate team, while the Steelers merged with the Chicago Cardinals for the 1944 season.

What author once played quarterback for the Detroit Lions?

Famous for his first-person looks at the world of professional sports, George Plimpton worked out with the Lions at their training camp in 1966 and played quarterback during an exhibition game. The story of his dering-do was told in the book *Paper Lion*. Plimpton also once played goaltender for the Boston Bruins.

223

What is the **Arena Football League**?

Founded in 1987, the Arena Football League (AFL) is a frenetically paced indoor version of the game of football that fans have long been familiar with from hours of NFL and major college football viewing. There are some respects in which arena football is the same as regular football—the ball is the same, a touchdown is worth six points, basic principles of passing, catching, and tackling are the same, etc.—but even a quick glimpse at an Arena League game makes it clear that there are some pretty significant differences, too.

Field: An Arena Football League field is 85 feet wide and 50 yards long, with eight-yard end zones. The goalposts are considerably smaller than those in the NFL, too: nine feet wide, with a crossbar height of 15 feet; NFL goalposts, on the other hand, are 18 1/2 feet wide, with a crossbar height of 10 feet. Another unique component of arena football is the presence of huge (30 feet wide, 32 feet high) nets at the back of both end zones. In the event that a kickoff, a missed field goal, or an errant pass hits the net, the players on the field are allowed to catch the rebound and run with the ball.

Players: Each team plays with eight players at a time, and fields a total roster of 20 players. Most of the players play both offense and defense. The only players who don't pull such double duty are the quarterback, the kicker, and three players—called specialists—who are designated to play on only one side of the ball (each team can pick one exclusively offensive player and two exclusively defensive players). Each team can make only one non-specialist substitution per quarter.

Scoring: The awards for touchdowns (six points), extra points (one point), field goals (three points), and safeties (two points) are all the same as what one would find in the NFL or college football. But teams interested in going for a two-point conversion after a touchdown can either pass or run the ball into the end zone or drop kick the conversion through the uprights. Finally, arena football teams can also score four points by successfully kicking a field goal via a drop kick.

Change of possession: Offensive teams are given four downs to either a) gain ten yards and another first down; b) score a touchdown; or c) attempt a field goal. Punting is illegal.

Who is the **winningest coach in Arena Football** League history?

Tim Marcum is the AFL's winningest coach. In the league's inaugural season he guided the Denver Dynamite to a championship triumph, and since then he has led his teams to five more ArenaBowl championship victories. In 1988, 1989, and 1992, he marched the Detroit Drive to the title. In 1995 Marcum took over the reins for the Tampa Bay Storm and promptly pushed the team to two ArenaBowl titles in 1995 and 1996.

What former Heisman Trophy winner became a perennial MVP in the **Canadian Football League**?

Doug Flutie enjoyed a storybook career at Boston College, but his professional career seemed doomed to pale in significance until he headed north to the CFL, where he became the most exciting player in the league during the 1990s.

When Flutie left B.C., memories of his fabulous 1984 season—and especially his dramatic Hail Mary touchdown pass that beat the powerhouse Miami Hurricanes—were still fresh in the memories of all football fans. But Flutie's relatively small stature (five feet, ten inches) convinced many NFL coaches and personnel directors that he would never be able to make an impact in the pros. He did spend five years in the NFL, but he bounced to three different teams during that time. Dogged by the skepticism of coaches and teammates alike, Flutie was never able to claim outright leadership of any of the clubs for which he played.

Finally, after being released by the New England Patriots in 1989, Flutie looked northward to the Canadian Football League. To the surprise of just about everyone (except perhaps Flutie himself), the former B.C. Eagle proved to be a one-man wrecking crew in the Great White North. From 1990 to 1997 Flutie starred for three teams—the British Columbia Lions, Calgary Stampeders, and Toronto Argonauts. During that time he won six awards as the most outstanding player in the league and became its highest-paid player. He led the league in passing yardage in five of those seasons, and helmed his teams to three victories in the Grey Cup (Canada's version of the Super Bowl). In 1997 alone he threw 47 touchdown passes.

Imagine how shocked CFL fans were, then, when Flutie suddenly announced early in 1998 that he was returning to the U.S. to play. Lured by the desire to prove his mettle in the NFL, Flutie signed a two-year contract with the Buffalo Bills, even though the terms of the contract meant a pay cut. But the former CFL superstar soon was hit with a nasty surprise as well. Only weeks after signing Flutie, the Bills traded a number one draft pick for Jacksonville Jaguars quarterback Rob Johnson, a trade that left NFL observers wondering once again whether Flutie's professional luck is destined to once again turn sour south of the U.S.-Canada border.

How is the **Canadian version of football** different from the American game?

Canadian football differs from American football in several fundamental respects. These differences make the northern version a much more wide open game, though the arctic conditions in which late-season and post-season games are often played mitigates this somewhat. For example, the size of CFL fields is considerably larger than those in the NFL. CFL fields are 110 yards long, 65 yards wide, and feature end zones that are 20 yards deep. NFL fields, by contrast, are only 100 yards long and 53 yards wide, and feature end zones that are only 10 yards deep. In addition, the Canadian Football League plays with 12 players on a side, rather than the 11 that line up in the NFL. Also, the CFL only provides for three downs before a team must make a first down or score, while the NFL allows four downs. Another feature of CFL ball, which can be disconcerting to American viewers used to the strict illegal motion regulations of the NFL, is that offensive players are allowed to sprint toward the line of scrimmage—in effect giving them a running start—before the ball is snapped. Finally, the Canadian version of the game maintains a completely different system for scoring and penalties.

COLLEGE FOOTBALL

What is the **option**?

The option is an offensive scheme utilized by many college teams at all levels of competition. With this play, the quarterback snaps the ball and rolls out to one side of the line with a running back keeping pace a few yards behind him. As the defensive players converge, the quarterback has the option of either keeping the football himself and trying to advance it upfield, or pitching the ball to the trailing running back who will then turn upfield to try to gain yardage. This play is a staple of football programs blessed with strong running quarterbacks, and some teams—such as Nebraska and Oklahoma—have made it a perennial cornerstone of their offensive strategy.

What does it mean to be **redshirted**?

Players who are redshirted are held out of intercollegiate competition for a year even though they continue to attend practices and school. In return, they are granted another year of playing eligibility down the road. This practice, which is commonly applied to freshman who would not see much playing time during their first year, is also sometimes used when a player suffers an injury that will take him out of action for a significant portion of the season.

BOWLS AND CHAMPIONSHIPS

What is the **Bowl Alliance**?

After years of bickering and complaining about the fact that Division I-A football was the only NCAA sport on any level that did not have a sanctioned national champion, the powers that be decided to form a Bowl Coalition in an attempt to eliminate the seemingly annual controversy over who was the top squad in Division I-A. The Coalition, which was formed in 1992, sought to keep the popular bowl system intact while forcing an annual championship game between the regular season's two top-ranked teams. All of the major bowls signed on, with the notable exception of the Rose Bowl, where the winners of the Big Ten and PAC-10 conferences annually clashed. But the Coalition hoped for the best, since it included four other major bowls (the Fiesta, Cotton, Orange, and Sugar), champions of five conferences (ACC, Big Eight, Big East, Southeastern, and Southwest), and the consent of independent powerhouse Notre Dame.

In 1993 and 1994 the Coalition worked as planned, as the nation's two top-ranked teams met in the 1993 Sugar Bowl (in which number two Alabama knocked off the top-ranked Miami Hurricanes) and the 1994 Orange Bowl (in which number one Florida State held off number two Nebraska). In 1995, however, the Coalition had to settle for a No. 1 versus No. 3 headline game, for second-ranked Penn State played in the non-Coalition Rose Bowl. The 1995 Orange Bowl, in which the Cornhuskers defeated the Hurricanes, was a dandy, but Penn State's absence caused much gnashing of teeth among college football fans and media.

An updated version of the Coalition called the Bowl Alliance was introduced in the fall of 1995. The big difference between this arrangement and the one of the previous few years was that it was able to enlist the participation of the Rose Bowl (and the Big Ten and PAC-10 conferences) beginning with the 1998 season. Under the new rules, if a Big Ten or PAC-10 team is ranked first or second in the country, it will move to another bowl if necessary to create a number one versus number two match-up for the undisputed national title. By agreeing to join the Alliance, the Rose Bowl will also join the rotation of major bowls that get to host the title game.

Unfortunately, the delay in incorporating the Rose Bowl into the Bowl Alliance until the 1998 season created another controversial situation at the end of the 1997 season, which ended with two teams sharing the national title one last time. Alliance participant Nebraska went undefeated during the regular season (thanks in large measure to a last-second victory over the Missouri Tigers that ranks among the most miraculous in college football history), but Division I-A's only other unbeaten team, the Big Ten Michigan Wolverines, were obligated to go to Pasadena to face the PAC-10 champ one final time. Both Nebraska and Michigan won their bowl games, leading to a split title as the AP poll named Michigan the national champs and the ESPN/*USA Today* voters gave the nod to the Cornhuskers.

Which teams have made the **most appearances in the major bowl games**?

Some of college football's most enduring dynasties have made their reputations in large part because of their associations with one of the games "big four" bowl games—the Rose Bowl, the Sugar Bowl, the Orange Bowl, or the Cotton Bowl.

The USC Trojans, for instance, have appeared in a whopping 28 Rose Bowl contests, posting a gaudy 20–8 record in those games. The Big Ten representative with the most appearances in Pasadena is Michigan, which has won eight out of the 17 games they've played. Other teams that have been a significant part of Rose Bowl history include Washington (6–6–1), Ohio State (6–7), Stanford (5–5–1), and UCLA (5–6).

The Alabama Crimson Tide, meanwhile, hold the record for most Sugar Bowl appearances with 12. The Tide has gone 8–4 in those contests, making them the winningest team in Sugar Bowl history as well. Other teams that have made frequent appearances in the bowl include Louisiana State (3–7) and Mississippi (5–3).

The Cornhuskers of Nebraska are the most frequent visitors to the marquee of the Orange Bowl. The Huskers have made 17 appearances in the bowl, winning 8 and losing 9. Other frequent visitors to this high-profile bowl include Oklahoma (11–5), Miami of Florida (5–3), and Alabama (4–3).

Down in the Lone Star State, meanwhile, the Longhorns of Texas are the team that has been most often spotlighted in the Cotton Bowl. Texas has a .500 record in 19 appearances, posting a 9–9–1 record. No other team has played in the Cotton Bowl more than nine times.

How many times has the **No. 1 team in the AP poll played the No. 2 team**?

Thirty-one times, 11 of which were bowl games. No. 1 holds an 18–11–2 advantage, but No. 2 is 10–6 since 1979, including No. 2 Florida State's 24–21 victory over No. 1 Florida in 1996.

What were **the results when the No. 1 and No. 2 teams met** in bowl games?

Here are the results of the 11 times that has happened:

In 1963, No. 1 USC defeated No. 2 Wisconsin 42–37 in the Rose Bowl.
In 1964, No. 1 Texas defeated No. 2 Navy 28–6 in the Cotton Bowl.
In 1969, No. 1 Ohio State defeated No. 2 USC 27–16 in the Rose Bowl.
In 1972, No. 1 Nebraska defeated No. 2 Alabama 38–6 in the Orange Bowl.
In 1979, No. 2 Alabama defeated No. 1 Penn State 14–7 in the Sugar Bowl.
In 1983, No. 2 Penn State defeated No. 1 Georgia 27–23 in the Sugar Bowl.
In 1987, No. 2 Penn State defeated No. 1 Miami 14–10 in the Fiesta Bowl.
In 1988, No. 2 Miami defeated No. 1 Oklahoma 20–14 in the Orange Bowl.

In 1993, No. 2 Alabama defeated No. 1 Miami 34–13 in the Sugar Bowl.
In 1994, No. 1 Florida State defeated No. 2 Nebraska 18–16 in the Orange Bowl.
In 1996, No. 1 Nebraska defeated No. 2 Florida 62–24 in the Fiesta Bowl.

Will the **Bowl Alliance** promise more of these match-ups?

After the 1998 season, all major conferences are included in an alliance in which a designated bowl will host a showdown between the nation's No. 1 and No. 2 teams. This should guarantee a national title game. In the past, some conferences were locked into certain bowls—the Big Ten and PAC Ten with the Rose Bowl, for example.

However, some questions still persist. What if there are three or more undefeated teams at season's end, or only one undefeated team and several teams with only one defeat? Which poll is going to be used—the AP, ESPN/*USA Today,* or another? At press time, such questions were still unanswered.

When have **unbeaten teams met in bowl games**?

Unbeaten teams have met 15 times in bowl games. In addition to the 1972, 1987, 1988, 1993, and 1996 games listed in the answer above concerning No. 1 versus No. 2, the other ten are

1921 Rose Bowl, when California defeated Ohio State 28–0.
1922 Rose Bowl, when California tied Washington & Jefferson 0–0.
1927 Rose Bowl when Stanford tied Alabama 7–7.
1931 Rose Bowl when Alabama defeated Washington State 24–0.
1939 Orange Bowl when Tennessee defeated Oklahoma 17–0.
1941 Sugar Bowl when Boston College defeated Tennessee 19–13.
1952 Sugar Bowl when Maryland defeated Tennessee 28–13.
1956 Orange Bowl when Oklahoma defeated Maryland 20–6.
1973 Sugar Bowl when Notre Dame beat Alabama 24–23.
1989 Fiesta Bowl when Notre Dame beat West Virginia 34–21.

Which 10 teams have **finished in the AP Top 10 the most**?

The top 10 of the top 10 (with No. 1 rankings in parentheses) are:

Notre Dame	34 (8)
Michigan	33 (2)
Alabama	30 (6)
Oklahoma	29 (6)
Nebraska	27 (4)
Ohio State	24 (3)
Penn State	21 (2)
USC	20 (3)

Which two perennial powerhouse teams won major bowl games in 1998 but don't have winning bowl records all-time?

Michigan and Nebraska finished the 1997 season undefeated, won their bowls games, and shared the national championship, with each claiming the top spot in one of the major polls. The wins brought Michigan's all-time bowl record to 14–15, Nebraska's to 18–18.

Tennessee	20 (1)
Texas	19 (2)

Which colleges have **won the most bowl games**?

1. Alabama	28–17–3
2. USC	25–13
3. Tennessee	21–17
4. Penn State	21–11–2

Which **Division I-AA** team has won the most national championships?

Georgia Southern has won four national titles since the NCAA established a playoff format for the division in 1978. Their victories took place in 1985, 1986, 1989, and 1990. Other Division I-AA teams with multiple championships include Youngstown State, Eastern Kentucky, and Marshall.

Which **Division III** program has won the most championships in NCAA history?

Augustana College of Illinois won four straight championships from 1983 to 1986. Other Division III teams that have won multiple championships are Ithaca (NY) with three; and Dayton (OH), Mt. Union (OH), Widener (PA), Wisconsin-La Crosse, and Wittenberg (OH), all of which have claimed two crowns.

The Heisman and Other Awards

What are the **major college awards** besides the Heisman?

The Maxwell Award: Beginning in 1937, the Maxwell Memorial Football Club of Philadelphia presented its award to the outstanding football player in the nation. The award is named after Robert (Tiny) Maxwell, who was a great lineman for the University of Chicago at the turn of the century. The Maxwell and the Heisman are similar awards and have gone to the same player in the same season 32 times. The Maxwell voters have shown more variety than the Heisman voters, who have chosen either a quarterback, running back, or receiver every year except one (1997, Charles Woodson, defensive back, Michigan; the Maxwell for 1997 went to Peyton Manning, quarterback, Tennessee). A center (Chuck Bednarik, Penn State, 1948), a tackle (Bob Reifsnyder, Navy, 1957), two linebackers (Tommy Nobis, Texas, 1965; Jim Lynch, Notre Dame, 1966), a defensvie tackle (Mike Reid, Penn State, 1969), and two defensive ends (Ross Browner, Notre Dame, 1977; Hugh Green, Pittsburgh, 1980) have won the Maxwell.

O'Brien Quarterback Award: The O'Brien Memorial Trophy was first presented in 1977 to the outstanding player in the Southwest Conference; in 1981 it was renamed the O'Brien Quarterback Award and has since been given to the nation's outstanding quarterback. The award is bestowed by the Davey O'Brien Educational and Charitable Trust of Fort Worth, Texas and is named after 1938 Heisman-winning quarterback Davey O'Brien of Texas Christian University.

The Outland Trophy: Presented by the Football Writers Association of America since 1946 to the nation's outstanding lineman. The award is named for its benefactor, Dr. John H. Outland (graduate of Kansas, 1898). Center Dave Rimington of Nebraska is the only two-time winner (1981–82), and he, Ross Browner (defensive end, Notre Dame, 1976), Steve Emtman (defensive tackle, Washington, 1991), and Orlando Pace (offensive tackle, Ohio State, 1996) are the only juniors to win the award.

Lombardi Award: Presented since 1970 by the Rotary Club of Houston to the best lineman. Named after Vince Lombardi, coach of the Green Bay Packers and a college football player (he was one of the famed "seven blocks of granite" linemen at Fordham during the 1930s). The Outland and Lombardi both honor linemen, and a player has won both awards in the same year 10 times.

Butkus Award: Presented since 1985 by the Downtown Athletic Club of Orlando, Florida, to honor the nation's outstanding linebacker. The award is named for Dick Butkus, two-time All-American linebacker at Illinois.

Thorpe Award: Presented since 1986 by the Jim Thorpe Athletic Club of Oklahoma City to the nation's outstanding defensive back. Named after Olympic champion and football great Jim Thorpe.

Payton Award: Presented since 1987 by the Sports Network and Division I-AA Sports Information Directors to honor the nation's outstanding Division I-AA player. Named after Walter Payton, an All-American at Jackson State and the NFL's all-time leading rusher.

Hill Trophy: Presented since 1986 by the Harlon Hill Awards Committee of Florence, Alabama, to the nation's outstanding Division II player. Named after Northern Alabama and NFL star Harlon Hill.

Walter Payton, the NFL's all-time leader in career and single-game yardage, is the namesake of the award given to the outstanding Division I-AA player.

Who are some of the **defensive players** (besides 1997 winner Charles Woodson) to have garnered significant Heisman voting?

Don Whitmire, a tackle for Navy, finished 4th in 1944; Alex Karras, a tackle for Iowa, finished 2nd in 1957, and another tackle, Lou Michaels of Kentucky, finished 4th that year; Bobby Bell, a tackle from Minnesota, finished 2nd in 1962; Rich Glover, a middle gaurd from Nebraska, finished 3rd in 1972; Hugh Green, a defensive end from Pittsburgh, finished second in 1980; Brian Bosworth, a linebacker from Oklahoma, finished 4th in 1986; Gordie Lockbaum, a two-way player (receiver/defensive back) from Holy Cross finished third in 1987; Steve Emtman, a defensive tackle from Washington, finished 4th in 1991; and Marvin Jones, a linebacker from Florida State, finished 4th in 1992.

Has anyone ever **won the Heisman Trophy twice**?

Archie Griffin of Ohio State is the only multiple winner of the Heisman, taking it in 1974 and 1975. He finished college in 1975 as the nation's all-time leading rusher with 5,179 yards. He still ranks fourth, behind Tony Dorsett (6,082), Charles White (5,598) and Herschel Walker (5,259), who won their Heismans in 1976, 1979, and 1982, respectively. Billy Sims of the University of Oklahoma came close to winning the award twice, winning it in 1978 as a junior and then finishing second to White in 1979.

How many times has the player who won the **Heisman Trophy** played on a team that **won the national championship the same year**?

Eleven times, the most recent occurring in 1997 when Charles Woodson of Michigan became the first defensive player to win the trophy, leading his team to a 12–0 record and a share of the national championship. Other players to pull off the double play include Danny Wuerffel, quarterback, University of Florida, 1996; Charlie Ward, quarterback, Florida State, 1993; Tony Dorsett, running back, University of Pittsburgh, 1976; John Huarte, quarterback, Notre Dame, 1964; Leon Hart, end, Notre Dame, 1949; Johnny Lujack, quarterback, Notre Dame, 1947; Doc Blanchard, fullback, Army, 1945; Angelo Bertelli, quarterback, Notre Dame, 1943; Bruce Smith, quarterback, Minnesota, 1941; and Davey O'Brian, quarterback, Texas Christian, 1938.

FAMOUS GAMES

What game ranks as the most famous in the storied rivalry between **Harvard and Yale**?

On November 23, 1968, the Harvard and Yale squads clashed in a classic contest, a tie game that still brings smiles to Harvard alumni and prompts dark mutterings from Yale grads.

The Harvard-Yale game is a perennial highlight of every Ivy League season, but in 1968 the contest was particularly meaningful. Both teams entered the game unbeaten and untied, marking the first time since 1909 that both squads began the contest with unblemished records. An undisputed Ivy League title was on the line. As kickoff approached, banter between opposing fans increased in intensity, and scalpers commanded ridiculous prices for mediocre seats within Harvard Stadium. Yet when the game itself commenced, it at first appeared that all the pre-game hoopla would give way to a disappointing contest. Led by quarterback Brian Dowling and halfback Calvin Hill, Yale pushed out to a commanding 22–0 lead in the second quarter. Yalies were delighted, while the home fans started glancing at their watches.

Desperate to jump-start his floundering offense, Harvard Coach John Yovicsin sent second-string quarterback Frank Champi out into the fray. Champi promptly led the Harvard offense down the field on their best drive of the day, concluding the drive with a touchdown strike to receiver Bruce Freeman. The conversion failed, however, leaving the Crimson with an imposing 16-point halftime deficit.

Harvard narrowed the lead to 22–13 with a third quarter score, but hopes of a late comeback seemed to be squelched once and for all when Dowling (who would serve as the model for the character B.D. in Garry Trudeau's *Doonesbury* comic strip) punched in a touchdown with less than 11 minutes left in the game to push the margin back up to 16 points. Yale fans reveled in the stands, chanting "You're Number 2!" to Harvard backers. But Harvard didn't give up. Champi took the ensuing kickoff and marched his team to a touchdown with 42 seconds left. A successful two-point conversion closed the gap to 29–21.

But Harvard still needed a miracle. Down by eight points with less than a minute to go, an onside kick was their only hope. Yet to the horror of Yale fans, their team lined up in their normal kickoff formation instead of crowding the front line with sure-handed players. Harvard pounced on the miscue, recovering the onside kick at midfield. On first down, Champi scrambled for 14 yards before being pulled down by the face mask. The infraction cost Yale another 15 yards, bringing the Crimson down to the 20-yard line with 26 seconds left on the clock. The stadium was in an uproar, as Yale fans screamed for their defense to hold and Harvard supporters prayed for a tie.

Each subsequent play was a titanic struggle, and by the time that Champi got Harvard down to the 8-yard line, only three seconds remained on the clock. There was only enough time for one more play from scrimmage. After snapping the ball, Champi was forced out of the pocket by a strong pass rush. Scrambling to and fro, he finally found team captain Vic Gatto alone in the end zone for a touchdown. Bedlam ensued, as Harvard fans rushed out onto the field. But both sides knew that the TD pass had only closed the score to 29–27. Harvard would have to try for a two-point conversion to gain a tie and a share of the Ivy League Championship. The Yale defenders lined up with fire in their eyes. But Champi would not be denied. He connected with one of his receivers in the end zone, giving Harvard a miraculous tie and ensuring his place in Ivy League history.

"It's been a strange day from the beginning," Champi admitted after the game. "I'm an intuitive guy and when I woke up this morning, I was sort of in a dream. It felt like something great was going to happen to me. Then when I got [to the stadium], I still felt strange. It didn't feel like I was here but someplace else. I still don't feel like I'm here. It's all very strange."

What college football team needed a **fifth down** to win a share of the national championship?

On October 6, 1990, the 12th-ranked University of Colorado Buffaloes traveled to Missouri to meet the lightly regarded Tigers. The Bufs were heavily favored, but Missouri put on a spirited performance and took a 31–27 lead late into the fourth quarter. Colorado drove to the Tiger three-yard line in the final minute. After quarterback Charles Johnson spiked the ball to stop the clock on first down, Buffalo running back Eric Bieniemy carried the ball down to the one-yard line. The Bufs took a timeout with 18 seconds to go, but unnoticed in the excitement was the fact that the officials never changed the sideline down marker after the play. Rather than showing an upcoming third down, it stayed at second down and Colorado was able to run an additional play. Bieniemy was stopped on that play for no gain, but an official stopped the clock with eight seconds to play because the Missouri defenders were so slow in letting the Colorado runner get up. On what should've been fourth down (though the marker said third down), Johnson once again spiked the ball to stop the clock. Two seconds remained on the clock, and the erroneous sideline marker indicated that Colorado had one more down to try and punch the ball in the end zone. On the last play of the game, Johnson dived forward on a quarterback sneak, and when none of the officials signaled touchdown immediately, Missouri fans went crazy. They poured onto the field to celebrate, tearing down the goal posts at the far end of the field. But amid all the pandemonium, the line judge signaled a touchdown in front of the suddenly outraged Tiger fans.

Around this same time, the game officials and the Missouri coaching staff huddled together, for everyone had finally figured out that the Buffaloes had been awarded an extra down during their last offensive series. But NCAA rules clearly state that once the fifth-down play had been mistakenly run, it counted. Missouri coaches, players, and fans were beside themselves, but there was nothing to be done. Colorado was named the victor by a 33–31 score.

In subsequent weeks, the significance of Colorado's "fifth down" victory increased. The club kept winning, and their season-ending 10–9 victory over Notre Dame in the Orange Bowl gave the Bufs a 11–1–1 record and lifted them to national champion status in the eyes of the Associated Press (United Press International named Georgia Tech

"RED" GRANGE STARTS FOR THE GOAL LINE
ILLINOIS 39 — MICHIGAN 14
1924

Harold "Red" Grange of the University of Illinois (with the ball) played perhaps the finest game ever by a college running back in 1924, running for 402 yards and five touchdowns against then-unbeaten Michigan.

their national champion). But Colorado's national crown remained a controversial one. Critics contended that the Missouri game should have been a loss for the Bufs, and they pointed out that Colorado had dodged another bullet in the Orange Bowl thanks to an official's call. In the last minute of the game, Notre Dame's Raghib Ismail had returned a punt 91 yards for an apparent game-winning touchdown, only to have it wiped out by a clipping penalty.

Which player **gained 262 yards in the first quarter** alone against a Michigan team that had allowed only 32 points in its previous 20 games?

Illinois halfback Harold "Red" Grange shredded the Wolverines for a total of 402 yards in an October 18, 1924, contest that ranks among the most famous in Big Ten history. The Galloping Ghost's performance pushed the Illini to a startling 39–14 victory over a team that had not been beaten in two seasons. Grange gave Michigan defenders a taste of what was to come with the opening kickoff, which he returned 95 yards for a touchdown. Before the first quarter was over, he had added weaving touchdown runs of 67, 56, and 44 yards. The last of these gave him four touchdowns in 12 minutes against a defense that had only allowed a total of four touchdowns over the previous two seasons.

Michigan never recovered from Grange's first quarter onslaught, even though he sat out the second quarter. He returned to the game after halftime, and by the time the game was over the All-American back had added a fifth touchdown run and a touchdown pass. Illinois went on to post an 8–1–1 record for the season, while Michigan registered five shutouts in a 6–2 season. They only gave up 54 points the entire season, but 39 had come at the hands of Grange and his Illini teammates. "I don't think I ever played in any other game where every man did exactly what he was supposed to do," Grange later said. "In the first quarter, if a man was supposed to block the end, he blocked the end, If he was supposed to hit the tackle, he hit the tackle. I don't think any college team in the nation could have licked us on that day. Maybe on the Friday before or the Sunday afterward, they might have beat our brains in, but not on that one Saturday."

What **shocking pass play** lifted the run-oriented Texas Longhorns to a national championship in 1969?

The December 6, 1969, clash between Coach Darrell Royal's top-ranked Longhorns and Coach Frank Broyles' number two-ranked Arkansas Razorbacks turned out to be one for the ages, as a desperation fourth down pass put the Longhorns in position to pull out a victory in the game's final minutes.

The game itself was one of the most eagerly anticipated in college football history, and as dignitaries such as President Richard Nixon, Henry Kissinger, and Billy Graham filed into the stadium, fans across America tuned in via television (it was later estimated that half of the nation's TV sets were tuned to the game). The contest didn't disappoint, as both squads fought tooth and nail for any edge they could get. Arkansas' ability to shut down the Longhorns' vaunted wishbone running attack, though, enabled them to build a 14–8 lead midway through the fourth quarter. With about four minutes to go, Texas found itself facing a dangerous fourth down. Stationed on their own 43-yard line, they needed three yards for a first down. Texas considered punting the ball, but they worried that Arkansas would eat up all the remaining time on the clock. Coach Royal decided to go for the first down. But instead of calling a running play, as everybody in America—including Arkansas—expected, Royal amazed his coaching staff and players by calling a surprise pass. "We hadn't moved the ball all day long," he later explained. "I felt we had to get something big."

As the play unfolded and Texas quarterback James Street dropped back to pass, the capacity crowd in Arkansas rose to their feet with a roar. Street hurled the pass downfield to tight end Randy Peschel, who cradled it in for a 44-yard gain despite the close coverage of two defenders. "There were six hands up there and two of them belonged to us," said Royal. "It was like putting the ball through a keyhole, but it got to him and he caught it. Had [the pass] been unsuccessful, it would have been the most criticized call of all time. They would never have forgiven me for it."

But the pass play worked, advancing Texas deep into Arkansas territory. A few plays later, running back Jim Bertelsen plunged in from the two-yard line, giving

Texas a pulse-pounding 15–14 victory. Texas went on to win the national championship with a perfect 11–0 record that was capped by a 21–17 victory over Notre Dame in the Cotton Bowl.

What player **returned a fumble the wrong way** in a Rose Bowl?

During the second quarter of the 1929 Rose Bowl between California and Georgia Tech, Golden Bear running back Stumpy Thompson coughed up the ball on Tech's 36 yard line. Roy Riegel, the California center, caught the ball in the air and headed toward the end zone, but in trying to elude tacklers he got turned around and headed toward open field—toward the opposite end zone. Georgia Tech players ran along for the show, but Riegel's teammates took up the chase; quarterback Benny Lom caught him inside the 10 yard line, but Riegel shook him off, alledgedly yelling, "Get away from me, this is my touchdown!" But Riegel realized something was wrong and stopped short of the goal line. Georgia Tech players hoping to congratulate him tackled Riegel instead on the one-yard line—resulting in a 64 yard loss for Cal. The Golden Bears punted on the next play, but it was blocked and resulted in a safety. "Wrong Way" Riegel became a Rose Bowl legend.

Why were there 14 years between the **first Rose Bowl and the second**?

The first Rose Bowl was played on January 1, 1902, as an adjunct to the town of Pasadena's annual Rose Festival. That inaugural game pitted Stanford against Michigan, which had gone 11–0 in the regular season and scored 555 points while shutting out every opponent. It was only a postseason exhibition game, but many people thought Stanford didn't belong on the same field as the Michigan team. As it turns out, they were right. The Wolverines knocked most of the Stanford starters out of the game, then went to work on the second- and third-stringers. With the score 49–0 and eight minutes left in the game Stanford surrendered and walked off the field. The Tournament of Roses committee was humiliated. They dropped football from the Rose Festival until the West Coast was able to put together a stronger team.

Why did the referee **award Dick Moegle** a touchdown in the 1954 Cotton Bowl even though Tommy Lewis had tackled him?

Lewis had jumped off the bench to make the tackle.

PLAYERS AND COACHES

What school was known as **"Tailback U,"** and how did it earn its name?

The University of Southern California (USC) became known as "Tailback U" during the late 1960s and 1970s, when it produced one legendary running back after another—including O.J. Simpson, Ricky Bell, and Charles White. Marcus Allen, who had come to USC as a defensive back in 1978, became yet another in the school's long line of great runners when head coach John Robinson made the decision to switch him to running back after his first week of practice. "Since the first time he put on our uniform," Robinson said at the time, "it's been obvious that Marcus has three things you need to be a tailback at USC: the personal ambition, the magnetism, and that tailback look in his eyes." The move meant that Allen—playing behind junior Charles White— sat the bench his freshman year and played fullback his sophomore year. Allen was rewarded for his patience during his junior year, when he became the Trojans' starting tailback and gained 1,563 yards rushing—second in the country to George Rogers of South Carolina, who won the Heisman Trophy that year. In his senior season, Allen became the first running back in history to rush for more than 2,000 yards in a single season, finishing with an NCAA-record 2,342 yards to shatter the old record of 1,948 yards held by Tony Dorsett of the University of Pittsburgh. He averaged more than 212 yards per game and scored 23 touchdowns while winning every major college football award there was to win, including the Heisman Trophy.

What is the **"Elway Cross"**?

No, it's not a fancy pass pattern featuring crossing receivers. Instead, it's the nickname that was given to the distinguishing red marks on the chests of the Stanford Universi-

239

> **Bo Schembechler, legendary head coach of the Michigan Wolverines, was known to yell at his players. But he started yelling at one of his quarterbacks when he was only 10 years old. Which one?**
>
> Jim Harbaugh, who quarterbacked the Wolverines to a Big Ten Championship in 1986, first raised the gruff coach's ire as a young boy. His father, Jack Harbaugh, was a defensive backfield coach at Michigan under Schembechler in the 1970s. Jim often tagged along to watch the Wolverines' practices as a kid. "I would play games by myself on the sidelines," he explained. "I would play with the tackling dummies, trying to dodge and jump over them. Make it like a real game. I made like I was older in college. I was in my own little world." Schembechler remembered his future quarterback during these years as "a devil, running on the field when he shouldn't, playing with his friends. One time he did that, I screamed 'GET THAT KID OUT OF HERE ... NOW!' I think he was 10 years old. So, for the record, that is the youngest I ever yelled at one of my quarterbacks."

ty receivers during the time that Elway was the star quarterback for the Cardinal. In practice, he threw the ball so hard that his receivers had to worry about breaking their fingers if they caught a pass wrong. It became easy to spot the receivers in the Stanford locker room because they all had red marks where the nose of the football had hit them when they caught a hard pass from Elway. By his sophomore season at Stanford, Elway and his rifle arm had gained national attention. He completed 248 of 379 passes (65.4 percent) for 2,884 yards, 27 touchdowns, and only 4 interceptions that year, and became the first sophomore in 18 years to be named first team all-America at quarterback. Though an ankle injury limited his effectiveness as a junior, Elway had another strong year as a senior and finished his career at Stanford in 1983 with 774 completions in 1,246 attempts, good for 9,349 yards and 77 touchdowns. He set five national passing records and 17 PAC 10 Conference records in the process.

Who was **Knute Rockne**?

Rockne, head coach of the Notre Dame Fighting Irish from 1918 to 1930, is still considered by many to be the greatest college coach in history. Rockne's record of 105–12–5, a winning percentage of .881—still the best of all-time—certainly bears this out. "The Rock" was not particularly known as an innovator, but he was a master at studying the work of coaches who preceded him and implementing the best of their ideas. For instance, his masterful use of the new forward pass was instrumental in gaining national attention—and a winning record—for his early teams. His one major innovation was the Notre Dame Shift, a finesse move intended to allow his smaller, faster players to outmaneuver bigger, clumsier opponents.

But, above all, Rockne had a magnetic personality, and he is still widely known as the best motivator in football history. He knew when to stroke players' egos and when to berate them for sloppy performance, and his halftime pep talks are the stuff of legend. His most famous halftime talk came in a game against Army in 1928, when his team entered the locker room with a 0–0 tie. Rockne told his players about the time in 1920 when George Gipp, the Notre Dame All American, had looked up from his deathbed and related his last request: "Some day . . . when the odds are against us, ask a Notre Dame team to win a game for me—for the Gipper." Said Rockne, "This is the day, and you are the team." Whether the Gipper story was true or not, the pumped-up team went out and upset Army 12–6.

Who are the **five winningest coaches** in college football history?

Eddie Robinson of Grambling closed out a 55-year career in 1997 with 411 victories; Bear Bryant had 323 victories, Pop Warner 319, and Amos Alonzo Stagg 314; Joe Paterno at Penn State has 298 and is the leader among active coaches.

What famous college football players were known as **"Mr. Inside" and "Mr. Outside?"**

The two star running backs from the powerhouse Army teams of the 1940s—Doc Blanchard and Glenn Davis earned those nicknames while winning back-to-back Heisman Trophies—Blanchard won in 1945 and Davis turned the trick in 1946. The pair combined for 97 touchdowns in their college days at West Point.

Who were the **Four Horsemen**?

The most famous football backfield of all time, the Four Horsemen played for Notre Dame under head coach Knute Rockne from 1922 to 1924. The group consisted of quarterback Harry Stuhldreher, halfbacks Don Miller and Jim Crowley, and fullback Elmer Layden. They were named by sports writer Grantland Rice in a *New York Times* story on October 18, 1924. Rice wrote: "In dramatic lore [the Four Horsemen] are known as famine, pestilence, destruction, and death. These are only aliases. Their real names are: Stuhldreher, Miller, Crowley, and Layden."

A week after the story appeared, a Notre Dame student publicity aide posed the players on four horses from the school's farm. The photo was published nationwide, and by the mid-point of their senior-year schedule the Four Horsemen had become legends.

They began playing together in their sophomore year, and during the three years they played on the varsity team, Notre Dame compiled a record of 26–2–1. In their senior year, the team went 9–0 in the regular season and went on to a victory over Stanford in the Rose Bowl to claim Notre Dame's first national championship.

Who is the **career rushing leader** in college football?

Tony Dorsett amassed 6,082 yards from 1973 to 1976 for Pittsburgh.

Who is the NCAA's **career passing leader**?

Ty Detmer lit up opposing defenses for 15,031 yards for Brigham Young University between 1988 and 1991. Detmer also holds the record for most yards in a single season with 5,188 in 1990.

Who was the first college player to **catch more than 100 passes in a season**?

Howard Twilley of Tulsa caught 134 passes for 16 touchdowns in 1965.

Has anyone ever **passed for 700 yards**?

David Klingler tossed for 716 yards for Houston in a 1990 game against Arizona State. His own Houston team was lit up for 690 yards passing that year by Matt Vogler of TCU. They both topped the 631 yard mark set by Scott Mitchell of Utah against Air Force in 1988.

Who kicked the **longest field goals** in a college game?

In 1977, Steve Little of Arkansas kicked a 67-yarder against Texas; not to be outdone, Texas's Russell Erxleben kicked a 67-yarder that year against Rice; Joe Williams of Wichita State tied them with a 67-yarder against Southern Illinois in 1978.

Who holds the record for the **longest field goal without using a kicking tee**?

In 1991, Washington State Huskies' kicker Jason Hanson boomed a 62-yard field goal through the uprights against the University of Nevada-Las Vegas.

Who holds the record for **most points** scored in a single college game?

Four players in college football history have scored 48 points in a single game. The first player to do it was Panhandle State's Junior Wolf, who racked up the points in a November 8, 1958, Division II contest against St. Mary's (Kansas). Ten years later, on October 12, 1968, another Division II player, North Park College's Paul Zaeske, rolled up 48 points against North Central. On September 22, 1990, Howard Griffith of Division I-A Illinois matched the mark in a rout of Southern Illinois. The most recent player to tie the record was Carey Bender of Coe College (Division III) in a November 12, 1994, tilt against Beloit.

Brian Griese and his father Bob constitute perhaps the most successful father-son combination ever in the sport of football.

Which **father-son quarterback combo** can claim a Super Bowl ring, two undefeated seasons, a Rose Bowl victory, and a National Championship between them?

In 1971–72, Miami Dolphin quarterback Bob Griese led his team to a perfect 17–0 season and a 14–7 victory over the Washington Redskins in Super Bowl VII. Twenty-six

How many coaches have taken teams to all four major bowls?

Only four coaches have managed the feat of guiding teams to the Rose, Orange, Sugar, and Cotton Bowls. The first to do so was Georgia Tech's Bill Alexander, who guided the team from 1920 to 1944. He was followed by Tennessee's Bob Neyland, who had three different stints as head coach of the Volunteers (1926–34, 1936–40, 1946–52). Frank Thomas of Alabama, who led the Crimson Tide from 1931 to 1946 with a year off in 1943, became the third. The last to do so was Penn State's legendary Joe Paterno, who has roamed the sidelines for the Nittany Lions since 1966. Paterno is the only one of the four to secure victories in all four major bowls.

years later, his son Brian culminated his progression from walk-on to college star by throwing three touchdown passes in the Michigan Wolverines' 21–16 win over the Washington State Cougars in the Rose Bowl. The win clinched a perfect 12–0 season for the Wolverines and enabled them to secure the AP half of the national championship.

What two coaches **coached national champions** in college and also **coached in the Super Bowl**?

Barry Switzer coached the 1975 and 1985 national champion Oklahoma teams and won the 1996 Super Bowl with Dallas, while Jimmy Johnson coached the 1986 University of Miami national nhampions as well as the 1993 and 1994 Dallas Cowboys championship teams. Johnson's Miami Hurricanes defeated Switzer's Sooners in the 1987 Orange Bowl for Miami's national championship.

Bobby Ross, on the other hand, was twice a bridesmaid. Ross's 1990 Georgia Tech team (11–0–1) was UPI champ but was outpolled in the AP by Colorado (11–1–1), and Ross's San Diego Chargers lost Super Bowl XXIX (1995) to San Francisco.

Who was the only person to be enshrined in the **college football, pro football, and baseball halls of fame**?

Cal Hubbard was a star at Centenary College in Louisiana before going on to become a four-time All-Pro in the NFL. After his football career was over, Hubbard switched sports and was a professional baseball umpire for 16 seasons.

244

What quarterback engineered **the largest comebacks ever** in NCAA and NFL football?

Frank Reich. In the 1992 AFC playoffs, Reich replaced Bills all-time great quarterback Jim Kelly in the second half in a game against Houston, with the Bills trailing 35–3. By the final gun, the score was tied 38–38, then Buffalo won in overtime. It was an incomparable turnaround: just the week before, in the final regular season game, Houston had beaten Buffalo 27–3. Buffalo made the second half playoff comeback without quarterback Jim Kelly, running back Thurman Thomas, and linebacker Cornelius Bennett—all All-Pros that year.

In college at Maryland, Reich completed 62.9 percent of his passes for 2,097 yards and ranked among the top passers in the country as a senior. He rallied the Terrapins to a comeback 42–40 victory after being down 31 points to the Miami Hurricanes. While at Maryland, Reich roomed with another great college and pro quarterback, Boomer Esiason: they later went into business together, owning and operating a boot store.

Who holds the Division I-A record for **most interceptions in a season**?

In 1968 Washington defensive back Al Worley snagged 14 interceptions for the Huskies. Another player from the Pacific Northwest, Oregon defensive back George Shaw, holds second place with his 13 interceptions during the 1951 campaign. The all-time leader in career interceptions, though, is Illinois back Al Brosky, who nabbed 29 errant passes from 1950 to 1952.

ODDS AND ENDS

What is the **longest winning streak** in college football history?

From early 1953 until 1957, the University of Oklahoma went, 47–0. The Sooners actually went 48 games without a loss, having tied Pittsburgh 7–7 in 1953 before winning the next 47.

The streak came to an end on November 16, 1957, when Dick Lynch of Notre Dame scored with four minutes left in the game to give the Irish a 7–0 win. The loss also brought an end to an Oklahoma scoring streak of 123 consecutive games.

What was the **worst team** in college football?

Depending on how you count, there are a couple of choices. The Macalester College Scots lost 50 games in a row, from 1974 through 1980, setting an NCAA record for consecutive losses. Macalester, a small liberal arts college in St. Paul Minnesota, best known for its academic excellence, lost big during that streak. In 1977, they lost all eight of their games by a combined score of 532–39; in one game that year they were defeated 97–6. The torture finally ended on September 6, 1980, when Macalester defeated Mount Scenario College of Ladysmith, Wisconsin, 17–14.

The Northwestern Wildcats of 1976–82 went 3–65–1 and set a major-college record of 34 losses in a row. The Wildcats' worst year was 1981, when they were outscored a total of 505–82 (average game score: 46–7). Northwestern has since fielded some fine football teams, but on November 7, 1981, the Wildcats broke the existing major-college record of 29 straight losses—and the excited fans mobbed the field, tore down the goalposts, and carried them through the streets of Evansville chanting, "We are the worst. We are the worst."

As for losing streaks, Prairie View A&M lost 68 in a row between 1989 and 1996, breaking Columbia's streak of futility of having lost 44 straight between 1983 and 1988.

What is the **worst football defeat** on record?

On October 7, 1916, Tennessee's Cumberland College lost to Georgia Tech, 222–0. Cumberland had a pickup team coached by a law student. Georgia Tech, coached by John Heisman (for whom the Heisman Trophy is named), was coming off an unbeaten season. The suggestion was made that the game be called off before it started, but Cumberland stood to forfeit $3,000 in good-faith money if it withdrew, so officials decided to give it a try.

On the first play of the game, the Cumberland quarterback was knocked unconscious and carried off the field. Things went downhill from there. Georgia Tech scored on every one of its possessions, racking up 32 touchdowns—13 on interceptions, fumbles, kickoff returns, and punts. Cumberland failed to make a single first down, rushed for minus 45 yards, connected on two of 11 passes, threw four interceptions, and fumbled nine times.

At halftime, with a 63–0 lead, Heisman told his players to keep up the pressure in the second half: "You never know what those Cumberland players have up their sleeves." It's not that he was a sadist. Sportswriters at the time rated teams solely on the total points they scored, a system Heisman disagreed with. So he wanted to run up the score as much as possible to demonstrate how meaningless it was to humiliate a weaker team.

What is the **oldest active athletic conference**?

The Big 10. In 1895 the presidents of seven Midwestern universities gathered in Chicago to discuss ways to maintain better control of intercollegiate athletics. This led to the formation, in February 1896, of the Intercollegiate Conference of Faculty Representatives, known informally as the Western Conference and later the Big 10.

The charter members of the Big 10 included Illinois, Chicago, Michigan, Minnesota, Purdue, Northwestern, and Wisconsin. Indiana and Iowa were added in 1899. Michigan left the conference in 1907, then returned in 1917. Ohio State entered in 1912. Chicago dropped football in 1939 and left the conference in 1946. Michigan State was admitted in 1949. Membership remained stable until 1990, when Penn State joined, taking membership in the Big 10 to 11 schools.

Many schools play for a trophy or prize when they face off against one of their heated rivals. What are some of the **unique trophies** that are a part of college football?

The oldest of the well-known rivalry trophies is the Little Brown Jug, which goes to the winner of the Michigan-Minnesota game. The jug was first contested in 1909. Other popular trophies include the Axe (California vs. Stanford); the Beer Barrel (Tennessee vs. Kentucky); the Commander-in-Chief Trophy, which goes to the head-to-head winner of the games between the Army, Navy, and Air Force Academy; the Floyd of Rosendale trophy (Minnesota vs. Iowa); the Golden Egg (Mississippi vs. Mississippi State); the Old Oaken Bucket (Indiana vs. Purdue); the Paul Bunyan Axe (Minnesota vs. Wisconsin); the Tomahawk (Illinois vs. Wisconsin); and the Victory Bell (Southern Cal vs. UCLA).

What **college stadium** known as "The Big House" is the largest in college athletics?

Michigan Stadium, home to the Michigan Wolverines, currently seats 102,501 people and is undergoing a renovation in 1998 that will raise the capacity to 107,701. The Stadium, which was built in 1927 at a cost of $950,000 originally held 72,000 fans. The stadium holds the NCAA record for highest single—game and season attendance and has led college football in attendance for 23 consecutive seasons. The last crowd of less than 100,000 to watch a game there was on October 25, 1975 when the Wolverines defeated Indiana University 55–7.

What is *Touchdown Jesus*?

Looming over Notre Dame's home football stadium in South Bend, Indiana, is a huge painting of Jesus with his arms raised up to the heavens. The several-story-high painting, which is on the side of a building, is quite popular with Notre Dame fans, some of whom like to claim that the painting shows Jesus signaling yet another touchdown for the Fighting Irish.

What Heisman Trophy runner-up was a **regular cast member on the hit series** *Hill Street Blues*?

As a running back for Cornell, Ed Marinaro finished second to Auburn quarterback Pat Sullivan in the balloting for the 1971 Heisman Trophy. He moved on to the NFL, playing with unremarkable results for the Minnesota Vikings, New York Jets, and Seattle Seahawks. After a few years of pro ball he moved on to acting, and eventually landed the role of officer Joe Coffey in the long-running series.

What was the **worst halftime show** ever put on during a football game?

Tough call, but there are a couple good contenders. On October 28, 1967, the Columbia Marching Band engaged in some sociological analysis on a major development of the era: the birth control pill. They formed a giant calendar and played "I Got Rhythm" (dedicating the song to the Vatican), then reformed into a shotgun to the tune of "Get Me to the Church on Time."

But then on September 14, 1985, the Stanford University band (known for some outrageous halftime antics) did a "Tribute to Presidential Diseases." They began with a commemoration of the removal of a cyst from President Ronald Reagan's nose by forming a large nose with a bump on it. Then other band members formed gigantic pincers that squeezed the bump until it burst. They followed this with an even more unbelievable homage to the removal of part of Reagan's colon, spelling out the word "benign" to the tune of the song "Kick It Out."

GOLF

GENERAL

ORIGINS AND HISTORY

What are the **origins of golf**?

Golf, as we know it by today's rules, equipment, and even the 18-hole course layout, evolved over several centuries in Scotland. It has been played there since the early 1400s, and it was in Scotland where rules were first codified: the *Rules of Golf* was published in 1754 by the St. Andrews Golfers, later called the Royal & Ancient Golf Club.

Previous to the 1400s, variations of golf and field hockey had been played in many· different societies. Romans, for example, had turned their penchant for hitting things with sticks into a game called *Paganica* that involved knocking a stone toward a target. Variations on the game of field hockey (without the running) were played in the 1300s in several western European countries, including Holland, where they played a game called *kolf* with balls and clubs, and France, where they played a stick and ball game called *chole*. As trade increased between western European nations, such games spread fairly quickly.

The first recorded reference to *chole* in Flanders (Belgium) occurred in 1353, and around 1420 *chole* was introduced to a Scottish regiment aiding the French against the English at the Siege of Bauge. Hugh Kennedy, Robert Stewart and John Smale, three of the players, are credited with introducing the game of *chole* back in Scotland.

What was the **first club of golfers**?

The Honourable Company of Edinburgh Golfers was formed and began playing at Leith links in 1744.

> ### When and why was golf banned?
>
> In 1457, golf (referred to as "golfe" and "the gouf") and football were banned by the Parliament of King James II of Scotland because the games were interfering with military training for the wars against England. The ban was not seriously enforced, and in 1502, with the signing of the Treaty of Glasgow between England and Scotland, the ban on golf was lifted altogether.
>
> The banning of golf from the streets of Albany, New York, in 1659 is the first known reference to golf in America.

Where was the **first club of golfers** in the **United States**?

The South Carolina Golf Club was formed in Charleston in 1786. As early as 1743 a shipment of 96 clubs and 432 balls arrived in Charleston from the Port of Leith in Scotland.

What is the **oldest surviving golf hole** in the United States?

The first hole at The Homestead, White Sulphur Springs, West Virginia, survives from the original Oakhurst Golf Club, founded in 1884, and is, thus, the oldest golf hole in the United States.

When was golf first played at St. Andrews, and why is it referred to as **The Royal and Ancient Golf Club of St. Andrews**?

The first recorded evidence of golf being played at St. Andrews in Scotland is 1552. A license was granted by John Hamilton, Archbishop of Sanctandros, to the city's people allowing them "inter alia to play at golf, futball, schuting at all gamis with all uther manner of pastime." Since this act was a matter for record and reference is made to "the common Links where golf was played," golf was obviously played there before that date, perhaps as early as 1413, when the University of St. Andrews was founded.

In 1754, the Gentlemen of Fife invited the Gentlemen of Leith to join them in forming the St. Andrews Society, which eventually became the Royal & Ancient that developed as the governing body for the rules of golf. The Royal and Ancient Golf Club of St. Andrews was so named in 1834 with the permission of King William IV. Golf had long been called "a royal and ancient game."

When was the Ryder Cup competition established?

In 1926, an unofficial match between a group of professionals from the United States and a team made up of golfers from England and Ireland was played in Wentworth, England. British seed merchant Samuel Ryder, an avid golfer, was so impressed with the competition that he donated the Ryder Cup to be awarded to the winning side in the biennial Ryder Cup competition. The first official Ryder Cup match was played at the Worcester Country Club in Massachusetts and was won by the host U.S. team.

In 1979, the competition changed to a United States *vs.* European team format. The competition had been dominated by the U.S., but the European team won four and tied another competition while only losing twice from 1979 to 1997.

When did **stroke play** originate?

The earliest reference to stroke play is 1759, occurring at St. Andrews. Previously, all golf was match play. In match play, players or teams compete on a hole-by-hole basis rather than going by their total scores for eighteen holes. The winner in match play is determined by who has the lowest score on the most holes. In stroke play, golfers compete on the basis of who has the lowest individual score for 18 holes, or some multiple of 18 (72 holes for tournaments).

What was the first **18 hole golf course**?

The number of holes on a golf course wasn't settled as 18 until 1764. Previous to that, most courses had seven holes, and as late as 1851 Prestwick, which hosted the first 12 British Opens, was formed with only 12 holes. The Opens at Prestwick consisted of three rounds of 12 holes.

St. Andrews originally had 12 holes, then one of the original holes was abandoned. Because the land of the course was so narrow, golfers played rounds of 22 holes—11 holes going out, away from the clubhouse, then turning around and playing the same 11 in reverse order coming in. In 1764, the first four holes were combined into two, leaving nine holes and reducing the round from twenty-two holes to 18. St. Andrews thus became the first 18-hole golf course and set the standard for future courses.

The greens on six of the nine holes were later expanded to accommodate two holes, creating the famous two-hole greens (2 and 16, 3 and 15, 4 and 14, 5 and 13, 6 and 12, 7 and 11, 8 and 10) in the 18-hole layout of 1842, still in place today.

253

Was golf ever an **Olympic competition**?

Golf was played during the second modern Olympiad, held in 1900 in Paris. Margaret Abbott won the competition by shooting a 47 in the nine-hole event, becoming the first American athlete ever to win an Olympic medal.

Where was the first **miniature golf course**?

The first miniature golf course opened in 1916 in Pinehurst, North Carolina.

TOURNAMENTS

When did the **British Open** begin?

After the first British Amateur Championship was held in 1859 (and won by George Condie of Perth), The Prestwick Club hosted a Professional's Championship played at Prestwick in 1860. Contenders played for a trophy—a belt of red Morrocan leather with silver inlays, including one depicting four golfers on a green—presented by the Earl of Eglington. The first Championship Belt was won by Willie Park. In 1861, The Professional's Championship was opened to amateurs, thus becoming the first true British Open.

When was the first **U.S. Open** played?

The first U.S. Open Championship was held in 1895 on the Rocky Farm Course at the Newport (Rhode Island) Golf Club, which was founded by Theodore Havermeyer. He was President of the United States Golf Association and reportedly covered all expenses to ensure that the best golfers would compete. The first Open was scheduled for early September but was moved back to October so it wouldn't be overshadowed by the America's Cup yacht races being held out in a huge water hazard near the course.

An Open competition for professionals was held at St. Andrews Golf Club in Yonkers, New York, in 1894, and both Saint Andrews and Newport Golf Club held Amateur Open competitions that year as well. The United States Golf Association was formed late in 1894 by representatives from those two clubs as well as The Country Club (Brookline, Massachusetts), Shinnecock Hills (Southampton, New York), and the Chicago Golf Club to conduct national golf championships in the United States. The first U.S. Open was won by Horace Rawlins, who shot a 173 for the tournament, which was played in four, nine-hole rounds during one day.

What is the **Grand Slam of Golf**?

Four tournaments, collectively referred to as the Majors, form the Grand Slam of Golf: the British Open, begun in 1860 and usually held during the end of the third week of July; the U.S. Open, begun in 1895 and usually held during the end of the second week of June; the PGA Championship, begun in 1916 and usually held during the end of the second week in August; and the Masters, begun in 1934 and usually held during the end of the second week of April.

What are the tournaments that make up the **Grand Slam of Women's Golf**?

The first Women's Open was organized by the Women's Professional Golf Association, which began with efforts immediately after World War II to organize a professional women's golfing tour. The first Open was played in 1946 and consisted of qualifying rounds leading to match play competitions. Patty Berg defeated Betty Jameson, 5 and 4, to become the first Open champion. The Open switched to stroke play in 1947.

The LPGA Championship began in 1955 with a match play format: Beverly Hanson won in the final over Louise Suggs, 4 and 3. The format turned to stroke play in 1956 and delivered immediate drama, as 22-year old Marlene Hagge topped Patty Berg in a sudden death playoff.

The Colgate Dinah Shore Tournament began play in 1972 and became a major in 1983. The Peter Jackson Classic, played in Canada, was designated as a Major in 1979; it was originally called La Canadienne (1973), then the Jackson from 1974 to 1982, and became the du Maurier Ltd. Classic in 1983.

The Titleholders Tournament, which ran from 1937 to 1966, was considered a Major on the LPGA Tour. Patty Berg won the event seven times, Louis Suggs was a four-time winner, and Babe Zaharias was a three-time champion. The Western Open ran from 1937 to 1967 and was also considered a Major. Multiple winners include Patty Berg (7), Louise Suggs and Babe Zaharias (4 each), Mickey Wright (3) and Betsy Rawls (2). Considering the Titleholders and the Western Open as Majors, Babe Zaharias completed a Slam (or The Triple) in 1950, winning those two tournaments plus the Open—all the women's Majors that year.

GOLF TERMS

How did the term **caddie** originate?

Mary, Queen of Scots, generally credited as being the first woman golfer, is also credited as having been the source of the word caddie. She was raised in France and returned to Scotland at age 19. Her royal assistants, called pages in English, retained their French

Mary, Queen of Scots is said to have been the first woman golfer, and is also credited with the origin of the term "caddie."

title—cadets. Among other duties, the Cadets (pronounced ka-day in French) lugged her golf clubs.

What is the **Slope Rating** on a golf card?

The Slope Rating is one way to measure a course's difficulty. The Slope Rating is calculated by dividing the average score of "bogey golfers" by the average score of scratch players (a scratch player has a zero handicap—meaning he/she usually shoots par) over 27 holes from the back and front tees. The lowest Slope Rating is 55, and the highest is 155; a course of standard playing difficulty would have a USGA Slope Rating of 113. Examples of slope ratings on famous courses: Pinehurst #2—131/135; Pebble Beach—142/130.

What does the phrase **"up and down"** mean in golf?

"Up and down" is most commonly used to describe reaching the green and holing out, with one approach shot (up) and one putt (down). A confident golfer (often deluded) might step into a greenside bunker and say, "I can get up and down from here," meaning he thinks he can place the ball close enough to the hole to putt it in.

What is a **bogey** in golf and how did the term originate?

To bogey a hole means to play it in one over par. The term bogey comes from the Great Yarmouth Golf Club in England, where Major Charles Wellman referred to fail-

What is the Vardon grip?

Also called the overlapping grip, the Vardon grip is a way of holding the golf club so that the little finger of the right hand overlaps the space between the forefinger and middle finger on the left hand for a right-handed golfer. Six-time British Open winner Harry Vardon developed the grip around the end of the nineteenth century, when slimmer shafted clubs became widely used. The Vardon grip remains the most widely-used method for gripping golf clubs. Vardon promoted and demonstrated the grip in his book, *The Complete Golfer*, published in 1905.

ure to achieve par as "getting caught by the bogey man." Club members created an imaginary Colonel Bogey, who would always play each hole in one over par.

Why is the word **"Fore!"** used as a warning call?

Use of the word "Fore!" to warn golfers that a ball is heading their way probably derives from a phrase yelled in the British military. Artillery men called out "Beware before!" to warn the infantry ahead that a volley of cannonballs were about to be discharged at the enemy.

What are the odds of getting a **hole-in-one**?

For an amateur, the odds are generally given at about 12,600 to 1; the chances of a touring professional hitting a hole-in-one are about 3,708 to one. A hole in one is also called an ace.

The only golfer to record consecutive holes-in-one was Bob Hudson, who aced the 11th and 12th holes at the Martini International at Norwich, England, in 1971. He probably ended up buying quite a few double martinis that afternoon: tradition has it that a player who makes a hole in one should buy a round of drinks for everyone in the clubhouse when he concludes his round of golf.

What was golf's **"Shot heard 'Round the world?"**

After the fanfare of the opening of Augusta National and the playing of the first Masters Tournament in 1934, the tournament still needed to be established as a major event. Less than two dozen people were in the gallery when Gene Sarazen reached the 15th hole of the final round of the 1935 Masters. Sarazen was trailing leader Craig Wood, who was already in the clubhouse. Sarazen conferred with his caddie, Stovepipe,

What is an albatross, and what are the odds of getting one?

An albatross describes a hole completed in three strokes under par—shooting a two on a par five, for example. The more common term is a double eagle (an eagle being two under par for a hole). The odds of making an albatross have been put at 1 in 5.85 million. An amateur named John Cook did it on the 14th hole (475-yard par 5) at the Ocean Course on Hilton Head Island using a 3 Wood and an 8 Iron. That was in the morning; in the afternoon he did it again on the same hole, using a 3-Wood and a Wedge. Only one player ever scored an albatross in a U.S. Open: T. C. Chen achieved it in the opening round of the 1985 championship at Oakland Hills in Michigan. Chen had a more unfortunate rarity later in that tournament: he hit the same ball twice on one swing—a double hit, and both count—on the 5th hole of the final round, taking an 8 for the hole and losing his four-stroke lead; he finished tied for second.

One of the most famous golf strokes ever—called "the shot heard 'round the world"—was an albatross.

and the two figured that Sarazen would need a birdie four on 15, birdie two on 16, then a birdie three on either 17 or 18 for a tie. Sarazen thought he had a decent chance, until he saw his lie in the rough after his drive on 15. It was, as he says in his book, *Thirty Years of Championship Golf,* "None too good." He and his caddie huddled, again, and he decided on hitting a 4-wood, the rough lie eliminating his 3-wood from consideration. What occurred next has been called the "Shot Heard Round the World" and is considered by some as the most spectacular shot in the history of golf.

With the flag 220 yards away, Sarazen was concerned about the possible loss of yardage with the 4-wood and toed the club in to decrease loft and seek the extra distance. He tore into the shot with everything he had and the ball rose no more than 30 feet off the ground, heading straight for the flag. Sarazen began running to watch the flight and saw the ball hit the green on a perfect line. When he heard the tiny crowd explode in cheers, he knew he'd scored an albatross.

That shot wiped out the 3-stroke deficit and Sarazen played the final three holes in par to force a playoff, then took the 36-hole playoff by five strokes.

EQUIPMENT AND THE
FIELD OF PLAY

GOLF BALLS

How have **golf balls** evolved?

The first golf balls were probably small stones, later small wooden balls. Some 15th century Dutch paintings show golf being played with wooden balls, probably made of beech. Leather balls stuffed with wool or feathers were most common from the early 1600s through the mid-1800s. The leather was cut in strips and then soaked in a solution of alum. The strips were then sewn together and turned inside out, leaving a small hole through which feathers were stuffed with an awl. The feathers, usually from goose and chickens, were boiled first to soften them. After the hole was sewn up, the ball was left to dry, during which the feathers expanded and the leather shrunk, creating a hard ball.

Around 1848 the gutta-percha ball was introduced. Gutta-percha is Malaysian for "tree sap," and the balls were formed from the sap, an early form of rubber. William Montgomerie, a surgeon employed by the East India Company, had traveled to Malaya and brought back samples of gutta-percha to the Western world, and gutta-percha was soon applied to golf balls. The gutta-percha ball was cheaper than the featherie and lasted longer, but it didn't fly as well until after being scratched up. This led a St. Andrews ballmaker, Robert Forgan, to hammer in regular patterns on the ball's surface.

Two improvements occurred around 1870: golf balls were being made by machine and became more uniform, and the introduction of cork, leather, and metal fillings ground together with gutta-percha formed a more lively ball called the gutty. Many other improvements and experimentations took place through the end of the century, but the Haskell Ball of 1898 was the next major improvement. Developed in Akron, Ohio, by Coburn Haskell, a bicycle manufacturer, and Bertram Work, a rubber worker, the Haskell ball consisted of a small rubber core wound over with elastic thread and covered with gutta percha. Since then, the insides of the ball have remained the same while manufacturers have experimented with the outer covering, developing such rubber-based products as balata and Surlyn.

When did **dimples** first appear on a golf ball?

In 1880, molds were used to dimple the gutta-percha ball. Golfers had long noticed that the guttie flew much better after it had been hit several times and scuffed up. The first dimple pattern for golf balls was patented by William Taylor in England.

What is the **standard size and weight** of a golf ball?

The maximum weight is 1.62 ounces and the minimum diameter is 1.68 inches. The United States Golf Association sets the requirements for maximum weight, minimum size, spherical symmetry, initial velocity, and overall distance. Historically, American golf balls have tended to be somewhat larger that those used internationally.

Clubs and Holes

Why do golf club heads have **grooves**?

The grooves help prevent the ball from sliding up and over the face of the club on impact. The grooves hold the ball on club, helping to propel the ball forward. However, the grooves hold on only long enough to prevent slipping and sliding: a golf ball stays on the face of a driver for only .0036 seconds.

When were **wooden tees** first used, and what preceded them?

Wooden tees came into use in 1922. Previously, golfers used sand or dirt to build a small mound from which they hit their first drive. Sandboxes were common at tee areas until the tee came into use.

Courses

What are some of the different **layouts of golf courses**?

The layout, or routing, of a golf course is dictated by the course architect. The greatest course architects are almost always masters at routing the course to attain the best natural locations for holes on a piece of property. Golf courses set beside the sea and exhibiting terrain with sandy soil and odd dune shapes are called Links.

Some of the strategies for routing used by famous architects include the Heroic style, the Penal style, and the Strategic style.

What is the **Heroic style** of design?

Heroic is a term coined by renowned architect Robert Trent Jones, Sr., to describe holes where the design rewards or punishes a player for taking chances: for example, the player must decide whether to try to reach a green by hitting over a hazard or play safe and try to keep the ball in the fairway.

When did the size and depth of a golf hole become standardized?

The games that evolved into golf usually involved hitting a round object—a stone, wooden ball, or a stuffed leather ball—toward a target, usually a post. Playing the game in fields required continual trimming of grass around the pole so that the ball could be maneuvered toward it, thus you have the first greens. Holes replaced poles, and knives or other cutting implements were used to form the hole, usually by tracing around the bottom of a flowerpot. A turf cutting tool developed in the eighteenth century was designed to cut a hole 4 1/4 inches wide, and the Royal and Ancient decreed in 1894 that 4 1/4 inches shall be the uniform size of the hole, with a depth of not more than four inches.

What is the **Penal style of design**?

Penal designs force golfers to hit over hazards instead of giving them options of whether to risk hitting over a hazard or playing around it. Courses designed by Pete Dye and C. B. Macdonald best exemplify this style of design.

What is the **Strategic style of design**?

Augusta National and the Old Course at St. Andrews showcase the Strategic style of design, which provides players with various options and routes, with different rewards depending on the shot that is carried out. Miss-hit shots usually aren't as severely penalized by the Strategic style as they are by the Heroic style.

Where can the **largest green** be found?

The largest single green on any golf course is on the fifth hole of the International Golf Club in Bolton, Massachusetts. It has an area of more than 28,000 square feet, big enough for three average suburban houses and yards.

What famous course was developed on **land that had been a nursery**?

You know it's spring when the magnolias, azaleas, and dogwoods are in bloom during the annual Masters tournament in April. Augusta National was built on 365 acres of land that had been developed by a Belgian-born horticulturalist. Golfing great Bobby Jones designed the course with noted golf architect Alister Mackenzie.

261

Mackenzie died in 1934, not long after Augusta National was completed. His ashes were spread over the Pasatiempo course in Santa Cruz, California, another of his brilliantly designed courses.

RULES

When were the **rules of golf first codified**?

The Society of St. Andrews Golfers spelled out their "Thirteen Basic Rules of Golf" in 1754:

1. You must tee your ball within a club length of the hole.
2. Your tee must be on the ground.
3. You are not to change the ball which you strike off the tee.
4. You are not to remove stones, bones, or any break-club for the sake of playing your ball, except upon the fair green, and that only within a club length of your ball.
5. If your ball come among water or any watery filth, you are at liberty to take out your ball and throw it behind the hazard six yards at least; you may play it with any club, and allow your adversary a stroke for so getting out your ball.
6. If your balls be found anywhere touching one another, you are to lift the first ball until you play the last.
7. At holing you are to play your ball honestly for the hole, and not to play upon your adversary's ball, not lying in your way to the hole.
8. If you should lose your ball by its being taken up or any other way, you are to go back to the spot where you struck last and drop another ball and allow your adversary a stroke for the misfortune.
9. No man at holing his ball is to be allowed to mark his way to the hole with his club or anything else.

10. If a ball is stopped by any person, horse, dog or anything else, the ball so stopped must be played where it lies.
11. If you draw your club in order to strike and proceed so far with your stroke as to be bringing down your club, if then your club should break in any way, it is to be counted a stroke.
12. He whose ball lies farthest from the hole is obliged to play first.
13. Neither trench, ditch, nor dike made for the preservation of the links, nor the Scholar's Holes, nor the Soldier's Line shall be counted a hazard, but the ball is to be taken out, teed, and played with an iron club.

How is **par for a hole** determined?

Par is the number of strokes a good golfer can expect to make on a particular hole. Guidelines for par are based on distance:

Par 3: holes up to 250 yards for men, 210 for women.

Par 4: holes from 250 to 470 yards for men, 210 to 400 for women.

Par 5: holes over 470 for men, over 400 for women.

Instead of reporting their scores in raw numbers, golfers may say that they shot so many strokes over or under par, or they shot even par. Par didn't become part of golf parlance until the early 1900s. Until then, playing the equivalent of bogey golf was considered good. An informal system for rating holes was in effect at least as early as 1870 when a newspaper reported that Young Tom Morris' opening round in the British Open that year was achieved 2 strokes "in excess of absolutely faultless play." His 149 total in the three rounds of 12 holes format was the lowest score ever achieved with the gutty ball.

How are **handicaps** established?

A handicap is a golfer's average score over 18 holes, expressed as strokes over par (a 3 handicap golfer will usually shoot in the mid-70s, an 18 handicap golfer will shoot around 90). Handicaps allow golfers with different abilities to compete, as scores are adjusted based on a player's established handicap. A "Course Handicap" is the number of handicap strokes a player receives from a specific set of tees at the course being played.

In order to obtain a handicap, golfers must join a golf club and post their adjusted scores, which are subject to peer review; an authorized golf association may simply be a group of people who play golf together on a regular basis. They must establish a Golf Committee and follow all the requirements of the USGA Handicap System. After at least five scores have been posted, the club will issue a USGA Handicap Index to the golfer.

The formula used for determining a USGA handicap:

1. Take the best 10 of your last twenty scores.

2. Subtract the USGA Course Rating from the sum total of your 10 best scores; multiply the difference by 113 (the Slope Rating of a course of standard difficulty); then divide the resulting number by the USGA Slope Rating for the course. Round to the nearest tenth.

3. Average the differentials.

4. Multiply the average by .96.

5. Delete all numbers after the tenths digit, but do not round to the nearest tenth. This will give you your Handicap Index, but unless you establish it through the United States Golf Association procedures no one will take it seriously.

For more information, call the USGA (908)234-2300 and/or visit their web site: http://www.usga.org

What is the regulation concerning the **number of clubs a golfer may carry** in his bag?

A player is allowed to carry a maximum of 14 clubs in his bag. He can replace a damaged club during a round. The player selects among three types of clubs: Woods— broad-headed clubs used for longer shots and numbering 1 to 9; irons, numbered 1-9, have metal clubheads with faces of increasingly severe angles as the numbers increase, plus various wedges for pitching and sand play; and putters.

FAMOUS GOLFERS

Who was the **first woman golfer**?

Mary, Queen of Scots (1542–1587), is generally credited as being the first female golfer. She was reportedly seen playing golf, in fact, shortly after the death of her husband, Lord Darnley, who had been found strangled in a house blown up by gunpowder in 1567. Mary didn't have much time for golf after that: she was involved in various intrigues, eventually imprisoned, and was beheaded (but that has nothing to do with the fact that golfers are often told to keep their head down).

However, another woman golfer may have preceded her. Catherine of Aragon (1485–1536), the first wife of Henry VIII, wrote in one of her many correspondences with Thomas Cardinal Wolsey, the Archbishop of York, that the king's subjects would be happy that she would be busy with golf, "for my heart is very good to it."

Who was the **first amateur to win the U.S. Open**, and why was it so memorable?

Even though the U.S. Amateur Open was considered more prestigious than the U.S. Open Championship during the early years of the twentieth century, an amateur didn't win the U.S. Open until 1913. That win, called the "Ouimet Miracle," was accomplished by little-known Francis Ouimet, who outdueled the two greatest golfers of the day, Harry Vardon and Ted Ray, in a playoff. The win began a trend that changed golf dominance from Great Britain to the United States. When the U.S. and British Opens resumed after being canceled during World War I, Americans won 11 of the next 13 British Opens.

Ouimet grew up in Brookline, Massachusetts, just across the street from The Country Club where the 1913 U.S. Open was held. He learned golf as a young boy, frequently sneaking onto the course at The Country Club to play and also caddying there. He also played at the Franklin Park public course, but getting there involved a mile-and-a-half walk with his golf clubs, three street car changes, and another walk of a mile to the course. Only 13 at the time, he would play 54 holes there and then come home.

Ouimet won the 1909 Boston Interscholastic championship when he was 16. He failed to qualify for the U.S. Amateur for three years before finally making it in 1913, just prior to the U.S. Open. He gave eventual winner Jerry Travers a good match in the second round but finally lost, 2–3. His play was observed by Robert Watson, president of the USGA, who asked Ouimet to enter the U.S. Open at The Country Club in Brookline. Ouimet was reluctant to enter because he had already taken time off work to play in the U.S. Amateur. Enter he did, though, and his understanding boss gave him the necessary time off.

Ouimet followed up his surprise victory in the U.S. Open with a win in the 1914 U.S. Amateur. His career was disrupted when the USGA revoked his amateur status because of a business association with a sporting goods concern. The outcry over Ouimet's banishment caused the USGA to rescind the ban in 1918, and Ouimet returned to amateur competition. He reached the finals of the U.S. Amateur in 1920 and took his second victory in the 1931 U.S. Amateur. Ouimet was a member of the Walker Cup team in 1922 and played on eight Walker Cup teams between 1922 and 1934. He also served as non-playing captain of the Walker Cup team five times between 1936 and 1949. He was subsequently elected captain of the Royal & Ancient in 1951, the first American to hold the post.

Who was the first golfer to amass **$1 million in lifetime earnings**?

Arnold Palmer, who had 61 Tour victories, became in 1968 the first golfer to amass $1 million in career earnings.

Who was the **first woman golfer to amass $1 million in lifetime earnings**? Who was the first to do it in a **single year**?

Kathy Whitworth was a dominant force on the LPGA Tour from 1962, when she won her first tournament, to 1981, when she became the first woman golfer to surpass $1 million in career earnings. She won the most LPGA tournaments from 1965–68, taking 35 during that span and never fewer than eight in a season.

In 1996, Karrie Webb became the first woman to win $1 million is a single year, reflecting her great talent as a 22 year old rookie and also the tremendous growth in purses on the LPGA Tour. Webb won three tournaments and finished second in five others.

Who holds the record for **most PGA tournament wins in a year**?

Byron Nelson won 19 tournaments, including an astounding eleven in a row, during the 1945 Tour. At one point he carded 19 consecutive sub-70 stroke rounds and he had a stroke average of 68.33 per round for the season.

How many **majors** has **Greg Norman** won, and how many times has he been the runner up?

The Shark has won 2 British Opens: in the 1986 Open he won by a whopping 5 strokes, helped by a record-tying 63 in the second round, and in 1993 his British Open victory came in record-setting fashion with an all-time tournament total score of 267, including a closing-round 64.

Norman's second place finishes have been dramatic. One of his three second-place Masters finishes includes the 1987 tournament when Larry Mize chipped in a 140-foot shot on the second playoff hole. Norman had a playoff loss in the U.S. Open in 1984 and finished second again in 1985. His 64 final round in the 1989 British Open was enough to force a playoff, but Mark Calcavecchia completed a round of amazing shots in a four-hole playoff to win. In the 1986 PGA Championship, Norman lost on the final hole when Bob Tway holed a shot from a bunker, and in 1993 he lost a sudden death playoff to Paul Azinger. That's 10 Top-2 finishes for Norman in Majors, with 2 wins.

What Hall of Fame golfer had the **greatest final round comeback in U.S. Open** history?

Arnold Palmer thrilled fans with his rousing comeback in the 1960 U.S. Open.

During the first three rounds of the 1960 Open, Arnold Palmer had turned in a respectable, but not spectacular performance, 72–71–72, which left him seven strokes behind the tournament leader, Mike Souchak. Palmer started out the fourth round by driving the green on the 346-yard, Par-4 first hole; he missed the eagle putt but left himself a tap-in for birdie. On the 410-yard second, he hit another long drive, just missed the green with his pitch, but chipped in for another birdie. Palmer smashed his tee shot again on the next hole, a 348-yard dogleg left, and put a wedge shot a foot from the pin: birdie. His fourth consecutive birdie came on the 426-yard fourth hole when he sank an 18-foot putt. He settled for a par on the Par-5 fifth but came back with another birdie after a 25-foot putt on the Par-3 sixth. On the 411-yard, Par-4 seventh hole, Palmer stopped a wedge shot six feet from the stick and holed out for his sixth

Mickey Wright took 34 of her 82 career tournament victories in a three-year span (1962–1964).

> ## Who has won the most majors?
>
> Jack Nicklaus, "The Golden Bear," has the most impressive professional resume in golf history. Named "Golfer of the Century" by *Sports Illustrated*, Nicklaus has recorded 70 wins on the PGA Tour, including an astounding 18 Major wins (six Masters, four U.S. Opens, three British Opens, and five PGA Championships). Just as amazing are the 18 times he finished as runner up or tied for second in Majors (three Masters, four U.S. Opens, seven British Opens, and four PGA Championships).

birdie in seven holes. Parring the eighth and ninth, he turned in a 30 for the front nine and solidified his reputation for final-round charges, with "Arnie's Army" vigorously cheering him on. Arnie's Army was a term coined by sportswriter Johnny Hendrix to describe the swarm of fans cheering Arnold Palmer on to victory at the 1958 Masters.

Even after this spectacular front nine performance in the 1960 Open, Palmer's win was far from a done deal. At this point in the tournament, Souchak was tied for the lead and several other players had a chance to win the Open, including young Jack Nicklaus (still in college) and the legendary Ben Hogan, who were playing together two groups ahead of Palmer. Arnie arrived at the seventeenth needing pars on the last two holes to win. He played the Par-5 seventeenth conservatively, laying up short of the water with his second shot and ensuring the par. Then, although he missed the green with his second shot on the Par-4 eighteenth, his neat little chip and four-foot putt won the Open for him. Palmer's final-round 65 (30 for the front and 35 on the back) was the lowest ever score by an Open winner on the last round of the tournament.

Has anyone achieved the **Grand Slam**?

Previous to the inception of the Masters in 1934, golf's four most prestigious tournaments were the British and U.S. Opens and the British and U.S. Amateur Opens. Bobby Jones won all four events in 1930. His other legendary season was 1926, when he won the British and U.S. Opens, finished second in the U.S. Amateur, and made it to the fifth round of the British Amateur match play competition. Two men have won three majors in a given year: Lee Trevino won the PGA, British Open, and U.S. Open in 1974, and Ben Hogan took the Masters, U.S. Open, and British Open in 1953.

Who won the **most LPGA tournaments in a single year**?

Mickey Wright won 13 tournaments in 1963. Wright also won 10 events in 1962 and eleven in 1964 among her 82 tournament victories that also included four U.S. Womens Open triumphs.

What track and field gold medalist, college basketball All-American, and professional baseball player also won 32 professional golf tournaments?

Babe Didrikson Zaharias won gold medals in the javelin, high jump, and 80-meter hurdles during the 1932 Summer Olympics at Los Angeles. She also played pro baseball in a women's league and toured with an exhibition team of male players and was a basketball All-American in 1930 and 1932.

Babe didn't take golf seriously until she was in her twenties, winning the Texas Amateur in 1935. It was said she could drive the ball over 250 yards and sometimes as far as 300. She lost her amateur status in 1935 because of her professional activities in other sports and would not regain it until 1943. By then she had married wrestler George Zaharias and had tried and given up tennis. In 1946 and 1947 she is said to have won 17 consecutive golf tournaments. She took both the 1946 U.S. Amateur and the British Amateur.

Zaharias and Patty Berg reorganized the struggling Women's Professional Tour and set up eight events in 1948, three of which Zaharias won, including the U.S. Women's Open by 8 strokes. She was the leading money winner from 1948 to 1951 and was the biggest draw on the Tour. In 1953 Zaharias underwent a major operation for cancer. She made an astounding comeback in 1954, winning five events. She won her tenth and final major with her third U.S. Women's Open championship (by 12 strokes). Her cancer reappeared in 1955 and limited her schedule to eight events. She won her final two golf tournaments that year, then died of cancer in 1956 while still in the top rank of female American golfers.

In the film *Tin Cup*, Roy McAvoy loses his chance at winning the U.S. Open by repeatedly hitting his ball into the water on the final hole. What pro golfer hit five consecutive tee shots into Rae's Creek at the par-3 12th hole of Augusta National during the 1980 Masters Tournament?

Tom Weiskopf couldn't keep his tee shot on the 12th green, which slopes dramatically toward the creek, during the 1980 Masters. A fiery competitor, Weiskopf tried again, and again his shot took a dive and bath. After three more dumps, Weiskopf finally kept it on the green and putted out for a 13. It was on that same hole, usually put in around 155 yards from the tee and placed between tough bunkers in front and behind the hole, that Greg Norman found the water during the final round of the 1996 Masters, completing a swoon that saw him go from a six stroke lead over Nick Faldo at the beginning of the round to two strokes behind Faldo after the 12th hole.

At the 1998 Bay Hill Invitational tournament, John Daly hit six consecutive shots into the water on the sixth hole (par 5, 543 yards) of the final round. Daly had managed to carry the corner of a lake that runs along the left side of the nearly L-shaped fairway in the practice rounds, but couldn't do it in the final round. Daly used a driver

Jack Nicklaus, *Sports Illustrated*'s "Golfer of the Century," has won 18 Majors in his illustrious career.

on his tee shot, then moved up 30 yards after that shot found the water, then hit water five more times with a 3-wood. His sixth 3-wood shot barely cleared the water but was buried in an adjacent hazard. He took the penalty drop for stroke number 14, hit his next shot into the bunker, blasted out to the green, then two-putted for 18.

Who are the only golfers to **win the same event four years in a row**?

Only two men have pulled off the feat and one woman. The most recent is Laura Davies, who won the Standard Register Ping tournament in Phoenix, Arizona four straight years between 1994 and 1997. Prior to her quad, the only men to do the same were the legendary Walter Hagen and Gene Sarazen. Hagen's wins are even more impressive because they came in one of the four major championships when he won the PGA Championship four straight times beginning in 1924, when the PGA was a match-play tournament. Davies and Hagen both lost in their bids to win the same tournament five straight years, but Sarazen never got a chance to go for five. He won the Miami Open four straight times in the late 1920s; after his last win, the tournament was dropped from the PGA schedule.

Who is recognized as the **first golf architect**?

Old Tom Morris (1821-1908), a four-time British Open champion, ball and club manufacturer, and groundskeeper is recognized as the first golf course architect. He created the basic routings and designs of Muirfield, Prestwick, and Dornach, and he redesigned the Old Course at St. Andrews, Carnoustie, and Machirihanish—all landmarks in Scotland. Several renowned architects were mentored by Old Tom, including Donald Ross, C. B. Macdonald, Aleister Mackenzie and A. W. Tillinghast.

Who is the **youngest golfer to score a hole in one**?

The youngest acer on record was four-year-old Scott Statler, who had a hole in one on a par-three course in Greensburg, Pennsylvania, in 1962.

Who is the **oldest golfer to score a hole in one**?

99 and 3/4 year-old Otto Bucher scored a hole in one at La Manga Golf Course in Spain in January of 1985. The Swiss native was on vacation at the time.

Who was the **oldest golfer** ever to **score an ace during a Major**?

Gene Sarazen capped a brilliant career by acing the famous Postage Stamp green (the 126-yard 8th hole) at Troon during the 1973 British Open. He was 71 at the time.

Tiger Woods took the PGA by storm in his rookie year of 1996, winning two tour events and bringing younger fans to the game.

What are some of the records Tiger Woods holds?

In 1997, Tiger Woods became the first golfer to earn $2 million in a season and at age 20 the youngest golfer to win the Masters Tournament. In 1996, after having won an unprecedented three straight U.S. Amateur Championships, he won two of eight PGA Tour events and became the youngest golfer ever to earn $1 million.

In 1995, Tiger won the NCAA individual title, and in 1993 he became the first three-time U.S. Junior National Champion (having been the youngest ever Junior National Champion in 1991). There will be plenty more to come.

What club works best **on the moon**?

In 1971, Alan Shepard, an astronaut on the Apollo 14 moon mission, chose a six iron to launch a drive from the dusty surface. He claimed it went for miles and miles, but it likely landed in the Sea of Tranquility, which may or may not have led to a penalty stroke.

In technical terms, what makes **Tiger Woods** such a great golfer?

A comprehensive study of Woods and his golf-swing properties by Titleist at a testing site near New Bedford, Massachusetts, concluded that Woods generated more golf-ball speed at one of the lowest rates of golf-ball spin ever recorded—an optimum combination that reflects a near-perfect launch angle at impact. That helps explain why a man of 6 foot 2, 155 pounds, can hit a tee shot 350 yards, or reach a 500 yard green (such as the par 5 15th at Augusta), with a drive and a wedge shot.

Along with efficient method of striking the ball for long distances from the tee and the fairway, Woods is also deadly accurate with his wedges, which often follow his booming and accurate drives. Woods also has a great putting touch and superb concentration—a rare, complete package of golf skill and attention.

HOCKEY

FACE OFF

ORIGINS AND HISTORY

What are the **origins of hockey**?

Hockey has its roots in several ball and stick field sports played in the British Isles, including: shinny, an English game; hurley, an Irish game; and shinty, a Scottish game. Ice hockey's first appearance on the North American mainland is speculated to have happened in the 1870s. There is no doubt that Canada was the birthplace of hockey, although the cities of Kingston, Ontario, and Halifax, Nova Scotia, both claim to be the sites of this historic occurrence. The first organized game—replete with rules—is thought to have been coordinated in December of 1879 by J.G.A. Creighton in Montreal, Quebec, for students of McGill University. Several amateur clubs and leagues were established in Canada by the late 1880s.

From where does the word **hockey** derive?

It is generally held that the word hockey was adapted by the British in the 18th century from the French word *hoquet* (shepherd's crook) to describe a kind of stick used in shinty. The word was applied to the ice sport in 19th century Canada.

How has hockey developed **outside of North America**?

Seven European countries—Sweden, Belgium, Switzerland, Czechoslovakia, France, Russia, and Slovakia—took part in the first Olympic hockey tournament, which was held during the summer games in 1920 at Antwerp, Belgium.

What are the origins of hockey in the United States?

The first professional hockey team found a home in the United States, taking shape in 1903 in the city of Houghton, Michigan. Frank and Lester Patrick later brought professional franchises to the Pacific Northwest, including Portland, Oregon (the Rosebuds, 1914-15), and Seattle, Washington (the Metropolitans, 1915-16). The Seattle Metropolitans of the Pacific Coast Hockey Association (PCHA) defeated the Montreal Canadiens of the National Hockey Association (NHA) in 1917 to claim the Stanley Cup. The first U.S.-based NHL club still in existence is the Boston Bruins, founded in 1924. Three other U.S. clubs, the Detroit Cougars (later the Red Wings), Chicago Black Hawks, and New York Rangers, began play in 1926-27.

In Russia, the sport of hockey had its origins in a game called bandy, which was reminiscent of field hockey on ice. There were eleven players on each team, and no substitutions were permitted. The first public game of hockey took place in 1946 in an outdoor stadium in Moscow. Although the Russians wanted to compete and challenge in international tournaments, they had few resources in terms of coaches, players, and playing sites. They centralized their training system, bringing the best people associated with the sport to Moscow. This mindset was the genesis of the 16-team Soviet league. The Red Army Club, or CSKA, is recognized as the best, having won the national championship 31 times in 43 years. Other top teams are Dynamo, Spartak, and the Soviet Wings. By 1954, the Soviets were ready to take part in the World Championships, where they stunned Canada 7-2 in the final.

When did **professional hockey** begin, and what leagues predate the NHL?

The first professional team took shape in 1903 in the city of Houghton, in Michigan's Upper Peninsula. Called the Portage Lakers, the team was run by Americans, but its roster was purely Canadian. The following year saw the formation of the International Pro Hockey League (IPHL). The first Canadian-based professional team, the Sault. Ste. Marie Soos, was a member club of the IPHL. Four years later, Canada could boast of its first professional league, the Ontario Professional Hockey League (OPHL). In 1909 the Canadian Hockey Association (CHA) joined the professional ranks, housing five teams that each paid a fee of $30 to join the association. In 1910, the five-team National Hockey Association (NHA) had its genesis. One club from the National Hockey Association remains to this day: the Montreal Canadiens. It was the NHA that introduced the six-player team (previously, seven players were allowed on the ice for one team at the same time) in the 1911-1912 season. In 1911, the legendary Patrick

What was the Gondola?

The term "gondola" referred to the custom-built broadcast booth at Toronto's Maple Leaf Gardens that was 56 feet above ice level. It was reachable only via a catwalk with no railing. Canadian broadcasting legend and Hall of Famer Foster Hewitt announced from this spot. The most storied announcer for Canada's Saturday night tradition of *Hockey Night in Canada*, Hewitt served as the hockey announcer for 50 years. When the gondola was demolished to make room for luxury boxes in 1979, Hewitt is reported to have broken down in tears.

brothers—Lester and Frank—organized the Pacific Coast Hockey Association (PCHA). To attract fans, the Patricks lured big-name players away from eastern Canadian clubs.

When did the **National Hockey League** begin?

On November 22, 1917, the NHL was organized, and on November 26th, its five member clubs received charters. Those teams were the Montreal Canadiens, the Montreal Wanderers, the Ottawa Senators, the Quebec Bulldogs, and the Toronto Arenas. According to legend, the NHL was formed by the leaders of four former NHA clubs in a calculated attempt to oust Toronto Blueshirts' owner Eddie Livingstone from professional hockey. There had been such animosity between Livingstone—who was angry, in part, because the league would not allow him to run two clubs—and the other NHA owners that in 1916-17 the league had cancelled Toronto's games and reassigned its players to other clubs. Although Livingstone took legal action against the new league, he lost his court case.

Where were the early hockey **rinks**?

The first rinks were outdoors and their dimensions were much smaller than today's NHL standard of 200 by 85 feet. The ice surface was surrounded by low boards and the goals consisted of a set of stakes without netting to join them.

When did hockey move **indoors**?

Canada's Pacific Coast province of British Columbia boasted the first two indoor rinks in 1911. Built under the supervision of Frank and Lester Patrick, the arenas were located in the cities of Vancouver and Victoria. Indoor rinks were not common, however, until the 1920s.

When were the first hockey games **broadcast on radio and television**?

Starting on January 1, 1933, the games of the Toronto Maple Leafs were broadcast across Canada via radio. On March 21, 1951, the Canadian Broadcasting Company (CBC) produced the first television broadcast of a game; the contest was the Leafs versus the Montreal Canadiens. As it was a test run, only six people—those in the Maple Leafs Gardens' radio-control room—actually saw the game. Regular television coverage began during the 1951-52 season. At that time it was necessary for teams to wear contrasting white or dark uniforms when they faced off against each other for the benefit of the home viewer.

Who first uttered the famous line, **"He shoots! He scores!"**

Tha same man who made his living in the Gondola—Foster Hewitt. With a voice that was known across Canada, Hewitt first used his now-signature line during the 1933 playoffs. The Toronto Maple Leafs were facing the Boston Bruins in the Stanley Cup semifinals. The five-game series was tied 2–2 at the end of three periods. Overtime dragged on and on—five of them—with no score. Finally, in the sixth overtime, Hewitt made the call to end what was the longest game ever at that point:

"There's Eddie Shore going for the puck, in the corner beside the Boston net. Andy Blair is on for the Leafs now. He hasn't played as much as the others and seems a little fresher than some. He's moving in on Shore, in the corner.

"Shore is clearing the puck. Blair intercepts! Blair has the puck! Ken Doraty is dashing for the front of the net! Blair passes! Doraty takes it! He shoots! He scores!"

After 104 minutes and 46 seconds of overtime play, Toronto had finally won the marathon game. Unfortunately for Toronto fans, the Maple Leafs went on to lose to the New York Rangers in the Stanley Cup finals.

When did NHL teams start painting the **arena's surface white** and why is the red, or center, line **checkered**?

These two innovations became necessary for the sake of hockey's television audience. Starting in the 1949–50 season the ice surface was painted white for contrast, so that television viewers—watching on black and white television—could better follow the (black) puck. The center-ice red line was checkered to distinguish it from the blue lines that border the neutral zone.

When did the NHL become a true **"coast-to-coast"** presence in North America?

From 1942 to 1967 the league operated with only six franchises—the Montreal Canadiens, Toronto Maple Leafs, Chicago Black Hawks, Boston Bruins, Detroit Red Wings, and New York Rangers. In 1967, however, the NHL launched a dramatic expansion effort that doubled the number of teams in the league and established beachheads on the West Coast with franchises in Oakland and Los Angeles. By 1979 the league had grown to 17 teams despite the presence of the rival World Hockey Association. Later that year, the NHL took four WHA clubs under its banner, raising the total number of clubs in the league to 21 only a dozen years after first dipping its toe into the expansion pool.

RULES, STANDARDS, AND TERMS

What is **forechecking**?

Forechecking is the action of aggressively attacking the opposition in the offensive zone in an effort to cause confusion and, ultimately, turnovers so that the forechecking team is able to gain possession of the puck and thus increase their number of good scoring chances. There are a wide variety of forechecking systems from which teams can choose, ranging from the simple standard triangle, which stresses positional play and putting pressure on the opposing puck carrier, to the complex 1–2–2 "everything to the net" approach, which attempts to push all action toward the opposition's goal area.

What is a **power play**?

This is a situation in which a team gains a numerical advantage on the ice over the opposition because of a penalty that has been called on a member of the opposing team. When a penalty occurs, the offending player has to serve a period of time (two minutes for most penalties, though some infractions require longer stays) in the so-called penalty box. During the duration of the penalty, the team that still has its full complement of players out on the ice is said to be on a power play. Teams with a power play opportunity typically send their top offensive players out on the ice for the penalty, since their superior numbers (usually six players to five, or five players to four) gives them an opportunity to mount a sustained attack on the opponent's goalie in hopes of scoring a goal. If a goal is scored by the team with the extra player, then any remaining time left in a two-minute minor penalty is wiped out and the penalized team can return to "full strength."

A team that is forced to send a player to the penalty box, meanwhile, will send its best defensive players out on the ice in an effort to "kill" the penalty, i.e., prevent the other team from scoring while it has its numerical advantage. This penalty-killing unit tries to burn valuable seconds off the penalty by shooting the puck far down the ice whenever possible. This forces the team on the power play to go through the time-consuming process of bringing all of its players back to their side of the blue line and regrouping their offense. Every once in a while, a team that is "shorthanded," (has fewer players on the ice because of a penalty) will score a goal despite this disadvantage. This kind of goal is called a shorthanded goal, but unlike power play goals, it does not wipe out the remaining time on the penalty.

What is a **face-off**?

A face-off is a method of putting the puck in play. A referee or linesman drops the puck to the ice between the sticks of two opposing players, each with their back to their team's goal. Each player awaits the dropping puck with the blade of their stick on the ice surface, and when the puck is dropped, the two players attempt to gain possession of the puck for their team, either by gaining possession themselves or by passing it to a teammate. No other players are allowed inside the face-off circle or within 15 feet of the puck until the puck has been dropped.

There are nine different face-off spots that are used on the ice depending on the circumstances that led to the face-off. At the start of a game or period, and after a goal, the face-off is held at center ice. If the game is stopped by action of the attacker in his team's attacking zone, the face-off is held at the nearest face-off spot in the neutral zone. If the game is stopped as a result of action of a defender in his team's defensive zone or in the neutral zone, the face-off takes place at the point where play stopped. If the game is stopped between the end face-off spots and the end of the rink, then the face-off will take place at the nearest end face-off spot.

What is a **plus/minus** rating?

The plus/minus (also designated as the +/- rating) rating is a statistic that measures the performance of a team when an individual player is on the ice. It's regarded as a measurement of overall performance that takes into consideration elements of the game (such as checking, defense, etc.) that are hard to measure. Every time a team scores a goal, the players out on the ice for the scoring team are given a point in the plus category. Conversely, every player on the ice for the team that gave up the goal is given a point in the minus category. A player at +22, then, has been out on the ice 22 more times when his team scored than when his team was scored upon. It should be noted, however, that even top-notch players may carry a minus rating if the team on which they play isn't very good.

What restrictions does the NHL impose on the length and shape of **hockey sticks**?

According to NHL regulations, hockey sticks have to be made of wood (or some other material approved by the league's Rules Committee), although adhesive tape may be wrapped around the stick at any place for the purpose of reinforcement or to aid in improving control of the puck. Sticks can be no longer than five feet (60 inches) long from the heel to the end of the shaft, and can not run more than $12\frac{1}{2}$ inches from the heel to the end of the blade.

In addition, league rules address issues surrounding both the curvature and the width of the blade itself. As far as curvature is concerned, the rule book states that "curvature . . . shall be restricted in such a way that the distance of a perpendicular line measured from a straight line drawn from any point at the heel to the end of the blade to the point of maximum curvature shall not exceed one-half inch." Moreover, the blade of the stick can not be less than two inches or more than three inches in width.

Finally, the NHL has a separate set of rules for sticks used by goalies. There are no restrictions on curvature of goalkeeper sticks, and the blade can be as long as 15 and 1/2 inches. The maximum width of the blade of a goalie stick is 3 1/2 inches except at the heel, which has a maximum width of 4 1/2 inches. In addition, the widened portion of the goalie stick extending up the shaft from the blade may not extend more than 26 inches from the heel and may not be more than 3 1/2 inches wide. Lastly, the top of the shaft of each goalkeeper's stick must be topped with a knob of white tape or other approved protective material at least half an inch thick.

Why did the NHL eliminate **overtime periods** in 1942?

The league discovered that overtime periods were wreaking havoc on team's travel schedules, which had to follow the restrictions that were imposed across the country in the wake of America's entrance into World War II following the December 7, 1941, bombing of Pearl Harbor.

What are the **dimensions of a hockey rink**?

In the NHL, the standard rink is 200 by 85 feet. Olympic rinks may legally reach a length of 200 feet and width of 98.5 feet. The rink is enclosed by boards about four feet high. Goals are four feet high and six feet wide. The playing area is divided into three equal-sized zones, set off by the blue lines. The center red line divides the rink into halves. The five face-off circles each have a 15-foot radius.

When and why did the NHL change the rule on **minor penalties,** allowing the penalized team to return to full-strength following a power-play goal?

Up until the 1956–57 season, a penalized player had to serve his full two-minute term regardless of how many goals were scored by the opposing team. The rule was changed because the Montreal Canadiens had such a powerhouse power-play unit that they frequently scored two or more goals during a power play, with a unit that featured Hall of Famers Jean Beliveau, Maurice "Rocket" Richard, Boom Boom Geoffrion, Bert Olmsted, and Dickie Moore, among others. Three of those players finished among the top four in league scoring during the 1955-56 season, and a fourth finished seventh (Beliveau led the league in goals and points, Richard tied for second in goals and finished third in points, Olmstead led the league in assists and finished fourth in points, and Geoffrion finished fifth in goals and seventh in points).

Who is the only member of an NHL team who can't serve as **captain**?

According to rule 14d of the NHL rule book, no goaltender is allowed to be either a captain or alternate captain. This rule came into effect in the late 1940s. Bill Durnan of the Montreal Canadiens was the last goaltender to serve as a captain of his team, a position he held during the 1947–48 season.

What are some **rule changes** under consideration for the 1998–99 season and beyond by the NHL?

Suggestions have been made for adopting the college and international rule of immediately stopping play for icing once the puck crosses the red line and for discouraging

Bill Durnan was the last goalie to serve as captain.

players from using their sticks to slow, tie up, or hit at opponents. The alternative icing rule eliminates hot pursuit between a defensive and offensive player where one player might aggressively body check the other player who becomes vulnerable when reaching for the puck. The stick rule helps alleviate "clutch and grab" defensive techniques that slow action and prevents the kinds of stick checks that can result in injuries, such as the meaningless hit Mighty Ducks' star player Paul Kariya endured during the 1997–98 season that knocked him out of the Olympics and led him to miss a significant number of games.

During the spring of 1998, the minor American Hockey League tested several possible NHL rule changes in live action during certain games. Those alternative rules include: 1) having penalized players serve the entire two-minutes for minor infractions instead of having the penalty terminated if the opposing team scores in their man-advantage situation; 2) not allowing goalies to go behind the net to stop a puck shot into the offensive zone by an opposing player, which would create more possibilities for the offensive team to gain possession and scoring opportunities; 3) not allowing players in possession of the puck in their defensive zone to stop behind the net, where they pause while time ticks away and can easily avoid possession challenges by offensive players; 4) having "hurry-up face offs," which under proposed new rules means immediately conducting neutral zone face-offs after play-stoppages instead of allowing players to skate around or teams to make line changes; 5) moving the red line up two feet, which increases behind-the-net play by creating more room and thus more offensive playmaking potential.

283

UNIFORMS AND EQUIPMENT

When did **numbers and names** first make their appearance on hockey jerseys?

In 1930 it became mandatory for players to have numbers on their jerseys. It was not until the 1977–78 season, however, that the league mandated that all players must have their names on the backs of their uniforms.

Which Hall of Fame goalie popularized the **goalie mask**?

Jacques Plante, who was one of the NHL's all-time great goalies. Winner of the Vezina Trophy an incredible seven times during his career, he singlehandedly won countless games for the Montreal Canadians. By the midpoint of his career, however, one glance at his scar-marked face made it clear that he was paying dearly for those Vezinas. By the late 1950s he had accumulated 200 stitches across his face, four broken noses, two broken cheekbones, and a fractured skull.

Plante was understandably interested, then, when he heard that a contoured mask had been developed that could fit snugly against a person's face and offer protection against rocketing pucks. Before the 1958–59 season began, he approached Montreal Coach Toe Blake about wearing the mask. Plante even pointed out that the idea of a goalie wearing a mask had been tried before, when Clint Benedict donned one for the Montreal Maroons in 1929. But Blake argued that the mask would be an affront to the game's traditional trappings, and he refused to let his netminder wear it.

Plante was disappointed with Blake's stand, but he didn't press the point. Instead, he simply continued to do his usual excellent job between the pipes for the Habs. But on November 1, 1959, Plante decided once and for all that a goalie mask had become a necessary piece of equipment for him. Montreal was playing the Rangers in New York that evening. Eight minutes into the contest, Ranger sniper Andy Bathgate stroked a 25-foot sizzler that Plante never saw because he was screened by a struggling mass of players in front of the crease. The rocketing puck ripped open his cheek and nose and knocked him to the ice. Within minutes he skated off the ice and to the locker room, where seven more stitches were added to the road map of scars.

As the time approached to return to the ice, Plante turned to Blake and with iron in his voice grumbled that he was staying put unless he was allowed to wear the mask. Blake knew that this was no idle threat, and also recognized that Plante held all the cards. Back in that era of hockey, NHL teams did not carry a spare goalie. Instead, the home team was responsible for making sure that a replacement was on hand in case either goalie was injured. Some teams utilized assistant trainers to fill this role, while others recruited teenage goalies from junior teams as emergency replacements. In New York, meanwhile, the role of replacement goalie was filled by a middle-aged weekend amateur named Joe Schaefer.

Jacques Plante (right) popularized the use of the goalie mask. He also was one of the first goalies to regularly leave the crease to play the puck forward to teammates.

Blake knew that if he had to put Schaefer between the pipes, the game would turn into a rout. He had no choice but to capitulate to his star goalie. Thus was hockey history made, for Plante proved just as effective with a mask as he had always been without one. He stopped the Rangers by a 3–1 score that night, and went on to win three of his seven Vezina Trophies after adding the mask. "I had to show good results to keep the mask," he later admitted.

It's safe to say that Plante's stand saved future generations of goalies a significant amount of money in plastic surgery costs. Plante's stature made it much easier for other goalies around the league to lobby for the right to wear one as well. And as time passed the goalie mask became a basic piece of equipment for netminders. Today, it seems incredible that goalies ever played without them.

Who was the first goaltender to **wear a mask during an NHL game**?

Although Jacques Plante is credited with popularizing the facemask by proving that it did not adversely affect his play, he was actually the second goalie to don a mask when he took to the ice in one on November 1, 1959. Almost 30 years earlier, in 1930, Montreal Maroon goalie Clint Benedict wore a leather facemask during an NHL game in the hopes of protecting his broken nose from further damage.

285

What other innovation, besides popularizing the facemask, was **Jacques Plante** responsible for?

A superior skater, Plante was the first goalie to leave the goal crease as a matter of strategy. Plante often skated behind the net when an opponent shot the puck into the corners. He would trap the puck and hold it in place for his defensemen. Gradually he became more courageous, skating out of his crease to deliver passes to his teammates.

When did NHL players first begin wearing **helmets**?

In the 1959–60 season, four players donned headgear: Charlie Burns and Vic Stasiuk of Boston, Warren Godfrey of Detroit, and Camille Henry of New York. By the 1979–80 season, all players entering the NHL were required to wear helmets.

Who was the **last helmetless player** in the NHL?

Craig MacTavish entered the league before the 1979–80 season and went hatless his entire career, which ended when he retired after the 1996–97 season.

PLAYERS AND AWARDS

What are the different **NHL awards** and for whom are they named?

Unless otherwise noted, the award is voted on by hockey writers and broadcasters.

Hart Memorial Trophy: Awarded to the player "most valuable to his team." The award has been presented by the NHL since 1960 after the original Hart Trophy (donated in 1923 by Dr. David A. Hart, father of Cecil Hart, former manager-coach of the Montreal Canadiens) was retired to the Hockey Hall of Fame.

Art Ross Trophy: Awarded to the player who compiles the highest number of scoring points during the regular season. If players are tied for the lead, the trophy is awarded to the one with the most goals. If still tied, it is given to the player with the fewer number of games played. If these do not break the deadlock, the trophy is presented to the player who scored his first goal of the season at the earliest date. The trophy was presented by Art Ross, the former manager-coach of the Boston Bruins, to the NHL in 1947.

Vezina Trophy: Awarded to the goalie voted most valuable by the hockey writers and broadcasters. Until the 1981–82 season, the trophy was awarded to the goalie or goalies for the team that gave up the fewest goals during the regular season. The trophy was presented to the NHL in 1926–27 by the owners of the Montreal Canadiens in memory of Georges Vezina, former Canadien goalie.

Frank J. Selke Trophy: Awarded to the forward "who best excels in the defensive aspects of the game." The trophy was presented to the NHL in 1977 in honor of Frank J. Selke, who spent more than 60 years in the game as coach, manager and front-office executive.

James Norris Memorial Trophy: Awarded to the league's best defenseman. Presented in 1953 by the four children of the late James Norris, Sr., in memory of the former owner-president of the Detroit Red Wings.

Calder Memorial Trophy: Awarded to the league's outstanding rookie. To be eligible for the trophy, a player cannot have participated in more than 20 games in any preceding season or in six or more games in each of any two preceding seasons. From 1932–33 to 1936–37 the top rookies were named but no trophy was presented. The Calder Trophy was originated in 1937 by Frank Calder, first president of the NHL. After his death in 1943, the league presented the Calder Memorial Trophy in his memory.

Conn Smythe Trophy: Awarded to the Most Valuable Player in the Stanley Cup playoffs. Selected by vote of the NHL Governors. The trophy was presented by Maple Leaf Gardens Ltd. in 1964 to honor the former coach, manager, president and owner of the Toronto Maple Leafs.

Lady Byng Trophy: Awarded to the player combining the highest type of sportsmanship and gentlemanly conduct plus a high standard of playing ability. Lady Byng, the wife of the Governor-General of Canada in 1925, presented the trophy to the NHL during that year.

Bill Masterton Trophy: Awarded by the Professional Hockey Writers' Association to "the NHL player who exemplifies the qualities of perseverance, sportsmanship and dedication to hockey." Named for the late Minnesota North Star player.

Jack Adams Award: Awarded by the National Hockey League Broadcasters' Association to the "NHL coach adjudged to have contributed the most to his team's success." Presented in memory of the late Jack Adams, longtime coach and general manager of the Detroit Red Wings.

King Clancy Memorial Trophy: Awarded the player who best exemplifies leadership qualities on and off the ice and has made a noteworthy humanitarian contribution to his community. Awarded in honor of the Hall of Fame defenseman, referee, and coach.

Lester Patrick Trophy: Awarded for outstanding service to hockey in the United States. Eligible recipients are players, officials, coaches, executives and referees. Selected by a six-man committee consisting of the President of the NHL, an NHL Governor, a hockey writer for a U.S. national news service, a nationally syndicated sports

Bobby Orr (left, with puck), who revolutionized the defense position with his speed and scoring ability, was rated number two in the *Hockey News*' 50 Greatest Players of All Time.

columnist, an ex-player in the Hockey Hall of Fame and a sports director of a U.S. national radio-television network. Presented by the New York Rangers in 1966 to honor the memory of the long-time general manager and coach of the New York Rangers.

Lester B. Pearson Award: Presented to the NHL's outstanding player as selected by members of the NHL Players' Association. Lester B. Pearson was Prime Minister of Canada.

Who was voted to the *Hockey News*' list of the **Top 50 Hockey Players of All Time**?

As part of the *Hockey News*' 50th anniversary celebration in 1997, the periodical commissioned a panel of 50 voters—including coaches, management officials, broadcasters, former players, hockey writers, and league historians—to assemble the league's top players into an ordered list. What follows is that numerical listing and a brief description of the player's accomplishments.

1. Wayne Gretzky: The NHL's all-time scoring leader holds 62 NHL records. He has been a part of four Stanley Cup-winning teams, won the Conn Smythe Trophy twice, and has appeared in 17 All-Star games through the 1997–98 season. Several of his most notable records include scoring 50 goals in only 39 games, scoring 92 goals in a season, scoring 215 points in a season, and compiling a 51-game scoring streak.

2. Bobby Orr: Credited with reshaping the game from his defense position, Orr won the Norris Trophy eight consecutive seasons and was the first defenseman to win the Art Ross Trophy as the league's highest scorer—a feat he accomplished twice. Orr's record of 139 points for a defenseman in a season still stands.

3. Gordie Howe: Played an unmatched 33 seasons of professional hockey, including a 25-year stint with the Detroit Red Wings. Howe held the NHL record for career points (1,850) until that mark was eclipsed by Wayne Gretzky. Howe was a six-time winner of both the Hart and Art Ross trophies, and he finished in the top five in league scoring for 20 consecutive years.

4. Mario Lemieux: Scored on his first shift in his first NHL game, a sign of prodigious scoring to come. Lemieux won the Art Ross Trophy six times, the Hart Trophy three times, and the Conn Smythe Trophy twice in leading the Penguins to two Stanley Cups. During his 12 NHL seasons he returned from both back surgery and Hodgkin's disease. Lemieux retired following the 1996-97 season and was inducted into Hockey's Hall of Fame without the usual waiting period.

5. Maurice Richard: Played 18 years for the Montreal Canadiens, earning 17 NHL records before he retired. An intense competitor, he was a part of eight Stanley Cup-winning teams. Richard was the first player to score 50 goals in 50 games, a feat he accomplished in the 1944–45 season.

6. Doug Harvey: Known as a highly skilled passer, Harvey was an integral component of the Montreal Canadiens' power play. He led the league's defensemen in scoring three times, won the Norris Trophy seven times, and the Stanley Cup six times.

7. Jean Beliveau: Captain of the Montreal Canadiens for ten seasons, Beliveau also was a part of ten Stanley Cup-winning teams. He was the first-ever recipient of the Conn Smythe Trophy as playoff MVP. In addition to his athletic accomplishments, Beliveau was known as one of the classiest players in NHL history.

8. Bobby Hull: Known for blazing speed and a high-speed shot that intimidated goaltenders, Hull lead the league in goal scoring seven times. A charismatic figure, Hull helped legitimize the World Hockey Association (WHA) when he signed an unprecedented, multimillion-dollar contract with the Winnipeg Jets in 1972.

9. Terry Sawchuk: Holds the career record for victories by a goalie with 447. Sawchuck backstopped his teams to four Stanley Cups and earned 103 shutouts in 971 career games.

10. Eddie Shore: Distinguished both by his feistiness and his scoring prowess, Shore was considered the best offensive defenseman of his day. Shore was designated the league's most valuable player four times, something no other defenseman has accomplished.

11. Guy Lafleur: Part of the Montreal Canadiens team that won four consecutive Stanley Cups, Lafleur led the league in scoring three times. He was defined by his speed and grace on the ice and the fact that he was an equally talented goal scorer or playmaker.

12. Mark Messier: Deemed one of the greatest leaders in sports, Messier has captained two clubs to Stanley Cup championships and was a part of four other championship teams. He has appeared in more playoff games than any other NHL player.

13. Jacques Plante: The goalie who popularized the facemask, Plante won the Vezina Trophy seven times. His career record of 434 wins ranks second in NHL history.

14. Ray Bourque: Considered one of the most well-rounded defenseman of his era, Borque has spent his entire career with the Boston Bruins.

15. Howie Morenz: Despite having won three Stanley Cups, three Hart Trophies, and two scoring titles, Morenz has been immortalized by the circumstances surrounding his death. A month after breaking his leg in a game, Morenz died in the hospital; 40,000 people passed through the Montreal Forum to view his casket in a service on the Forum ice.

16. Glenn Hall: Hall is credited with originating the butterfly style of goaltending. A three-time winner of the Vezina, Hall battled nerves before every NHL start, yet still managed to play in 502 consecutive regular-season games.

17. Stan Mikita: Played 21 seasons with the Chicago Black Hawks, retiring as the team's record-holder for games played, assists, and points.

18. Phil Esposito: Won the Art Ross Trophy five times as the league's leading scorer. As of 1997, Espo stood as the fourth leading goal scorer of all time. In 1970–71, he scored 76 goals in 78 games.

19. Denis Potvin: In nine seasons, Potvin scored 20 or more goals and ranks second among defensemen in career scoring.

20. Mike Bossy: One of only three players to score 50 goals in 50 games and the lone player to record nine consecutive 50-goal seasons.

21. Ted Lindsay: When he retired, "Terrible" Ted held the NHL record for career penalty minutes. He was also an eight-time All-Star who was part of Detroit's famed Production Line (with Gordie Howe and Sid Abel). Lindsay spearheaded the attempt to create the first players' union.

22. Red Kelly: The first winner of the Norris Trophy, Kelly led the NHL in goals by a defenseman eight times.

23. Bobby Clarke: Captain of Philadelphia's Broad Street Bullies, Clarke led the expansion team to two Stanley Cup championships.

24. Larry Robinson: In every year of his 20-year career, Robinson and his team qualified for the playoffs. This streak is an NHL record. This high-scoring defenseman was the winner of six Stanley Cups.

25. **Ken Dryden:** Goalie Dryden won the Vezina Trophy five times and was part of six Stanley Cup-winning teams in Montreal.

26. **Frank Mahovlich:** A nine-time All-Star who won the Cup four times with the Maple Leafs; since he was traded away, Toronto has not yet recaptured the Cup. The "Big M" was part of two more championship teams in Montreal during the twilight of his career.

27. **Milt Schmidt:** Won two Stanley Cups, the Art Ross Trophy in 1940, and was part of Boston's famed "Kraut" Line. During World War II, he left the NHL to serve for three years in Canada's Royal Canadian Air Force.

28. **Paul Coffey:** A three-time Norris Trophy winner, the smooth-skating Coffey is the NHL's top-scoring defenseman of all time.

29. **Henri Richard:** Part of eleven Cup-winning teams, Richard was a great all-around player who was a steady, but not flashy or prolific, scorer.

30. **Bryan Trottier:** In his 15 years with the New York Islanders, Trottier won four Cups and emerged as the club's all-time leading scorer. He came back from retirement to win two more Cups with Pittsburgh.

31. **Dickie Moore:** With the grit of a utility player, Moore fit in effortlessly with the Canadiens' offensive stars of the 1950s and 1960s and once turned in a 96-point season. Considered by his teammates as a great team player, Moored helped the Habs to six Stanley Cup championships.

32. **Newsy Lalonde:** During an NHL career that spanned the first decade of the league's existence, Lalonde led the league in scoring five times.

33. **Syl Apps:** In a ten-year career interrupted by service in World War II, Apps captained the Maple Leafs for six years and became a nationwide star with exposure from the newfound medium of radio broadcasts.

34. **Bill Durnan:** Won the Vezina Trophy six times in a seven-year career. He was also distinguished by his ambidexterity and the fact that he was the last goaltender to serve as captain of his team.

35. **Patrick Roy:** In both the AHL and NHL, Roy led his clubs to championships in his rookie season. A four-time Vezina winner and two-time playoff MVP, Roy holds the NHL record for postseason wins by a goaltender.

36. **Charlie Conacher:** Part of the famed "Kid" Line, Conacher played for the Maple Leafs for twelve years, earning two scoring championships and one Stanley Cup.

37. **Jaromir Jagr:** The youngest player on the top-50 list, Jagr (born in 1972) has already scored more than 650 career points, won two Stanley Cups, earned an Olympic gold medal, and set an NHL record for season assists by a right winger.

Gretzky has re-written just about every page of the NHL record book. Here's a record of his records: most career goals, assists, points, scoring titles, and hat tricks; most points in a season (the top four totals and the only 200 + point seasons by an individual), most assists in a season (the top eight totals and eleven of the top 12), and most goals in a season (the top two totals).

38. Marcel Dionne: The third-leading scorer in NHL history, Dionne racked up impressive offensive statistics—including six 50-goal seasons—but never had the chance to play with a championship team.

39. Joe Malone: Played during the first seven years of the NHL's existence, and in one season averaged an unmatched 2.20 goals per game. He scored what remains an NHL record of seven goals in one game; this occurred at an outdoor rink in Quebec when the temperature was minus 20.

40. Chris Chelios: A three-time Norris winner who is considered one of the league's feistiest players and most intense competitors, Chelios has tallied at least 60 points in seven of his 14 NHL seasons.

41. Dit Clapper: The first NHLer to play 20 seasons, the Bruins' Clapper served 11 years as a forward and nine as a defenseman. He was named an All-Star at both positions.

42. Bernie Geoffrion: Credited with introducing the slap shot, "Boom Boom" Geoffrion was overshadowed by other star players on the Montreal Canadiens, yet was a prolific goal scorer and six-time Stanley Cup winner.

43. Tim Horton: In 22 NHL seasons, Horton averaged slightly more than one penalty minute per game. A dominating defenseman with offensive skill, Horton was killed in an auto accident on the way home from a game.

44. Bill Cook: A scorer with renowned toughness, Cook captained the New York Rangers for ten years and won two Stanley Cups.

45. Johnny Bucyk: Bucyk spent 21 season with the Boston Bruins and is the oldest player—at age 35—to have scored 50 goals in a season.

46. George Hainsworth: The first-ever recipient of the Vezina Trophy (and successor to the goalie for whom the award is named), Hainsworth won two Stanley Cups. He posted 94 career shutouts and finished with a career Goals-Against-Average under 2.0.

47. Gilbert Perreault: In a 17-year career with the expansion Buffalo Sabres, Perreault hit the 30-goal mark ten times.

Wayne Gretzky has turned the NHL record book into his personal resume. That could explain why his nickname is simply "The Great One."

Dave Schultz (right) gives Gary Smith the business. Schultz's rough style of play epitomized the "Broad Street Bullies" Flyer teams of the early 1970s.

48. Max Bentley: An outstanding puck handler who played with Chicago, Toronto, and New York, Bentley was a premiere finesse player and won the Art Ross Trophy twice.

49. Brad Park: A rugged defenseman who finished second in Norris Trophy voting six times (behind either Bobby Orr, Denis Potvin, or Larry Robinson—all listed above), Park led his Rangers and Bruins teams to playoff in each season of his 17-year career.

50. Jari Kurri: The Finnish winger joined an elite group when he reached the 600-goal plateau during the 1997–98 season as a member of the Colorado Avalanche. A member of five Stanley Cup-winning teams, Kurri led the league in postseason goal-scoring four times.

The NHL has been known throughout its history for the colorful **nicknames** of its players, lines, coaches, teams, etc. Some of the most unique, personal nicknames over the years include The Flower, The Rat, The Great One, The Roadrunner, The Golden Jet, The Rocket, The Hammer, and The Pocket Rocket. Who were the players to whom these monikers referred?

The Flower was the Montreal Canadiens' Guy Lafleur: it was the literal English translation of his name. The name Rat was an honest, if disparaging, nod to Ken Linesman's feisty style of play. The Great One is none other than Wayne Gretzky, the NHL's all-time leading scorer. The Roadrunner, Yvan Cournoyer, was so named because of his speed. Bobby Hull was dubbed the Golden Jet because of both his blond hair and skating speed. Due to his quick acceleration, the Montreal Canadiens' Maurice Richard was christened The Rocket by his teammates. Dave Schultz's numerous fisticuffs earned him the label of The Hammer. As a member of Philadelphia's Broad Street Bullies, Schultz led the league in penalty minutes during the 1973–74 season. The Pocket Rocket was the logical name for Henri Richard, the younger—and smaller—brother of Maurice Richard.

What NHL all-time great had his **most productive season after turning 40**?

Gordie Howe reached the 100-point plateau the only time in his NHL career during the 1968–69 season (he turned 41 as the season ended). Previous to that season Howe had scored 703 goals, 1,624 assists, and 2,327 points. In 1968–69 he tallied 44 goals and added 59 assists.

How many **NHL All-Star games** did Gordie Howe appear in?

"Mr. Hockey" appeared in an astounding 23 All-Star games. He was 51 years old when he played in his last All-Star game in 1980. The game, played at the Joe Louis Arena in Detroit featured the largest crowd ever to watch an NHL game at that time.

Who are the only NHL **goaltenders to score a goal**?

Philadelphia Flyer netminder Ron Hextall made history on December 8, 1987, when he became the first goalie to successfully shoot a puck into the opposition's net. Chris Osgood of the Detroit Red Wings joined Hextall in the record books when he scored an empty-net goal against the Hartford Whalers on March 6, 1996. Another goaltender, Billy Smith of the New York Islanders, is credited with scoring a goal, but this feat occurred on a technicality: Smith was the last Islander player to touch the puck before Colorado's Rob Ramage accidentally put the puck into his own team's net during a game on November 28, 1979.

Which player holds the record for **most points in a season by a goaltender**?

During the 1983–84 season, Edmonton Oilers' goalie Grant Fuhr tallied 14 points during the club's drive to their first ever Stanley Cup Championship.

Who was the last **goalie to serve as a team captain**?

In the long history of the NHL, only six goalies have ever served their teams as captains. The last of these netminders was Bill Durnan, who wore the big "C" for the Montreal Canadiens way back in 1947–48. Actually, it was Durnan who was primarily

295

Gordie Howe, one of hockey's all-time greats, had his most productive season after he turned 40.

> ## Who is the only NHL goalie to post a goals-against average of under 2.00 in five straight seasons?
>
> A number of legendary netminders have roamed NHL ice over the years, but Terry Sawchuk is the only goalie to manage this feat. Amazingly, he did it in his first five seasons, earning five All-Star appearances and three Vezina Trophies in the process. In 1950–51 Sawchuk posted a 1.99 goals-against average in 70 games. A year later, he lowered his GAA to 1.90, again in 70 games. He duplicated his amazing feat during the 1952–53 campaign, where he again tallied a 1.90 GAA (in 63 games). In 1953–54, Sawchuk posted a 1.94 GAA in 67 games, and in 1954–55, the Hall of Famer finished the season with a 1.96 GAA in 68 games.

responsible for ensuring that he would be the last of the "C"-wearing goalies. His tendency to leave the crease to question calls by the referee angered opponents, who increasingly argued that Durnan's skates out to the official slowed the game down and often seemed to serve as unscheduled time-outs for the Canadians. After reviewing the complaints, NHL officials were forced to agree, and the following year passed a rule that prohibited goalies from captaining teams.

What players formed the NHL's **Production Line**?

The Detroit Red Wings line of Gordie Howe, Sid Abel, and Ted Lindsay was formed on November 1, 1947, and played together through the 1951-52 campaign. The trio reigned as the highest-scoring forward unit in the NHL in the early 1950s. The name was also a reference to the city's automotive industry, which Henry Ford had revolutionized by implementing the assembly line.

What team featured the **Punch Line** and who were its members?

The Montreal Canadiens were the home team of this line, formed in the 1943-44 season, that consisted of Toe Blake, Elmer Lach, and Maurice Richard.

What team boasted the **Kid Line** and who were its members?

The Toronto Maple Leafs dubbed the forward line of 19-year-old Charlie Conacher, 23-year-old Joe Primeau, and 18-year-old Harvey "Busher" Jackson the Kid Line. Formed midway through the 1929-30 season, this trio is considered the league's first superstar unit. In the 1931–32 season, they finished first (Jackson), second (Primeau), and fourth (Conacher) in overall league scoring.

Who made up the Soviet Union's KLM Line?

This famous international unit of Vladimir Krutov, Igor Larionov, and Sergei Makarov was christened the KLM line, based upon the players' initials. After stellar international and Olympic careers, all three forwards were drafted by NHL teams. Krutov was a pick of the Vancouver Canucks; Larionov was also picked up by Vancouver in the 11th round (214th overall) of the 1985 NHL Entry Draft; and Makarov was Calgary's 14th choice (231st overall) in 1983.

What players made up the famed **"French Connection"** line?

Gilbert Perreault, Richard Martin, and Rene Robert formed the high scoring line that would help take the Buffalo Sabres to the Stanley Cup finals in 1975, a mere five years after entering the league. The Sabres have not reached the finals since.

Who was the first great **European star** in the NHL?

Borje Salming, a Swedish defenseman, was the first European-trained player to enjoy considerable success in the NHL. Starting in 1973-74, he played 17 NHL seasons, 16 with the Maple Leafs and one with the Red Wings. Salming scored 150 goals and had four seasons where he tallied more than 70 points.

Who was the first non-North American to be voted into Hockey's **Hall of Fame**?

Vladislav Tretiak, a Russian goalie and later a coach. He led the Soviet team to three gold medals in the Winter Olympics and made a lasting impression on those who watched the 1972 Canada-Russian Summit Series as well as that year's Winter Olympics in Sapporo, Japan, where he led the Soviets to the gold medal. He was not the opposing goalie when the United States team won against the Soviets in the 1980 Olympics in Lake Placid. Tretiak was drafted by the Montreal Canadiens in 1983 and received offers to coach in the NHL, but Soviet authorities would not allow him to play outside the USSR. In 1991, Tretiak became a coach for the Chicago Black Hawks.

Who was the **first European to win the Vezina Trophy** as the NHL's best goalie?

Sweden's Pelle Lindbergh of the Philadelphia Flyers won the Vezina in 1984–85 with a 3.02 goals-against average and two shutouts.

Lindbergh was killed in a car accident during the 1985–86 season.

Mario Lemieux kept Wayne Gretzky from taking all the Hart Trophies of the 1980s by winning the MVP in 1988.

Who was the **first American to win the Hart Trophy**?

Billy Burch of the Hamilton Tigers. The Yonkers, New York native scored 20 goals in 27 games in the 1924–25 season to win the second Hart Trophy ever awarded.

Who was the only player not named Gretzky to win the **Hart Trophy** as the NHL's MVP in the 1980s?

Pittsburgh's Mario Lemieux was the MVP in 1988, on the strength of his 70 goals and 98 assists in 77 games.

Who was the only player to ever **average two or more goals per game** in a single season?

Joe Malone of the Montreal Canadiens. In the 1917–18 season Malone scored 44 goals in a 20 game season. At that pace he would have scored 172 goals with today's 80 game schedule.

Who was the first player in NHL history to score **300 career goals**?

Bruising forward Nels Stewart, who played for a total of 15 years, broke the 300-goal mark in a St. Patrick's Day game against the New York Rangers in 1938. Stewart began his career with the Montreal Maroons, where he immediately proved his mettle. As a rookie, he won the 1925–26 scoring title with 42 points, won the Hart Trophy, and was the team's leading goal scorer in their playoff drive to the Stanley Cup Championship. He also led the team in penalty minutes, a direct result of his gritty style of play. An average-sized player by today's standards, Stewart was one of the game's behemoths back in the 1920s and 1930s, and he was not shy about muscling his way around the ice.

Teemu Selanne holds the rookie record for goals (76) and points (132) in a season.

After seven seasons with the Maroons, where he won another Hart Trophy as a member of the team's dangerous S Line, Stewart was traded to the Boston Bruins. The big forward put up big numbers in Boston, too, but he retired as a member of the New York Americans. Indeed, he was wearing a New York uniform when he shattered the 300-goal mark. Stewart retired on March 24, 1940, after playing his 650th game. He finished with career totals of 324 goals, 515 points, and 953 penalty minutes.

Who is the only player in NHL history to put together a **100-point season for a team with less than 20 wins** in a season?

Before the Quebec Nordiques moved on to Colorado and became the Avalanche, forward Joe Sakic spent some pretty lean years skating up in Quebec. But in two successive years he managed to score 100 points, even though his team failed to get close to 20 victories. In the 1989–90 campaign—a year that saw the Nordiques struggle to a measly 12 wins—Sakic registered 102 points. A year later, he tallied 109 points for a team that managed a mere 16 victories. Sakic was eventually rewarded for those long, hopeless nights, however, when the team moved on to Colorado and began to build a championship-caliber squad. Sakic was instrumental in guiding the team to the 1995–96 Stanley Cup. Indeed, he was awarded the Conn Smythe Trophy for his performance in the playoffs that year.

Who was the first player to score **hat tricks in consecutive periods**?

On February 7, 1976, Toronto Maple Leaf forward Darryl Sittler rang up hat tricks in both the second and third periods against the Boston Bruins to lead the Leafs to an 11–4 victory. Sittler's six goals, coupled with four assists, vaulted him to the top of the NHL's single-game scoring record books. His ten points shattered the single-game record of eight points that had been shared by Maurice "Rocket" Richard and Bert Olmstead.

Sittler's feat was particularly noteworthy because he had been in the midst of a slump when it occurred, and because he registered the ten points against a Bruin club that had lost only once in its previous 17 outings. But the Bruins had placed rookie goalie Dave Reece between the pipes that evening, and the inexperienced netminder suffered through a nightmarish evening. "It was a night when every time I had the puck something seemed to happen," recalled Sittler, who took ten shots to get his six goals. "Sure, I got some bounces, and I don't think it was one of their goalie's greatest nights."

Who is the only player to tally **five points in his very first game**?

On February 14, 1977, Al Hill scored five points for the Philadelphia Flyers in his first NHL action. A day earlier, he had been toiling for the Springfield Indians in the AHL, but as soon as he hit the ice for the Flyers he seemed intent on proving that he belonged on the big stage. His first point came only 36 seconds into the game, when he drilled a 40-foot slap shot past St. Louis Blues goalie Yves Belanger. Eleven minutes later he scored another goal on his second shot of the game, and as the game unfolded he added three assists to lead the Flyers to a 6–4 victory.

Hill's amazing feat proved to be a bittersweet one, as the magic of that first night never really returned. He managed just one more point in the next eight games, prompting the Flyers to send him back to Springfield. Hill was called back to the Flyers several more times after that, but he was never able to gain a secure spot on the team. Instead, he spent the remaining eight years of his career bouncing back and forth between the NHL (where he scored a total of 95 goals for Philly) and the minors.

Which Detroit Red Wing once responded to a pre-game **death threat** by pointing his stick up into the crowd and pretending to shoot it?

Ted Lindsay. A legendary member of Hockeytown's vaunted "Production Line," Lindsay was a fearless competitor who time and again proved a formidable foe to opponents and NHL owners alike (he was a leader in the effort to establish a players' union in the NHL). Little wonder, then, that when an anonymous caller telephoned Toronto newspapers in the middle of a Red Wings-Maple Leafs playoff series with a promise to shoot both Lindsay and fellow star Gordie Howe at Maple Leaf Garden later that night, the rugged forward shrugged it off.

News of the threat became public, and plainclothes policemen were assigned to guard the two players in the hours before game time. The atmosphere in the Red Wing locker room became tense, and when it came time to skate into the arena, Lindsay, Howe, and the other Red Wings must have felt a tremor or two of apprehension. By the third period, Detroit had fallen behind by a 4–2 score, and some observers were clucking that the threat, horrendous as it was, seemed to have had its desired effect. But Howe and Lindsay proved their mettle in the game's waning moments. Each player scored a goal in the third period to send the game into overtime. Then, less than five minutes into the extra period, Lindsay pushed the winning score in past Toronto goalie Harry Lumley. He then skated around the Toronto ice, pointing his stick up into the stands as if it were a rifle and pantomimed shooting it. Lindsay's gesture further solidified his reputation as one of hockey's all-time toughest customers.

Which player holds the NHL's all-time **highest plus/minus rating** for one season?

Boston Bruin Bobby Orr, who's almost universally regarded as the best defenseman ever to lace up skates, registered an incredible plus/minus rating of +124 during the

303

Which four-time Most Valuable Player had his nose broken an astounding 14 times during his NHL career?

Boston Bruin defenseman Eddie Shore was one of the chippiest players in the history of the NHL. A four-time MVP and seven-time member of the NHL All-Star team, he was also one of the game's more controversial figures during his 14-year career, which began in 1929. In fact, Shore's penchant for attacking opposing players sometimes got more attention than his unparalleled defensive abilities. The defenseman's unceasingly aggressive style of play took its toll over the years—he accumulated 978 stitches, five broken jaws, and a mouthful of broken teeth in addition to his 14 broken noses—but Shore played at the same feverish pitch until his retirement in 1943. Four years later, he was named to the Hockey Hall of Fame.

1970–71 season. The best rating ever put together by a forward in a season, meanwhile, was the +89 notched by Guy Lafleur for the Montreal Canadians in 1976–77.

Who holds the NHL record for **career penalty minutes**?

Dave "Tiger" Williams spent 3,966 minutes (the equivalent of 66.1 games) in the penalty box during a 14-year career with the Toronto Maple Leafs, Vancouver Canucks, Detroit Red Wings, Los Angeles Kings, and Hartford Whalers. Williams had six seasons in which he surpassed the 300 minute mark, and another three seasons in which he was over 290.

The 6-1, 190 lb. left winger also racked up 455 penalty minutes in the post-season.

Who invented the **slap shot**?

Bernie Geoffrion is credited with introducing this now-standard shot. Geoffrion's nickname, "Boom Boom," is said to have mimicked the sound of his hard shot rattling off the end boards.

What **family** boasts the most NHL players?

The Sutter family of Viking, Alberta, Canada, produced six NHL players: brothers Brian, Darryl, Duane, Brent, Rich, and Ron. The first Sutter, Brian, came to the NHL in 1976. In 1982, all six of the brothers were active players.

> ### Who are the only father and son to win the Hart Trophy as the NHL's most valuable player?
>
> **B**obby Hull won the award twice—in 1965 and 1966—as a member of the Chicago Black Hawks. His son, Brett Hull, won the award following the 1991-92 season, in which he recorded 131 points for the St. Louis Blues.

What is the largest number of **brothers playing in the same game at the same time**?

Six Sutter brothers played in the NHL at the same time. During the 1983–84 season, four played in the same game (Darryl and Brent with the Islanders, Rich and Ron with Philadelphia). Brian was born in 1956 and scored 303 goals for the St. Louis Blues, with whom he played 12 seasons; Darryl was born in 1958 and scored 161 goals during eight seasons with Chicago; Duane was born in 1960 and scored 139 goals during 11 seasons, eight with the Islanders, three with the Chicago; Brent was born in 1962 and scored 305 goals, mostly with the Islanders, with whom he played 11 seasons; twins Rich and Ron were born in 1963, and Rich scored 124 goals and played 10 seasons with four teams, while Ron scored 156 goals during a 10-year career, nine with Philadelphia, one with St. Louis.

Who are the only **father and sons to play together** in professional hockey?

Gordie Howe and his sons, Marty and Mark, all played for the World Hockey Association's Houston Aeros during the 1973–74 season.

Who was the **youngest player** in NHL history?

Armand Guidolin played for the Boston Bruins as a 16-year-old starter in 1942. He had a nine-year career.

Who was the first NHL player to become a **millionaire**?

Bobby Orr earned this distinction in the 1971–72 season.

Who was the first player to score **50 goals** in an NHL season?

Maurice "Rocket" Richard reached the 50-goal plateau in the 1944–45 season. Prior to that, no player had scored more than 45 goals in one year.

> **In a 16 year period between 1972 and 1988 only five head coaches won the Stanley Cup. Who are they?**
>
> In an era of dynasties, Scotty Bowman won five Cups with the Montreal Canadiens, Fred Shero won two with the Philadelphia Flyers, Al Arbour won four with the New York Islanders, as did Glen Sather with the Edmonton Oilers, and Jean Perron won one with the Montreal Canadiens.

THE STANLEY CUP PLAYOFFS

Who is the **Stanley Cup** named for and what are its origins?

The cherished championship trophy is the namesake of Canadian Governor General Frederick Arthur, Lord Stanley of Preston. At an 1892 banquet honoring the Ottawa Hockey Club, which was Lord Stanley' favorite team, he announced: "I have for some time been thinking it would be a good thing if there were a challenge cup which could be held from year to year by the leading hockey club in Canada." Not long after the banquet, he was called back to England, but as a parting gift, he paid $50 to have a silver bowl handcrafted in London and sent to Canada. He named the bowl the "Dominion Challenge Trophy." The trophy was first awarded in 1893 amidst a swirl of controversy. The men in charge of awarding the trophy knew that Lord Stanley would like to see his favorite team win the cup, so they arranged for the Ottawa club to travel to Toronto to meet the Osgoode Hall Team for the championship. The Ottawa club felt it should have the home-ice advantage in the game, however, and refused to play. As a result, the cup was quietly awarded to the Montreal Amateur Athletic Association Hockey Club, which had won a smaller league title. By 1910, however, professionals vied for the trophy. The Stanley Cup is the oldest trophy for which North American-based athletes compete.

How **big** is the Stanley Cup?

The Stanley Cup weighs 32 pounds and stands almost three feet (35 1/2 inches) tall.

During a 26-year span, 1962–1988, only **six different franchises won the Stanley Cup.** Who were they?

Toronto (1962–64, 1967), Montreal (1965–66, 1968–69, 1971, 1973, 1976–79), Boston (1970, 1972), Philadelphia (1974–75), New York Islanders (1980–83), Edmonton (1984–88).

The Stanley Cup. Hockey teams have been battling for the Cup since 1893.

The 1973–74 season marked the first time an **expansion team won the Stanley Cup.** What was that team?

The Philadelphia Flyers, known as the "Broad Street Bullies" for their rugged play, was the first expansion team to win the cup. Proving it was no fluke, they repeated the feat the very next season.

In 1994, the New York Rangers won the Stanley Cup for the first time in 53 years; in 1997, the Detroit Red Wings won their first Cup in 41 years; what team going into the 1998–99 season has gone **longest—37 years—without winning the Cup?**

The Chicago Black Hawks last won the Stanley Cup in 1961. Toronto is next, having last won in 1967. Of the original six expansion teams, only Pittsburgh and Philadelphia have won Cups: Los Angeles, St. Louis, and Dallas (originally Minnesota) face passing 30 years Cup-less in 1998. Although they began play in the 1990s, the San Jose Sharks' lineage includes the original expansion California Golden Seals franchise, which relocated to Cleveland, then merged with Minnesota, then began play in San Jose after being allowed to take several Minnesota players with them.

Which teams have **won and played in the most Stanley Cup finals?**

The original six have made the most appearances in the finals through 1997, led by Montreal (32 finals, 23 Cups), Toronto (21 appearances, 13 Cups), and Detroit (21 appearances, nine Cups). The Bruins have won five Cups, same as the Edmonton Oilers, the Rangers have four, same as crosstown rivals the Islanders (and also the original Ottawa Senators), and the Black Hawks have won three.

What was the **longest NHL game** ever played?

The Detroit Red Wings defeated the Montreal Maroons 1-0 on a goal by Mud Bruneteau in the sixth overtime of Game One of a 1936 semifinal series. The two teams had nearly played a tripleheader, as the goal came late in the sixth overtime— 116 minutes and 30 seconds of play after the 60 minutes of regulation time.

That game eclipsed the old record of 104:46 of overtime in a 1933 semifinal game between Toronto and Boston, which Toronto won 1–0 in the sixth OT. More recently, the third longest game occured in a 1996 first round playoff contest between Pittsburgh and Washington, which featured 79:15 of overtime before Petr Nedved tallied the winner for Pittsburgh.

What Hall of Fame defenseman **played every position** during a single Stanley Cup playoff game?

In the early days of the NHL, when a goalie drew a penalty, he had to serve it himself. That was the rule in 1923 when the Ottawa Senators faced the Edmonton Eskimoes in the final game of the Stanley Cup playoffs. When Ottawa's goalie was whistled off for a penalty, the Senators were in trouble. Injuries had already sidelined five starters, and the Senators had only dressed eight healthy skaters. Leave it to King Clancy to save the day. The star defenseman had already played center, both winger positions, and defense in the game, and he immediately volunteered to play goal during the penalty. Not only did he shut out the Eskimoes during the power play, but he nearly scored a goal himself, scooping up a loose puck in front of his own net and skating the length of the ice to take a shot that just missed. Thanks to Clancy's heroic efforts, Ottawa won the game 1–0 to clinch the Stanley Cup.

What player has been a member of the most **Stanley Cup**-winning teams?

Henri Richard of the Montreal Canadiens raised the Cup eleven times.

What player won an Olympic gold medal and the Stanley Cup in the same year?

Through the 1996–97 season, only Ken Morrow has had the double pleasure. He was a member of the U.S. "Miracle on Ice" 1980 gold medal team and then went down the road from Lake Placid to help the New York Islanders win the Cup.

Who is the only coach to win an **NCAA college hockey championship and a Stanley Cup**?

Bob Johnson won three NCAA titles with the University of Wisconsin (1977, 1981, 1983) and led the 1990–91 Pittsburgh Penguins to Lord Stanley's Cup eight months before dying of a brain hemorrhage.

Who is the youngest goalie to guide his team to a Stanley Cup?

Veteran All-Star Patrick Roy was a tender 20-year-old rookie when he minded the net for the Montreal Canadians during their 1986 championship drive. Roy won 15 of 20 playoff games for the Habs that year, posting a gaudy 1.92 goals-against average in the process. In recognition of his performance, he was awarded the Conn Symthe trophy as that year's playoff MVP.

What was the **greatest team comeback in Stanley Cup** history?

The 1942 Toronto Maple Leafs were down three games to none in the finals to Detroit before rallying back with four straight wins to take the Cup.

Which famous **coach was forced into action** during one of his team's playoff games?

In the 1928 Stanley Cup playoffs, the New York Rangers appeared to be in trouble when goalie Lorne Chabot was injured in the second period of the team's game with the Montreal Maroons. When Chabot had to leave the game, Patrick was stuck with no goaltender. Knowing that Alex Connell, talented goalie for the Ottawa Senators was at the game, Rangers' coach Lester Patrick asked the Maroons if he could use Connell as his goalie. Needless to say, the Maroons said no. "If you need a goalkeeper, why the hell doesn't Lester play?", shouted Montreal manager Eddie Gerard. Without another word, the 44-year-old Patrick did just that. During his professional career, Patrick had played goalie only once, but that didn't stop him. Somehow, Patrick made 18 saves and allowed only one goal, and the Rangers won the game in overtime. With a new goalie in place the next game, the Rangers would go on to win their first Stanley Cup.

Why do fans in Detroit toss **octopi** onto the ice during playoff games?

The tradition, which has been discouraged by the NHL by allowing referees to penalize a home team when fans interrupt a game by tossing items to the ice surface, began during a 1952 playoff game: an octopus was tossed onto the ice to symbolize the eight playoff wins needed to capture the Stanley Cup at that time.

What was **Yellow Sunday**?

The term refers to the Stanley Cup playoff game between the Boston Bruins and New

Jersey Devils on May 8, 1988, that was officiated by replacement officials—Paul McInnis, Vin Godleski, and Jim Sullivan—wearing yellow practice jerseys (instead of the normal black-and-white striped shirts). In the previous game, Devils' coach Jim Shoenefeld had insulted NHL referee Don Koharski in front of live television cameras by shouting the now-infamous phrase, "Hey Koharski, have another donut, you fat pig!" Shoenfeld was suspended by the NHL for one game, but a New Jersey judge granted an order allowing Shoenfeld to take his regular spot behind the bench. As a protest, the NHL officials scheduled to work the game refused to take the ice, and the league had to scramble to find replacements. Although delayed more than an hour, the game took place with the substitutes keeping order. After a league hearing, Schoenfeld was suspended for the fifth game of the series, and the NHL officials returned to work.

Which Toronto Maple Leaf player **scored a Stanley Cup-winning goal, only to mysteriously disappear** a few short months later?

On April 21, 1951, steady defenseman Bill Barilko scored an overtime goal to lift the Toronto Maple Leafs to a 4–1 championship series victory over the rival Montreal Canadians. His goal, which he fired past goalie Gerry McNeil from the blue line, made him a hero throughout Ontario. Unfortunately, he apparently was only able to savor his newfound celebrity for a few short months. In August 1951 he and a pilot friend vanished on a flight into northern Canada to go fishing. The two men were never heard from again, and an extensive search of their projected flight turned up no clues as to their whereabouts. Finally, 15 years after Barilko's mysterious disappearance, wreckage from a plane that was believed to be the one carrying the Maple Leaf defenseman was discovered in a remote area of northern Canada. The circumstances surrounding the crash, however, continue to be veiled in mystery.

ODDS AND ENDS

GENERAL

Which **coach** has won the most games?

With each win, Scotty Bowman adds to his lead—having passed the 1,200-win mark in 1997. Bowman has won eight Stanley Cups, five with Montreal, two with Detroit, and one with Pittsburgh. Bowman's eighth cup (his second with Detroit) ties him with his mentor Toe Blake for most Stanley Cups.

Al Arbour ranks second with 902. Bowman also has the top winning percentage.

How is one voted into hockey's Hall of Fame?

A person can be elected to the Hall of Fame in one of four categories: players, builders, referees or linesmen, and media. Players are selected by a special committee that includes former players, officials, and hockey writers. Originally a player had to wait five years before he was eligible for membership. As of the late 1990s there is a three-year waiting period that can be waived if deemed appropriate. Builders are selected by the Hall of Fame's board of directors. The media category includes writers and broadcasters; they are selected by the Professional Hockey Writers Association and the NHL Broadcasters' Association, respectively.

What are the **records** for most goals, assists, and points in one game?

Joe Malone scored seven goals for Quebec in a 1920 game against Toronto. Seven players have scored six goals in one game, the most recent being Darryl Sittler of the Maple Leafs in a 1976 game against Boston.

Seven is also the lucky number for assists in a game. It's been done four times, by Billy Taylor for Detroit in 1947 and by Wayne Gretzky of Edmonton on three occasions, 1980, 1985, and 1986.

In his six goal game, Darryl Sittler added four assists—a 10 point performance that is the most ever recorded in one game. On 12 occassions a player has recorded 8 points in a game, with Gretzky and Mario Lemieux performing the feat twice each.

What is the NHL record for **most combined goals** scored in a game?

In 1920, the Montreal Canadiens beat the Toronto St. Patrick, 14–7. The record was tied in 1985, when the Edmonton Oilers beat the Chicago Blackhawks 12–9.

Where is hockey's **Hall of Fame**?

Since 1943, Toronto, Ontario, Canada has been the home of the Hockey Hall of Fame and Museum. Originally, the Hall of Fame was in Kingston, Ontario.

Who was the first **American-born referee** to be inducted into the Hockey Hall of Fame?

In 1964 legendary referee William L. "Bill" Chadwick was elected to the Hall. A native of New York, Chadwick officiated for 16 NHL seasons and was widely regarded as the

Bill Chadwick, the first American-born referee to be inducted into the Hockey Hall of Fame.

finest ref of the 1940s. A steady penalty caller, he also introduced the use of hand signals to explain penalties such as tripping and holding.

What is the significance of **September 28, 1972**, for Canadian hockey fans?

This date marked the clinching game of the Canada-Russia "Summit Series," which included eight games in each country. It was a confrontation between a country that took immeasurable pride in originating the sport and filling NHL rosters versus a country that, in only 25 years, had gone from introducing the game to its denizens to dominating competition at the world amateur level. The professionals and amateurs proved surprisingly well matched. Going into game eight, the series was deadlocked at three wins, three losses, and one tie for each club; Canada had scored 25 goals, while the Soviets had put in 27. At least 7.5 million of Canada's 21.8 million population watched the afternoon broadcast of the series-clinching game (and another five million watched the replay). In the second period of the eighth game, the Soviets led 5-3. Canada came back to tie the game at five with less than a minute to play. And then, in a play emblazoned on the Canadian psyche, Paul Henderson scored a goal with 34 second to go to win both the game and the series. Henderson later remarked to Ken Dryden for the book *Home Game*, "I still talk about that goal 300 days a year...I mean, it's gotta die, but it's not going to die. I mean, it's just indelibly written in Canadians' hearts." In 1997, the country marked the 25th anniversary of the "Summit Series" with a Canadian postage stamp.

Who is the **first woman** to play in one of the four major sports leagues (NHL, NFL, NBA, MLB)?

Manon Rheaume. On September 23, 1992, Rheaume started in goal for the Tampa Bay Lightning in a pre-season game against the St. Louis Blues.

Has the NHL **schedule** ever been interrupted?

Yes. The members of the NHL's Player Association went on strike on April 1, 1992, threatening that year's Stanley Cup playoffs. An agreement was reached, however, and the players returned to the ice on April 12th. During the 1994–95 season owners essentially locked out the players, although the NHL's wording was that the season was delayed. Play resumed on January 19, 1995, with all clubs playing a condensed 48-game schedule featuring only intra-conference games.

Another, more positive, break in play took place when the NHL voluntarily interrupted its schedule in February of 1998 to allow its players to take part in the Olympic games. The NHL did not suspend play, however, during either world war. Although the Winter Olympics were canceled during World War II, NHL officials decided to maintain their regular schedule, regardless of the fact that many players were pressed into service for their countries.

Who is the Zamboni machine named for, and what does it do?

The Zamboni is the creation and namesake of Frank Zamboni, an ice-rink operator from California, who introduced the revolutionary vehicle in 1949. The four-wheel-drive machine resurfaces the ice by scraping it and then laying down a thin layer of water. Previously, the maintenance of the ice during the game had consisted of flooding the rink between periods. The Zamboni makes its appearance during each of the two intermissions of a typical hockey game, but because it scrapes the ice before flooding it, the resulting sheet of ice is smoother and freezes more quickly than previous methods. This innovation improved the quality of play by allowing for more speed, because the ice was less likely to turn slushy, or melt in warmer weather.

What is the origin of "**the Habs,**" the nickname of the Montreal Canadiens, and of their logo, the intertwined letters C and H?

There are several unofficial explanations for the Canadiens' nickname and logo. The nickname is generally regarded to be the shortened English pronunciation of les Habitants, the French term for "those who live there." The C and H that appear on the Montreal sweater are officially said to be initials standing for the name Club de Hockey Canadien. Other unofficial explanations are that the C and H stand for "Canadian habitants," or that the logo has its origins in a French-Catholic cursing expression— "p'tit criss d'hostie," meaning "tiny Christ of the host."

What were the names of the NHL's **division and conferences** in the 1992–93 season and why is this significant?

In 1992–93, the Prince of Wales Conference consisted of the Adams and Patrick divisions, and the Clarence Campbell Conference consisted of the Norris and Smythe divisions. The 1992–93 season was the last in which historical hockey names were used to designate groupings within the NHL. Starting in 1993–94, the NHL adopted a generic and geographical system—the Eastern and Western conferences and the Northeast, Atlantic, Central, and Pacific divisions.

Which NHL club holds the record for the **longest undefeated streak**?

From October 14, 1979, through January 6, 1980, the Philadelphia Flyers emerged with at least one point in 35 consecutive games. The team registered 25 victories during the amazing run while settling for ties on 10 other occasions. The longest home

315

and road winning streaks, meanwhile, are both owned by the Montreal Canadians. From November 1, 1976, through April 2, 1977, the Habs delighted hometown fans by flying through 34 consecutive games with either a win (28 times) or a tie (six times). A few years earlier, the club also posted the NHL's all-time longest undefeated streak on the road by playing 23 games without a loss from November 27, 1974, through March 12, 1975.

Who is the only NHL player from the league's six-team era (1942–67) to be signed to **play for all six teams**?

Bronco Horvath is the only player who managed this feat, although he only actually *played* for five of the teams. Originally signed by the Detroit Red Wings, he was traded to the New York Rangers before he actually played any games for the Wings. After a relatively brief stint with the Rangers, Horvath moved on to Montreal, Boston, Chicago, and Toronto. He ended his career just as the NHL embarked on its first expansion effort, spending his last ice time with the fledgling Minnesota North Stars in 1967–68.

Which NHL team became the first in league history to **score on two penalty shots in one game**?

The Vancouver Canucks, in a February 11, 1982, game against the Detroit Red Wings. Remarkably, both goals came in the third period. The first penalty shot goal was scored by Thomas Gradin, who was awarded the shot after Red Wing Jody Gage gloved the puck in the Detroit crease. The second penalty shot came after Canuck Stan Smyl was hauled down from behind on a breakaway. Smyl was injured on the play, so Ivan Hlinka was appointed to take the shot. Both goals were notched against goalie Gilles Gilbert.

Who were the **Broad Street Bullies**?

In the mid-1970s the Philadelphia Flyers skated to two consecutive Stanley Cup championships on the strength of a bruising, intimidating style of play fueled by stingy defense and a notable eagerness to drop the gloves. Indeed, the team lived by the motto of Coach Fred Shero, who was fond of saying, "If you can't beat 'em in the alley, you can't beat 'em on the ice."

During the 1973–74 season, the Flyers led the NHL with an amazing 1,750 penalty minutes, 600 more than the next most-penalized team. The Flyer who was most often escorted over to the penalty box was Dave "The Hammer" Schultz, whose goon-like ways earned him 348 minutes. But the Flyers also had some talented hockey players, most notably goalie Bernie Parent and center Bobby Clarke. These two were the cornerstones of the Philadelphia squad that defeated the Bruins for the Cup. A year

> ## How did a Hall of Famer's jersey and Stanley Cup ring end up going for a trip on the space shuttle *Columbia*?
>
> In the spring of 1996 Canadian astronaut Robert Thirsk, who was scheduled to serve a mission later that year on the *Columbia*, asked former Boston Bruin great Bobby Orr if he could take along a totem from his playing days. Orr had always been a childhood hero of his, and as Thirsk put it, "I finally got the nerve to call him up and ask him, out of respect, if I could fly something for him." Orr agreed to send something along, and Thirsk was thrilled when, over the course of the next few days the hockey legend sent along both a blood-spattered Bruin jersey from his playing days and his 1970 Stanley Cup ring.

later, the Flyers stuck with their ugly but winning formula to repeat as champs. Philly knocked off the Buffalo Sabres in six games to become the NHL's first repeat champions since the 1967–68 and 1968–69 Canadians.

Which two teams hold the record for **most penalties committed by both teams in one period** of a game?

On February 26, 1981, the Minnesota North Stars and the Boston Bruins combined for a mind-boggling 67 penalties in one period. The North Stars tallied 34 of the penalties, while the Bruins generously contributed 33 to the total.

Which NHL team once **bought an entire hockey league** in order to add a single player to their team?

In 1953 the Montreal Canadiens purchased the entire Quebec Senior League and the professional rights to all of its players in order to add forward Jean Beliveau to their roster. The Habs took this dramatic step because even though they held the NHL's negotiating rights to the young star, Beliveau rebuffed all of their advances. He was the highest paid player in the Quebec Senior League at the time at $20,000 a year (even though the league was classified as "amateur," its players did receive salaries) and he claimed that he would suffer financially if he moved on to the NHL ranks.

Montreal fans raised such a fuss about seeing the powerful and graceful Beliveau in a Canadiens uniform that the team's management took the unusual step of buying the entire Quebec Senior League and turning it professional. This effectively pulled the rug out from under Beliveau and forced him to sign with Montreal. Still, the Canadiens were generous with their newest addition. The club gave him a $20,000

317

Jean Beliveau was so highly-regarded by the Canadiens that they bought a whole league just to acquire his services.

bonus just for signing, and awarded him a five-year, $105,000 contract that made him the envy of players around the league.

The Canadiens' dramatic efforts to obtain Beliveau proved to be one of the club's all-time best moves over the next several years. The big center became one of the finest players of his era. Beliveau was twice named the league's Most Valuable Player, and was the highest-scoring center in NHL history (1,219 points) when he retired in 1971 after 18 seasons.

How many **nationalities** are represented in the NHL through the 1997–98 season?

Hockey players from at least 17 countries have taken part in league games. Those nations represented in the NHL include Canada, the United States, Russia, Sweden, the Czech Republic, Finland, the Ukraine, Slovakia, Germany, England, Latvia, Belarus, Northern Ireland, Poland, Scotland, South Africa, and Lithuania.

How much has it cost for teams to enter the NHL in each phase of **expansion**?

During the NHL's first expansion in 1967–68, prospective owners were charged $2 million. In each of the next four expansions—1970–71, 1972–73, 1974–75, and 1979–80—the price tag was $6 million (except for the New York Islanders, who were required to pay an extra $4 million to the New York Rangers for territorial indemnification). In 1990 the expansion fee climbed to $50 million, and those teams seeking to enter the NHL via the 1997 expansion were charged $80 million.

Which team did the Wayne Gretzky once refer to as a **"Mickey Mouse Operation?"**

The New Jersey Devils. Gretzky made the controversial comment in 1983 after his team had inflicted a 13–4 drubbing on the hapless Devils. While creating controversy, Gretzky's words had unexpectedly done the troubled franchise a favor. The next time the teams played, the Byrne Arena was a sea of mouse ears and chanting fans. While not inspiring the team to change it's losing ways, his words did help at the box office as fans began to come out in larger numbers to see the home team.

Which International Hockey League coach was **suspended for attacking an opposing team's mascot**?

On February 4, 1995, Cincinnati Cyclones Head Coach Paul Jackson attacked Sir Slap Shot, the mascot of the Atlanta Knights, after the mascot knocked Jackson into his players by slamming the glass partition against which the coach had been leaning. An enraged Jackson responded by climbing over the partition and battering Sir Slap Shot,

319

to the amazement of watching fans. Needless to say, this sort of behavior did not go over too well with the IHL front office. Jackson was suspended for ten games and fined $1,000. But in recognition of Sir Slap Shot's role in triggering the whole ugly incident, the league also fined Atlanta $1,000 for their mascot's conduct.

WORLD HOCKEY ASSOCIATION (WHA)

What was the **World Hockey Association**?

The WHA was a rival professional league to the NHL from 1972–79. Four teams—the Edmonton Oilers, Hartford Whalers (later moved to Carolina), Quebec Nordiques (later moved to Colorado), and Winnipeg Jets (later moved to Phoenix)—merged with the NHL after the WHA folded. Bobby Hull was the first great player to change leagues. Gordie Howe played in the league for six seasons, including stints with his sons, Marty and Mark. Wayne Gretzky and Mark Messier are among the NHL greats whose careers started in the WHA.

The Stanley Cup is well known as the NHL's championship trophy. What was the name of the **trophy awarded to the WHA's championship team** and who was the first team to win the trophy?

The Avco Cup, sponsored by Avco Financial Services was won by the New England Whalers in the WHA's inaugural season (1972–73).

Which player won the World Hockey Association's first **scoring title**?

Center Andre Lacroix of the Philadelphia Blazers led the way with 124 points on 50 goals and 74 assists. Two years later—after finishing second to Mike Walton during the 1973–74 season—Lacroix took the scoring crown once more with 147 points (41 goals and 106 assists). Between the pipes, meanwhile, Cleveland's Gerry Cheevers set the league standard with a league-low 2.83 goals against average during the WHA's inaugural season.

What **exhibition series** lent credence to the WHA's long-standing contention that their teams were comparable to those fielded by the NHL?

Prior to the 1976–77 season, the owners of the WHA and NHL agreed to a 21–game exhibition series that would in effect serve as the preseason for both leagues. The decision was a popular one among fans, for while the games would technically not mean

> ## Which WHA team selected Soviet Premier Alexei Kosygin with one of its 1972 draft choices?
>
> When the 12 WHA teams got together for their first draft in 1972, the teams selected a combined 1,081 persons. But while a number of the selections raised eyebrows among fellow WHA officials or observers over in the established NHL, surely the strangest was the playful decision by Scotty Munro of the Calgary Broncos to pick Kosygin.

anything, the rivalry between the two leagues made it likely that the atmosphere during the contests would be a little more lively than what one usually found at a pre-season contest. Certainly the WHA teams took the series seriously, for when it was all over and the dust had settled, the WHA had posted a 13–6–2 record against their NHL foes.

COLLEGE HOCKEY

When did hockey make its **first college appearance** in the United States?

While there is speculation that hockey may have been imported and played as early as 1882 in the Northeast, there is more verifiable evidence that points to 1893 as the year hockey first arrived on at least two college campuses in the United States. In that year, a student who had come to study at Johns Hopkins University from Canada invited a Quebec team to square off against a hockey team of his fellow students. Coincidentally, that same year two Yale tennis players, Arthur Foote and Malcolm Chace, introduced hockey to their school after encountering it while playing in a Canadian tennis tournament. These two events are looked at as not only the first arrival of hockey on college grounds, but also the meager beginnings of hockey in the United States.

In what year did the **first NCAA Men's Hockey Tournament** take place?

The first NCAA Hockey Tournament took place in Colorado Springs back in 1948. While forward Joe Riley of Dartmouth won the award for most outstanding player in the tournament, his Dartmouth team was no match for the University of Michigan. The final match that year saw legendary coach Vic Heylinger lead his Wolverines to an 8–4 romp over Dartmouth. Not only did the wild, high-scoring affair give the Wolverines the distinction of being the first national collegiate hockey champions, but it also saw them score two consecutive goals in just five seconds—a record that has yet to be matched or broken in the over fifty years since the inaugural tournament was played.

321

What are the Pairwise Rankings (PWR)?

At the conclusion of the regular season, the NCAA uses the Pairwise Rankings (PWR) as a statistical tool to determine which Division I teams should be invited to the championship tournament. In order to do this, the PWR method compares every team with a .500 record or better against every other team that meets that qualification. A team is then awarded one point each time it is deemed superior to another on the combined basis of Ratings Percentage Index (RPI), win-loss record over the last 20 games, overall record against other eligible teams, record against common opponents, and victories when competing head-to-head. The higher a team's point total, the higher they will be seeded in the tournament. The lower the total, the better the chance they'll be watching the tournament on television.

What are the major **awards given to college players**?

The Hobey Baker Award has been given annually since 1981 to honor the outstanding college hockey player of the year. Hobey Baker was a Princeton hockey and football star killed in World War I. A Most Outstanding Player award is given annually for each NCAA tournament.

Who was **Spencer T. Penrose**?

Spencer T. Penrose was a wealthy businessman who built one of college hockey's most historic arenas. Penrose made his fortune with gold and copper mines in the early part of the 1900s. After traveling the globe for a period of time with his wife Julie, Spencer returned to Colorado Springs and founded the Broadmoor Resort and Broadmoor World Arena. Although renowned for its opulence, the Broadmoor offered something even more important to the NCAA—a world-class venue for its fledgling hockey tournament. For the first ten years, from 1948 to 1958, the Broadmoor World Arena was the only site to host the NCAA Championships. Today, the American Hockey Coaches Association commemorates Penrose's invaluable support and contributions to collegiate hockey by presenting the Spencer T. Penrose Award to the year's top college hockey coach.

Boston University has a student population nearly ten times that of Lake Superior State University. Why do they both play **Division I** hockey?

When it comes to evaluating what separates a Division I school from a Division II or III school, the NCAA criteria for hockey tries to account for more than overall student population or school size. Due possibly to the fact that sports like college hockey have historically been non-revenue generating, not all schools have emphasized their hockey programs equally. For this reason, the NCAA also weighs the playing level and hockey affiliation of a school to determine what division they should play in. That's why there are over a dozen schools playing Division I hockey that are institutionally considered to be Division II or III schools. Conversely, six Division I-sized schools are currently playing hockey at the Division II or III level.

I thought my favorite college team would play in the Big Ten Conference, but instead they're in something called the **Central Collegiate Hockey Association**. How can that be?

There are four different collegiate conferences that play Division I hockey. As confusing as it may seem, teams in any given conference are often brought together more by their team's level of play than by any geographical proximity to one another.

The Central Collegiate Hockey Association (CCHA) is made up of teams from the University of Michigan, Miami (of Ohio) University, Michigan State, Lake Superior State, Bowling Green, Western Michigan, Ohio State, Alaska-Fairbanks, Ferris State, and Notre Dame.

The Western Collegiate Hockey Association (WCHA) is comprised of North Dakota, Minnesota, St. Cloud, Colorado College, Denver, Minnesota-Duluth, Wisconsin, Northern Michigan, Alaska-Anchorage, and Michigan Tech.

The Hockey East conference teams are Boston University, New Hampshire, University of Maine, Providence, Merrimack, Boston College, University of Massachusetts-Lowell, University of Massachusetts-Amherst, and Northeastern.

The Eastern College Athletic Conference (ECAC) consists of Clarkson University, Cornell, Vermont, Rensselaer, Princeton, Union College, Colgate, Harvard, St. Lawrence, Yale, and Dartmouth. In addition to these four conferences, ten independent schools also play Division I hockey.

What are the various categories of **penalties** that are called in NCAA hockey?

Hockey penalties can be arranged in several different categories, depending on their severity. The most common penalties are called *minor penalties*. These penalties, which are two minutes in length, are given out for the following infractions:

Unsportsmanlike conduct

Excessive violence (roughing)

Cross-checking (holding the stick in both hands off the ice and blocking an opponent's movement with a hit)

Slashing (hitting or attempting to hit an opponent with a stick)

323

Obstruction

Body-checking (illegal use of the body to block an opponent's movement)

Delay of game

Falling on the puck (goalies are not subject to this rule)

Interference with an opponent not in possession of the puck

Hooking (using the blade end of the stick to interfere with an opponent)

Use of illegal equipment (such as a stick with excessive curvature of the blade)

Extra player on the ice

Displacing the goal cage

Holding

Keeping stick away from opponent

Deliberately firing the puck out of the rink

Spraying the goalkeeper

All bench minor penalties also count as minor penalties.

Major penalties, meanwhile, are five minutes in length. Some violations may be categorized as minor or major, depending on the severity of the infraction. These violations include: board checking, cross-checking, charging, elbowing, hitting from behind, fouling the goalie, kneeing, charging, slashing, and high-sticking. In addition, the following violations are always categorized as major penalties:

Hooking (if injury results)

Grabbing an opponent's face mask

Head butting

Refusal to start play

Misconduct penalties are 10 minutes in length, and may be called for the following infractions:

Abuse of officials

Equipment violations

Player interference with official or penalty shot

Shooting a puck after the whistle has blown

Intentionally breaking a stick

Deliberate illegal substitution

Obscene gestures

Use of ethnic or racial slurs

A *game misconduct* penalty calls for the suspension of a player for the remainder of the game, but a substitute is permitted to replace the player immediately. Infractions that will result in a game misconduct include:

Further disrespect of officials

A third equipment violation

Interference with spectators

Abusive language, acts of disrespect, or other willful violations by coaches and/or nonplaying persons

Disqualification is the most serious penalty that can be called. When this is called, the player in question is suspended for the balance of the game and hit with a major penalty. In NCAA hockey, the ramifications of a disqualifications are particularly great because they extend beyond the game in which the penalized actions took place. A player who receives a disqualification not only is forbidden from playing in the game in which the action took place, but also is disqualified from playing in his team's next game. This disqualification rule is progressive, meaning that a player who is repeatedly disqualified will receive progressively longer suspensions. Moreover, game-disqualification penalties carry over to the next season if the player still has remaining eligibility.

Penalties that are punishable by disqualification include the following:

Spearing or butt-ending (pushing the top of the stick into an opponent)

Altercation off the ice surface

Any attempt to injure an opponent

Continued abuse of officials

Fighting

Causing an injury by high-sticking

Kicking

Leaving the bench during an altercation

Swinging a stick during an altercation

Physical or verbally abusing an official at the end of a contest

Fans of professional hockey will no doubt have noticed that the penalties for infractions committed in NCAA action sometimes vary considerably from those meted out for similar behavior in the NHL. The most obvious difference lies in how the two organizations approach fighting. In the NCAA, the penalties for fighting are so severe that altercations are exceedingly rare, although detractors sometimes claim that the restrictions on fighting encourage excessive stickwork by some players. In the NHL, meanwhile, fighting is relatively commonplace—especially during the regular season—since the penalties imposed are pretty modest.

Which team has claimed the most **NCAA Division I championships**?

The Michigan Wolverines won the first Division I hockey championship back in 1948, and they haven't looked back since. In the 50 years since that first title, the Wolverines have added eight more championships, in 1951, 1952, 1953, 1955, 1956, 1964, 1996, and 1998, giving them a total of nine. They're followed by North Dakota (six), Denver and Wisconsin (five), and Boston University (four). Lake Superior State, Michigan Tech and Minnesota have won three times, Colorado College, Cornell, Michigan State, and Renneslaer Polytechnic Intsitute each took the title twice.

In 1973, who did the **University of Wisconsin** hockey team have to defeat in the NCAA Finals to become the champions?

Nobody. Bob Johnson had coached Wisconsin team to an impressive 29–9–2 record with one game left to go for the championship. Unfortunately, the title game that was supposed to take place in Boston Garden between Wisconsin and Denver never came about. The NCAA Committee disqualified Denver from the tournament, citing rule infractions, and made them vacate their position. Wisconsin forward Dean Talafous was named the tournament's most outstanding player, Wisconsin became the national champions, and, for the first and only time in the NCAA's 50-year tournament history, no final match was played to determine the overall winner.

Which famous hockey player was sent to the **penalty box** only once in his entire collegiate career?

Hobart "Hobey" Baker, who captained Princeton's hockey and football teams from 1911 to 1914. Baker, considered by many of his contemporaries to be the most talented hockey player to ever lace up skates, is a celebrated figure not only for his physical prowess but also his good sportsmanship. In addition to only paying one career visit to the penalty box, the standout athlete always made a point of visiting the opposition team's locker room after a game. He was a charter member of the United States Hockey Hall of Fame and is one of the few Americans to be inducted into the Canadian Hockey Hall of Fame.

Who is the **winningest coach** in college hockey history?

Ron Mason of Michigan State University holds the record of most wins by a collegiate hockey coach. On March 12, 1993, Mason surpassed former Boston College coach Len Ceglarski's mark of 673 career coaching victories when the Spartans beat Kent by a score of 6–5 in the first round of the CCHA tournament. Still an active coach, Mason's number of total victories stood at 806 at the end of the 1997–98 season.

Mason began coaching college hockey back in 1966, when he was appointed the first head coach of Lake Superior State. In 1973, he moved to Bowling Green State

> ## Why did the Great West Hockey Conference last for only three seasons?
>
> If you consider the geographical location of the four schools that made up this conference from 1985 through 1988, you may wonder how they even lasted that long. Comprised of the only independent hockey teams west of the Mississippi (except for Air Force), the Great West Hockey Conference (GWHC) had four teams—Northern Arizona, U.S. International (located in San Diego), Alaska-Fairbanks, and Alaska-Anchorage. Due in large part to difficulties in scheduling games with other opponents—as well as the expense of flying the team to every away game—Northern Arizona left the GWHC at the end of the first season, dropping their varsity hockey program altogether. U.S. International followed Northern Arizona's lead two seasons later. With only two teams left, the GWHC folded.

University, and then, in 1979, joined the Michigan State Spartans. In addition to his career win mark, Mason has won an NCAA title (with Michigan State in 1986), an NAIA championship (with Lake Superior State in 1972), and has led 18 teams to the NCAA tournament.

What was the **longest game** in the history of Division I college hockey?

While the Colorado College men's hockey team did battle through four overtime periods before beating Wisconsin 1–0 on March 8, 1997, the distinction of the longest Division I game ever played belongs to a showdown of two women's collegiate hockey teams that took place a year earlier. It happened at the ECAC Women's Championship Game in Durham, New Hampshire, on March 10, 1996. New Hampshire and Providence had ended regulation deadlocked at two goals per side when the 20-minute overtime periods started. They played four of them when, deep into the fifth overtime period, Brandy Fisher scored the game winner for New Hampshire. Total time of play: 145 minutes and 35 seconds.

What did **Raymond C. Chaisson** do that helped give him a spot in the United States Hockey Hall of Fame?

Let's just say that during his junior and senior years he had the mother of all hot streaks. Over the course of 1939 and 1940, Raymond Chaisson averaged just under two goals a game for Boston College, scoring 62 goals in just 32 games, and racking up a whopping eight hat tricks! Thanks to these impressive numbers, he was among the first collegiate players to be honored with induction into the United States Hockey Hall of Fame.

Who is Terry Flanagan?

Terry Flanagan was an assistant coach for 11 seasons at Bowling Green, beginning in 1981. Serving as a full-time assistant coach, a graduate assistant, and a devoted family man, Flanagan helped lead the Falcons to six visits to the NCAA Tournament with one NCAA Championship crown in 1984, four CCHA regular-season championships, nine trips to the CCHA playoffs and one CCHA playoff title. On top of his already generous committment of time, Flanagan was known for spending additional hours after practice helping players further develop their talents.

In recognition of Flanagan's accomplishments and perseverance on and off the ice, the Terry Flanagan Memorial Award is awarded annually by the CCHA to a player who has overcome personal adversity to achieve success on and off the ice. Past winners include Wes McCauley of Michigan State (1992–93), Chuck Thuss of Miami (1994–95), and Bryan Adams of Michigan State (1997–98).

Why was there **no league play** during the 1958–59 season in the Midwest Collegiate Hockey League?

The Midwest Collegiate Hockey League originated as the Midwest College Hockey League in 1951. During the 1950s, the league won every NCAA championship except for 1954, but it disbanded in 1958 because of a dispute over the recruiting practices of some of its members. At the time, the MCHL was comprised of Colorado College, Denver, North Dakota, Minnesota, Michigan, Michigan State, and Michigan Tech. The Michigan and Minnesota schools accused the western members of recruiting over-age Canadians. Although the practice was not in violation of any MCHL or NCAA rules, the schools felt it was not in the spirit of the league. Eventually, Michigan, Michigan State, Minnesota, and Michigan Tech withdrew from the league over the dispute. The following year, the Western Collegiate Hockey Association was founded on more informal grounds: schools were allowed to schedule games with whomever they wanted. The wounds caused by the schism took a number of years to heal. Denver and Minnesota, for instance, refused to play one another until more than ten years after the 1958 split.

Who are some of the **great NCAA players** of all time?

During the 50th NCAA Tournament in 1997, the NCAA unveiled its All-Time Tournament team—21 players elected by a group of current Division I coaches, past coaches who participated in the NCAA Tournament, and members of the Division I Hockey Committee. Players named had to have participated in at least one tournament. The team included the following players with their university and year(s) in the tournament in parentheses:

Forwards

Tony Amonte (Boston University, 1981, 1983)
Lou Angotti (Michigan Tech, 1960, 1962)
Red Berenson (Michigan, 1962)
Bill Cleary (Harvard, 1955)
Tony Hrkac (North Dakota, 1987)
Paul Kariya (Maine, 1993)
Bill Masterson (Denver 1960–61)
John Matchetts (Michigan, 1951, 1953)
John Mayasich (Minnesota, 1954–54)
Jim Montgomery (Maine, 1990–93)
Tom Rendall (Michigan, 1955–57)
Phil Sykes (North Dakota, 1979–80, 1982)

Defensemen

Chris Chelios (Wisconsin, 1982–83)
Bruce Driver (Wisconsin (1981–83)
George Konik (Denver 1960–61)
Don Lodboa (Cornell, 1970)
Keith Magnuson (Denver, 1968–69)
Jack O'Callahan (Boston University, 1976–78)

Goalies

Marc Behrend (Wisconsin, 1981, 1983)
Ken Dryden (Cornell, 1967–69)
Chris Terreri (Providence, 1983, 1985)

When was the first national **collegiate championship for women's hockey** held?

The first national women's hockey championship—called The American Women's College Hockey Alliance National Championship—was held in Boston on March 21, 1998. In the final game, the New Hampshire Wildcats beat Brown by a score of 4–1 after falling behind early in the contest. The championship was seen as an important step in drawing attention to the women's game. Women's collegiate hockey requires the creation of another ten varsity teams to meet the NCAA requirement of 40 for it to stage its own national tournament. New Hampshire player Brandy Fisher won the Patty Kazmaier Memorial Award as the nation's best player, while her teammate Winny Brodt was awarded the tournament's Most Valuable Player.

HORSE
RACING

AND THEY'RE OFF!

What does it mean to win "hands down"?

The term originated in horse racing and means to win without using the whip. To win hands down has since been used more generally to refer to a win without significant challenges from competitiors.

What is pari-mutuel betting?

The type of gambling typically allowed at horse racing tracks takes its name from French terms meaning "mutual wager." All the money that's bet on a race is combined into one large pool of funds. The odds, or likelihood of winning, for each horse are determined by the relative amounts wagered on each horse. The horse on which the most money is wagered is called the favorite, and those on which the least amount is wagered are called long shots. After the race has been run, the money in the pool is divided among the people who bet on the top three finishers. Of course, a certain percentage is subtracted first to pay track expenses, purses to the winning horses, and the state gaming commission.

Are jockeys allowed to bet on horse races?

Surprisingly, yes—making horse racing one of the few professional sports that allows participants to wager on the outcome. Jockeys are even allowed to bet on their own races, as long as they bet on the horse they're riding rather than on the competition.

What is the birthdate of every thoroughbred race horse?

For racing purposes, every thoroughbred is considered to have been born on January 1 of the year in which it was born. Regardless of what time of year a horse was actually born, that date is used to establish its official age. A horse is considered a foal until it is one year old. Between the ages of two and five, male horses are called colts and female horses are called fillies. Beyond the age of five, male horses are simply known as horses while female horses are known as mares. A male horse that has been neutered is called a gelding, while one that is intact for breeding purposes is called a stallion. These designations are significant because thoroughbred racing divides horses into different divisions based upon their age.

What kind of **weight** are thoroughbred race horses required to carry?

It depends on the type of race. In races between equally matched competitors in the same age group, all the horses usually carry the same weight. For Triple Crown races, that weight is 126 pounds. The total weight includes the jockey and the saddle, and lead weights may be added to the saddle to increase the weight if needed. In handicap races, horses may carry different weights in order to even the competition. For example, a horse that had won several races would carry several pounds more than one that had not won a race. Some races that include horses of various ages will assign different weights based on age as a form of handicapping. In addition, apprentice jockeys often receive a ten-pound weight advantage. Jockeys and their equipment are always weighed both before and after a race to ensure that the proper weight was carried.

In which **direction** are horse races run?

Any race that takes place on a standard oval in the United States is always run counterclockwise. Some European races are run in the other direction.

How many yards are in a **furlong**?

The furlong, which is a standard unit of measurement in horse racing, is 220 yards.

What are the **Eclipse Awards**?

Sponsored by the *Daily Racing Form*, the Thoroughbred Racing Associations, and the National Turf Writers Association, the Eclipse Awards honor the champions of the sport in several categories on an annual basis. The sponsoring organizations released separate Horse of the Year Awards for many years, until they combined their efforts to create the Eclipse Awards in 1971. The awards are named after Eclipse, an 18th century racehorse that went undefeated in 18 starts and also sired winners of 344 races. The award categories include Horse of the Year, Two-Year-Old Colt or Gelding, Two-Year-Old Filly, Three-Year-Old Colt or Gelding, Three-Year-Old Filly, Older Male Horse, Older Filly or Mare, Champion Male Turf Horse, Champion Female Turf Horse, Best Sprinter, Best Steeplechase or Hurdle Horse, Outstanding Jockey, Outstanding Apprentice Jockey, Outstanding Trainer, Outstanding Owner, Outstanding Breeder, and Award of Merit. In both 1995 and 1996, Cigar was named Horse of the Year, Jerry Bailey was Outstanding Jockey, and Bill Mott was Outstanding Trainer.

What is the **Breeder's Cup**?

The Breeder's Cup has been held since 1984. Seven races are held at a different track each year to determine the year's champions in seven categories.

HORSES

What famous racehorse was affectionately known as **Big Red**?

Man o' War, the American thoroughbred that helped popularize horse racing in the United States in the early 20th century, was called Big Red because of his glistening chestnut coat. His ancestry could be traced back to both the Byerly Turk and the Godolphin Arabian—the founding sires of the thoroughbred line. He was bred by August Belmont I, for whom Belmont Park was named.

Man o' War lost only one race in his illustrious career.

Did Man o' War ever **lose**?

Believe it or not, a horse named Upset handed Man o' War the only defeat of his career on August 13, 1919. It was Man o' War's seventh race, and he was left at the post because of the actions of an inexperienced starter. Man o' War ended up winning 20 races in 21 starts as a two- and three-year-old, beating some of the best horses of his day by 15 lengths or more and setting eight records.

What Triple Crown winning horse went on to **sire** another Triple Crown winner?

Although several Triple Crown winners became highly successful studs, 1930 winner Gallant Fox was the only one to father another Triple Crown winner. His son Omaha claimed the top prize in thoroughbred racing in 1935. Both father and son were bred in Kentucky by Belair Stud and trained by J. E. ("Sunny Jim") Fitzsimmons.

What racehorse is the **biggest money winner** of all time?

Cigar owns this title outright, having won 19 races in 33 starts and earned close to $10 million in his career. Alysheba is next on the list, with 11 wins in 26 starts and career earnings of $6.68 million. John Henry ($6.6 million), Best Pal ($5.67 million), and Sunday Silence ($4.97 million) round out the top five.

Why was Man o' War retired as a three-year-old, at the peak of his career?

Because his owner, Samuel D. Riddle, was unhappy at the amount of weight handicappers were requiring the great horse to carry. Man o' War routinely raced at 130 pounds during his impressive career. But when the burden was increased to 138 pounds in 1920, his owner decided to retire him to Faraway Farms in Lexington, Kentucky, before he broke down under the strain. It was a good decision. Man o' War lived to be 30 and became one of the greatest sires in the history of horse racing. One of his offspring, War Admiral, won the Triple Crown in 1937. Another son, Battleship, became the first American horse ever to win the Grand National Steeplechase in England. Man o' War also became quite a tourist attraction in his later years—more than one million people visited his stables and listened to his old groom, Will Harbut, tell colorful tales about the great horse and his offspring.

Secretariat posted the fastest times ever in the Kentucky Derby and the Belmont. What horse holds the **record time in the Preakness**?

Tank's Prospect covered the 1 3/16-mile distance at Pimlico Race Course in 1:53 2/5 during the 1985 running of the Preakness Stakes. Louis Quatorze tied this record in 1996. Two other horses have run the race just a fraction of a second slower at 1:53 3/5—Gate Dancer (1984) and Summer Squall (1990). Secretariat's winning time in the 1973 Preakness was 1:54 2/3, the tenth-fastest in history.

What thoroughbred was horse racing's **first million-dollar winner**?

Citation—winner of the Triple Crown in 1948—became horse racing's first millionaire on July 14, 1951, after claiming the $100,000 purse for the Hollywood Gold Cup. Citation was six years old at the time and not as sound as he once was, but his retirement was postponed so that he could fulfill the dying wish of his owner, baking soda magnate Warren Wright, and top $1 million dollars in career earnings.

What athlete became the first ever to grace the **covers of *Time*, *Newsweek*, and *Sports Illustrated*** simultaneously in 1973?

Secretariat was the remarkable athlete to achieve this feat. It was the week before the Belmont Stakes, in which Secretariat had a good chance to become the first Triple Crown winner since Citation had claimed the prize 25 years earlier. Secretariat soon

How did Secretariat come to belong to Mrs. Penny Tweedy of Virginia's Meadow Farm?

She lost a coin toss with Ogden Phipps, owner of Kentucky's Claiborne Farm. For many years, Claiborne's stallion, Bold Ruler, had been bred to two of Meadow's brood mares. Tradition dictated that the two owners would flip a coin every other year to see who got first choice of the resulting foals. The loser would automatically get the first choice the following year. Phipps won the toss in 1970 and chose The Bride, a filly out of Somethingroyal. When Tweedy's turn came the following year, she chose a colt from the same parents and named him Secretariat. The Bride ended up racing six times and never finishing better than fourth. Secretariat ended up being probably the fastest horse in history.

proved that all the attention was well-deserved. He won the Belmont by an amazing 31 lengths over Twice A Prince. He also set a new record with a time of 2:24, which was 2 3/5 seconds faster than the previous record (the equivalent of 20 lengths).

Which Triple Crown winner was the only horse to reach that pinnacle **undefeated**?

Seattle Slew, the 1977 Triple Crown winner and Horse of the Year. He managed this feat partly because he was so lightly raced, making only six starts prior to the Kentucky Derby. In fact, Seattle Slew lost his first race just three weeks after winning the third jewel at Belmont.

Who was the first **filly to run all three legs of the Triple Crown**, and how did she do?

Genuine Risk became the first filly to run against the boys in all three Triple Crown races in 1980, and she performed admirably. She became only the second filly in history to win the Kentucky Derby (Regret was first in 1915, and Winning Colors became the third in 1988), and she finished a close second in both the Preakness and the Belmont. A 13–1 shot in the Derby, she trailed in the early going but began moving up on the back stretch. Jockey Jacinto Vasquez made a great move on the outside in the far turn to overtake five opponents, and Genuine Risk took the lead and held it with a blistering final quarter. As she approached the finish line, the track announcer shouted, "It's Genuine Risk, and she's genuine!" Unfortunately, her hopes for becoming the first filly to win the Triple Crown were dashed in the Preakness. In the final turn before the home stretch, running neck and neck with Codex, Genuine Risk was bumped by the

336

colt. Her momentary lapse of concentration was enough to ensure Codex the victory. Whether the interference prevented her from winning a Triple Crown became a moot point, however, when she took second again in a clean race at Belmont. Still, she was inducted into racing's Hall of Fame in 1986—her first year of eligibility.

What happened the first time **two Kentucky Derby winners were ever bred**?

In 1982, following her retirement from racing, Kentucky Derby winner Genuine Risk was bred to the great Secretariat, who had won the Triple Crown nine years earlier. "It was a great moment in racing history," said the manager of Claiborne Farm, where the event took place. Everyone with even a passing interest in horse racing waited anxiously for the pedigreed baby to be born. Unfortunately, Genuine Risk gave birth to a stillborn foal in April 1983. Then the great racing filly developed a number of other breeding problems. Another attempt with Secretariat failed the following year, as did the next three attempts with other prominent stallions. She conceived but could not carry a foal to term in several other years. Finally, in 1993, Genuine Risk gave birth to her first live foal.

There is a mystery surrounding the **death of a famous Triple Crown contender**. Which one?

Alydar—the only horse to finish second in all three legs of the Triple Crown (to Affirmed in 1978)—was found in his stall with a broken right hind leg in November 1990 and had to be destroyed. When the financial problems of his owners, Calumet Farms, came to light a short time later, some people began to speculate that the horse had been killed for the insurance money. Alydar became one of the world's top breeding stallions after his retirement from racing, siring two Kentucky Derby winners (Alysheba and Strike the Gold) and seven horses that won more than $1 million in purses. At a fee of $350,000 per mare, Alydar was bred up to 100 times per year (most top stallions are bred only 50 to 60 times per year) and his breeding rights were sold years in advance.

The initial investigation into Alydar's injury found that he had probably kicked the sliding door of his stall loose and then caught his hoof in the metal bracket that held it in place. But it was later learned that—despite the stud fees commanded by Alydar—Calumet Farms was more than $120 million in debt and faced cancellation of their insurance coverage for nonpayment of premiums. Upon Alydar's death, Calumet collected a $36 million insurance settlement. The mystery continued as of 1998, when a Houston grand jury indicted the groom on duty that fateful night on charges of lying about what happened.

As Ann Hagedorn Auerbach—author of the book *Wild Ride*, which chronicles the rise and fall of Calumet Farms—explained: "I believed what everyone was saying: You

337

don't kill the goose that lays the golden egg. But the more research I did, the more I was persuaded that the horse could have been killed…. By the time he died, Alydar wasn't the goose laying the golden egg anymore. He was like a maxed-out credit card."

JOCKEYS

What jockey has ridden to victory in the most **Triple Crown races**?

Eddie Arcaro, who retired in 1961, won 17 Triple Crown events in his storied career as a jockey. He won the Kentucky Derby five times, and the Preakness and Belmont each six times. Arcaro also piloted two of the 11 horses that have won the Triple Crown—Whirlaway in 1941 and Citation in 1948—making him the only jockey ever to claim two Triple Crowns. Bill Shoemaker, who retired in 1990, is second on the all-time list for victories in Triple Crown races with 11. As of 1997, Pat Day was the leader among active jockeys with eight wins in Triple Crown events. Day's total includes five Preakness wins.

Jockey **Eddie Arcaro's riding style** changed when he won the third leg of the Triple Crown aboard Citation in 1948. What was different, and why?

After winning the Kentucky Derby and the Preakness with Citation, Arcaro suffered an injury to his right shoulder, severely limiting the use of the arm he usually used to wield the whip. But he chose to conceal the injury from Citation's owner, fearing that he'd be replaced as the horse's jockey for the Belmont. So Arcaro carried the whip in his left hand for the first time that day, as Citation won the Belmont by eight lengths to become the eighth Triple Crown winner in history. As it turned out, Arcaro favored a left-hand whip for the remainder of his career.

Who is the top **female jockey** of all time?

Julie Krone has the most career wins (3,158) and career earnings ($70.6 million) of any female jockey. She began riding professionally in 1980 and has been the top money winner on 12 occasions since then. From 1986 to 1996, she won 2,511 races in 13,782 starts. In 1993, she became the first woman jockey ever to win a Triple Crown race when she took the Belmont aboard Colonial Affair.

Who was the first **woman jockey to compete in the Kentucky Derby**?

Diane Crump made the first-ever appearance for a woman jockey in the Derby in 1970. Unfortunately, she and her mount, Fathom, finished in 15th place. Just a year earlier,

Eddie Arcaro won a record 17 Triple Crown races in his career.

> ## What jockey holds the title for most career victories?
>
> The legendary Bill Shoemaker, known as "The Shoe," won 8,833 races in a career that spanned over 40 years, from 1949–1990. His first victory came aboard Shafter V on April 20, 1949, and his last aboard Beau Genius on January 20, 1990. Shoemaker also earned an impressive $123.4 million for his efforts. An active jockey is approaching Shoemaker's record, however. Laffit Pincay Jr., who started his racing career in 1967, has won 8,547 races through 1997 and earned over $196 million. Angel Cordero, Dave Gall, and Pat Day are the other jockeys who have notched more than 7,000 career wins.

Crump was the first woman jockey ever to ride at a pari-mutuel track. She made the historic ride at Hialeah and finished in tenth place.

What jockey set a record by winning **eight races in one day**?

A four-time winner of the Eclipse Award as Outstanding Jockey, Pat Day won eight of the nine races he entered on September 14, 1989, at Arlington International. "It was rainy and the track was muddy," he recalled of that memorable occasion. "It was a great accomplishment, but to be honest I've had no time to reflect on it. My intention is always to try and win." Day originally hoped to become a rodeo bull rider. When that career path closed, he got a job cleaning stalls and grooming horses at a thoroughbred farm in California. He appeared in his first horse race at age 19, and the rest is history. Day was inducted into the Racing Hall of Fame in 1991.

Who was the **first jockey to be named Athlete of the Year** by the Associated Press?

Steve Cauthen, who rode Affirmed to the Triple Crown in 1978, won this and many other awards for his achievement. He claimed the Eclipse Award as Jockey of the Year, as well as Sportsman of the Year awards from many publications. He was also the youngest jockey—at 18—ever to win the Triple Crown, and the first jockey ever to earn more than $6 million in a single year. As Barney Nagler described Cauthen's unique rapport with his mounts in *The Racing Form*, "He endows a horse with a sense of urgency that other riders know about but cannot catch, much as they cannot imprison lightning in a bottle."

FAMOUS RACES

What horse race is considered by some to be an early indication of the rivalry that led to the American **Civil War**?

In the spring of 1823, the first national horse racing event held in the United States pitted American Eclipse, representing the North, against Sir Henry, representing the South. The race came about because of a challenge issued by Colonel William Ransom Johnson, one of the top horse owners of the South, to Cornelius Van Ranst, the owner of American Eclipse. Van Ranst accepted the challenge and sent word that his horse would race any Southern competitor Johnson chose. Both owners put up $20,000 to seal the deal. At that time, many Americans thought that all the top breeding stock had gone to the South, and this race was meant to settle the question of which part of the country had the best horseflesh. When news of the race was announced, it attracted the attention of the whole nation. More than 50,000 people gathered at the Union Race Course on Long Island, New York. Since all the hotels within 50 miles were booked well in advance, people slept in wagons, camped in the woods, and even stayed on boats anchored offshore. People bet everything they could afford, and then some. When the race finally went off, eight-year-old American Eclipse defeated four-year-old Sir Henry rather handily. Newspapers played up spectators' reactions—even claiming that one ruined Southerner had taken his own life following the race—but in reality the Southern contingent took the defeat gracefully.

What is the **traditional beverage of the Kentucky Derby**? What song is always sung before the race begins?

Drinking and singing associated with the Derby seems to have a strong Kentucky theme. The traditional drink consumed by the Southern ladies and gentlemen who attend the race is a mint julep. It consists of Kentucky bourbon mixed with sugar and poured over ice, garnished with a sprig of mint. Prior to the start of the race, a well-known Kentucky native always leads the crowd in a rendition of "My Old Kentucky Home."

Through 1997's 123rd run for the roses, 48 favorites finished first. Thirty-nine did not even pay, finishing fourth or worse. Spectacular Bid in 1979 was the last favorite to wear the roses in the winner's circle.

What one-on-one exhibition race is known as **horse racing's battle of the sexes**?

The year was 1975, just two years after Billie Jean King defeated Bobby Riggs in tennis's celebrated battle of the sexes. More than 18 million people watched on television

Jockey Bill Shoemaker holds the record for most career victories.

as Foolish Pleasure—the colt that won that year's Kentucky Derby and was runner up in the other two legs of the Triple Crown—faced off against Ruffian—the two-year-old filly of the year in 1974. She had led from the start in all of her 10 victories. Ruffian was leading by half a length and giving women's libbers a thrill when she broke her right front leg. Sadly, she had to be destroyed after the race.

What are some of the most famous **international horse races**?

Perhaps the best known is England's Grand National, which has taken place annually since 1839. It's a steeplechase run over a four-mile course with 30 fences at Aintree, Liverpool. The most prestigious thoroughbred race in Europe is France's Prix de l'Arc de Triomphe, which has been run annually since 1920. It is run at Longchamps, Paris, on a one mile, 864-yard track. The one-and-a-half mile Irish Derby is another European classic, having been staged since 1866 at The Curragh, County Kildare. Finally, Australia has held a prestigious annual race, the VRC Melbourne Cup, at the two-mile Flemington Racetrack in Victoria since 1861.

What do the thoroughbreds **Aristides, Survivor, and Ruthless** have in common?

Each of these horses was the winner of an inaugural Triple Crown race. Aristides won the first Kentucky Derby in 1875, Survivor was the winner of the original Preakness in 1873, and Ruthless was the first champion at Belmont in 1867.

Affirmed (third from right) won the Triple Crown in 1978, with Alydar finishing as the runner-up in all three races.

THE TRIPLE CROWN

What is the history of **horse-racing's Triple Crown**?

The Kentucky Derby, held at Churchill Downs in Louisville, Kentucky, was first run in 1875. The Preakness States, held at Pimlico Race Course in Baltimore, Maryland, started in 1873. The Belmont Stakes, held at Belmont Park in Elmont, New York, was first held in 1867. The Kentucky Derby is held during the first Saturday in May, the Preakness is held two weeks after the Derby, and the Belmont is held three weeks after the Preakness. The length of the Kentucky Derby is 1 1/4 miles (1 1/2 miles from 1875–1895), the Preakness has been at 1 3/16 miles since 1925, and the Belmont has been 1 1/2 miles since 1926.

The first horse to win all three races in one year was Sir Barton in 1919, but the term Triple Crown was coined in 1930 by sportswriter Charles Hatton to describe the three wins of Gallant Fox, the second horse to win the three races.

How many **horses** have won the Triple Crown?

Eleven. In addition to Sir Barton and Gallant Fox, Triple Crown winners include Omaha (1935), War Admiral (1937), Whirlaway (1941), Count Fleet (1943), Assault (1946), Citation (1948), Secretariat (1973), Seattle Slew (1977), and Affirmed (1978).

How many horses have won two jewels of the Triple Crown?

42. 15 horses won the Derby and Preakness but not the Belmont (two didn't race because of injuries). Zev, in 1923, won the Derby and the Belmont but finished 12th in the Preakness (which was the first of the three races run that year), and Hansel finished tenth in the Derby, then won the Preakness and Belmont. A horse has won the first two legs of the Triple Crown only to finish second in the Belmont 14 times, including Silver Charm in 1997. Through 1922, eleven horses won the the Preakness and Belmont but did not race in the Derby, including the legendary Man o' War (1920). Alydar in 1978 finished second to Triple Crown winner Affirmed in each race.

Which horse has **record times in two of the three races**?

Secretariat (1973) is the only horse to run the 1 1/4 mile Derby in under two minutes, and his 2:24 in the Belmont is still two seconds faster than any other horse has run since 1926—when the length of 1 1/2 miles became standard—through 1997.

How many **fillies have won the Triple Crown**?

None. Three have won the Derby, four took the Preakness, and two at the Belmont.

What is the **attendance record** for a Triple Crown event?

163,628 showed up at Churchill Downs in 1974. Capacity for the Downs is 148,500 (48,500 seats, 100,000 in the infield). Pimlico holds 100,000 (40,000 seats, 60,000 infield) and Belmont holds 82,491 (32,491 seats, 50,000 infield).

Why have the **1997 and 1998 Triple Crown campaigns** been called the best in 20 years?

In 1987, Silver Charm had a chance to become the first Triple Crown winner since Affirmed in 1978. With Gary Stevens aboard, Silver Charm won the Kentucky Derby by a head over Captain Bodgit. He then took the Preakness by a head over Free House. Touch Gold, a horse that had not run the Kentucky Derby, gained attention in the Preakness by falling to his knees at the break and then coming on toward the end to finish fourth. Silver Charm came to Belmont in good health for the final leg of the Triple Crown, while some of his main competitors experienced problems. Captain Bodgit was retired after suffering an injury in the Preakness, and Touch Gold's readiness was uncertain after his fall. As expected, Silver Charm looked like a sure winner

345

Secretariat, thought by many to be the greatest thoroughbred ever.

through the stretch run in the Belmont. But then—in one of the most exciting finishes in recent memory—Touch Gold, with Chris McCarron up, managed to run the favorite down in the last 50 yards to deny him the prize.

In 1998, the story was much the same. Real Quiet, who was trained by Bob Baffert, the same man who trained Silver Charm. With jockey Kent Desormeaux aboard, Real Quiet easily won the first two legs of the Triple Crown. Then, in the Belmont, it appeared that the horse was on his way to another easy win when Gary Stevens brought Victory Gallop up from back in the pack to catch Real Quiet at the wire. With the crowd waiting breathlessly, the judges had to go to a photo finish before declaring Victory Gallop the winner. It turned out that Real Quiet would have been moved to second place even if he had won for bumping Victory Gallop down the stretch.

HARNESS RACING

In **harness racing**, what's the difference between trotting and pacing?

The two main styles of harness racing are distinguished by the gaits of the horses involved. The high-stepping gait of a trotter involves moving the two legs that are diagonally opposite from each other at the same time. In other words, a trotter would move its right front and left rear, then left front and right rear, etc. as it moved down the track. In contrast, the swinging gait of pacers involves moving the two legs on one side (for example, the right front and right rear) at the same time, then the two legs on the other side. Both types of harness racers are attached to a lightweight, two-wheeled sulky and controlled by a driver.

Is there a **Triple Crown for harness racing**?

In fact, there are two harness racing Triple Crowns—one for pacers and one for trotters. Like the thoroughbred racing Triple Crown, both of the premier harness racing series are intended for three-year-old horses. The Pacing Triple Crown, which was established in 1956, consists of the Cane Pace, the Little Brown Jug, and the Messenger Stakes. Seven horses had won all three legs going into 1997: Adios Butler (1959), Bret Hanover (1965), Romeo Hanover (1966), Rum Customer (1968), Most Happy Fella (1970), Niatross (1980), and Ralph Hanover (1983). Seven other pacers had won two of the three legs. No driver or trainer has won the Pacing Triple Crown more than once. The Trotting Triple crown, established in 1955, consists of the Yonkers Trot, the Hambletonian, and the Kentucky Futurity. Six horses have won all three races in one year: Scott Frost (1955), Speedy Scot (1963), Ayres (1964), Nevele Pride (1968), Lindy's Pride (1969), and Super Bowl (1972). Stanley Dancer, the driver/trainer of both Nevele Pride and Super Bowl, is the only man to have won the Trotting Triple Crown twice. Seven other horses have won two of the three legs.

THE OLYMPICS

GENERAL

What are the **origins of the Olympic games**?

The Olympian Games date from 776 BC as one the four great national festivals of the ancient Greeks. The Olympian Games were celebrated in the summer every four years in the sanctuary of Zeus at Olympia. Greek city-states sent delegations to compete with one another and to celebrate athletic feats. The competitions included footraces, wrestling, boxing, and the pancratium (a combination of wrestling and boxing), horse racing (with owners competing as jockeys), the pentathlon (a series of five events described below). The victors were awarded crowns of wild olive. The Olympian Games were stopped late in the fourth century AD by the Roman emperor Theodosius I.

The Games were revived in Athens, Greece, in 1896. French educator Pierre de Coubertin had proposed the resumption as a means to promote a more peaceful world. The 1896 games featured summer events (the Winter Olympics was established in 1924). About 300 athletes competed in 43 events in nine sports. More than 10,000 athletes from more than 190 countries competed in 271 events in 29 different sports during the 1996 Summer Olympics in Atlanta, Georgia.

Who was the first athlete to take the **Olympic oath**?

In the 1920 Olympic Games held in Antwerp, Belgium, Belgian fencer and water polo player Victor Boin took the first Olympic oath. The Olympic oath thus became an established part of the Olympic experience. Today, the Olympic oath is still taken on behalf of all competitors by a representative of the host nation, who makes a pledge that all of the athletes will take part in the Olympic Games "in the true spirit of sportsmanship."

Who designed the symbol of interlocking multi-colored rings that has long represented the Olympic games?

The French educator Baron Pierre de Coubertin, who was instrumental in bringing the Olympics to life in 1896, was also the man who designed the Olympic rings. According to de Coubertin, the five interlocking rings of blue, green, red, yellow, and black were meant to symbolize all nations of the five continents, since at least one of the colors appeared in the flag of every Olympic country. The rings themselves were meant to symbolize the joining of athletes from all areas of the globe in joyful, fair competition.

De Coubertin's interlocking ring symbol is the most visible reminder of his influence on the Olympic movement, but it is by no means the only legacy the Frenchman left behind. The president of the International Olympic Committee (IOC) until 1924, de Coubertin authored the Olympic Charters, the athlete's Olympic Oath, and put together the procedures for the opening and closing ceremonies.

In which Olympics did the **Olympic flame** become a part of the Games' opening and closing ceremonies?

The 1928 Summer Games in Amsterdam were the first to use the Olympic torch as a symbol of the beginning and ending of the Games. The flame quickly became a major symbol of the entire Olympics, as did the carrying of the Olympic torch. Olympic tradition calls for the torch, which is used to light the flame during the opening ceremonies, to be lit in Olympia, Greece, approximately one month before the games begin. The torch is then transported to the host city via a relay of runners (as well as other modes of transportation when necessary). The Olympic torch is then carried into the host stadium during the opening ceremonies to light the flame. The honor of carrying the torch on this last leg of the journey is one that is reserved for only the most legendary athletes.

What **act of nature** gave London the opportunity to host the 1908 Olympic Games?

The 1908 Olympics had initially been awarded to Rome, Italy, but the devastation caused by the 1906 eruption of Mount Vesuvius forced Italy to give up its claim as host.

Was the **tug-of-war** ever an Olympic event?

Actually, yes. From 1900 until 1920 the tug-of-war was featured in every Olympic competition. In the very first tug-of-war event, a combined team featuring representa-

> ## Which Olympics was the first at which representatives from all five continents competed?
>
> The 1912 Olympic Games held in Stockholm, Sweden, were the first to enjoy this distinction. Historians regard this fifth Olympiad as one that established a model for future Olympic organizers to emulate. The Swedish organizers did a great job of heading off several incidents of political bickering that threatened to mushroom into major distractions, and they introduced a number of technological innovations—including the electronic timer and the photo-finish—that proved invaluable in officiating the games. Finally, the 1912 Games marked the first time that women participated in swimming events and the first appearance of Japanese athletes.

tives from both Sweden and Denmark (neither team could come up with the required six athletes on their own) joined forced to defeat American (silver) and French (bronze) teams. In 1904 American teams claimed all three medals, but four years later the U.S. was trumped by Great Britain, which managed its own sweep of the medals during the London Games. In 1912 Sweden defeated the Brits for the gold, and in 1920 (no Olympics were held in 1916 because of World War I) Great Britain out-tugged a team from the Netherlands for the last Olympic tug-of-war gold medal.

Who was the **first American woman to carry the American flag** in an Olympic ceremony?

Fencer Janice Lee York Romary, who was a member of six U.S. Olympic teams from 1948 to 1968, was the first woman to be so honored. She carried the flag during the 1968 Summer Games at Mexico City, the last Olympic competition in which she participated. Still regarded as one of the best female fencers ever to come from the United States (she won ten national championships during the 1950s and 1960s), she finished just out of the medal running in both the 1952 and 1956 games with fourth-place finishes.

Which nations garnered the **most gold medals** in each Olympiad?

Over the course of the last century, the impact of a number of nations on the Games has waxed and waned with the winds of political and social change, even as other countries—most notably the United States—have kept their spot at or near the top of the medal count. Following is a rundown of the top three gold medal-winning nations for each Olympiad:

351

Athens, 1896:

USA	11 gold (6 silver medals and 2 bronze medals)
Greece	10 gold (19 silver, 18 bronze)
Germany	7 gold (5 silver, 3 bronze)

Paris, 1900:

France	29 gold (41 silver, 32 bronze)
USA	20 gold (14 silver, 9 bronze)
Great Britain	17 gold (8 silver, 10 bronze)

St. Louis, 1904:

USA	80 gold (86 silver, 72 bronze)
Germany	5 gold (4 silver, 6 bronze)
Cuba	5 gold (3 silver, 3 bronze)

London, 1908:

Great Britain	56 gold (50 silver, 39 bronze)
USA	23 gold (12 silver, 12 bronze)
Sweden	7 gold (5 silver, 10 bronze)

Stockholm, 1912:

Sweden	24 gold (24 silver, 17 bronze)
USA	23 gold (19 silver, 1 bronze)
Great Britain	10 gold (15 silver, 16 bronze)

Antwerp, 1920:

USA	41 gold (26 silver, 27 bronze)
Sweden	17 gold (19 silver, 26 bronze)
Great Britain	15 gold (15 silver, 13 bronze)

Chamonix, 1924 (winter):

Norway	4 gold (7 silver, 6 bronze)
Finland	4 gold (3 silver, 3 bronze)
Austria	2 gold (1 silver)

Paris, 1924 (summer):

USA	45 gold (27 silver, 27 bronze)
Finland	14 gold (13 silver, 10 bronze)
France	13 gold (15 silver, 10 bronze)

St. Moritz, 1928 (winter):

Norway	6 gold (4 silver, 5 bronze)
USA	2 gold (2 silver, 2 bronze)
Sweden	2 gold (2 silver, 1 bronze)
Finland	2 gold (1 silver, 1 bronze)

Amsterdam, 1928 (summer):

USA	22 gold (18 silver, 16 bronze)
Germany	10 gold (7 silver, 14 bronze)
Finland	8 gold (8 silver, 9 bronze)

Lake Placid, 1932 (winter):

USA	6 gold (4 silver, 2 bronze)
Norway	3 gold (4 silver, 3 bronze)
Sweden	1 gold (2 silver)
Canada	1 gold (1 silver, 5 bronze)
Finland	1 gold (1 silver, 1 bronze)

Los Angeles, 1932 (summer):

USA	41 gold (32 silver, 30 bronze)
Italy	12 gold (12 silver, 12 bronze)
France	10 gold (5 silver, 4 bronze)

Garmisch-Partenkirchen, 1936 (winter):

Norway	7 gold (5 silver, 3 bronze)
Germany	3 gold (3 silver)
Sweden	2 gold (2 silver, 3 bronze)

Berlin, 1936 (summer):

Germany	33 gold (26 silver, 30 bronze)
USA	24 gold (20 silver, 12 bronze)
Hungary	10 gold (1 silver, 5 bronze)

St. Moritz, 1948 (winter):

Norway	4 gold (3 silver, 3 bronze)
Sweden	4 gold (3 silver, 3 bronze)
Switzerland	3 gold (4 silver, 3 bronze)
USA	3 gold (4 silver, 2 bronze)

London, 1948 (summer):

USA	38 gold (27 silver, 19 bronze)
Sweden	16 gold (11 silver, 17 bronze)
France	10 gold (6 silver, 13 bronze)
Hungary	10 gold (5 silver, 12 bronze)

Oslo, 1952 (winter):

Norway	7 gold (3 silver, 6 bronze)
USA	4 gold (6 silver, 1 bronze)
Finland	3 gold (4 silver, 2 bronze)
Germany	3 gold (2 silver, 2 bronze)

Helsinki, 1952 (summer):

USA	40 gold (19 silver, 17 bronze)
USSR	22 gold (30 silver, 19 bronze)
Hungary	16 gold (10 silver, 16 bronze)

Cortina d'Ampezzo, 1956 (winter):

USSR	7 gold (3 silver, 6 bronze)
Austria	4 gold (3 silver, 4 bronze)
Finland	3 gold (3 silver, 1 bronze)
Switzerland	3 gold (2 silver, 1 bronze)

Melbourne, 1956 (summer):

USSR	37 gold (29 silver, 32 bronze)
USA	32 gold (25 silver, 17 bronze)
Australia	13 gold (8 silver, 14 bronze)

Squaw Valley, 1960 (winter):

USSR	7 gold (5 silver, 9 bronze)
Germany (combined team)	4 gold (3 silver, 1 bronze)
USA	3 gold (4 silver, 3 bronze)
Norway	3 gold (3 silver)
Sweden	3 gold (2 silver, 2 bronze)

Rome, 1960 (summer):

USSR	42 gold (28 silver, 29 bronze)
USA	34 gold (21 silver, 16 bronze)
Italy	13 gold (10 silver, 13 bronze)

Innsbruck, 1964 (winter):

USSR	11 gold (8 silver, 6 bronze)
Austria	4 gold (5 silver, 3 bronze)
Norway	3 gold (6 silver, 6 bronze)
Finland	3 gold (4 silver, 3 bronze)
France	3 gold (4 silver)

Tokyo, 1964 (summer):

USA	36 gold (28 silver, 28 bronze)
USSR	30 gold (31 silver, 35 bronze)
Japan	16 gold (5 silver, 8 bronze)

Grenoble, 1968 (winter):

Norway	6 gold (6 silver, 2 bronze)
USSR	5 gold (6 silver, 3 bronze)

| France | 4 gold (3 silver, 2 bronze) |
| Italy | 4 gold (no silver or bronze) |

Mexico City, 1968 (summer):

USA	45 gold (28 silver, 34 bronze)
USSR	29 gold (32 silver, 30 bronze)
Japan	11 gold (7 silver, 7 bronze)

Sapporo, 1972 (winter):

USSR	8 gold (5 silver, 3 bronze)
East Germany	4 gold (3 silver, 7 bronze)
Switzerland	4 gold (3 silver, 3 bronze)
Netherlands	4 gold (3 silver, 2 bronze)

Munich, 1972 (summer):

USSR	50 gold (27 silver, 22 bronze)
USA	33 gold (31 silver, 30 bronze)
East Germany	20 gold (23 silver, 23 bronze)

Innsbruck, 1976 (winter):

USSR	13 gold (6 silver, 8 bronze)
East Germany	7 gold (5 silver, 7 bronze)
USA	3 gold (3 silver, 4 bronze)
Norway	3 gold (3 silver, 1 bronze)

Montreal, 1976 (summer):

USSR	49 gold (41 silver, 35 bronze)
East Germany	40 gold (25 silver, 25 bronze)
USA	34 gold (35 silver, 25 bronze)

Lake Placid, 1980 (winter):

USSR	10 gold (6 silver, 6 bronze)
East Germany	9 gold (7 silver, 7 bronze)
USA	6 gold (4 silver, 2 bronze)

Moscow, 1980 (summer):

USSR	80 gold (69 silver, 46 bronze)
East Germany	47 gold (37 silver, 42 bronze)
Bulgaria	8 gold (16 silver, 17 bronze)

Sarajevo, 1984 (winter):

East Germany	9 gold (9 silver, 6 bronze)
USSR	6 gold (10 silver, 9 bronze)
USA	4 gold (4 silver)
Finland	4 gold (3 silver, 6 bronze)

Sweden   4 gold (2 silver, 2 bronze)

Los Angeles, 1984 (summer):

USA	83 gold (61 silver, 30 bronze)
Romania	20 gold (16 silver, 17 bronze)
West Germany	17 gold (19 silver, 23 bronze)

Calgary, 1988 (winter):

USSR	11 gold (9 silver, 9 bronze)
East Germany	9 gold (10 silver, 6 bronze)
Switzerland	5 gold (5 silver, 5 bronze)

Seoul, 1988 (summer):

USSR	55 gold (31 silver, 46 bronze)
East Germany	37 gold (35 silver, 30 bronze)
USA	36 gold (31 silver, 27 bronze)

Albertville, 1992 (winter):

Germany	10 gold (10 silver, 6 bronze)
Unified Team	9 gold (6 silver, 8 bronze)
Norway	9 gold (6 silver, 5 bronze)

Barcelona, 1992 (summer):

Unified Team	45 gold (38 silver, 28 bronze)
USA	37 gold (34 silver, 37 bronze)
Germany	33 gold (21 silver, 28 bronze)

Lillehammer, 1994 (winter):

Russia	11 gold (8 silver, 4 bronze)
Norway	10 gold (11 silver, 5 bronze)
Germany	9 gold (7 silver, 8 bronze)

Atlanta, 1996 (summer):

USA	44 gold (32 silver, 26 bronze)
Russia	26 gold (21 silver, 16 bronze)
Germany	20 gold (18 silver, 27 bronze)

When did the Olympics first use a **tri-level podium** for the medal award ceremonies?

The 1932 Summer Games held in Los Angeles, California, were the first to feature this innovation.

What is a **demonstration sport**?

According to IOC rules, the host city of an Olympic Games has the option of petitioning the IOC to include one or two "demonstration sports" during the games that they host. Only sports that are recognized by the IOC and adhere to the committee's rules are eligible for this consideration, however. Over the years, several events that first appeared as demonstration sports have eventually gained full Olympic sport status, including baseball, basketball, canoeing/kayaking, badminton, and tennis.

Which Olympic competition eventually came to be known as the **Intermediate Games**?

The 1906 Olympic Games, successfully held in Athens, Greece, provided a much needed boost to the Olympics, which had been dogged by poor planning and small crowds in both 1900 and 1904. The 1906 Games also marked the first appearance of traditions that are today regarded as among the games' most cherished, including the awarding of gold, silver, and bronze medals and the appearance of athletic teams in the opening ceremonies. But the 1906 Athens Games were also controversial. In 1901 the IOC had decided to stage Olympics at two-year intervals beginning in 1906. Many people objected to this arrangement, however, and even though the 1906 Games went well, · the status of those games was eventually downgraded and the Athens competition came to be known as the Intermediate (or Intercalated) Games.

To what degree have **world events impacted the Olympic Games** over the years?

Given the very nature of the Olympics, which pits athletes from various nations against one another in sporting competitions, it is perhaps inevitable that the games often feel the reverberations of political clashes and other world events. Following is a rundown of some of the Olympic games to have felt the impact of political events on the larger world stage:

1916 Summer Olympics: Not held because of World War I.

1920 Summer Olympics: Countries held responsible for "The Great War" are excluded from participating. Athletes from Germany, Austria, Bulgaria, Hungary, and Turkey are thus relegated to bystander status.

1924 Summer Olympics: Germany once again excluded from participating because of its leading role in starting World War I. Their athletes were finally readmitted to the games in 1928.

1932 Winter Olympics: The Great Depression takes its toll, as only 17 nations are able to send a total of 252 athletes to compete at Lake Placid. Only four years earlier, 464 athletes from 25 nations had participated in the Winter Games.

1932 Summer Olympics: The worldwide economic strains caused by the Depression are felt here, too, as only 1,400 athletes from 37 countries compete (the 1928 Summer Olympics featured more than 3,000 athletes from 46 countries).

1936 Winter and Summer Olympics: The rise of the Nazis in Germany, which hosted both of these games, cast a pall over both events. Various efforts to mount a boycott fail and both games are well-attended by the world community.

1940 Winter and Summer Olympics: Not held because of outbreak of war between Japan and China and onset of World War II.

1944 Winter and Summer Olympics: Not held because of World War II.

1948 Winter and Summer Olympics: Germany and Japan excluded from competing because of their roles in starting World War II (athletes from both nations returned to the Olympic fold for the 1952 games).

1968 Summer Olympics: In order to head off a threatened boycott by other African nations, the IOC withdraws its invitation to the apartheid regime of South Africa. Four years later, a similar boycott threat leads the IOC to forbid Rhodesia from participating.

1972 Summer Olympics: A terrorist attack by Palestinian guerillas on Israel's national team in the Olympic Village ultimately results in the deaths of 11 Israeli athletes, one policeman, and five terrorists. This event continues to stand as by far the most shocking and terrible incident in Olympic history.

1976 Summer Olympics: Twenty-two African countries and Guyana boycott the games because of their objections to the participation of New Zealand, which had allowed its national rugby team to play in apartheid South Africa earlier in the year. In addition, Taiwan withdraws its athletes after a political dispute with host Canada.

1980 Summer Olympics: A huge boycott of the Moscow Games is held to protest the Soviet Union's 1979 invasion of Afghanistan. The United States, Japan, and West Germany are among the dozens of nations that refuse to send their teams to compete.

1984 Summer Olympics: Still annoyed at the U.S.A. for its leading role in organizing the boycott of the 1980 Summer Games in Moscow, the Soviet Union and many of its allies refuse to send teams to the 1984 Games in Los Angeles.

1992 Winter Olympics: The collapse of the Soviet empire and the Iron Curtain is evident, as Germany sends a unified team for the first time in 28 years, several former satellites of the USSR fly their own flags for the first time ever in Olympic competition, and other parts of the former Soviet Union participate together as "the Unified Team (EUN)."

1992 Summer Olympics: South Africa is allowed to participate for the first time in 32 years in recognition of political reforms made within the country.

1994 Winter Olympics: A number of newly independent Soviet republics, including Georgia, Russia, and the Ukraine, send individual teams to the games, marking the end of the Unified Team arrangement.

1996 Summer Olympics: A terrorist bomb goes off in Atlanta's Centennial Olympic Park, killing one woman and injuring 111 others.

Who was the **first athlete to win** an Olympic competition?

American triple jumper James Brendan Connolly claimed the very first victory of the 1896 Olympic Games in Athens, Greece. He won the triple jump event with a total of 44 feet and 11 3/4 inches (13.71 meters).

Which individual **won the most gold medals in the first Olympics** games?

Carl Schuhmann of Germany won four different events in the 1896 games. In addition to registering victories in three gymnastics events, Schuhmann also took the first Olympic wrestling championship. Interestingly enough, though, Schuhmann and the other victors of 1896 did not actually receive gold medals for their triumphs; event winners at the Athens games were instead presented with a silver medal, an olive branch, and a certificate.

The athlete who took home the most total medals in the 1896 games, meanwhile, was Schuhmann's countryman Hermann Weingartner, who won a total of six medals (three golds, two silvers, and a bronze) in a variety of gymnastics events.

SUMMER GAMES

GENERAL

What is the world's **fastest racket sport**?

Competitive badminton is ranked as the world's fastest racket sport, featuring shuttlecocks zooming off the surface of lightweight rackets at speeds approaching 200 miles per hour. Players require dexterity and lightning-quick reflexes. Like the backyard version of badminton, the Olympic event involves hitting a shuttlecock (the bird) over a net with a racket.

Badminton was a demonstration sport in 1972, an exhibition sport in 1988, and a full medal sport in 1992. Badminton most certainly began on the Asian continent, but the exact origins are unknown. In 5th-century BC China the game of *Ti Jian Zi*, or shuttlecock kicking, was played, and the modern version of badminton can be traced to India, where *poona* matches were contested during the 1800s. British military officers stationed in India during that time became interested in *poona* because of its similarities to lawn tennis. The officers brought the game with them when they returned home. The game became a popular pastime on the Gloucestershire estate of the Duke of Beaufort, beginning at a party he gave in 1873. The estate's name was "Badminton" and participants were given to referring to the sport as "that game at Badminton."

The shuttlecock weighs less than two ounces and is just under three inches in length. The bird is constructed of 16 goose feathers, taken from the identical wing of four different geese to ensure that the shuttle flies true. The base where the shuttle is struck is cork wrapped in kid leather. The accuracy and speed of the bird is paramount: hidden inside is a small metal screw that may be adjusted for weight and altitude considerations.

What are the three **weapons used in fencing** competitions?

The foil is the sword of choice for the majority of fencers. Designed as a training weapon, the foil still serves as the introductory weapon for virtually all fencers. However, it should not be regarded only as a beginner's weapon: the foil is often said to be the most difficult of the three to master.

Foils feature four-sided blades, rectangular in cross-section, a circular hand guard, and a handle that can vary according to the preference of the individual fencer. A foil can reach up to 1100 millimeters (43.307 inches) in total length and up to 500 grams (17.637 ounces) in weight, although the modern emphasis on quickness leads competitors to favor much lighter foils.

The épée (pronounced *eh*-pay in English, or eh-*pay* in proper French), like the foil, is a thrusting weapon only and is the same length as the foil. But the épée is considerably heavier, weighing up to 770 grams (27.16 ounces). The blade of an épée is triangular in cross section, making it quite a bit stiffer than a foil, and its hand guard is significantly larger.

The sabre is the only weapon that can score points by cutting, or slicing, in addition to thrusting. Its blade is V-shaped and narrow, fairly stiff when used with a cutting motion but quite flexible in the flat plane (that is, when moved side to side). The maximum overall length of the sabre is 1050 millimeters (41.338 inches) and it has the same maximum weight as the foil. While in the *en guard*, or "ready," position, a foil or épée fencer's arm is generally in line with the blade, while the sabre is held perpendicular to the arm. As a result, the sabre's hand guard sweeps around the back of the hand to the pommel and protects the fencer's knuckles against cuts.

What does one watch for in **fencing** competitions?

Foil: Foil fencing is characterized by a group of "conventions," rules that have evolved from the desire to make the sport resemble a real sword fight as closely as possible. Once an attack has been started, the defender must neutralize, or "parry" the thrust before beginning a counterattack. If a defender attacks into an attack (a very dangerous and foolhardy move that could, in a real duel, result in the death of both opponents), that defender does not score a legal touch. The determination of "right of way" is made by a tournament official called the president or director.

Épée: Since the épée evolved from dueling weapons, and since the object of many duels was to draw first blood and not necessarily deliver a fatal thrust, the épée has no invalid target. Hits from head to toe count as touches. It is, therefore, the simplest of the three weapons to follow in a bout, and it was the first of the three fencing competitions to be electrified—by adding a rudimentary plunger on the end of the blade. The only thing remotely sophisticated about electric épée equipment is its ability to "lock out" a second light within a split second, thus eliminating constant simultaneous touches and, incidentally, making this the easiest type of fencing for the novice viewer to understand: The light signals a point.

Sabre: Having evolved from the cavalry sabre, the fencing sabre takes as its target area the entire body above the waist, the most logical targets for a mounted warrior. As in foil competition, sabre bouts are regulated by conventions, with the same right-of-way rule in effect. Unlike foil and épée bouts, however, sabre matches until very recently were officiated manually, since this weapon proved to be the most complicated to electrify. The director presided over the bout with four judges watching for touches. But new advances in technology have finally allowed the sabre to catch up with the other weapons, and in the 1992 Olympic sabre matches were officiated with the aid of electrical equipment for the first time.

Sabre fencing is often considered the most exciting of the three weapons to watch. Since the sabre offers a wider variety of targets than the foil, as well as cutting attacks not possible with either the foil or the épée, sabre movements tend to be noisier and more flamboyant. The movements are also larger than the quick maneuvers of the other competitions, making sabre bouts easier for casual fans to enjoy.

How is scoring determined in **Olympic judo**?

After a ceremonial bow, the contestants await the referee's command of *"hajme,"* which means "begin fighting." Olympic matches last 10 minutes and are won by a single point, which may be scored if one contestant throws his or her opponent to the mat so that the opponent's back strikes the canvas. If the throw is executed with perfect form, a point is awarded and the match is over. If the form is not perfect, half a point may be awarded; another half can be gained by holding the opponent on the mat 20 seconds. Thirty seconds of holding is worth a full point as well.

If no point is scored in the full 10 minutes, the decision is up to the referee and judges. An extra three minutes of competition may be held at the judges' request.

What Olympic athletes later became **U.S. Congressmen**?

Senator Bill Bradley (D-New Jersey), elected to Congress in 1978, played on the 1964 gold-medal basketball team in Tokyo. Bradley, a three-time All-American at Princeton and a Rhodes scholar, went on to play for the NBA New York Knicks. He averaged 10.1 points per game for the U.S. team in 1964.

Representative Tom McMillen (D-Maryland) was elected to Congress in 1986 and served six years. McMillen averaged 7.6 points and 4.3 rebounds for the 1972 silver-medal team that suffered a crushing, controversial, last-second defeat to the Soviets, 51–50, in Munich. McMillen played college hoops at Maryland, was a Rhodes scholar, and played in the NBA for 11 years, with stops in Buffalo, New York, Atlanta, and Washington. His book *Out of Bounds*, a critique of professional and youth sports, was published in 1992, and in 1993 he was named co-chairperson (with fellow Olympian Florence Griffith Joyner) of the President's Council on Physical Fitness.

Ben Nighthorse Campbell (R-Colorado) was elected to the House as a Democrat in 1986 and to the Senate in 1992. In 1995, he switched parties to become a Republican. Campbell, a member of the Black Belt Hall of Fame in Burbank, California, captained the 1964—and first—U.S. Olympic judo team.

What made New Zealand **archer Neroli Fairhall** different from all other athletes competing in Olympic history?

Competing in the 1984 Olympics, she was the first Olympic athlete to perform from a wheelchair.

What are the various **Olympic yachting** events?

The number of yachting competitions has proliferated over the years. By the 1996 Summer Games hosted by Atlanta, events in ten different divisions had been granted Olympic status. Modern Olympic yachting divisions include the following:

Which Olympian won three consecutive single scull competitions in the 1970s and 1980s?

Finnish rower Pertti Karppinen claimed the gold in singles sculling in the 1976 (Montreal), 1980 (Moscow), and 1984 (Los Angeles) games, twice relegating his legendary West German rival Peter-Michael Kolbe to the second spot on the medal podium. In 1976 Karppinen registered a time of 7:29.03 to edge Kolbe, who finished in 7:31.67, and in 1984 Karppinen again slipped past Kolbe by about two seconds (7:00.24 to 7:02.19). In 1980, meanwhile, Kolbe was absent because of the Western boycott of the Games. As a result, Karppinen's closest competitor was Soviet sculler Vasily Yakusha, who finished two seconds behind the Finnish rower's winning time of 7:09.61.

Finn Class: This men's competition pits single sailors against one another in boats outfitted with a single sail.

Europe Class: A women's event, this competition also features solo sailors who compete in dinghies.

470 Class: This event, which is held for both women and men, features 470-centimeter-long fiberglass boats sailed by two crew members. Formerly open to mixed teams, this event was divided into separate competitions for men and women in 1988.

Star Class: Competition in this event takes place on boats that are 22 feet, 8 inches long and manned by a two-person crew.

Soling Class: This competition features the largest boats in the yachting events and uses three-person crews.

Tornado Class: Sailed by two-person crews, this event features 20-foot-long catamarans. It's the fastest of all Olympic classes.

Flying Dutchman: This class uses two-person crews on centerboard dinghies that are 19 feet, 10 inches long. A fan favorite, this competition allows one member of each crew to use a rope and trapeze to attach himself to the boat and lean far outside the craft so that they're horizontal to the water.

Boardsailing: Also known as windsurfing, this division has both men's and women's events.

What are the various **canoeing and kayaking** Olympic events?

Canoeing and kayaking competitions have been around since 1936, when canoeing/kayaking on a flatwater course became an official Olympic sport. Women began competing for medals on flatwater courses twelve years later, in the London games. Whitewater slalom events were added to the official Olympic program in 1972.

Flatwater Events: A variety of flatwater events are held in both kayaking and canoeing. Men compete at both 500 meters and 1,000 meters in both singles and doubles kayaking events (K-1 and K-2) and singles and doubles Canadian canoeing events (C-1 and C-2). The men's competition also includes a four-man kayaking race of 1,000 meters (K-4). Women, meanwhile, compete only at 500 meters and only in singles, doubles, and fours kayaks (K-1, K-2, and K-4).

Whitewater Slalom Events: This exciting sport requires participants to charge downriver and negotiate a series of buoys and markers (called "gates") on their way to the finish line. The only women's event in whitewater slalom is the single kayak (K-1). Men compete in three different events: single kayak (K-1), single Canadian canoe (C-1), and pairs Canadian canoe (C-2).

Why was the bronze medal won by Canadian **rower** Silken Laumann in the 1992 Summer Games so remarkable?

In the months leading up to the 1992 Games at Barcelona, Laumann was among the favorites to win the gold in the women's single sculls competition. After all, she was the 1991 world champion in the event, and her pre-Olympic training had gone well. But only ten weeks before the games were to begin, her shell was accidentally rammed by the shell of a German coxless pair's team. The impact drove a piece of splintered wood right through Laumann's leg, severing muscles and ligaments and shattering bone. The German rowers assisted Laumann to shore and helped her out of her shell, but when the gruesome damage to her leg was revealed, both of the Germans fainted on the spot.

Doctors subsequently told Laumann to take a minimum of six months off, but the Canadian rower wouldn't hear of it. She had trained too long and hard for the Olympics to watch the games pass by without participating, and though she recognized that the injury would make it impossible for her to win a gold medal, she decided that if she could beat just one other competitor she would be satisfied. As it turned out, she did far better than that. Showing the spirit and skill that had made her a world champion, Laumann rowed her way to a bronze medal. Four years later, she earned a silver in the single sculls event at the Atlanta Games.

Who won a silver medal in an **equestrian event** despite suffering from a malady that required her to be lifted on and off her horse?

Danish rider Lis Hartel, who rode to a silver in the 1952 Summer Games in Helsinki in the Grand Prix (Dressage) competition atop her horse, Jubilee. At the time, she was

Canada's Silken Laumann came back from a gruesome leg injury to take the bronze medal in the single sculls event at Barcelona in 1992.

suffering from a condition known as poliomyelitis that caused inflammation of the spinal cord. The condition made it impossible for her to mount or dismount on her own, but she was determined to compete, and she and her coaches eventually realized that there were no rules that forbade her from receiving assistance in getting on or off her horse. Hartel made the necessary arrangements, enabling her to eventually establish her place in Olympic history.

Why were the equestrian events of the 1956 Summer Games held in Stockholm, Sweden, when all the other events took place in Melbourne, Australia?

The Australian government refused to waive their stringent six-month quarantine period for horses entering the country. Since participants in the Olympics' equestrian events were understandably not willing to spend that amount of time "down under" prior to the Games, Olympic officials had no choice but to schedule the horse riding events in another country.

Who won the inaugural men's and women's mountain biking competitions in the 1996 Games?

Dutchman Bart Jan Brentjens won the men's gold medal in mountain biking, while Italy's Paolo Pezzo took the first-ever women's title.

How many athletes have earned medals in both the Winter and Summer Olympics?

Only three athletes have managed this feat in the entire history of the Games. The first athlete to do so was America's Eddie Eagan, who punched his way to a gold medal in the light-heavyweight division in 1920 and was also a member of the four-man bobsled team that took a gold medal in the 1932 games. Norway's Jacob Tullin Thams duplicated Eagan's accomplishment in 1936, when he won a silver medal in yachting to go with his 1924 gold medal in ski jumping. The only woman to earn medals in both the summer and winter games is Christa Luding-Rothenberger of East Germany, and she managed to do it in the same year (1988). She won a total of four medals in winter competition during her Olympic career, including gold medals in 500-meter speed skating in 1984 and 1,000-meter speed skating in 1988 (she also won silver in the 500-meter event in 1988 and bronze in the 500-meters in 1992). She obtained her sole medal in the summer games in Seoul, taking a silver medal in the match sprint cycling event.

> ## What Olympic gold medalists went on to become professional prizefight champions?
>
> **A**mong the most noted are Floyd Patterson (1952, middleweight gold), Muhammad Ali, then known as Cassius Clay (1960, light heavyweight gold), Joe Frazier (1964, heavyweight gold), Sugar Ray Leonard (1976, light welterweight gold), brothers Michael (1976, middleweight gold) and Leon Spinks (1976, light heavyweight gold), Pernell Whitaker (1984, lightweight gold), Mark Breland (1984, welterweight gold), Virgil Hill (1984, middleweight silver), Evander Holyfield (1984, light heavyweight bronze), Riddick Bowe (1988, super heavyweight silver), and Oscar De La Hoya (1992, lightweight gold).

BOXING

What was early **Olympic boxing** like?

It is unclear what kind of boxing was contested during the early Olympics, but in 688 BC, during the 23rd Ancient Olympiad, the boxers wore headgear and wrapped their fists with long leather thongs known as *caestus* to protect their hands and increase the power of their punches. The fights were not divided into rounds; the boxers fought until one combatant dropped or conceded by raising a fist in the air.

Who was the first **boxer** in Olympic history to win three gold medals?

Hungarian Laszlo Papp won gold medals in the 1948, 1952, and 1956 Olympic Games. In the 1948 competition in London, Papp defeated Great Britain's John Wright to take the middleweight title. Four years later in Helsinki, Papp switched to the light-middleweight division, where he outfought Theunis van Schalkwyk for the gold. In 1956, the 30-year-old Hungarian claimed his third gold medal by successfully defending his light-middleweight Olympic crown against America's Jose Torres.

SWIMMING AND DIVING

How is scoring determined in **diving**?

There are seven judges in Olympic diving contests. After each dive, each judge determines the point total for the dive on a scale of 0 (lowest) to 10 (highest), in half or whole point increments. The seven point scores are displayed and the highest and lowest scores are eliminated. The remaining five scores are totaled and then multiplied by the degree of difficulty. The result is reduced by 3/5 (0.6), in keeping with the tradition that a diver's score comes from three judges.

For example, a dive earns scores of 6–5–5–5–5–5–4. The sum, after high (6) and low (4) scores are eliminated, is 25. Let's say the degree of difficulty is 2.0: 25 x 2 = 50, 50 x 0.6 = 30—the score for the dive.

The degree of difficulty is a rating from 1.1 to 3.5. for executing a specific dive. Beginning with the 1996 Summer Games, divers no longer had to choose their dives from a list that had set degrees of difficulty. Instead, they can create their own dives using the different categories—forward, reverse, or twisting. With the new dives, competitors can potentially raise their scoring ability, since they are choosing as much difficulty as they desire.

At the beginning of a dive, the diver's body should be straight, head erect, heels together and arms straight to the sides. Once the diver stands on the front end of the board to perform a standing dive, the judges assume the dive has begun. The parts of each dive are analyzed and evaluated by the judges.

Who is considered the **greatest diver of the late 20th century**?

Greg Louganis had a record-breaking two gold medals in each of two successive Olympic diving competitions, an unprecedented platform score of more than 700 points, and gold-medal success in every major national and international diving event he entered during the 1980s.

Though he couldn't compete in the 1980 Olympics in Moscow, which the United States and other Western nations boycotted to protest the Soviet invasion of Afghanistan, he had already begun building his reputation as the greatest diver in the world.

Having won twenty-six U.S. championships, four Pan American events, and three world championships, Louganis was clearly favored to win the platform and springboard diving contests in the 1984 Olympic Games. Louganis won gold medals in both events (becoming the first man to do so in 56 years). He won the springboard competition by more than 90 points over the silver medalist, and he set a record for points scored in the platform event.

Four years later, at the Summer Olympics in Seoul, Louganis' competitive edge was complicated by physical problems, including an injured wrist, a fever, and a three-inch head wound he sustained by striking the springboard during a preliminary competition dive. Nonetheless, Louganis finished the springboard event and won the gold, and he performed a superior final platform dive, which ensured him that gold medal, too. For his gutsy performance at the 1988 Olympics, Louganis was also given the Olympic Spirit Award.

What are the Olympic **medley swimming** competitions?

The individual medley features all four competitive strokes. The swimmer begins with the butterfly, changes to the backstroke for another quarter, then breaststroke, and finally finishes with the freestyle. The new "no-touch" backstroke turn may not be used in the backstroke to breaststroke exchange in an individual medley race. Both men and women swim 200m and 400m individual medleys.

In the medley relay, all four strokes are swum by four different swimmers, covering 100m each. No swimmer may swim more than one leg of the relay, which is swum in backstroke, breaststroke, butterfly, then freestyle order. The men and women each compete in their own 400m race. An important part of any relay race is the exchange between the swimmer in the water and the next swimmer on the relay team. In a perfect exchange, the finishing swimmer's hand will alight on the touch pad at the same time as the starting swimmer's feet are still just touching the starting block, with the body extended over the water in the last instant before takeoff.

What are the different **swimming styles** used in Olympic competition?

In the freestyle, competitors may use any stroke they wish, and their wish is usually the Australian crawl, characterized by the alternate overhand motion of the arms. Individual freestyle events for men and women include 50m, 100m, 200m, and 400m. Women also swim an 800m individual race, while the men engage in a 1500m event. Additionally, both women and men swim 400m and 800m freestyle relays in which no individual may swim more than one leg of the race.

The butterfly features the simultaneous overhead stroke of the arms combined with the dolphin kick, and both the arms and legs move up and down together. No flutter kicking is allowed. The butterfly, perhaps the most beautiful and physically demanding stroke, was developed in the early 1950s as a loophole in the breaststroke rules and in 1956 became an Olympic event at the Melbourne Games. Butterfly races include a men's and women's 100m and 200m.

Popularized by Harry Hebner of the United States in the 1912 Olympics, the backstroke requires the swimmer to remain on his or her back at all times. The backstroke is the only race in which the competitors are in the water at the start, taking a handgrip on the edge of the pool while resting on their back. The stroke is an alternating motion of the arm, resembling an upside-down crawl. Starting in 1991, a swimmer no longer must touch the wall with his or her hand before executing the turn maneuver, a change that may cause many Olympic backstroke records to fall. Backstroke events include the men's and women's 100m and 200m races.

369

One of the most difficult strokes to master is the breaststroke, which requires simultaneous movements of the arms on the same horizontal plane. The hands are pushed forward from the breast or under the surface of the water and brought backward in the propulsive stage of the stroke simultaneously. The kick is a simultaneous thrust of the legs called a "frog" or breaststroke kick. No flutter or dolphin kicking is allowed. At each turn a swimmer must touch with both hands at the same time. The breaststroke races include a men's and women's 100m and 200m.

Who are the Olympic recordholders in the **women's freestyle swimming** events?

50 meters: Yang Wenyi, China (24.79 seconds)
100 meters: Zhuang Yong, China (54.64 seconds)
200 meters: Heike Friedrich, East Germany (1 minute, 57.65 seconds)
400 meters: Janet Evans, United States (4 minutes, 3.85 seconds)*
800 meters: Janet Evans, United States (8 minutes, 20.20 seconds)
*also a world record

Which Olympic swimmer won **six gold medals in six starts** at the 1988 Summer Olympics in Seoul?

East Germany's Kristin Otto put on an amazing show in Seoul, earning gold in every event in which she participated. In addition to lending a hand in two relay wins for the East Germans (the 4 x 100-meter freestyle and 4 x 100-meter medley), Otto won the first Olympic 50-meter freestyle, the 100-meter freestyle, the 100-meter backstroke, and the 100-meter butterfly.

Which Olympic medalist became the first woman to **swim the English Channel**?

On August 6, 1926, American Gertrude Ederle became the first woman to cross the English Channel. Even though she had won three swimming medals at the 1924 Summer Olympics, the accomplishment still shocked the world. Many observers—the male ones, anyway—had scoffed at her chances, especially after she was forced to abandon her first bid in 1925 because of seasickness. But Ederle remained undaunted, and the next year she made the journey from France to England in 14 hours and 31 minutes, beating the best time recorded by a man up to that time by nearly two hours. Ederle's time stood as the women's record for nearly 40 years, until 1964.

Who was the first American woman to win **four Olympic gold medals in swimming** events?

Janet Evans, who won three golds in the 1988 Seoul Games and another gold at the 1992 Games at Barcelona (she also won a silver in the 1992 competitions). Evans was one of those children who lived for the water from the time she was a toddler. By the time she was two years old, she could swim the length of the local pool, a sure sign of things to come. As she grew older, it became clear that her strengths lay in the longer distance events, such as the 400-meter freestyle, the 800-meter freestyle, and the 1,500-meter freestyle. In 1987 she set new world records in all three events, making her the odds-on favorite for gold in Seoul the following year.

As expected, Evans cruised to gold in both the 400-meter freestyle and 800-meter freestyle in the 1988 Games. In the first event, she posted a time of 4:03.85, more than two seconds faster than her nearest competitor. In the 800-meter event, meanwhile, she won with a time of 8:20.20 to defeat Astrid Strauss of East Germany (8:22.09). The 1,500-meter competition was not an Olympic event for women, but Evans found another way to get a third gold medal, as she whipped the field in the 400-meter medley with a time of 4:37.76 (the silver medalist was Romania's Noemi Lung, who finished in 4:39.46). Evans' awesome performance in Seoul made her a celebrity across America.

Four years later, she returned to Olympic competition in an effort to add to her medal total. But unlike the '88 Games, she wasn't the big favorite to win. She was older, and her qualifying times weren't as good as they had been in the past. Nonetheless, Evans put together a great performance in the 800-meter freestyle to become the first American woman in Olympic history to win four gold medals in swimming. She crushed the field in the event, winning by nearly five seconds. Evans also added a silver in the 400-meter freestyle, losing out on the gold to Germany's Dagmar Hase by .19 seconds.

In 1996 Evans made one final appearance at the Olympics. She qualified for the team that competed in Atlanta, and even though it was clear that she was past her swimming prime (she didn't win a medal), she was warmly greeted by appreciative American crowds wherever she went.

Has any swimmer ever won **five individual gold medals**?

On July 25, 1996, Krisztina Egerszegi of Hungary won the 200-meter backstroke competition at the Atlanta Summer Olympics, making her the first swimmer in history to win five individual gold medals.

Which American athlete yelled "This is a victory for all the **nerds** out there" after winning a gold medal?

In the 1996 Summer Olympics, U.S. swimmer Amy Van Dyken became the first American woman to win four gold medals in one Games. She didn't get off to a particularly auspicious beginning. In her first event, the 100-meter freestyle, Van Dyken finished just shy of a medal finish with a fourth-place effort that left her gasping and cramping at the side of the pool. But in subsequent events, Van Dyken would not be denied. Over the course of the next week, she won the 100-meter butterfly, the 50-meter freestyle, and helped the U.S. women win two golds in relay events (the 400-meter freestyle and the 400-meter medley). After winning her record-breaking fourth gold medal in the 50-meter event, the young woman joked about the progress that she had made since her high school days, when she had struggled to be accepted by her teammates. "This is a victory for all the nerds out there," she shouted. "To all the girls who gave me a hard time in high school, I say, 'Thank you.'"

Which **American swimmer** spent his days swinging through Hollywood jungles after collecting five Olympic gold medals?

Johnny Weissmuller won three gold medals in the 1924 Olympic Games in Paris, France, recording the Olympics' first sub-one minute time in the 100-meter freestyle in the process (he also struck gold in the 400-meter freestyle and in the 4 x 200-meter freestyle relay, and won a bronze medal as a member of the American water polo team). Four years later, in Amsterdam, Weissmuller added to his gold medal total with

Mark Spitz entered seven events in the 1972 Olympics—four individual and three relays—and took the gold in all of them, setting world records every time.

a victory in the 100-meter freestyle and the 4 x 200-meter relay. After retiring from the pool, Weissmuller parlayed his Olympic exploits into a long film career as Tarzan the Ape Man.

Who dominated the first Olympic **synchronized swimming** events?

American Tracie Ruiz won gold medals in both of the synchronized swimming events that debuted in the 1984 Games in Los Angeles. In the solo competition, she took the gold with a score of 198.467. Canada's Carolyn Waldo (195.300) and Japan's Miwako Motoyoshi (187.050) rounded out the medal winners in that category. Ruiz also teamed with Candy Costy to win the gold medal in the duet competition, once again edging competitors from Canada and Japan.

GYMNASTICS

How are **gymnastic** competitions scored?

Artistic gymnastic competition is divided into compulsory and optional movements. For each routine, the gymnast begins with less than a perfect score (for women, 9.40,

373

Amy Van Dyken brought home four Olympic gold medals in 1996.

and for men 9.00). In awarding their scores, judges take into consideration the degree of difficulty of a gymnast's program along with aesthetic appeal. Points are deducted for such faults as poor execution, lack of control, falling, missing requirements, or exceeding the time limit. Judges may award up to 0.60 bonus points for women and up to 1.00 for men. The "perfect 10.00" score was first awarded in world-class competition to Nadia Comaneci at the 1976 Olympic Games.

The individual all-around (combined) champions for men and women are determined by totaling scores on all the apparatuses. For the men's and women's team combined, the total of the top six scores on each apparatus is the team's score.

Why is the **order of competitors** crucial in women's gymnastics?

As gymnastics routines become more complex and difficult, the maximum score of 10 does not mean perfection so much as it means a better and harder performance than the previous competitor's. For that reason, the order in which gymnasts compete is crucial: coaches send out their lineups of six team members in inverse order of accomplishment. The weakest competitor in an event goes first, and her score becomes the base against which the rest are compared. If the first scores well and the second a bit better, the judges' scores escalate until, finally, the top performer goes out last in hopes of building on a base now escalated to 9.90 or 9.95.

What are the different **exercises** in a gymnastic competition?

Floor Exercise: Floor exercise routines for men consist of tumbling skills that only a few years ago were performed solely on the trampoline. Multiple saltos (flips or somersaults) and twists are increasingly common. The best will incorporate three or four tumbling passes of substantial difficulty, performing twisting double saltos on the second or third passes. Unlike the women's competition, the men's floor exercise is not performed to music.

Always a crowd favorite, women's floor exercise is best identified with Nadia Comaneci's perfect precision and Mary Lou Retton's powerful tumbling. The most important aspect to the floor exercise is grace. Look for dancer-like command of music, rhythm, and space. The gymnastics elements should flow freely into each other—the leaps covering impressive distances, the pirouettes and turns adding excitement to the music, the displays of strength, flexibility and balance all complementing each other. Difficult tumbling, ranging from triple twists to double-back somersaults with a full twist, are expected.

Vault: Men's and women's vaults begin with a strong, accelerated run. The best vaulters explode off the board, getting their feet up over their head with tremendous quickness during the first flight phase of the vault—from the springboard to contact with the horse. The judges are looking for proper body, shoulder, and hand position and instantaneous repulsion. The second flight phase and the landing are critical. Watch for height and distance of travel, as well as the number of saltos and twists— usually the more of each, the higher the difficulty value of the vault. The sudden impact of a no-step, "stuck" landing creates a favorable impression. Note that male gymnasts are not allowed to perform the round-off vault, or Yurchenko, named after the Soviet woman who invented the maneuver. The women's horse is set perpendicular to the approach while the men's horse is set in line with the launching board.

Pommel Horse (men only): Considered by many to be the most difficult of all men's gymnastics events, the pommel horse is also the most subtle. Each move is defined by complex hand placements and body positions. The difficulty stems from two factors. First, the gymnast is performing moves that differ from the swinging and tumbling skills of the other five events. Second, he spends most of each routine on only one arm, as the free hand reaches for another part of the horse to begin the next move. Look for a long series of moves in which the gymnast reaches his hands behind his back, or places both hands on a single pommel. The hand placements should be quick, quiet, and rhythmic.

Rings (men only): The rings are the least stable of the men's apparatuses. Stillness is paramount and those with the best command of the event will display extraordinary skill in arriving at all holds with absolute precision. The rings should not wobble or swing, the body should not sag or twist, and the arms should not waver or shake.

Parallel Bars (men only): Although not a requirement, some of the better gymnasts move outside the two rails, performing handstands, presses, kips, and hip circles on only one bar. The most difficult skills require the gymnast to lose sight of the bars for a moment, as in front and back saltos.

Horizontal Bar (men only): Watch for blind releases, in which the gymnast loses sight of the bar while executing a salto or twist. One-arm giants are extremely difficult, and if the gymnast performs several in succession as he changes directions, or if he performs a blind release out of one-arm giants, he has performed admirably.

Uneven Bars (women only): The most spectacular of the women's events. Watch for the big swings that begin in handstands on the high bar—two, three, or four in succession, incorporating multiple hand changes, pirouettes, and release/flight elements.

Balance Beam (women only): The overall execution should give the impression that the gymnast is performing on a floor, not on a strip four inches wide. The beam is sixteen feet, three inches long, four inches wide, and almost four feet off the floor. Watch for variations in rhythm, changes in level (from sitting on the beam to jumping head-height above it) and the harmonious blend of gymnastics and acrobatic elements.

When did **women's gymnastics** become so popular?

The popularity in participation and viewing women's gymnastics erupted during the 1970s and was fueled further by dynamic competitors of the 1980s and 1990s. Olga Korbut injected new daring and dash into the sport in the 1972 Olympics, and Nadia Comaneci followed in 1976 with her flawless work on the uneven parallel bars and the balance beam. Mary Lou Retton, watching those performances on television as a child, vowed to do the very same thing, and did so during the 1980s.

Olga Korbut was perhaps the first notable example of a changing trend in women's gymnastics. As international competitions intensified during the 1960s, coaches began to look for younger and younger children who could be trained to perform daring stunts before natural fear processes set in. Korbut, born in 1955, was nine when she began to work out at a gymnastics club in Grodno, near the Polish border. A mere five years later she was a national star, the first athlete ever to perform a back flip on the balance beam. She became the entire world's darling at the 1972 Olympics, earning gold medals for Soviet team victories in the balance beam and floor exercises, and she won a silver medal for her performance on the uneven bars.

Nadia Comaneci's daring in the Olympics in 1976 on the uneven bars and balance beam made history with the first perfect scores ever awarded. Comaneci left Montreal that year with two gold medals, a silver for team finish, and a bronze for floor exercise. As Walter Bingham put it in *Sports Illustrated*, the youngster compiled routines "that had the audience first gasping, then roaring with applause."

Nadia Comaneci's 1976 performance is one of the reasons for the surge in popularity of women's gymnastics

Retton's showdown in the 1984 Olympics was one of the closest ever. With her scores hovering within .10 of opponent Ecaterina Szabo—and coming off knee and wrist injuries—Retton earned the all-around gold, silver in team and vault, and bronze in uneven bars and floor exercise, earning a place in the record books next to the champions who had inspired her.

Youth is an absolute premium now in gymnastics, thanks to the exploits of Korbut, Comaneci, and Retton. It is no coincidence that each of the three champions retired before the age that most people go to work. As Retton declared in 1989: "I just can't do it [anymore]. My body's strong enough, but I don't have the discipline. The girl who won those medals was a machine. Gymnastics was her life. I've found other things now—that you actually can go to a movie on a Thursday night, and it can be very nice. Just go to a movie."

Has the **U.S. women's gymnastics team** ever won a gold medal at the Olympics?

In 1996 the U.S. women won their first gymnastics gold medal in Olympic history, and in the process provided perhaps the single most memorable moment in the Atlanta Games. Prior to the competition, 90-pound gymnast Kerri Strug had a far more modest public profile than did some of her teammates, including Dominique Moceanu, Dominique Dawes, and Shannon Miller. But as the competition unfolded, events thrust her squarely into the spotlight. The American team moved into the lead, but in the final stages of the event, it seemed they were in danger of losing the gold to the Russians. By the time Strug came forward to make her last appearance in the team event, it was clear that if she didn't score at least a 9.5, the Russian team would have an opening to wrest the gold from the American women. Strug sprinted toward the vault, but she landed awkwardly and injured her left ankle, posting only a 9.162 score in the process. Hardly able to put any weight on her foot, she knew that she was badly injured. But after wiping away a few tears of pain, she returned to the top of the runway to make a second vault attempt. She performed magnificently, holding her landing position despite the pain that shot out from her ankle (where she had torn two ligaments) when she landed. The judges posted her gold-clinching score of 9.712 and she was quickly whisked off her feet by her coach, Bela Karolyi, as the Atlanta crowd roared its approval. Strug's gritty "take-one-for-the-team" performance ensured her of an enduring place in the history of the Olympic Games, and made her America's favorite athlete of the 1996 Games.

Who was the first gymnast in Olympic history to **score a perfect 10 in the horse vault** event?

Soviet gymnast Aleksandr Dityatin scored a perfect 10 in the horse vault on his way to a haul of eight medals (three gold, four silver, and a bronze) at the 1980 Summer

Kerri Strug's heroic performance on the vault brought a team gold to the U.S. Women's Gymnastic team in 1996.

Games in Moscow. But the absence of many countries—including the United States, Japan, and West Germany—from the games because of unhappiness over the USSR's 1979 invasion of Afghanistan cast a shadow over the entire Moscow games.

TRACK AND FIELD

Which nations have won the **most track and field medals**?

The United States leads in this category by a wide margin, with Germany's total (including medals won by East and West Germany from 1968 to 1988) ranking a distant second:

1) United States   694 medals (299 gold, 217 silver, 178 bronze)
2) Germany   245 medals (67 gold, 86 silver, 92 bronze)
3) USSR/Unified Team   214 medals (71 gold, 66 silver, 77 bronze)
4) Great Britain   172 medals (43 gold, 72 silver, 57 bronze)
5) Finland   113 medals (48 gold, 35 silver, 30 bronze)

Who are the current Olympic recordholders in the **women's running** events?

100 meters: Florence Griffith Joyner, United States (10.62 seconds)
200 meters: Florence Griffith Joyner, United States (21.34 seconds)*
400 meters: Olga Bryzgina, USSR (48.65 seconds)
800 meters: Nadezhda Olizarenko, USSR (1 minute, 53.42 seconds)
1,500 meters: Paula Ivan, Romania (3 minutes, 53.96 seconds)
5,000 meters: Wang Junxia, China (14 minutes, 59.88 seconds)
10,000 meters: Olga Bondarenko, USSR (31 minutes, 5.21 seconds)
Marathon: Joan Benoit, United States (2 hours, 24 minutes, 52 seconds)
*also a world record

Which Olympic athlete triumphed over a childhood bout with **polio** to capture a record ten individual gold medals?

American Ray Ewry won a total of ten individual gold medals in a variety of standing jump events from 1900 to 1908, despite the fact that he had spent a portion of his childhood years partially paralyzed with polio. Determined to fight off the disease, young Ewry embarked on a course of athletics training that eventually became the foundation of his future international success. In 1900 he won the gold in all three standing jump events (high jump, long jump, and triple jump), and over the course of the 1904 and 1908 games, he added five more number one finishes. Those eight gold medals, coupled with the two titles he won at the "Interim Games" of 1906, gave him a

Who are the current recordholders in the various Olympic men's running events?

100 meters: Donovan Bailey, Canada (9.84 seconds)*
200 meters: Michael Johnson, United States (19.32 seconds)*
400 meters: Michael Johnson, United States (43.49 seconds)
800 meters: Vebjorn Rodal, Norway (1 minute, 42.58 seconds)
1,500 meters: Sebastian Coe, Great Britain (3 minutes, 32.53 seconds)
5,000 meters: Said Aouita, Morocco (13 minutes, 5.59 seconds)
10,000 meters: Haile Gebrselassie, Ethiopia (27 minutes, 7.34 seconds)
Marathon: Carlos Lopes, Portugal (2 hours, 9 minutes, 21 seconds)
*also a world record

total of ten gold medal finishes during his sterling career. After the 1908 London games, the 34-year-old wonder retired from competitive sports.

Who was the **first American woman to win three gold medals** in Olympic track and field competition?

Sprinter Wilma Rudolph overcame a lifetime of adversity to win three gold medals at the 1960 Summer Olympics in Rome, Italy. The 17th of 19 children in her family, Rudolph was struck down by polio at the age of four. The disease decimated her immune system, leaving her vulnerable to bouts of pneumonia and scarlet fever that nearly killed her. She survived these illnesses, but they did take their toll, for she completely lost the use of her left leg. After five years of treatment, though, she stunned her doctors—who had been certain that she would be permanently disabled—by removing the brace on her leg and walking around the room. "By the time I was 12," she later recalled, "I was challenging every boy in our neighborhood at running, jumping, everything."

Rudolph's first exposure to the Olympics came in 1956, when she won a bronze medal as a member of the U.S. women's 4 x 100 meter relay team. It was in Rome, however, that she really showed her stuff, becoming an international celebrity in the process. She brought home gold for America in both the 100-meter and 200-meter sprints (setting a new Olympic record in the latter event), and helped lift the U.S. to a gold medal in the 4 x 100 meter relay. Rudolph's performance, especially given her childhood bout with polio, made her one of America's brightest Olympic stars and attracted attention around the globe.

What are the origins of the **marathon**?

Though not part of the ancient Games, the marathon commemorates the 25-mile run by Greek soldier and Olympic star Pheidippides. He ran that distance from Marathon to Athens with news of the Athenian victory over the Persians. "Rejoice, we conquer," he announced. Then, according to legend, he fell over dead.

Which Games saw the **first major marathon drama** in Olympic history?

In the 1908 London Games, Italian marathoner Dorando Pietri seemed poised for victory. As he entered the stadium where the marathon finish line lay and began his final lap, Pietri had a comfortable lead over his nearest competitors. But it soon became clear to the stadium crowd that the race had taken its toll on the Italian runner. He collapsed to the ground on four separate occasions on the final lap. Each time, he dragged himself back to his feet and staggered on as the crowd roared encouragement. But after regaining his feet for the fourth time, it was not at all clear whether the semi-conscious Pietri would be able to cross the finish line and claim the gold. Thus, two officials scurried out to the track and helped him across the line. One of these officials was the stadium announcer, while the other was, according to some accounts, none other than Sir Arthur Conan Doyle, creator of the Sherlock Holmes character.

After Pietri staggered across the finish line, the London crowd roared its approval and congratulations. But Olympic officials reluctantly decided that they could not give the gold to him, since he had "used external support" to finish the marathon. He was disqualified, even though he vehemently denied that he had asked for help from anyone. Pietri's disqualification meant that the winner of the 1908 Olympic marathon was American John Joseph Hayes, who finished with a time of 2:55:18.4. Pietri was tremendously disappointed by the turn of events, but he did receive some salve for his emotional wounds the day after the race, when Queen Alexandra arranged a ceremony at which she awarded him a golden trophy in recognition of his gutsy performance.

Who was the "**Mechanical Man**"?

Finnish distance runner Paavo Nurmi, who set 22 world records and won 12 Olympic medals (nine gold and three silver) during his legendary athletic career. Dubbed the Mechanical Man because of the odd upright stance that he maintained when he ran, Nurmi dominated the distance events in the 1920, 1924, and 1928 Olympics. Nurmi had many glorious Olympic moments, but none could match his performance of July 10, 1924, when he took the gold in both the 1,500- and 5,000-meter running events despite having only one hour of rest between the two events.

In 1932, however, Nurmi was permanently banned from Olympic competition by the IOC because he had claimed travel expenses to finance his trips to track meets around the world. The IOC ruled that those claims were a violation of amateur regula-

Wilma Rudolph finishes off the U.S. Women's victory in the 4x100-meter relay at the 1960 Olympics.

tions. Finland was outraged by the decision, and 20 years later, when the Fins hosted
the 1952 Summer Games, they made it clear that they had not forgotten the IOC's rul-
ing. Finland featured Nurmi on the official poster for the 1952 Helsinki Olympics and
chose the runner to carry the Olympic torch into Helsinki Stadium to start the games.

Who won the highly anticipated clash between British distance runners **Steve Ovett and Sebastian Coe** at the 1980 Summer Olympics?

At the end of 1979, Coe was the world record holder in the 800 meters, 1,500 meters, and
the mile. But in the months prior to the opening ceremonies in Moscow, Ovett served
notice that he wasn't going to meekly accept second-best status. He bettered Coe's record
mark in the mile, and tied his countryman's best-ever time in the 1,500 meters.

As it turned out, the two British track stars shared the spotlight. Coe grabbed the
gold in the 1,500 meters, even though most track observers felt that Ovett was better
in the longer distance. Coe finished with a time of 3:38.4, barely edging East Germany's Jurgen Straub (3:38.8) and Ovett (3:39.0). But Ovett managed to win the gold
at 800 meters, Coe's preferred distance. Ovett took the top spot with a time of 1:45.4,
while Coe was forced to settle for silver with a finish of 1:45.9.

Who was the **"Flying Housewife"**?

Fanny Blankers-Koen of the Netherlands, who starred in the 1948 Summer Olympics in
London. A 30-year-old mother of two children, she won a total of four gold medals (80
meter hurdles, 100 meter sprint, 200 meter sprint, 4 x 100 meter relay). Blankers-
Koen's great performance was all the more remarkable because it came in an era when
women with children were often discouraged from taking part in athletic competition.

Finnish runner Paavo Nurmi lights the Olympic torch at the 1952 Summer Games hosted by Helsinki, Finland.

Abebe Bikila (on podium) won Olympic marathon gold in 1960 and 1964.

Her performance inspired countless young women who did not wish to leave sports behind upon entering motherhood. It also led many historians to wonder how many medals she might have won had the Olympics not been suspended in 1940 and 1944, the prime of her athletic career.

Why were American sprinters **Tommie Smith and John Carlos** kicked off the 1968 team after posting medal-winning performances?

Smith won the gold medal in the 200-meter sprint at the 1968 Games in Mexico City, while teammate Carlos snagged the bronze medal in the same event. But their actions during the subsequent medal ceremony caused a firestorm of controversy and led the managers of the American contingent to ban both athletes from the national team. During the playing of the American national anthem, both Smith and Carlos had raised black-gloved fists in the air from their positions on the awards dias. This salute was a recognized symbol of the radical black power movement, a controversial movement that had risen in the 1960s to protest the treatment African Americans often received in the United States. U.S. officials were infuriated by the actions of Carlos and Smith, and both athletes were permanently banned from all future Olympic competition.

Who won the **first women's 400-meter hurdles** race in the Olympics?

Nawal El Moutawakel of Morocco became the first ever women's gold medal winner in this event when she topped the field at the 1984 Summer Olympics in Los Angeles.

British rivals Steve Ovett (279) and Sebastian Coe (254) shared the spotlight in the 1980 Olympics, each one winning the event in which the other was favored.

How does the modern pentathlon differ from the pentathlon?

Five events comprise the modern pentathlon: equestrian, fencing, pistol shooting, swimming, and cross-country running. The only contemporary event of the five that has changed significantly from the 1912 Olympic format is the equestrian competition, which is now a 350-to-450-meter stadium-jumping course instead of a 5000-meter cross-country course. The scoring system has been completely revised to produce a points award for each individual performance, and the highest point total after five events is the winner. Both individual and team competitions have traditionally been held, but only the individual competition survives for the contemporary Olympic Games.

She wasn't a favorite to win gold in the event, but rose to the occasion by posting a time of 54.61 seconds, edging American Judi Brown (silver, with a time of 55.20 seconds) and Romania's Cristina Cojocaru (bronze, 55.41 seconds). El Moutawakel's victory was also noteworthy because it marked the very first time that a Moroccan woman had won a gold medal in Olympic competition.

What are the origins of the **pentathlon**?

The pentathlon was designed for the soldier athlete and included discus, spear or javelin throwing, broad jumping, running, and wrestling. Unlike the modern pentathlon, in which every person competes to the end, the original pentathlon was an elimination contest. All participants took part in the broad jumping contest. Those who jumped a certain distance entered the second event, spear or javelin throwing. The four best in that event qualified for the sprint. The top three in the sprint entered the discus throw, and the two surviving athletes wound up the grueling competition wrestling each other to a finish. The exhausted winner was crowned the Olympic pentathlon champion.

How are **Pentathlon events** structured?

Shooting: Competitors fire air pistols. The targets, 10 meters away, face the shooter for three seconds, then rotate away for seven seconds. During the three seconds, the contestant must raise the pistol, aim, and fire one shot. After four rounds of five shots each, the scores are totaled. Each bullet is worth up to 10 points, with the highest possible target score being 200 points. Only twice in Olympic history has a perfect score been achieved.

Fencing: This is the only event of the five in which the athletes engage in one-on-one competition. The dueling sword, or épée, is used in one-hit, sudden death bouts, which are limited to two minutes but often end in a matter of seconds. Scoring is determined by percentage of wins.

Swimming: A three-hundred-meter freestyle heat in which athletes are swimming against the clock: the faster the time, the more points the pentathlete earns.

Riding: On horses selected by random draw immediately before the competition, the riders are allowed a maximum of 20 minutes to practice with their mount. Horse and rider take on a 350- to-450-meter course of 15 obstacles. Points are taken off for refusals, falls, knockdowns, and for riding too slowly.

Running: A 4000-meter cross-country course is run, which begins with a staggered start: competitors take their places according to their standings going into this final event. Whoever crosses the finish line first is the winner of the entire Pentathlon event.

Has anyone **won the decathlon and the pentathlon**?

Jim Thorpe won both at the 1912 Summer Olympics in Stockholm. At the medal ceremony, King Gustav V of Sweden presented him with the golds and said, "You, sir, are the greatest athlete in the world," to which Thorpe replied, "Thanks, King." A 1950 poll of Associated Press sportswriters agreed, voting Thorpe the greatest athlete of the first half of the twentieth century.

How many times has an American won the Olympic **decathlon** competition?

Americans have won 11 of 19 gold medals in this event since 1912. Following is a list of the winners, along with their point totals (pre-1996 point totals have been retabulated based on adjusted tables approved by the International Amateur Track Federation):

> 1912: Jim Thorpe (6,564 points)
> 1924: Harold Osborn (6,476 points)
> 1932: Jim Bausch (6,735 points)
> 1936: Glenn Morris (7,254 points)
> 1948: Bob Mathias (6,628 points)
> 1952: Bob Mathias (7,580 points)
> 1956: Milt Campbell (7,565 points)
> 1960: Rafer Johnson (7,901 points)
> 1968: Bill Toomey (8,158 points)
> 1976: Bruce Jenner (8,634 points)
> 1996: Dan O'Brien (8,824 points)

Of the above gold medal-winning performances, nine of them set new world or Olympic records at the time. Only Bob Mathias's 1948 victory and Dan O'Brien's gold-medal performance in 1996 did not come on the strength of a new world or Olympic record.

What is the **Fosbury Flop** and when did it become popular?

The Fosbury Flop was invented by high-jumper Dick Fosbury during the 1960s. It involves the jumper twisting his body during flight over the bar so that he clears it while manuvering his back over the bar, rather than the more traditional side twisting. The "Fosbury flop" became the talk of the town at the 1968 Games when Fosbury won the gold medal with an Olympic record-breaking jump of 7ft, 4.25in. Soviet Yuri Tarmak won the gold in Munich in 1972, but still fell one inch short of Fosbury's mark. At Montreal in 1976, Dwight Stones, who had placed third in the Munich Games, placed third again, although the world record he had set prior to the 1976 Games remained untouched. Poland's Jacek Wszola set a new Olympic record that year with his gold-winning 7ft, 4.5in jump. Between 1972 and 1992, 13 of the 15 men's Olympic high jumping medalists used the Fosbury Flop.

What is a **discus** made of, and how is the discus competition arranged?

Today's discus is made from wood and metal and shaped like a saucer. It has a metal rim and metal center for added weight. The men's discus is about 22 centimeters (0.66 inches) and weighs two kilograms (4 pounds, 6.5 ounces). The women's discus weighs one kilogram and measures 18 centimeters (7.13 inches).

The athlete holds the discus flat against the palm and forearm while standing in the 2.5m (eight foot, 2.25-inch) throwing circle. The throw begins with one and a half spins that leads to a sidearm release. The discus spins through the air at an upward angle, the spin helping to propel it further. Throws with a strong wind will carry the discus further, but there is no rule against wind-aided throws. This makes it difficult to compare the distances of throws. Once the athlete enters the throwing circle, he or she must not leave until the discus has landed. Throws are measured from the landing point to the inside edge of the circle.

Too much spin on the thrower's part causes an uneven launch. Early discus throwers were strong but slow athletes who depended on pure power for throw length. Smaller but quicker athletes began to get better results by concentrating on form and spin. The winning distance for the discus has more than doubled since the modern Games began in 1896, when the winning throw was 95 feet, 7.5 inches.

What is a **shot put** made of, and how is the shot put competition arranged?

The shot is a ball of solid metal that weighs 16 pounds for men, and eight pounds, 13 ounces for women. The goal of this event is to "put" the shot as far as possible.

Who won the discus competition in four straight Olympic Games from 1956 to 1968?

American Al Oerter dominated the discuss for four consecutive Olympics, claiming gold for the U.S. in 1956, 1960, 1964, and 1968. He broke the world record for discus throwing on four different occasions during this incredible streak, which made him the first Olympic athlete to win four consecutive titles in the same event.

Because shots lose weight in use—tiny particles get chipped off when they land—the balls are weighed before each use. Additional tungsten chips can be added through a plugged hole to bring the shot back up to legal weight.

The shot must be pushed, or put, not thrown. The shot must not drop during the put below the athlete's shoulder. The putting technique begins with the contestant holding the shot in his or her hand, which rests against the shoulder. This is followed by a series of hops inside the putting circle, which is seven feet (2.1m) in diameter. The athlete then springs powerfully from a near-crouch, unleashes his or her arm, and lets loose the shot with a powerful push.

The athlete must remain within the circle during the throw. The ring is bounded by a board four inches (10cm) high at the top of the circle. The purpose is to allow the competitor's foot to hit the board without pushing beyond the circle. Measurement is from the point of impact to the inside circumference of the putting circle.

Like discus throwers, shot putters were originally physically powerful athletes who lacked technique. That changed as speed became important and as weight training improved performances. Additionally, shot putters were among the first athletes to abuse steroids, and many performances improved accordingly. Up until the early 20th century, most shot putters used the side-on hop favored by Scottish athletes since the beginning of the 19th century. A new putting technique was developed by American Parry O'Brien, who started with his back to the putting field to give more momentum before releasing the shot. He won gold medals in 1952 and 1956. Some putters use a relatively new technique of making one complete spin in the ring before putting.

Who was the most **dominant athlete** in a track and field event?

Hurdler Edwin Moses won the World Cup 400m hurdles in Dusseldorf, West Germany, in 1977, beginning a string of 122 consecutive victories and setting a record for dominance in a track event. It was ten years later, in June 1987, when he finally lost a race.

Moses won two gold medals at the Summer Olympic Games (1976 and 1984). In the 1976 Summer Olympics in Montréal, he won in record time—47.64 seconds—then went on to break that world record three times, reaching 47.02 seconds in 1983.

What is the **hammer**, and how is the **hammer throw** competition arranged?

The hammer is a 16-pound metal ball attached to nearly four feet (121.5cm) of a spring steel wire that leads to grips. The name apparently derives from the Scottish and English sport of sledgehammer throwing.

The throwing circle is seven feet (2.1m) in diameter. Inside the circle, with his feet stationary, the thrower grasps the handle in both hands and begins to swing the hammer. He swings the hammer in an arc so it passes below his knees and above his head several times. Before releasing the hammer he swings his body around to build up even more force, up to 500 pounds (227kg). Measurement of the throw is from the dent in the ground where the hammer landed to the inside circumference of the circle. A cage protects spectators from wild throws. Throws that land outside a marked field are not allowed.

Irish Americans won the hammer toss at the Olympics from 1896-1924. John Flanagan, a New York City policeman and Irish emigrant, won three golds, and Matt McGrath, also a policeman, won a gold and a silver. Europeans dominated the sport then until the mid-1950s. Soviet hammer throwers swept the event in the 1976, 1980, and 1988 Olympics, and again as the Unified Team in 1992.

How is the **javelin** competition organized?

A men's javelin must weigh at least 800 grams (one pound, 12.25 ounces) and measure 2.6-2.7 meters (eight feet, 6.25 inches and eight feet, 10.25 inches). A women's javelin weighs at least 600 grams (26.16 ounces) and measures 2.2-2.3 meters (seven feet, 2.66 inches and seven feet, 6.5 inches). The shaft can be either wood or metal, though the tip is always steel. For a throw to be counted, the metal tip must break the turf, and the distance is measured from the first touch-down point to a scratch line at the end of the thrower's runway.

Unlike competitors in other throwing events, javelin throwers wear spikes. They begin with a sprint down a runway, carrying the spear-like instrument by a grip in the shaft's center. As they near the line, throwers turn to one side, pull back the javelin and throw. Crossing the scratch line disqualifies the throw, and spinning before throwing the javelin is illegal because it endangers spectators.

In the Middle Ages, the javelin was thrown for accuracy. Throwing for distance was developed in Hungary and Germany in the mid-1800s. Most modern developments in the sport came in Sweden and Finland. Throwers from those two countries won all the Olympic competitions in javelin until 1936.

Franklin Held, an American, helped develop a more aerodynamic javelin. It floated farther but sometimes landed flat rather than at the point. He used this javelin to extend the world record to 263 feet. An East German athlete threw the javelin 16 feet, eight inches beyond the world record at the time, and in 1986 an amateur sports federation placed limits on javelins that emphasize aerodynamics over distance.

How do fellow Alabamans **Carl Lewis and Jesse Owens** compare in their **Olympic achievements**?

James Cleveland (Jesse) Owens, who was born in Danville, Alabama, and later attended Ohio State University, set a world record of 26 ft 83 in. for the running broad jump as a member of the Buckeyes' track squad in 1935, and the following year he set a new world record of 10.2 seconds for the 100m dash. At the 1936 Olympic Games held in Berlin, Owens won four gold medals: he ran the 100m dash in 10.3 seconds, equaling the Olympic record; he ran the 200m dash in 20.7 seconds, setting a new world and Olympic record; he won the running broad jump with a leap of 26 ft. 5I inches, setting a new Olympic record; and he was a member of the U.S. 400m relay team that set a new Olympic and world record of 39.8 seconds.

Frederick Carlton (Carl) Lewis, who was born in Birmingham, Alabama, and later attended the University of Houston, won nine gold medals spanning the Olympic Games of 1984, 1988, 1992 and 1996 (he had also qualified for the 1980 games in Moscow but was unable to compete because United States participation at the games was canceled to protest against the Soviet invasion of Afghanistan). At the 1984 Olympics in Los Angeles, Lewis won gold medals in the 100-meter and 200-meter dashes, the long jump, and the 4 x 100-meter relay—a feat that had only been accomplished once before, by Jesse Owens at the 1936 Olympics.

Lewis placed second in the 100-meter dash at the 1988 Olympics, but was declared the winner of this race when Ben Johnson was disqualified. Lewis also won the long jump. He won two more gold medals at the 1992 Olympics in Barcelona, Spain, in the 4 x 100-meter relay and in the long jump.

In which Olympic games did a **man compete in a woman's track and field event**?

One of the more bizarre episodes in Olympic history took place during the 1936 Summer Games in Berlin. Adolf Hitler's obsession with proving Aryan "superiority" was so all-consuming that German Olympic officials forced a young man on the team to hide his gender and compete in the women's high jump event in order to increase Germany's total medal count. The subterfuge didn't work, though, since he could do no better than fourth in the event. Hungary's Ibolya Csak (gold), Great Britain's Dorothy

Odam (silver), and Germany's Elfreide Kaun (bronze) all posted better jumps than the young man, who competed under the name Dora Ratjen.

Two years later, in 1938, German officials barred Ratjen from future athletic competition, charging that he was a hermaphrodite. It was not until the late 1960s, when Ratjen admitted that he had never been a hermaphrodite but had in fact been coerced into hiding his gender and competing in the women's high jump during the 1936 Games, that his strange secret was revealed.

Which Olympic sprinter was **stripped of his gold medal** after he tested positive for performance-enhancing drugs?

Canadian runner Ben Johnson lost his gold medal three days after winning the men's 100-meter race in a world-record time of 9.79 seconds. The decision to take the award (and the world record) from Johnson, who had been hailed throughout Canada as the nation's newest national hero, made the case the most spectacular drug incident in Olympic history. It also made American Carl Lewis the gold medal winner (9.92 seconds). The shocking turn of events angered and saddened all of Canada, and their national team quickly announced that Johnson had been banned from ever representing Canada again. That lifetime ban was, however, later reduced to two years.

WINTER GAMES

Who first came up with the idea of holding a **separate Winter Olympics**?

An Italian fellow named Eugene Brunetta d'Usseaux suggested the idea after the 1908 Games in London, which featured figure skating as one of its events. Even though they were certain to win just about everything in sight, the Scandinavian countries registered the most resistance to the idea. They worried that instituting a Winter Olympics might spell the end of the Nordic Games, a Scandinavian athletic competition that had been held in Sweden since 1901.

But as time passed and competitions in winter sports like figure skating and ice hockey became part of the Games, more and more people threw their support behind the institution of separate winter and summer competitions. The final push came in 1924, when an International Winter Sports Week was staged in Chamonix, France. It attracted 258 athletes from 16 countries to compete in five major areas—bobsled, ice hockey, speed skating, figure skating, and Nordic events. As expected, athletes from Scandinavian countries dominated the competition, which was a tremendous success.

Why did the 1932 Winter Olympics become a financial disaster for organizers?

The 1932 Games, which were held in Lake Placid, New York, were unable to overcome the Great Depression, which devastated the economies of nations all around the world. Many countries couldn't afford to send their athletes to America (over half of the athletes who competed were from Canada or the U.S.), while the U.S. itself found that economic worries convinced most Americans to hold on to what little money they had rather than spend it on the Games. Finally, the events were cursed with warm weather that transformed ice and snow into slush and forced repeated reschedulings of competitions. Unable to catch a break, the Games' organizers got financially soaked.

The IOC was forced to admit that the time had come for a Winter Olympics, and in 1925 it officially sanctioned a winter version of the Games. Some time later, the 1924 gathering at Chamonix was retroactively recognized as the world's first Winter Olympics.

Which nation has **hosted the most Winter Olympics** Games?

Both the United States (1932, 1960, and 1980) and France (1924, 1968, and 1992) have hosted the Winter Games three times. The only other countries that have hosted the Winter Games more than once are Norway (1952 and 1994), Austria (1964 and 1976), Switzerland (1928 and 1948), and Japan (1972 and 1998).

In which Winter Olympics did the United States post its **poorest performance**?

At the 1988 Winter Games in Calgary, the United States national team struggled to a tie for eighth place among the 57 participating nations. Those games mark the USA's worst place showing at any Olympic competition (the United States has finished no worse than third in any Summer Olympics competition).

Which gold medal-winning team was composed primarily of women who had **given birth within the previous 20 months**?

Of the five women that won the inaugural women's team curling event for Canada at the 1998 Winter Olympics, four had delivered children within the past 20 months.

HOCKEY

What countries have won the most **Olympic hockey medals**?

Since hockey debuted as a full-medal sport at the Winter Olympic Games in Chamonix, France, in 1924, Canada and Russia (the former Soviet Union) have won the most medals, garnering 11. Canada's yield includes five golds, four silvers, and two bronzes, while Russia has earned eight golds. The United States and the Czech Republic have both won eight medals (with the Czechs earning their first gold in 1998), and Sweden has earned seven.

Women's hockey became a full-medal sport in 1998, so three countries—the United States with gold, Canada with silver, and Finland with bronze—share the lead with one medal apiece.

How do **Olympic and NHL rules differ**?

Olympic hockey rules differ in several respects from those of the National Hockey League. An offside pass crossing the center, or red line, is called immediately in the NHL and play stops. In the Olympics, extenuating circumstances may permit play to continue at the referee's discretion. Similarly, play is stopped in the NHL for any offside or when a player enters the faceoff circle at the time of a faceoff. But in the Olympics, no whistle is blown if the non-offending team gains possession of the puck.

In Olympic hockey, a second major penalty carries an automatic game misconduct and a trip to the locker room. Any Olympian starting a fight is assessed a match penalty.

In which Olympics did the United States send **two different ice hockey teams** to compete for the gold?

In 1948 the U.S. sent two teams to St. Moritz, Switzerland, each of which claimed to be the true representative of their country. One of the teams was put together by the U.S. National Olympic Committee, while the other was organized by the Amateur Hockey Association of the United States (AHAUS). Despite IOC concerns about the amateur status of some of the players on the AHAUS squad, both teams were allowed to compete. Neither team was able to secure a medal, and in 1949 the IOC announced that the AHAUS team (which had finished fourth in the games) had been retroactively disqualified.

What was the "**Miracle on Ice**"?

In the 1980 Winter Olympics at Lake Placid, New York, an upstart group of young Americans defeated the heavily favored Soviet team on their way to claiming the gold

How is the 12-team Olympic field determined?

For the Winter Olympics, ten countries are eligible based on their finish in the previous year's world championships. The defending Olympic champion is given an automatic berth, as is the host nation. The 12 countries are split into two groups, with each group engaging in a five-game round-robin series. The two teams with the best records from each division advance to the semifinals, where the winner of each group meets the second place team of the other group. The two survivors then play for the championship.

medal. At the time, the U.S. team was composed of amateurs, while the Soviets were, essentially, professionals. Announcer Al Michaels immortalized the moment as the game clock ticked down by shouting, "Do you believe in miracles? YES!"

In which Olympic hockey gold-medal match were the game officials **pelted with snowballs**?

The 1948 Winter Games were held in St. Moritz, Switzerland, and when the Swiss hockey team advanced to the finals against Canada, a large crowd of Swiss hockey fans descended on the outdoor rink to cheer their team. But given the meager seating capacity around the rink, thousands of Swiss fans were forced to retire to the surrounding snowy hillsides. This proved to be an unfortunate development for the hockey referees, for as the game unfolded and the Swiss team fell behind, each officiating call that went against Switzerland aroused greater anger among the watching fans. By the third period, Swiss fans up on the hills were using the surrounding snow as ammunition, bombarding the refs with a blizzard of snowballs after any call with which they disagreed. Ultimately, though, the aerial assault was insufficient to turn the game around, as Canada cruised to a 3-0 victory and the gold medal.

Who did better at the 1998 Winter Olympics, the **U.S. men's hockey team or the U.S. women's hockey team**?

Not much debate about this one. The U.S. women's team took the gold medal in the first women's Olympic hockey tournament with a 3–1 victory over archrival Canada, displaying a virtuouso blend of talent, poise, and enthusiasm that delighted American viewers. Led by goalie Sarah Tueting, defenseman Angela Ruggiero, and forward Cammi Granato (who was chosen to carry the U.S. flag in the closing ceremonies), the women's team provided indisputable proof that hockey is no longer the exclusive domain of the male gender.

397

The U.S. hockey team stunned the world when it won the gold medal at the 1980 Winter Olympic Games in Lake Placid, NY.

Meanwhile, the U.S. men's team floundered, eventually leaving Nagano with a badly stained public image and little else (except an outstanding hotel bill). The squad never got untracked on the ice at Nagano, and after the tournament began the team was quickly eliminated from medal contention. They *did* manage to make some headlines with their boorish behavior at Nagano. Reports of late-night partying and Olympic Village rowdiness by some team members during the tournament caused more than a few raised eyebrows, but it wasn't until the team trashed a couple of hotel rooms before their departure that their behavior at the Games became a real issue. In the weeks following the vandalism, the NHL, USA Hockey, and the U.S. Olympic Committee all launched investigations to determine who on the team was responsible, but the responsible parties were never found. Sadly, the ugly incident—and the stonewalling that followed—tarnished the reputation of the entire men's hockey team.

Who was the netminder who led the **Czech Republic** to the 1998 Winter Olympics gold medal in men's hockey?

Buffalo Sabre goalie Dominik Hasek was invincible in Nagano. He allowed only six goals in six games, and was brilliant in a shoot-out win over Canada that advanced his team to the gold medal final. In that final against Russia, Hasek posted his second shutout of the tournament to lift the Czech Republic to a 1-0 victory and the gold medal.

SKIING AND SNOWBOARDING

What are the different types of **downhill skiing**?

Alpine, or downhill, takes place on steep slopes where the skiers follow a route and the best time wins. There are four types of Alpine races, plus a combined contest:

Downhill Racing—skiing down a sharply descending slope on a relatively straight course made up of poles with marker flags, placed in pairs. The racer passes through the gates while reaching speeds of 130 km/h (about 80 mph).

Slalom Racing—skiing in zigzags down and across the surface of a sloping course (in Norwegian, slalom means "sloping track") of about 536 m (about 1760 ft), maneuvering through 45 to 75 gates. A slalom race is run over two different courses and the winner is determined by who has fastest combined time for the two runs.

The Giant Slalom—a longer slalom, usually 1.6 km (1 mile) in length for men, run over two different courses, and the winner is determined by who has the fastest combined time for the two runs.

The Super Giant Slalom—also known as the Super G, this race combines downhill and giant slalom and features long, high-speed turns. The winner is decided in one run.

The Combined—skiers compete in downhill and slalom runs, with the best cumulative time over the two runs determining the winner.

What are the different kinds of **Freestyle Skiing**?

The Ballet—a 2 minute, 15 second program of jumps, spins, and gliding steps performed to music while the skier moves down a smooth slope. The routine is judged on its technical difficulty and the skier's overall performance and choreography.

Mogul—high-speed turns on a snow-bumped slope, where competitors are judged on the quality and technique of turns and their line down the slope, upright aerial tricks, and speed.

Aerial competitions—the skier makes an acrobatic leap from a specially prepared ski jump; the scoring is based on the takeoff, form and execution in the air, and landing, with the judges' scores multiplied by the degree of difficulty and the lowest and highest scores discarded.

Snowboarding's cool. What am I looking for?

Snowboarding, a cross-breed of skateboarding and surfing, debuted as an Olympic sport in the 1998 Games at Nagano, Japan, with two events—the half-pipe and the giant slalom. The sport began in the United States in the late 1960s when skis were tied together to create a winter surfboard. The equipment became more sophisticated, with symmetrically-shaped boards (for easier movement) made of fiberglass and wood and two bindings. Snowboarding grew rapidly in the late 1980s and the 1990s, and an estimated 40 percent of people who go to the snow will be snowboarding, rather than skiing, by the year 2000.

Beside the wild colors of gear and hair, look for similarities in giant slalom snowboarding with its skiing namesake, with the boarder passing through gates. The fastest boarder who doesn't miss a gate is the winner.

The half-pipe features a U shaped course, the name referring to its shape—like a pipe cut in half: boarders ride up to the lip of the pipe, leap off the edge, and perform aerial tricks—the more original and intricate the better. Judging categories include Standard Maneuvers, Rotational Maneuvers, Amplitude, Landings, and Overall/Technical Merit. Unlike figure skaters, snowboarders are not expected to execute pre-arranged jumps or rotations.

What is the **biathlon**, and what are its origins?

Perhaps the most unknown Olympic sport as far as Americans are concerned, the biathlon is a grueling discipline that combines furious cross-country skiing with expert marksmanship. Although not a Winter Olympic event until 1960, biathlon has its origins in ancient Scandinavian society. Early Scandinavians, after inventing skis for transportation across the snowy terrain, soon discovered that stalking prey was easier on skis than afoot. Later, when survival became less of a day-to-day struggle, the combination of skiing and shooting was included in the training of infantry soldiers, particularly in Finland. This led to the military ski patrol race, which began early this century among European armies.

In 1958, the first world biathlon championship was held in Austria. The 2km biathlon was added to the Olympics program in 1960; in 1968, the 30km relay was

Jean-Claude Killy dominated the skiing events of the 1968 Winter Olympics in Grenoble, France. He became a French national hero and helped organize the 1992 Albertville Games.

added. The 10km race made its Olympic debut in 1980. Olympic biathlon had been an all-male preserve, but in 1992 women made their skiing and shooting debut in three events: the 7.5km, 15km, and the 3 x 7.5km relay.

Which Olympic Games were dubbed the "**Killympics**"?

The 1968 Winter Olympic Games held in Grenoble, France, acquired this nickname after French skiing legend Jean-Claude Killy snared gold in all three Alpine skiing events. The dashing Frenchman took the gold in the slalom with a time of 1:39.73, barely edging Austria's Herbert Huber (1:39.82) on a course that was shrouded in fog. He also won the giant slalom, posting a time of 3:29.28 that was more than two seconds faster than the time posted by silver medalist Willy Favre of Switzerland (3:31.50). Killy needed a little good fortune to secure a sweep of the Alpine skiing events, though. Both Austrian Karl Schranz and Norwegian Haakon Mjoen lost their spots ahead of Killy (1:59.85) when they were disqualified for missing gates. Fellow Frenchman Guy Perillat ended up taking home the silver medal with a time of 1:59.93.

Killy's exploits, which unfolded before huge audiences of delighted countrymen, made him an enduring national hero. In subsequent years, the skier maintained his association with the Olympics. He was a major organizer of the 1992 Winter Games in Albertville, and in 1995 he was named to the International Olympic Committee.

> ## Which set of twin brothers
> ## grabbed the top two spots in the 1984 men's slalom?
>
> Americans Phil and Steve Mahre. Prior to the 1984 Winter Games at Sarajevo, no American skier had ever won the gold medal in the men's slalom. But Phil Mahre shattered that state of affairs by posting a time of 1:39.21, and his brother Steve grabbed the silver medal in the event by skiing to a time of 1:39.62 (France's Didier Bouvet took the bronze with a time of 1:40.20). The United States also took a gold in the downhill alpine skiing event that year, as Bill Johnson grabbed the top spot on the awards dias with a time of 1:45.59.

Which gold medal-winning **Alpine skier** became almost as well known for his late-night carousing as for his prowess on the slopes?

Italian playboy Alberto Tomba was a media magnet at the Winter Games of the late 1980s and 1990s. A fearless skier who barreled down the slopes in a wonderfully smooth but aggressive style, Tomba earned five medals from 1988 to 1994. It was during the 1988 competition in Calgary that he first exploded into the international spotlight, as he secured gold in both the slalom and giant slalom events. In the 1992 Games at Albertville, he won another gold in the giant slalom while tallying a silver in the slalom. And in the 1994 games at Lillehammer, Tomba added another silver in the slalom to his treasure chest (his efforts to win a sixth medal at the 1998 Winter Games at Nagano were unsuccessful).

But as impressive as Tomba's Olympic performances were, they were made all the more remarkable by the Italian skier's unique training regimen. While fellow Alpine skiers slumbered in the Olympic Village, Tomba became famous for his late-night partying. Indeed, Tomba reveled in his irrepressible playboy image and emerged as a favorite of television and print reporters. The Italian's colorful lifestyle apparently impressed his countrymen as well, for he attracted a fanatical following on the slopes at every Olympic competition.

Which American gold medalist at the 1998 Winter Games didn't even have a **first name** until she was six years old?

Fan favorite Picabo Street, who was a surprise winner of the Super G event at Nagano, went through the first six years of her life known simply as "Baby Girl" Street. The child of free-spirited hippie parents who raised their children in a household without television, Street was given the name Picabo (which is a Native American word for

Nikki Stone overcame severe back injuries to claim the freestyle ski jumping gold in Nagano.

"shining waters") only after her parents discovered that they wouldn't be able to take her into Mexico on a vacation if she didn't have a first name on her passport.

Today, her unique name—which is pronounced Peek-A-Boo—and her engaging personality have made her one of downhill skiing's most popular figures. Of course, Street's amazing talent on the slopes is a factor in her popularity as well. In 1994 she won a silver medal in the downhill, and many observers felt that she had as good a chance as anyone to win gold in the downhill in 1998. But she jolted everyone by winning the Super G event instead (she finished sixth in the downhill competition).

Which U.S. athlete won a gold medal at the 1998 Winter Olympics only a few years after suffering **back injuries** that threatened her ability to even compete in her event?

American Nikki Stone won a gold medal in freestyle ski jumping at Nagano, marking the culmination of a comeback from a series of back injuries that led doctors to tell her that she would never be able to ski jump again.

Which skier recovered from one of the most **spectacular crashes** in Olympic history to win two gold medals in the 1998 Winter Games?

Early in the downhill competitions at Nagano, Austrian Alpine skiing sensation Hermann Maier had lost control near the top of the course and flown off the mountain at roughly 65 miles per hour, plowing through two snow fences before finally coming to rest in a snowdrift. His coach, Werner Margreiter, later said that "[the crash] was the most incredible thing. I was watching, and then Hermann went sailing past, a couple stories above everything else." Amazingly, Maier suffered only a sprained right knee and a bruised left shoulder from the crash, and when bad weather delayed the Alpine events for three days, the Austrian received valuable time to recuperate, both physically and mentally. When the time came for him to make his run in the super giant slalom (Super G), Maier once again unveiled his pre-crash form, flying down the hill with the same mixture of grace and daring that had made him a pre-Olympic favorite to return home with gold. By the time the Alpine events were done, Maier had taken the gold in both the Super G and the giant slalom events.

Which was the **first non-European country to take all three medals** in a winter event?

In the 1972 Winter Games at Sapporo, Japan, three Japanese skiers took all three spots on the podium in the small (70 meters) hill ski jump. The gold medal winner for Japan was Yukio Kasaya. She was joined by Akitsugu Konno (silver) and Seiji Aochi (bronze).

Canadian Ross Rebagliati caused quite a stir when he won the gold in the first-ever Olympic snowboarding event, then tested positive for marijuana.

What was the margin of victory posted by the gold medal-winning Norwegian **cross-country ski** team in the 4 x 10-kilometer relay in the 1998 Winter Games?

Incredibly, Norway won by only two-tenths of a second in an event that routinely takes nearly two hours to complete. Chasing the Italian team for much of the event, Norway nosed out a gold medal by the slimmest of margins—the tip of a single ski—when anchor skier Thomas Alsgaard made a desperate lunge across the finish line.

Why was the inaugural Olympic **snowboarding** competition at the 1998 Games in Nagano so controversial?

Canadian snowboarder Ross Rebagliati won the gold medal in the event, only to have the medal taken away from him a couple days later when he tested positive for marijuana. The IOC decision triggered a tremendous controversy, especially after Rebagliati claimed that, while he had smoked marijuana in the past, he had quit in the months prior to the Olympics. He argued that the positive test was due to second-hand smoke exposure at parties in which some of his friends had smoked the illegal substance. Conflicting reports about the likely truth of Rebagliati's contention did nothing to quell the dust-up. Ultimately, the IOC relented and returned the gold medal to Rebagliati, who became the newest hero of snowboarding's infamously rebellious subculture as a result of the hubbub.

405

Bobsledding and Luge

Why is it called **Bobsledding**?

Bobsleds are named after the bobbing of crew members on straightaways to gain speed.

What factors affect **bobsled speed**?

The chief attractions of bobsledding are the speed of the sleds (approaching 90 miles per hour) and the danger to the crew (resting on a sled less than a foot above the ground while flying down an icy, mile-long course containing a series of curves designed to control speed as well as increase it). Bobsled speed is affected by three main factors: weight, air resistance, and friction. All things being equal, the heaviest sled/crew combination will run the fastest. Therefore, a maximum weight is set for each sled and crew combination. A four-man sled cannot exceed 630 kilograms (approximately 1,389 pounds), while two-man sleds cannot exceed 390 kilograms (859 pounds). Lighter crews can add weight to their sleds before a race, but heavier sleds can prove more difficult to start, a critical element to racers. Explosive starts result in fast finish times. Racers who beat a competitor's time by a fraction of a second at the beginning of the race can finish up to two or three seconds faster at the bottom. Considering this, adding weight to a sled for competition can be more detrimental than helpful to a lighter bobsled team.

Push time is the crucial factor—how long it takes the sledders to propel their craft and leap into it over the 50-meter starting run. A tenth of a second of saved push time can earn a third of a second off the entire run. Because bobsled requires a lot of upper-body strength and foot speed, it attracts cross-overs from football and track.

When did the **two-man bobsled** competition first appear?

The 1932 Winter Olympics at Lake Placid. Two American brothers, Hubert and Curtis Stevens, were the first to win gold in the event.

What speeds are attained in the **luge event**?

Luge has been described as the most dangerous of Olympic sports, with the sleds careening downhill at speeds up to 80 mph, the riders flat on their backs, feet extending beyond the runners of the sled. For roughly 40 seconds the pressure that flattens them against the sled could be up to five times the force of gravity, or twice that exerted on an astronaut during a shuttle launch. From a spectator's point of view, it looks like a mighty uncomfortable ride. A luge is so flexible that even a slight repositioning of the head can cause the sled to veer into a wall or off the track altogether.

> ### Which athlete has won the most
> ### Olympic medals in the history of the bobsled competition?
>
> Germany's Bogdan Musiol won a total of seven medals (one gold, five silver, and one bronze) in four Winter Olympics from 1980 to 1992. He competed for the East German national team in the first three of these games, but in 1992 he was part of the reunified German team that went to Albertville.

SKATING

What are the **various maneuvers in figure skating**?

Axel: the easiest jump to recognize because it is the only jump taken from a forward position. The skater glides forward on one foot, takes off from a forward outside edge, rotates (1.5 revolutions for a single, 2.5 for a double, and 3.5 for a triple axel), and lands on the opposite foot skating backward.

Loop: take off and landing on the same floor and edge. At the point of take-off, the skater's feet may look as if they are together. The free leg is then thrown sideways and upward in the direction of the jump.

Lutz: one of the few jumps that takes off counter to the natural rotation of the edge. The skater usually approaches in a long curve, takes off from the left back outside edge with assistance from the right toe, and turns counterclockwise, landing on the outside back edge of the right foot.

Salchow: a jump with a wide leg swing. At the moment before takeoff, the back inside edge of the skating foot curves sharply and the free leg is brought forward to initiate rotation. The skater lands on the back outside edge of the opposite foot of takeoff.

Split jump: the skater jumps and performs the splits in the air with hands touching the ankles or toes.

Which figure skater in the 1988 Winter Games became the first woman Olympian since Sonja Henie to successfully **defend her individual title**?

East Germany's Katerina Witt, who was nicknamed "Carmen on Ice," skated to gold at both the 1984 Winter Games in Sarajevo and the 1988 Winter Games in Calgary. She thus became the first woman skater since Sonja Henie—who won three straight gold

> ## Going into the 1998 figure skating competition at Nagano, many people thought that the United States had a great chance to sweep all three medals. Were they able to do so?
>
> Almost, but not quite. Tiny 15-year-old skating sensation Tara Lipinski took the gold for the Americans with a sensational finale, barely edging out fellow American Michelle Kwan, who won the silver medal. But the United States' third medal hopeful, Nicole Bobek, suffered through a performance that was punctuated with unfortunate spills, and she finished the competition in 17th place.

medals from 1928 to 1936—to successfully defend her spot at the top of the medal platform.

In which **movie** did gold medal-winning figure skater (and aspiring movie star) Carol Heiss take a leading role?

Mindful of Sonja Henie's success in parlaying Olympic figure skating gold into a rewarding movie career, Heiss decided to take a similar tack to make it big in Hollywood. Unfortunately, she decided to launch her new career with a starring role in *Snow White and the Three Stooges*. Not surprisingly, the part didn't exactly establish her as a serious actress. Other movie roles were not forthcoming, and Heiss eventually abandoned her Hollywood dreams.

Which gold medal-winning **figure skater** wore a variety of casts and corrective shoes as a child?

American Kristi Yamaguchi, who won the 1992 Olympic gold medal in figure skating at the Winter Games in Albertville, was born with legs that were turned in upon each other. By the time she was two weeks old, doctors had fitted her with casts that they hoped would mitigate the problem. These casts, which were changed every couple of weeks in recognition of her growth, were a constant part of her wardrobe until her first birthday, when doctors switched her to a pair of corrective shoes that were connected to one another with a bar.

Apparently, the efforts to correct the problem worked pretty darned well, for by the time Yamaguchi was nine years old, she was skating five hours a day, and as a teenager she emerged as one of the top young skaters in the United States. By the early 1990s she was one of the top figure skaters in the world, and her victory in the

Kristi Yamaguchi took the figure skating gold in Albertville in 1992.

1991 World Championships, along with her second-place finish behind the soon-to-be-infamous Tonya Harding in the 1991 U.S. Championships, made her one of the medal favorites for Albertville.

Yamaguchi established herself immediately once the figure skating competition began. Ignoring the firestorm of media coverage about Harding's role in a dastardly assault on Nancy Kerrigan in the months prior to the games, Yamaguchi skated flawlessly in the short program to take the lead over Kerrigan, Midori Ito (Japan), and Harding. She performed well in the long program as well. Skating to music from *Malaguena*, Yamaguchi skated gracefully and athletically. She had one fall during the program, but her closest competitors suffered mishaps as well, enabling her to hold on to the gold. Ito ended up finishing second to take a silver medal, while Kerrigan claimed a spot at the awards ceremony with a third place finish. Shortly after bringing home the gold medal for America, Yamaguchi decided to turn pro, and she is now a marquee name on various ice skating tours.

Who was the **youngest-ever** Olympic gold medalist?

Figure skater Tara Lipinski won the gold in the 1998 Olympics. She's younger by one month than the previous record holder, Sonja Henie, also a figure skater.

What techniques are used in **speed skating**?

The speed skater's body position—knees and waist bent, head lifted just enough to see down the track—reduces wind resistance. A top skater usually has his/her knee bent at a 90 degree angle, but Dan Jansen used a 78-degree bend and short-track skaters sit at a thigh-burning 70- to 75-degree angle.

The start is critical to the race's outcome. Racers run on their skates, lurching toward the first turn with a furious duck walk. Some races are decided within the first 100 meters: Bonnie Blair's wins, for example, are credited to her great starts.

While racing on a speed-skating oval, the racer's skates are almost constantly turning, usually with the skater not taking more than 10 strokes between curves, and a skater hits top speed when coming out of a turn: as both legs stroke outward, the skater creates an inward force through the turn. Leaning into the 180-degree turn, the skater pivots his left leg against centripetal force—which is why a speedskater's left leg is sometimes more than an inch larger in circumference than the right. The inward force coming out of the turn translates into speed, as the skater slingshots out of the turn with a burst of forward momentum.

A skater who's found a sweet spot seems to be hardly working: movements are measured, fluid, methodical. Signs that a skater is fading include more labored strides, elbows slipping away from the back, head lifted higher, and lack of full extension of the legs.

Bonnie Blair won five gold medals while participating in three Olympics—1988 in Calgary, Canada; 1992 in Albertville, France; and 1994 in Lillehammer, Norway.

Who is the United States' **most successful Olympic speed skater**?

Bonnie Blair won one gold medal at the 1988 Winter Olympics in Calgary, Alberta, Canada; two gold medals at the 1992 Winter Olympics in Albertville, France; and two gold medals at the 1994 Winter Olympics in Lillehammer, Norway.

She also won a bronze medal in the 1000m (1093 yard) race at the 1988 Winter Olympics. Her gold medal triumph in 1992 in the 1000m race was by an incredibly close two-hundredths of a second. Her five gold medals are the most for any American female Olympic athlete.

Which American skater won **five gold medals** and set four Olympic records in the 1980 Winter Games at Lake Placid?

Speed Skater Eric Heiden destroyed all comers in five different speed skating events for the U.S.A. Heiden, who took the Olympic oath at the opening ceremony on behalf of the 1,072 athletes gathered in New York state for the Games, took the gold in the 500-, 1,000-, 1,500-, 5,000-, and 10,000-meter events. He set a world record with his 10,000-meter time of 14:28.13, and broke four other Olympic speed skating records as well.

Which skater at the 1994 Winter Games in Lillehammer could only manage a bronze medal despite posting a faster time than the gold and silver medalists?

Canadian Marc Gagnon won the bronze medal in the 1,000-meter short track skating event even though he had actually clocked a considerably faster time than South Korean skaters Ki-Hoon Kim and Ji-Hoon Chae, who were awarded the gold and silver medals. The competition had been peppered with so many disqualifications and falls that only the gold and silver medals for the event were awarded in the usual fashion. To determine the bronze medal winner, another "B" final was held in which Gagnon posted a time that was better than the gold- and silver-winning times of the Koreans. As a result, the medal summary for the event had a distinctly odd appearance:

> Gold: Ki-Hoon Kim 1:34.57
> Silver: Ji-Hoon Chae 1:34.92
> Bronze: Marc Gagnon 1:33.03

Who was the first woman to win an Olympic **speed skating** event?

German Helga Haase won the gold in the 500-meter race, the first of the women's speed skating events that were unveiled at the 1960 Olympics in Squaw Valley. Haase, who was skating as part of a single team that included athletes from both East and West Germany, took the gold with a time of 45.9 seconds. In addition, three other women's speed skating events were run for the first time in 1960. The Soviet Union's Klara Guseva took the first-ever gold medal in the 1,000-meter race, and Soviet skater Lidia Skoblikova swept the 1,500- and 3,000-meter events.

In which Olympics did the **judges stop an ongoing event** to complain that the participating athletes were "loafing"?

The 1932 Winter Games at Lake Placid, New York. In one of the stranger incidents in Olympic history, the American judges apparently were so underwhelmed at what they saw during the second heat of the men's 1,500-meter speed skating event that they stopped the race in the middle and told the baffled skaters who were competing to quit "loafing" and race faster. The judges subsequently restarted the race and watched as American John Shea took the gold medal with a time of 2:57.5. Canadian skaters Alexander Hurd and William Logan took the silver and bronze medals, respectively. Shea's victory marked the last time an American skater would win the event until 1980, 48 years later, when Eric Heiden won during Lake Placid's second go-around as host.

SOCCER

RULES AND TERMS

What is the **origin** of soccer?

References to soccer-like games date back to ancient times in Greece and Rome. In these various contests, the use of hands was still allowed. Legend has it that the game developed further after a conquering army celebrated by booting a foe's severed head into a makeshift goal. Students in England organized games in the twelfth century, by which time the use of hands was forbidden. In the 1400s, the game itself was forbidden by Edward III, who deemed it a frivolous practice. Soccer flourished again during the Restoration and was introduced outside Britain as England developed into a global empire. The word "soccer," by the way, derives rather obscurely from the term "association football," used to distinguish the game from rugby.

What are "**The Laws of Soccer**?"

The Laws are a set of seventeen rules (with many amendments and clauses) dictating everything from field dimensions to game duration and player conduct. These laws distinguish various infractions and dictate their consequences.

How are **infractions** punished?

Minor fouls are punished by awarding the injured team an indirect kick, in which two players must touch the ball before a goal may be scored. More serious fouls are punished by a direct kick, in which only the player taking the kick must touch the ball before a possible goal is scored. Extreme fouls are punished by a yellow card. Two yel-

What are the dimensions of a soccer field, and what do the markings signify?

The length of a soccer field is 100 to 130 yards. The width is 50 to 100 yards. Goals are eight yards across and eight feet high. The goal area extends six yards either side of the goal and another six yards in front, stretching twelve yards across. The goal area lies within the penalty area, which is eighteen yards long and twenty yards wide. Infractions committed within this area are punished by penalty kicks taken from a spot centered twelve yards from goal. An arc with a radius of ten yards extends from the top of the penalty area to keep players away from the penalty kicker. In the center of the field, there is a circle with a ten-yard radius that opponents cannot enter until the ball has been kicked into play to commence the half or to resume play after a goal. In addition, there are corner arcs with one-yard radii: when the defending team kicks the ball out of bounds across the goal line, the attacking team kicks the ball back into play from the corner arcs. The ball is thrown back into play when it goes out of bounds from the sidelines, or touchlines.

low cards result in expulsion. Finally, the most extreme fouls are punished with a red card, which constitutes immediate expulsion from the game.

What is "offsides?"

Offsides is to soccer as cherry picking is to basketball, except that in soccer it isn't allowed. The furthest forward attacker cannot be closer to the opponent's goal than the furthest back defender when a ball is played forward. Intelligent players time their advances to avoid being offsides. Intelligent defenders will anticipate play and actually move forward to render the opponent offsides. This ploy is called "the offsides trap." When defenders incorrectly execute the trap, attackers find themselves with open space between them and the goal.

What are the player positions?

The essential positions in soccer are goalkeeper, defender, midfielder, and forward. Most contemporary formations use four defenders, with the central defenders marking (guarding) the opposition forwards. Flanking defenders may support the midfield, funnel play towards the center, and even attack. Central midfielders usually include a playmaker and a tackler capable of winning possession. Flanking midfielders may serve as wingers to hit crossing passes to the centered attackers. Forwards, also called

What tactics are employed?

Tactics have changed throughout soccer's history. Early in the century, teams favored a 2–3–5 setup light on defenders and strong on attackers. In the late 1950s, Brazil developed a 4–2–4 formation that still allowed for plenty of offense and short passing. Italy, meanwhile, developed an extremely defensive 1–4–3–2 formation with a safety valve called a sweeper playing behind the defense. Offensive play from this setup usually derived from swift counterattacks instead of systematic buildups. During the 1970s Holland played a freewheeling style called "total soccer" wherein players were required to be proficient in all positions. In more recent years, 4–4–2 and 4–3–3 formations have been most popular, with the defenders playing in unison to execute the offside trap.

strikers, are expected to score. They may play back to goal and jockey for position or face goal and pounce onto passes played through the defense.

What can **goalkeepers** do?

Goalkeepers can use their hands on the ball provided it doesn't come to them from a teammate's foot. They can catch the ball or punch it away. They can pick it up and punt it downfield.

How **long** are games?

Soccer games are played in two forty-five minute halves totaling ninety minutes. The referee, who maintains the only game clock, adds time at the end of each half if play had previously been interrupted (usually due to injuries). If tied at the end of regulation play, World Cup games continue for two fifteen-minute halves. If tied after extra time, games are resolved in penalty shootouts, with each team selecting five players to take penalty kicks. If tied after each team has taken five penalty kicks, teams take one kick each, continuing until the tie is ended.

When are **substitutions** allowed in soccer?

In major soccer competitions, each team is allowed to make only two substitutions per game. When the play is stopped, then a team may ask the referee for permission to make a substitution. After the player who is being replaced leaves the field, then the substitute enters the game at midfield. Once a team has reached its two-substitution limit, it is not allowed to replace additional players for any reason—including when players are sent off for rules infractions or must leave the game due to injuries. One wrinkle in the substitution rule is that any player on the field may exchange places with the goalie at any time, as long as they receive permission from the referee.

What is a **throw-in**, and when is it used?

A throw-in is a two-handed, overhead toss from out of bounds. It's used to return the ball to play after it has crossed the touch line (side boundary) of the field. A throw-in is made by a member of the team that did not touch the ball last before it went out of bounds. Upon returning to the field after making a throw-in, the thrower cannot play the ball until it has been touched by another player. Also, a goal cannot be scored directly from a throw-in.

What is a **corner kick**, and when is it used?

A corner kick, like a throw-in, is used to return the ball to play once it has gone out of bounds. But unlike a throw-in—which is used when the ball has crossed the touch (side) line—a corner kick is used when the ball has crossed the end line of the field, and only when it was last touched by a defensive player before going out of bounds. The ball is placed in the corner kick area close to where it went out of bounds. Any player on the attacking team may take the corner kick, but then he or she cannot kick it again until it has been touched by another player. The defensive players must stay at least 10 yards from the ball during the kick, while the attacking players can position themselves anywhere on the field. It is possible to score a goal directly from a corner kick.

What does the referee mean when he yells, **"Advantage, play on"**?

In soccer, the referee has the option of allowing play to continue after a foul has occurred when calling the penalty would benefit the offending team. In situations where stopping play on a penalty would provide the team committing the foul with an advantage, the referee will instead allow play to continue by shouting, "Advantage, play on!"

What is a **"friendly"**?

As opposed to some matches that are part of league play or tournament competition—which can at times be decidedly unfriendly—a friendly is a game that's played merely for fun or as an exhibition. Two teams may schedule a friendly in order to prepare for a tournament, to pay tribute to an individual, or to raise money for charitable purposes. Sometimes a friendly may be played simply to generate fan interest and increase the box office receipts for the teams involved.

What does it mean to **"jockey" or "mark" an opponent**?

A soccer player who's being marked or tracked is simply being defended very closely. The concept of jockeying or shepherding an opponent is very similar. It involves mark-

What is a bicycle kick?

The acrobatic maneuver known as a bicycle or scissor kick involves a player jumping into the air, rotating the body as if doing a backward somersault, and then kicking the ball above his or her own head. It got its name from the churning or snapping motion of the legs that occurs during its execution. As one foot moves to meet the ball, the other foot moves rapidly in the other direction to provide leverage. It is arguably the most exciting individual skill in the game of soccer. The first person to popularize the bicycle kick was Leonidas of Brazil, known as the "Rubber Man." The small center forward began performing the trick in the 1930s. He was so agile that he could control the ball with one foot and then kick it with the other during a bicycle kick. Carlo Parola, who played center halfback for Juventus and Italy in the 1940s, was one of the first to use the bicycle kick in Europe.

ing an opponent closely but not making any attempt to tackle him or her. The idea is to force a player with the ball to go wide or move into a poor position so that they can't score a goal or make a good pass.

What is an "own goal"?

Also known as a self-goal, an own goal occurs when a player scores a goal against his or her own team. Unfortunately for teams that find themselves victimized by this rule, it counts as a goal any time the ball goes into the net, regardless of which team puts it there. An own goal has decided the outcome of major international competitions on several occasions. For example, Hungary took the gold medal at the 1964 Olympic Games as a result of an own goal by Czechoslovakia. In 1975, an own goal prevented Colombia from achieving its first international honor in soccer. Columbia won the first leg of the South American Championship, then lost the second leg to Peru on an own goal to force a playoff, which Peru ultimately won.

WORLD CUP

What is the World Cup?

The World Cup is a championship contested every four years by more than 100 countries. Various geographic regions conduct qualifying rounds, then send representa-

What did exuberant fans do to Pele just after Brazil captured the 1970 World Cup?

In June 1970, over 110,000 soccer fans crowded into Azteca Stadium in Mexico City to watch their adopted home team, Brazil, face Italy in the World Cup finals. Pele scored the first goal of the game on a leaping header, but Italy came back to tie the score at the half. But Brazil proved too strong for their opponents, scoring three more goals in the last 23 minutes of play to seal the victory. Pele set up two of the goals. On the last one, he demonstrated his unselfish play by passing up a scoring opportunity and instead feeding a perfect pass to the captain of his team, defender Carlos Alberto. As time ran out, the fans rushed onto the field, picked up the Brazilian players on their shoulders, and began tearing at their clothing. Pele ended up wearing only his undershorts by the time the jubilant fans had all claimed a piece of their hero.

tives to compete in the finals. The first World Cup was held in 1930 in Uruguay, where 13 nations competed. The locations of ensuing competitions have been in both Europe and North and South America. More than 100 nations competed in qualifying games for the 1998 World Cup, held in France. The World Cup is routinely one of the most popular sporting events in the world.

What are the **top World Cup teams**?

Brazil, the 1994 world champion, is the only country to win four World Cups. West Germany and Italy have each won three, while Argentina and Uruguay have each won two. England won the only other World Cup. Argentina, Czechoslovakia, Holland, Hungary, and West Germany have all lost the final game on two occasions. Sweden is the only other team to lose a final game. Brazil, West Germany, and Italy have all played in five final games, and Argentina has played in four. Brazil is the only nation to triumph in a Cup held outside its own hemisphere.

What is the **history of the trophy** given to the World Cup champion?

The original trophy was named for the first president of FIFA (soccer's international governing body), Jules Rimet. After Brazil won the trophy three times—in 1958, 1962, and 1970—the original trophy was retired and the new trophy was called simply the World Cup.

What are some of the greatest World Cup games?

In 1950, Uruguay overcame their favored hosts Brazil 2–1. Four years later, West Germany upset Hungary 3–2 in another thrilling final. Brazil won impressively 1958, thrashing hosts Sweden 5–2, with Pelé scoring twice. England's victory in 1966, when they downed West Germany 4–2, came after extra time. The foremost match of the 1970 cup came in the semifinals when Italy defeated West Germany. In 1982 Italy overcame Brazil 3–2 in a quarterfinal and West Germany advanced to the final on penalties after tying France 3–3. In 1986 France went through on penalties after tying Brazil 1–1. The same score occurred in an enthralling 1990 semifinal between West Germany and England, with the German advancing on penalties.

What is the **highest scoring game** in World Cup history, and what is the **most lopsided** game?

In 1954, Austria defeated Switzerland 7–5 in the highest scoring game in Cup history. The score was 5–4 Austria at halftime.Three other games have totalled 11 goals, the most recent being Hungary's 10–1 win over El Salvador in the 1982 tournament. That game also represents the most goals scored by one team in a single game and is tied for the most lopsided win ever with Hungary's 9–0 win over South Korea in 1954 and Yugoslavia's 9–0 whitewashing of Zaire in 1974.

Who are the only men to win World Cup titles as **both a player and a coach**?

Mario Zegalo was a left wing on the great Brazilian team that won back-to-back World Cup titles in 1958 and 1962. In 1970, he was the coach of a victorious Brazilian team that many consider to be the finest national team ever. He was the only man to pull off the player-coach double until the legendary West german soccer star Franz Beckenbauer coached his team to a 1–0 victory over Argentina in 1990. As a player, Beckenbauer was an attacking sweeper who served as captain of the 1974 squad that defeated Holland for the title in 1974.

How many times has the **host country won** the World Cup?

There does seem to be a measure of home-field advantage attached to the World Cup tournament. The host country has prevailed six times in the 17 World Cup competitions held between 1930 and 1998. It all started with the very first World Cup, which was held in Uruguay in 1930. Although Uruguay offered to pay the travel expenses for all competing nations, only 13 teams showed up (the trip from Europe to South America took three weeks by boat in those days). Still, few people disputed that Uruguay had one of the best teams in the world when they defeated Argentina in the finals. The host country won again in the second World Cup, as Italy defeated Czechoslovakia in the finals. Host England was a significant underdog when it took the World Cup from West Germany in 1966. It happened again in 1974, when host West Germany defeated Holland, and in 1978, when host Argentina took another title away from Holland. In 1998, host France beat Brazil 3-0 in the final to take the last World Cup of the millenium. In the vast majority of World Cup competitions, a team from the same continent or region as the host country has taken the trophy. For example, Italy won in France and Spain, and Germany won in Switzerland and Italy. The main exception to this rule has been Brazil, which has proven that it can win a World Cup competition held in any part of the world. In addition to victories in nearby Uruguay and Chile, the Brazilians have won the tournaments held in Sweden, Mexico, and the United States.

Which is the only country to **qualify for all 15 men's World Cup tournaments**.

Brazil, the only nation to win four World Cups, is also the only country to qualify for the tournament in every year that it's been held.

What was unique about the **1994 World Cup finals** match?

It was the first time two teams had played to an overtime draw in the history of the Cup final. It was also the first Cup final to be decided by a shootout. Brazil and Italy were both making their fifth appearance in the finals that year. Brazil entered the championship match with a record of 6–0–1 in tournament play, while Italy had a 4–2–1 record. Their match was played before 94,000 fans at the Rose Bowl in Pasadena, California. After the overtime period ended in a scoreless tie, the two teams were allowed five shots each to determine the winner. Italy missed on its first shot, then Brazil's first shot was blocked. Both sides then scored on their second and third shots, evening the shootout score at 2–2. Italy missed its fourth shot, while Brazil managed another goal, raising the score to 3–2. Brazil was awarded its fourth World Cup championship when Italy missed its fifth and final shot. Romario, who had scored Brazil's first shootout goal, received the Golden Ball Award as the tournament's most valuable player.

How many players who participated in the 1994 World Cup are on the **All-Time World Cup Team**?

A poll of 991 soccer writers from 109 countries selected 22 players and three coaches for a World Cup "Dream Team." Only two of the players selected were still competing in the 1994 World Cup: Diego Maradona of Argentina, who received 907 votes for fourth place on the list; and Lothar Matthaus of Germany, who received 727 votes for ninth place on the list. Of course, Pele was a unanimous choice to head the list. Rounding out the top five were Franz Beckenbauer of West Germany (954 votes), Johann Cruyff of Holland (911), and Michel Platini of France (872).

What player has made the **most appearances in the World Cup finals** tournament?

Mexican goalkeeper Antonio Carbajal appeared in five consecutive World Cup finals tournaments between 1950 and 1966. He played in 11 games during that time. Four players are tied for World Cup finals games at 21: Uwe Seeler of West Germany, who did it between 1958 and 1970; Wladyslaw Zmuda of Poland, who played 1974–1986; Diego Maradona of Argentina and Lothar Matthaus of Germany, who both played 1982–1994.

What individual scored the **most goals** in the World Cup finals?

Geoff Hurst of England scored three of his country's four goals as the British defeated West Germany for the World Cup title by a score of 4–2 on July 30, 1966.

Who has scored the **most career goals** in World Cup competition?

Gerd Muller of West Germany scored 14 goals in two World Cup tournaments, in 1970 and 1974, to become the all-time career leader in World Cup goals. Just Fontaine of France is second in career goals, but first in goals scored in a single World Cup tournament. He scored all 13 of his goals in just 6 games in 1958. The great Pele of Brazil scored 12 goals in four World Cup tournaments between 1958 and 1970. Sandor Kocsis of Hungary is fourth on the all-time list but second to Fontaine in goals scored in a single tournament. He scored 11 World Cup goals, all of them in five games played in 1954.

What was the **largest crowd** ever to witness a women's sporting event?

Over 76,000 fans showed up to watch the American women's soccer team face China in the final round of the 1996 Olympic Games in Atlanta, Georgia. The Americans won, 2–1, to take the gold medal. Amazingly, the game wasn't shown live on television in the United States.

What is **"Total Football"** and where did it come from?

Total Football was the name given by the media to a new concept of team play in soccer that originated with Holland during the 1974 World Cup tournament. It was created by Stefan Kovacs and Rinus Michels, who were the leaders of one of the top Euro-

What was the infamous "hand of God" goal?

It was 1986, and the great Diego Maradona was in the midst of leading Argentina to its second World Cup championship. During a quarterfinal game against England, a leaping Maradona punched the ball with his fist and knocked it into the goal over the outstretched hands of the English goalkeeper. Of course, touching the ball with your hands is illegal in soccer, but it appeared to the officials as if Maradona had headed the ball. Afterwards, the star explained that "the hand of God" had determined the final score of the game.

pean soccer clubs of the day, Ajax Amsterdam. In a dramatic change over the more rigid, ball-control oriented style that had been used up to that point, the Dutch team emerged as contenders in the 1974 World Cup by emphasizing versatility and team play. Rather than having players stick to their assigned positions—for example, a defender would concentrate on defense, and a forward would concentrate on attacking—Holland made every player an interchangeable part of a fast-moving, physically imposing team. Every player could adopt an attacking or defensive posture as the situation required. The competition was caught off guard as Dutch fullbacks suddenly turned into wingers, or as Dutch teammates worked together to spring a sudden offsides trap. Holland was runner up to West Germany in the 1974 World Cup. By 1978, most other teams had imitated their new Total Football style of play. In fact, Argentina used it to beat Holland in the World Cup finals in 1978, and it has continued to be used in international competition ever since.

What was the only World Cup competition ever to be played in an **indoor stadium**?

When the U.S. hosted the World Cup in 1994, several qualifying matches were played at the Pontiac Silverdome in Michigan. The Silverdome is a completely enclosed indoor arena with a surface of artificial turf. But international soccer games have to be played on a natural grass surface. So agricultural researchers at Michigan State University came up with a system of interlocking, 3,500-pound trays of real grass and topsoil that served as a portable playing surface. The grass was grown outdoors, treated with special nutrients, and then relocated to the Silverdome, where it grew and was mowed and watered for two weeks during the World Cup competition.

What was the **"Battle of Berne"**?

It was a notorious quarterfinal match between Hungary and Brazil in the 1954 World Cup tournament, held in Berne, Switzerland. The game took place on a muddy field in a driving rain, which may have contributed to the players' short tempers. When Hidegkuti scored the first goal for Hungary, after just four minutes of play, his shorts were ripped off in the process. Later, a Hungarian player who was called for a foul laughed in the face of English referee Arthur Ellis. As the first half ended with Hungary leading by a score of 2–1, the game had already begun to degenerate into a shameful display of violence. An argument ensued early in the second half after a mix-up in the Brazilian penalty area. Both sides expected a free kick to be awarded to Brazil, but instead a penalty was awarded to Hungary, which scored. After Brazil scored to pull within a goal, at 3–2, two opposing players got into a fistfight and were sent off. It took a police escort to keep them separated. Before long, another Brazilian player was sent off for kicking an opponent. By the time Hungary prevailed in the match by a score of 4–2, the referee had called 42 free kicks, two penalties, four cautions, and three send offs.

The animosity between the two teams did not end with the conclusion of the game. The Brazilians hid in the dark players' tunnel after the game and attacked the Hungarians in their dressing room. The ensuing melee resulted in several injuries. Afterward, the Brazilian football authorities imposed stricter rules on their team, which would pay off in later years.

How did a dog named **Pickles** save the World Cup in 1966?

England hosted the World Cup tournament in 1966. As part of the hype leading up to the tournament, the World Cup trophy was displayed at various locations around the country. One time, when the British stamp dealer Stanley Gibbons displayed it at a stamp exhibition, it was stolen. All of England was engaged in the highly publicized hunt for the missing World Cup. Just over a week later, a dog named Pickles found the trophy undamaged in his garden. Pickles' owner fielded the media attention and collected the reward.

LEAGUES AND TOURNAMENTS

What other **important tournaments** exist for national teams?

The South American championship, the Copa America, commenced in 1910 and has been held irregularly in the ensuing years. In recent times, it has been played every two years. Argentina and Uruguay have each won this tournament on fourteen occasions. The European Championship began in 1960 and has since been held every four years. The Germans have won this tournament three times. No other country has won more than once. The African Nations Cup began play in 1957 and has continued irregularly; in recent times it has been contested every two years. Egypt has won the African Nations Cup three-times. The Asian Cup began in 1956 and has since been played every four years, with Iran as three-time winners. The CONCACAF Cup, contested by members of the Confederation of North, Central American, and Caribbean Football, has been held since 1941. Costa Rica leads the CONCACAF field with ten titles. Other prominent tournaments include the Olympics, where Hungary is a three-time winner of the gold medal. Women's tournaments include the World Cup, won by the U.S. in 1991, and the Olympics, in which the U.S. team scored the gold medal in 1996.

How are **domestic leagues** organized?

In Europe, most leagues usually hold between ten and twenty teams. One league is reserved for the very best teams, with other leagues also arranged based on talent. In a season, teams play each other home and away, earning three points for wins and one point for ties. The team with the most points at the end is the champion, period. At season's end, the bottom teams—anywhere from one to four—are relegated to the league that is one level below the teams' previous league. In turn, the top one to four teams from that league are elevated to the higher league. While competing in their domestic leagues, top teams may play other European teams in various competitions. South American leagues are organized in a similar manner, with the exception of Brazil, which has two top leagues. Major League Soccer, the top American league, holds playoffs to determine a champion. Many leagues conduct cup tournaments concurrent with league seasons. These tournaments, which include teams from lower leagues, may be held as a series of home-and-away or one-game rounds, with winners advancing.

What are some of the **world's greatest clubs**?

Among the most distinguished teams is Spain's Real Madrid, winner of six Champions Cups. Real's chief rival in Spain is Barcelona, past winners of all three of the major European tournaments. Among the most prominent Italian teams is A.C. Milan, five-time champions of Europe, and Juventus of Turin, which holds a record 25 domestic titles to add to two Champion's Cups. England's most accomplished club is Liverpool, which holds four Champion's Cups. Holland's most prominent team is Ajax of Amsterdam, four-time winners of the Champion's Cup, while Germany's most successful team is probably Bayern Munich, three-time winners of the same prize. Portugal's Lisbon club Benfica have a pair of Champion's Cup in addition to 30 domestic titles. In South America, many of the most accomplished clubs hail from Argentina. Notable here is River Plate, winner of more than 20 domestic championships. In Brazil, the most suc-

What are the most important tournaments in each region of the world?

In Europe, the most significant prize is the Champion's Cup, which is contested annually by the winners of the various leagues. Since the 1997–98 season, second-place teams from the eight highest-ranked leagues are also allowed to compete. Real Madrid lead the Champion's Cup field with six prizes, including the first five! The Cup-Winners Cup is played by the winners of the various leagues' cup competitions. Barcelona is the only four-time winner of this event. The third major tournament among European clubs is the UEFA Cup, which is contested by the best clubs absent from the other two competitions. Barcelona and Juventus of Turin have each won the UEFA Cup three times. South American champions vie for the Copa Libertadores, which has been in existence since 1960. Argentine teams have dominated this tournament, winning roughly as many titles as Brazilian and Uruguayan teams together. Other key competitions are the African Champions Cup and the CONCACAF Champions Cup.

cessful teams include Flamingo and Fluminense in Rio de Janiero and both Sao Paolo and Santos in Sao Paolo. Uruguay's greatest teams are Nacional and Penarol. Major League Soccer's best team has been D.C. United, winner of both league titles.

What team achieved the **longest undefeated run** in international competition?

This record belongs to Hungary, which played 29 soccer matches without a defeat between May 1950 and July 1954, when it lost in the World Cup finals to Germany. Throughout this impressive run, Hungary won 25 times and played to 4 draws. Hungary also holds the record for remaining undefeated at home. Excluding the war years, the Hungarians went 17 years without a home loss, from June 1939 to May 1956.

Some African soccer teams take **extreme and unusual measures** to ensure victory. What are some examples?

In some African nations—such as Kenya, Uganda, and Tanzania—many of the top soccer clubs employ witch doctors to cast spells on their opponents. Prior to an important match, the witch doctors will fast, meditate, and perform a series of chants. Sometimes they will create special potions consisting of herbs, roots, powdered animal and snake skins, and a variety of liquids. These potions might be eaten or worn by players or placed around the field prior to the game. In exchange for his services, the

425

witch doctor receives a generous payment. In some cases—at least in the minds of the opponents—the spells seem to have worked. Some players have reported seeing the ball turn into a snake as they were about to kick it, while an occasional goalkeeper has claimed to have seen two balls instead of one coming toward him at a critical moment. Although the African Football Conference has issued guidelines opposing the use of witchcraft in soccer games, and the Kenya Football Association has impounded materials used by team witch doctors, the phenomenon seems more likely to decline in popularity on its own.

When were the most **red cards** issued in a single game?

In a 1993 league game in Paraguay, referee William Weiler issued red cards to 20 players (that's right, only two players on the field were not ejected). The trouble started after two Sportivo Ameliano players were thrown out of the game against General Caballero. Then a fight broke out that took 10 minutes to get under control. Following the melee, Weiler ejected another 18 players, including the remainder of the Sportivo team. Obviously, the game could not resume.

Who scored the **first goal in Major League Soccer** history? Who scored the most goals in the **inaugural season**?

The first goal in MLS history was a dramatic one. Eric Wynalda put the ball in the net just moments before the scoreless first game had to be settled with a shootout. Roy Lassiter was the top goal scorer in the 1996–97 season with 27. He added four assists for a total of 58 points on the season.

PLAYERS

Who are the **greatest players in soccer history**?

The Brazilian Pelé is likely the most significant player in soccer history. His scoring exploits are astounding, and his success—both at national and club levels—is profoundly impressive. Alfredo di Stefano, the versatile Real Madrid forward, is also prominent, as is his Hungarian teammate, Ferenc Puskas. Diego Maradona, who led Argentina to the 1986 World Cup prize, and Dutch master Johann Cruyff, also figure among the all-time greats. The game's finest defensive player was probably Franz Beckenbauer, the West German sweeper who hoisted the World Cup, the European Championship Cup, and the Champion's Cup during his illustrious career. Among

Pele is one of the best-known soccer players in the world

What makes Pelé so special?

Pelé is credited with 1280 career goals! He holds the world record for most three-goal games (92) and the most international goals (97). He is the only player to play on three World Cup championship teams, first leading Brazil to victory as a 17-year-old in 1958 and then again leading them to the title in 1962 and 1970. He led the Brazilian Sao Paolo league in scoring from 1957 to 1965, with 127 goals in 1959 and another 110 in 1961. On nine occasions his club, Santos, won its league championship. Pelé inspired soccer enthusiasm in the United States when he emerged from retirement in the 1970s and led the New York Cosmos to three consecutive titles in the now-defunct North American Soccer League. He is widely regarded as an engaging, generous public figure, and he serves as an extraordinary goodwill ambassador for the game.

England's greatest players are Stanley Matthews, an astounding dribbler with Blackpool in the 1950s, and Bobby Charlton, a powerful forward for Manchester United in the 1950s and 60s. Charlton's flamboyant clubmate George Best also ranks at the top. Among the game's most celebrated goaltenders are Soviet Lev Yashin, credited with saving more than one hundred penalty kicks, and England's Gordon Banks, member of the 1966 world champions. Among female players, American Michelle Akers-Stahl is considered to be one of the best ever.

What is **Pele's real name**?

The man known around the world as Pele was born Edson Arantes do Nascimento on October 23, 1940, in the small town of Tres Coracoes, Brazil, near the port city of Santos. Growing up, he spent his free time kicking a rag ball (a real soccer ball was too expensive) around the streets and beaches near his home. At the age of 13, he scored nine goals in one game to lead his local club to an 11–0 victory. This performance led to a contract with the Santos team, and he became a starter at the age of 15. At 17, Pele led Brazil to its first World Cup title. He scored the winning goal against Wales in the quarterfinals, added three goals in the semifinals against France, and put two impressive headers into the net to ice the finals victory over host Sweden.

What **missed goal** contributed to Pele's legend?

In the 1970 World Cup, held in the heat and high altitude of Mexico City, Pele was brilliant as usual. But it was a missed goal that may have contributed the most to his legend that year. Brazil faced Czechoslovakia in the opening round of competition.

Mia Hamm of the United States is perhaps the best female soccer player in the world.

During the game, Pele noticed that the Czech goalie tended to wander far from the net when the play moved to Brazil's end of the field. To the amazement of fans and players alike, Pele took his first opportunity to rocket a powerful kick toward the Czech goal from 65 yards away. Sure enough, it caught the Czech goalie out of position and he was helpless to stop it. Unfortunately, the shot went just outside the corner post. Brazil went on to win the game, 4–1, and capture its third World Cup title.

Who are among the **best players in the game today**?

The Brazilian Ronaldo is widely considered the game's greatest player in the late 1990s. He has been a top scorer in the Dutch and Spanish leagues, and he currently plays for Italy's Internazionale Milan. Fellow Brazilian Roberto Carlos, who plays for Real Madrid, is among the game's finest defenders. Eric Cantona, a versatile playmaker and scorer, has led Manchester United to four English titles, while fellow Frenchman Youri Djorkaeff stars with Ronaldo at Internazionale. Liberian striker George Weah leads the attack at rivals A.C. Milan. Argentine striker Gabriel Batistuta is a feared scorer for Italian club Fiorentina, and Alessandro Del Piero is equally respected at rivals Juventus. In England, Alan Shearer is prominent at Newcastle United, while Dutchman Dennis Bergkamp impresses at London's Arsenal. Among the greatest goalkeepers are Peter Schmeichel, whose play spurred Denmark to a stunning triumph at the 1992 European Championship, and Paraguayan Jose Luis Chilavert, who even takes free kicks and penalties for his Argentine club Velez Sarzfeld. Stars of

Major League Soccer include Colombian Carlos Valderrama, Bolivian Marco Etcheverry, and Americans John Harkes and Eric Wynalda. Perhaps the top female player today is American Mia Hamm, who starred at the 1996 Olympics.

What **collegiate player** led her team to the NCAA championship four times?

Mia Hamm, undoubtedly one of the best women players in the world, began her impressive career by leading the University of North Carolina Tar Heels to four NCAA titles between 1989 and 1994. (She sat out the 1991 collegiate soccer season in order to focus on the first Women's World Cup.) During her time there, UNC posted an amazing record of 92–1–2, losing only one women's soccer match (to the University of Connecticut) in four years. The team also put together an incredible string of 70 consecutive victories. Hamm became the NCAA all-time career leading scorer with 103 goals and 72 assists. She also won the Hermann Award (given to the best female player in college soccer) in 1992 and 1993, and was named NCAA National Player of the Year in those two years as well as in 1994. In 1992—in what her coach called "the greatest season ever by a collegiate soccer player"—Hamm led the NCAA with 32 goals and 33 assists to set a single-season scoring record. UNC retired her jersey, number 19, at the end of her senior year.

Who was the **youngest player** ever to make the U.S. women's soccer team?

Star striker Mia Hamm was a 15-year-old high school student when she was picked for the national team. She was still the youngest player on the team, at 19, when the United States defeated Norway to win the first Women's World Cup soccer championship in 1991.

What member of the American women's soccer team holds the records for **most goals in a match, most goals in a season, and most points in a season**?

The great Michelle Akers set all three records in 1991, while leading Team USA to victory in the first-ever Women's World Cup. She scored five goals in one match, as well as 39 goals and 47 points over the course of the season. She even scored the game-winning goal in the gold medal match against Norway. Not surprisingly, she was named Female Soccer Athlete of the Year for the second time that year and also earned the Golden Boot Award.

What world-class female soccer player missed the 1995 World Championships because she was on her **honeymoon**?

Co-captain Julie Foudy, a four-time all-American midfielder at Stanford who helped the U.S. national team win the Women's World Cup title in 1991, took time out from her soccer career in 1995 to become Julie Foudy Sawyers.

> ## What top scorer took a turn playing goalie in a 1991 Women's World Cup game?
>
> **M**ia Hamm, widely viewed as the most dangerous scorer in the game, proved her versatility during a first-round match against Denmark. She took over for the regular American goalie, Brianna Scurry, after Scurry was ejected for a controversial rules infraction. "I was scared to death," Hamm admitted. "The goal is so much bigger when you're inside it than when you're shooting at it." She still managed to make a save late in the game.

Many people know that the World Cup, like many other international sporting events, was canceled in 1942 and 1946 due to World War II. But another **war was put on hold so that the combatants could watch a soccer game.** Which one?

In the late 1960s, during Pele's soccer heyday, Nigeria and Biafra declared a two-day truce in their ongoing civil war so that both sides could see his Brazilian team play.

What American soccer player loves **Slurpees from 7-Eleven** and plays in a band called **the Gypsies**?

These are traits of Alexi Lalas, a defender who helped the U.S. national team win a gold medal at the Pan-Am Games in 1991 and advance to the second round of the World Cup tournament for the first time in 1994. With his wild red hair, long goatee, outgoing nature, and unusual outlook on life, Lalas became a fan favorite leading up to the World Cup. He once told a reporter that "Without Slurpees, there is no humankind," which prompted hundreds of fans to send him the addresses of their favorite 7-Eleven stores. In his spare time he plays guitar and sings in a band, which led the media to label him the first "soccer rocker." But Lalas is more than just an eccentric: he won the Hermann Award as collegiate player of the year while at Rutgers in 1991, and was named U.S. Player of the Year in 1995. Many people hope that personalities like Lalas will help attract attention to soccer in America.

What brilliant **striker** who retired in 1997 was as well known for his temper as for his goal-scoring ability?

Eric Cantona, a Frenchman who starred on Manchester United of the English Premier League for five seasons, ended his colorful 13-year soccer career in 1997. Unfortunately, many Americans remember him best for an ugly confrontation with a fan that earned him an assault conviction and an eight-month suspension from the game. In a display of his temper, Cantona used his powerful legs to execute a Kung Fu-style kick on the fan.

OFF–FIELD CONCERNS

What are some of the most **disastrous soccer incidents**?

There have been many, may well-publicized disasters related to soccer. In 1967, for example, a disallowed goal in a Turkish game triggered a riot that left 41 people dead and 600 injured. In 1982, a spectator urinated from an upper deck in Cali, Colombia, and sparked a panic in which 22 died and 100 were injured. In one of the game's most notorious riots, 39 fans died and six hundred were injured when Liverpool supporters charged Juventus fans at the 1985 Champion's Cup final. Four years later, 95 Liverpool fans were crushed to death and nearly 200 were injured during crowd-control problems at Hillsborough in Sheffield.

What record was set by **Czech soccer nut Jan Skorkovsky** in 1990?

On July 8 of that year, Skorkovsky posted the fastest time ever for running a marathon while juggling a soccer ball. He completed the Prague Marathon in seven hours, 19 minutes, while also juggling a soccer ball nonstop with his feet, legs, and head. Of course, this is nothing compared to the all-time record for juggling a soccer ball without allowing it to touch the ground. Ricardinho Neves of Brazil kept a regulation soccer ball going for over 19 hours, five minutes in 1994. The women's record for juggling a soccer ball is seven hours, five minutes, set by Claudia Martini of Brazil in 1996.

AMERICAN SOCCER

How does the **United States** rate?

The U.S. has a surprisingly impressive history. The U.S. team played in the semifinals of the first World Cup, held in 1930, and beat highly-rated England 1–0 in the 1950 tournament. The U.S. also played in three consecutive World Cups in the 1990s. In

What are some of the largest stadiums and crowds?

The Maracana in Rio de Janeiro has held 200,000 spectators. The Morumbi, home to Sao Paolo, is likewise vast, holding 150,000. Among Europe's biggest stadiums are Barcelona's Nou Camp, which holds 130,000, and rival Real Madrid's Bernebau, which handles 105,000. In Italy, A.C. Milan and Internazionale share the Stadio Guiseppe Meazza, which holds 83,000, while Napoli's San Paulo holds 85,100 and Rome's Olimpico manages 80,000. In Lisbon, 130,000 have gathered to watch Benfica at the Estadio da Luz ("Stadium of Lights"). Glasgow's Hampden Park, meanwhile, held nearly 150,000 for a 1937 match in which Scotland beat England 3–1. London's Wembley, however, held more than 200,000 for a 1923 match in which Bolton beat Westham 2–1. Seating capacity for Wembley is now 80,000.

addition, the team has twice won the U.S. Cup, once in a field featuring Italy, Ireland, and Portugal, and beat England 2–0 in the 1993 competition. The U.S. has also fared well as an invited team in the Copa America. In the 1995 tournament, the U.S. upset mighty Argentina 3–0 then advanced on penalties against Mexico before succumbing 1–0 to eventual winners Brazil in the semifinals. The current team, led by Alexi Lalas and John Harkes, has achieved such notable successes as the team's recent upset of Brazil. The women's team has enjoyed even greater success, winning the World Cup in 1991 and the Olympic gold medal in 1996.

Who was the first player to make **100 appearances** with the U.S. national men's soccer team?

Defender Marcelo Balboa achieved this distinction on June 11, 1995. "I really didn't think I'd be the first one to break the century mark. There was someone else on the team who was up to 97 times," he noted. "I was very excited to find out that I had done it. To me that was something extremely special." He capped off his milestone day by scoring a goal in the team's 3–2 victory over Nigeria. By the beginning of 1997, Balboa—the son of Argentinean professional soccer player Luis Balboa—had notched 113 games with Team USA, and he did not plan to quit anytime soon.

What are the most successful **college soccer** programs in the United States?

Since the first NCAA men's Division I soccer tournament was held in 1952, the University of St. Louis has claimed the most national championships, with ten. But all of these titles came between 1959 and 1973, other teams have been more dominant in

Alexi Lalas has a distinctive look for the U.S. men's soccer team.

recent years. Indiana University has claimed three national championships over the last 15 years (in 1982, 1983, and 1988) and was also runner-up two additional times (in 1984 and 1994). The University of Virginia won an impressive four consecutive titles between 1991 and 1994, after tying for the championship with Santa Clara in 1989 (the final match between the two was declared a draw after two overtimes due to inclement weather). Clemson University (1984 and 1987) and UCLA (1985 and 1990) are other recent repeat national champions.

In women's college soccer, there's the University of North Carolina, and then there's everyone else. Since the first NCAA women's Division I soccer tournament was held in 1982, UNC has claimed all but two of the national titles awarded. The only defeats handed to the Lady Tar Heels came in 1985, when they lost to George Mason 2–0, and in 1995, when they lost a 1–0, triple-overtime thriller to Notre Dame.

What was memorable about the **1985 NCAA championship** men's soccer game?

The 1985 NCAA final match—between UCLA and American University at the Kingdome in Seattle—was the longest soccer game in collegiate history. The teams were locked in a scoreless tie after 90 minutes of regulation play. They remained tied through an amazing seven overtime periods. Finally, before the start of the eighth overtime, UCLA assistant coach Steve Sampson asked his players to "finish this thing so we can go home." And they did, when UCLA sophomore Paul Burke scored on a 13-yard shot with 3:55 left in overtime number eight. Altogether, the weary players were on the field for two hours, 46 minutes.

What is the likely **future of soccer**?

Soccer continues to increase in popularity throughout the globe. Television, especially satellite broadcasting, has made the game accessible everywhere. As the networks and broadcasting groups pump astounding sums into the game, salaries rise accordingly. The game, which has been largely attendance driven, even into the early 1990s, will doubtless become more similar to American sports, wherein the television-viewing fan is more valued than the paying spectator. In the United States, meanwhile, participation continues to increase, especially among children. If these same children develop an interest as spectators, then professional soccer will surely succeed in the United States. Otherwise, as the joke goes, "Soccer is the future of sports in America, and it always will be."

TENNIS

GENERAL

OK, one more time: explain **the scoring in tennis**.

To win a game a player must score four points and win by at least two. Love is a term equivalent to zero points, 15 is equivalent to one point, 30 to two points, 40 to three points. The server's score is called or listed first, so a server who has scored three straight points at the beginning is ahead 40–Love. If one person leads 40–30, or 30–40, he/she can win by scoring the next point. If the other person ties the game at 40–40, the score is referred to as deuce, and the first person to score two straight points wins. The first to win a tiebreaker point is referred to has having "advantage," which is followed either by a win or by returning to deuce.

What are we talking about when we talk about **"love?"**

Love means zero score, in tennis. The term love is thought to have derived from the French word "l'oeuf," meaning "the egg"—implying the goose egg, which looks like an 0 and is a slang sports term for saying zero.

What are the **different surfaces** on which tennis has been played?

Whether the playing surface is anthill grit (in Australia), dried cow dung (in India), wood, clay, grass, linoleum, canvas, concrete, asphalt or synthetic carpets, the dimensions are always the same. The game began on grass courts in England. That is an uncommon surface now, although the biggest tournament of all, Wimbledon, is still a grass event.

437

What are the dimensions of a tennis court and net?

At the center point the net is three feet high and at either end, three-and-a-half feet. The court is 78 feet long and 27 feet wide. It is 21 feet from the service line to the net in tennis. The alley, an addition to the singles court on both sides that provides space for doubles play, is 4 feet. This area, widening the court by nine feet, is in use during doubles play following the serve.

What's so different about **playing on grass** as opposed to clay or hard court?

The most distinguishing characteristic of natural grass courts is probably the high speed with which the ball skids off the surface. This feature tends to favor players with excellent serves and good net games while disfavoring baseline players. (There are always exceptions to the rule: baseliner Bjorn Borg won five consecutive Wimbledons, setting a modern-day record, and Steffi Graf—also primarily a baseliner—has won six Wimbledon titles.) In addition to the speed, grass courts can have treacherous footing compared to hard courts, particularly if the grass is damp. Also, especially toward the end of a long tournament when many matches have been played, a grass court will become chewed up and dirt-bound, especially in places where players naturally start and stop running. This last feature will cause numerous "bad" bounces of the ball—in other words, balls that bounce in unexpected ways (or sometimes not at all). Until the 1970s, numerous tournaments, including three of the four major tournaments—the French withstanding—were played on grass. However, the U.S. Open switched to hard court in the 1970s, and the Australian Open followed in the 1980s. By the 1990s, the only major tournament played all year on grass was the Wimbledon Championships.

Is **coaching** allowed in professional tennis?

Yes, but not during a match—until recently. The majority of players, especially top players, have coaches with whom they work on a part- or full-time basis. The rules have long stated that coaching is not allowed during a match. In other words, a player may not talk to his/her coach during a match. However, players and coaches have often sought to get around the coaching ban in subtle ways, such as with hand signals. As top men's pro Thomas Muster recently told *Tennis* magazine, "Let's face it, even though [coaching] was never allowed, it's always been there. It's like a known secret." Perhaps in response to the knowledge that coaching has "always been there," the men's touring body—Association of Tennis Professionals (ATP)—in 1998 voted to begin trying out the idea of allowing limited coaching. The ATP's move doesn't allow for unlimited coaching during a match but rather lets each player consult with a

Bjorn Borg won five consecutive Wimbledon titles.

> ## How can a player hit a winning shot without hitting the ball over the net?
>
> This can happen when a player hits the ball around the net and net post, as opposed to over it, and usually occurs when a player's opponent has hit a sharply angled-ball that pulls his opponent to the side of the court. In such a situation, a player may find it easier and more direct to hit the ball into the opponent's court without having to hit it over the net. This shot is perfectly legal. However, the ball cannot be hit through the net.

coach for two minutes after each of the first two sets. As of May 1998, the women's tour still disallows coaching in any form during a match.

Is it illegal to **hit the ball twice** during the same stroke?

Not unless the double-hit is intentional. If unintentional, play continues. Previously, even an unintentional double-hit (also called a "carry") was illegal and resulted in the loss of the point.

What is a **let**?

"Let" is called by the umpire if a point must be replayed. It's called if a serve hits the top of the net and still lands inside the service box. It's also called if a point is interrupted for any reason—a stray ball rolling onto the court during play, a piece of trash drifting onto the court during play, etc. Events or sounds that don't directly affect the court during play, such as a loud noise or exclamations from the crowd, do not result in a let.

Can pro players stop for a **restroom break** during a match?

Yes. Men may take one restroom break during a three-set match and two during a five-set match. Women, on the other hand, may take two breaks during a three-set match, either to visit the restroom and/or to change apparel (men simply change shirts on court). Amateurs playing for fun may take as many restroom breaks as they choose.

What is a **winner**?

A winner is a shot hit for a winning point that isn't touched by the opponent's racket. Virtually any sort of winning shot—a volley, an overhead smash, a passing shot from

What is a drop shot?

A drop shot is a delicately hit shot that's meant to barely clear the net in order to win a point outright, or to draw the opponent close to the net to make them more vulnerable to a lob or passing shot. Often, a drop shot is hit with underspin, so that when the ball bounces it will spin back toward the net, making it even harder for the opposing player to reach. A drop shot is considered a smart play when inside the baseline and the opponent is far behind the baseline. Conversely, if you're behind the baseline and/or if your opponent is inside the baseline, a drop shot is considered risky and unwise, because a drop shot that's easily reached by the opponent will allow the opponent a comfortable put-away. Using the drop shot against very speedy players is also dangerous.

the baseline, etc.—counts as a winner, as long as the ball isn't touched by the opponent's racket. One exception is a "service winner," which is a winning serve touched by the opponent's racket but not returned in play.

What is an **unforced error**?

As the phrase implies, an unforced error is an error not caused by anything other than a player's poor play, such as hitting the ball into the net or hitting it outside the lines. If a player hits an error as the result of a superior shot by his opponent—a shot hit with more pace or better placement than the opponent can handle—such an error is called a "forced" error and is no cause for shame.

What is an **ace**?

An ace is a winning service shot not touched by the opponent's racket. A winning serve that is touched by the opponent (but not returned in play) is called a "service winner."

What is a **break point**?

It's a point that holds the potential of a game being won by the person receiving serve in the game. In other words, if the receiver wins the break point, he/she wins the game and is said to "break" serve. If the score is 0–40 (with the server's score listed first), the point is said to be "triple break point," because the receiver actually has three consecutive break points if needed. Likewise, 15–40 is called "double break point," because the receiver has at least two consecutive chances to break serve.

What is a "kick" serve?

It's a serve hit with topspin that makes the ball bounce extremely high and jump away from the court. A right-handed player would typically hit the kick serve when serving into the "ad" court—the right-hand side of the court on the opposite side of the net. If the receiver is also right-handed, a well-hit kick serve will make for an extremely difficult backhand return. A left-handed server would typically hit the kick serve while serving to the "deuce" court—the left-hand side of the court on the opposite side of net.

What is a "poach" in tennis?

A poach is used in doubles and happens when the net player (assuming the standard doubles formation of one player at the net and the other at the baseline) crosses in front of his player in an attempt to intercept the ball and make a winning volley. The poach is often used when a team is serving, as the non-serving player at net will poach and try to intercept the return of serve. Poaching, however, is dangerous: by poaching, the player has to leave his side of the court open, at least briefly, which may allow the opposing team to place a winner in that open court. The best doubles teams are able to use poaching selectively as a surprise tactic, and they only do so after communicating their intention to one another, allowing the baseline player to cover the open court being left behind by the poacher.

What are the various types of spin with which the ball can be hit

There are essentially three types of spin: topspin (an overspin), slice (an underspin), and sidespin. As Bud Collins notes, topspin occurs when "the racket brushes the ball from low to high;" the result is a ball that bounces very high and that tends to jump when it bounces. Such a ball can also clear the net with a wide margin but still land inside the court, since the topspin will tend to cause the ball to dip toward the court in an arcing motion. Slice is the opposite of topspin and occurs when "the racket brushes from high to low;" the ball tends to bounce very low, and it tends to move through the air much more slowly than a top-spinning ball. Finally, sidespin occurs when "the racket brushes across the ball on either side;" depending on the direction of the brush, the ball will bounce either left or right when it lands. The vast majority of shots have either topspin or underspin on them. Topspin tends to be especially effective on a clay court, because its high bounce is enhanced; slice is extremely effective on grass, since it will tend to stay very low and even skid off of the slick grass court. Hard courts tend to play neutrally, favoring neither topspin nor slice.

What are tennis **strings** made of?

Tennis strings can be made with natural "gut"—literally, intestinal material from an animal, such as a cow—or synthetic (i.e. artificial) gut, or they can be made with other man-made materials such as nylon. Most top pros have long used natural gut because of the belief that natural gut provides the best "feel" for the ball. Natural gut has typically been more expensive than man-made string, which is why amateur players often opt for more-durable types of synthetic strings.

What is a **widebody**?

It's a style of racket design developed during the 1990s that features a frame with a thicker cross-section than standard frames. It's chief appeal is that it greatly enhances the player's ability to hit the ball with more power; it's chief drawback is that it increases arm strain. Widebodies have proven highly popular among amateur players but less so among professionals, who tend to generate enough power with conventional rackets and who look for frames that provide greater control than widebodies do.

What was the "**spaghetti" racket**?

It was a double-strung racket that used two sets of vertical strings, supported by five or six cross strings threaded through them. The strings were braced with adhesive tape, fish line, rope or other materials, including a plastic tubing that came to be referred to as "spaghetti." Because of their curious string pattern, these rackets generated a stunning amount of power. Invented by a West German named Werner Fisher, the racket was first used in a Grand Slam event by Barry Phillips-Moore at the French Open in 1977. As more players used the racket that summer, controversy increased from every part of the tennis establishment. The International Tennis Federation finally imposed a temporary ban on such rackets in October 1977 and a permanent ban a year later.

What other **good use for a tennis racket** is showcased in the 1960 movie, *The Apartment*?

Bachelor Jack Lemmon used his tennis racket to strain spaghetti.

What is **Cyclops**?

It's a computerized line-calling system, currently used only to call the service line (and rarely used outside of the major stadiums at major events). In this system, a machine directs an infra-red beam along the outer edge of the service line. When the ball crosses the beam, the machine beeps, signifying a fault. The system can only be used along the horizontal service line that's parallel with the baseline; humans must still call the vertical service line in the middle of the court and the sideline edge of the service box. Also, the system can only detect serves that are a few inches long; if the serve misses the service line by a larger margin, the umpire must call the fault manually. The system has been in use since 1980.

What four tournaments make up the **Grand Slam**?

In the order of play during a calendar year, the Grand Slam comprises the Australian Open, French Open, Wimbledon, and U.S. Open. The Opens were collectively called the Big Four because only those host countries had won the Davis Cup for the first 73 years of its existence. Grand Slam is a sports term for major accomplishments: a bases-loaded home-run worth four runs in baseball, and a set of major golf tournaments—the Masters, British Open, U.S. Open, and PGA Championship.

How many players have won **tennis' Grand Slam**?

Only two men, Don Budge (1938) and Rod Laver (twice—as an amateur in 1962 and as a professional in 1967), and three women, Maureen Connolly (1953), Margaret Smith Court (1970), and Steffi Graf (1988).

What players (male and female) have **won the most Grand Slam singles** titles?

Among the men, Roy Emerson leads the pack, with 12 titles: six Australian Championships, two French titles, two Wimbledons, and two U.S. Championships. Bjorn Borg is second, with 11 singles titles. Among active players, Pete Sampras has won 10 titles as of May 1998 (two Australians, four Wimbledons, and four U.S. Opens). For the women, Margaret Smith Court won 24 Grand Slam singles titles: 11 Australians, four French titles, two Wimbledons, and seven U.S. Championships. Still-active Steffi Graf is second with 21 titles as of May 1998: four Australians, five French Opens, seven Wimbledons, and five U.S. Opens.

What is the **Federation Cup**?

The Federation Cup is the women's version of the Davis Cup. It began in 1963, established by the International Tennis Federation. 32 teams competed annually at one site over the course of a week until 1994, when the Fed Cup adopted the Davis Cup format. The U.S. has won 15 Fed Cups, Australia seven, Czechoslovakia five, Spain four, and Germany has won twice.

Steffi Graf at the 1995 French Open. She is one of three women to win tennis's Grand Slam.

Which countries have **won the Davis Cup**?

The U.S. has won the Cup 31 times through 1997, Australia 20, France eight, Australia (Australia and New Zealand competed as one from 1920–24) six, British Isles and Sweden five, Great Britain four, and Germany three. Czechoslovakia won in 1980, Italy in 1976, South Africa in 1974.

Before which athletic showdown did one player give the opposing player a **live pig**?

Before "The Battle of the Sexes" (Billie Jean King gave it to Bobby Riggs). This 1973 Houston Astrodome spectacle—equal parts tennis, carnival, and sociological phenomenon—captured the fancy of America as no pure tennis match ever had. The crowd of 30,472, paying as much as $100 a seat, was the largest ever to witness a tennis match. Some 50 million more watched on prime-time television. The whole gaudy promotion was worth supposedly $3 million, and the 29-year-old King collected a $100,000 winner-take-all purse, plus ancillary revenues, for squashing 55-year-old, self-proclaimed "king of male chauvinist pigs" Riggs, 6–4, 6–3, 6–3. He earned a substantial prize as well.

Where is the **International Tennis Hall of Fame**?

Newport Casino, Newport, Rhode Island. The Hall of Fame was established to honor all-time greats of the game as well and to house a museum of tennis history and memorabilia. It was founded in 1953, conceived by tennis innovator Jimmy Van Alen as the National Tennis Hall of Fame, and until 1975 it enshrined only Americans. That year the name and scope went worldwide as the International Tennis Hall of Fame with the induction of Englishman Fred Perry. The first class of inductees was tapped in 1955.

MEN

What was the **longest match** ever played?

Dick Leach and Dick Dell beat Tom Mozur and Len Schloss, 3–6, 49–47, 22–20—an astounding 147 games—in the 1967 Newport (Rhode Island) Invitation. This was prior to adoption of the tie-breaker—death to deuce sets—played at six games all. The longest singles match went 126 games, when Roger Taylor of Great Britain defeated Wieslaw Gasiorek of Poland, 27–29, 31–29, 6–4, in the King's Cup in Warsaw, Poland, 1966.

Fred Perry was the first person inducted into the International Tennis Hall of Fame after it changed its name from the National Tennis Hall of Fame.

Who was Arthur Ashe?

A she grew up in Richmond, Virginia, where he could not play in the usual junior tournaments due to racial segregation. He persisted and enjoyed a glorious career, ranking in the top 15 for tournaments won. He won the 1970 Australian Open and Wimbledon in 1975. In 1968, he won the U.S. Open and the U.S. Amateur Open, becoming the first African-American to win the U.S. men's national tennis title. He lent himself, his name, and his money to various social causes and entered the Hall of Fame in 1985.

What tennis player received **No. 1 rankings in 1937 and 1938** and was the **first to win the Grand Slam**?

Don Budge. The red-haired young giant played a game of maximum power. His service was battering, his backhand considered perhaps the finest the game has known, his net play emphatic, his overhead drastic. Quick and rhythmic, he was truly the all-around player and, what is more, was temperamentally suited for the game. Affable and easygoing, he could not be shaken from the objective of winning with the utmost application of hitting power. He was elected to the Hall of Fame in 1964.

Who was the first **unseeded and youngest winner of Wimbledon** in 1985?

Boris Becker at age 17 years, 7 months. The redheaded phenomenon was the first German champ. A big man (6-foot-3, 180) playing a big carefree game of booming serves, heavy forehand, penetrating volleys, and diving saves, he was an immediate crowd favorite. Despite his youth, he showed sensitivity in rejecting an early, obvious nickname, "Boom Boom," considering it "too warlike."

Who was the first to win **five straight Wimbledon singles** tennis titles?

Bjorn Borg. Before he was 21, Bjorn Rune Borg had registered feats that would set him apart as one of the game's greats, and before he was 26, the head banded, golden-locked Swede was through. No male career of the modern era has been so brief and bright. Borg won six French Opens, Wimbledon five times, and was three-times runner-up at the U.S. Open.

Who is the only man to win the U.S. Open on **three different surfaces**?

Jimmy Connors, who won the tournament when it was played on grass in 1974, on clay in 1976 (both at Forest Hills), and three times on hard court (1978, 1982, 1983)

Arthur Ashe was a champion on and off the court. He ranks in the top 15 in tournament wins and was well known for his work on behalf of humanitarian and charitable causes.

after it moved to Flushing Meadow. In 1974, Connors's victim was Ken Rosewall, whom Connors routed 6–1, 6–0, 6–1. Connors beat Bjorn Borg in the finals in both 1976 and 1978, and he turned back Ivan Lendl in 1982 and again in 1983. Since no other Grand Slam event has been played on three different surfaces, Connors's record will likely stand for a long time. During his lengthy career (nearly 20 years), Connors also won two Wimbledon titles and one Australian Open title.

Who was the first **South American** man to be ranked number one in the world?

Marcelo Rios of Chile captured the number one ranking in March 1998, upon beating Andre Agassi to win the Lipton Championship in Key Biscayne, Florida. Rios's elevation to the top spot broke Pete Sampras's streak of 102 consecutive weeks at number one, and occurred without Rios having won a single Grand Slam title. However, Rios held the top spot for less than a month before Sampras moved back ahead of him.

Who was the first person to be **disqualified** from a Grand Slam tournament for bad behavior?

John McEnroe, who was disqualified from the 1990 Australian Open during his fourth-round match against Mikael Pernfors of Sweden. McEnroe's crime was hardly unusual behavior for him: uttering an "audible obscenity" and verbally abusing the

Who were tennis' version of the Musketeers?

Known as the "Four Musketeers," the legendary French quartet of Jacques Brugnon, Jean Borotra, Henre Cochet, and Rene Lacoste dominated men's tennis in the late 1920s. Jacques "Toto" Brugnon, the oldest of the group and essentially a doubles specialist, helped France win and keep the Davis Cup between 1927 and 1932. The elegant Borotra, who always played in his trademark beret and who was known as the "Bounding Basque," won five major singles championships. The small but enormously talented Cochet won seven major singles titles, including an amazing win over Bill Tilden in the 1927 Wimbledon semifinals, in which Cochet rallied from two sets down and 1–5 in the third set. The group's fourth member, Lacoste, nicknamed the "Crocodile," won seven major singles titles. In 1933, Lacoste founded a sportswear company whose logo was the crocodile.

umpire, Gerry Armstrong. Throughout his illustrious career, McEnroe was famous not just for his unsurpassed racket artistry but for his penchant for arguing line calls with officials. (Who can ever forget his legendary dispute with an umpire at Wimbledon in 1980, during which McEnroe complained that a linesperson had mistakenly called one of his shots out: "Chalk flew up!," Mac shouted.) But until the Australian Open in 1990, he had never been given any serious official flak for his behavior, despite a few suspensions and regular fines of a few thousand dollars—pittances for a player who won more than $12 million in prize money during his career. The decision to boot McEnroe was made by supervisor Ken Farrar, a former hockey referee, who ordered Armstrong to default McEnroe. This disqualification of a top player at a major event signaled a new era in the officiating of the game.

Who were the **"Handsome Eight"**?

They were the eight male pros who signed on as part of the first successful professional tennis circuit, known as World Championship Tennis (WCT). The year was 1967, and long-simmering tensions over the acceptance of professional players finally came to a head with the formation of WCT. The group included Dennis Ralston, Roger Taylor, Tony Roche, Pierre Barthes, John Newcombe, Niki Pilic, Butch Buchholz, and Cliff Drysdale, each of whom was a top player in 1967. With so many of the game's best players suddenly turning professional, the International Tennis Federation was forced to institute "open" tennis—competitions open to both amateurs and professionals. The "open" era came into being in 1968 and signaled the start of a period in which the

John McEnroe argues with the umpire at Wimbledon, which was a common sight during McEnroe's colorful career.

game would explode in popularity around the world. The WCT merged with the current men's circuit, the Association of Tennis Professionals (ATP), in 1990.

What prompted the majority of top male players to **boycott Wimbledon** in 1973?

The boycott was called in response to a decision by the International Tennis Federation (ITF) to ban Yugoslav player Nikki Pilic from the 1973 Wimbledon tournament because of his earlier suspension by the Yugoslav Tennis Federation. The Yugoslav Federation had taken action against Pilic for allegedly failing to play in a Davis Cup match to which he had previously committed. After the Yugoslav Federation's decision, the player's association—the ATP—urged the ITF not to take any action of its own to support the Yugoslav Federation, arguing that only the players' association should have authority to discipline an individual player. The ITF refused the ATP's request and suspended Pilic, daring the ATP's membership to boycott the game's most prestigious tournament. When the tournament opened, 79 men had withdrawn in protest, including 13 of the top 16 seeds. Among those who opted to play were Ilie Nastase, Jimmy Connors, and a Swedish teenager named Bjorn Borg. Czeck player Jan Kodes eventually won the tournament over a second-rate field, beating Alex Metreveli of the Soviet Union. The ATP's success with the boycott signaled a newfound power for the players' association at the expense of the old governing bodies and the various national tennis associations.

What player was the first to reach **$30 million in career earnings**?

Pete Sampras, who as of early 1998 had won more than $32 million in prize money. This figure represents the amazing growth in prize money in tennis since the advent of "open" tennis in 1968. Sampras's total, it should be noted, reflects only prize money earned at official tournaments; earnings from exhibition matches and off-court endorsements, which in the case of a top star like Sampras typically amount to far more than on-court prize money, are not included. As a measure of how much prize money has increased in the 1980s and 1990s, the great Bjorn Borg won a "mere" $3,600,000 during his illustrious career, which essentially ended in 1981.

Who was the first top player to hit with a **two-handed forehand**?

It was probably Pancho Segura who first used this unorthodox shot. While two-handed backhands have become commonplace, two-handed forehands are still rare, since the necessity to use two hands limits a player's ability to reach wide shots. Segura was born in Ecuador but moved to the United States to attend college. He began competing at the top levels of the tennis world in the mid-1940s. In 1947, though, he decided to turn pro, which meant that he would be unable to compete in major tournaments or to play most of the best players in the world. Nonetheless, he did win three U.S. Pro

Championships, beating such stars as Pancho Gonzalez. A small player, standing only 5-6, Segura's biggest weapon was his forehand. Since Segura, the most-notable player to hit with a two-handed forehand has probably been Monica Seles, who also hits with a two-handed backhand.

What superstitious player used to **refrain from shaving** during the Wimbledon fortnight?

Bjorn Borg, who thought that shaving his beard would be bad luck. Perhaps Borg was correct, since he set a modern-day record by winning an astounding five consecutive titles at Wimbledon between 1976 and 1980. Easily the most-significant of his victories at the tournament was his last, when he defeated John McEnroe in five thrilling sets to win the title in 1980. That match included a pulse-pounding fourth-set tiebreak that lasted for 34 points and continues to be regarded as one of modern tennis' most titanic clashes. During the tiebreak, Borg—who had won the second and third sets after losing the first—held five match points, while McEnroe held six set points before finally winning the set on his seventh. However, Borg regrouped to win the fifth and final set. A cool, restrained Swede with devastating foot speed and an unparalleled baseline game that relied on heavy topspin, Borg won eleven Grand Slam titles during his brief career, second only to Roy Emerson's twelve. Borg might have won more titles had he not retired abruptly at age 26; his retirement followed consecutive losses to McEnroe at Wimbledon and the U.S. Open in 1981.

Who was the last **British man to win Wimbledon**?

Fred Perry, who won eight major singles titles during the 1930s, including Wimbledon in 1934, 1935, and 1936. A relentless attacker with an unusual forehand—hit running forward toward the net—Perry also helped Britain win the Davis Cup every year between 1933 and 1936. In 1937, Perry turned pro, where he competed on the circuit with such luminaries as Bill Tilden and Ellsworth Vines. He's still considered the finest male player ever from Great Britain; Virginia Wade, who won Wimbledon in 1977, is the only British player since Perry to make a significant mark on the tennis world.

What player **threw up on court** during a fifth-set tiebreaker at the U.S. Open—and still won the match?

Pete Sampras, who not only won the match but went on to win the tournament. Playing clay-court specialist Alex Corretja from Spain in the quarterfinals in 1996, the top-seeded Sampras struggled all day in the humid heat, winning the first set in a tiebreak but then losing the next two sets. Sampras regrouped to win the fourth set, 6–4, setting up the decisive fifth set. The two battled into a tiebreak, where a visibly fatigued

Horst Skoff of Austria, who was banned for life from the men's tour for allegedly failing to take a drug test. The ATP (as well as the women's Corel tour) began instituting random drug testing at select tournaments in the 1990s, but its method of testing later resulted in a temporary restraining order and a lifting of the lifetime ban against Skoff by a Florida judge in 1998. The judge ruled that the ATP had violated many of its own testing procedures in the Skoff case; the decision forced the ATP's drug-testing administrator to remove himself from the position, although his company remained in charge of the overall drug-testing program for both the men's and women's tours. By May 1998, Skoff's $10 million civil suit against the ATP was going forward.

Sampras staggered to the back of the court and threw up early in the tiebreak. From then on, Sampras—slumping over between points, seemingly barely able to stand—somehow managed to stay even with Corretja. Trailing 6–7 (match point down) in the tiebreak, Sampras saved the match with a dramatic lunging volley at the net. He then electrified the crown with a terrifically placed second-serve ace, and won the match when Corretja double-faulted on the next point. The match remains one of the most dramatic ever televised, although some fellow players later speculated that perhaps Sampras wasn't as sick as he appeared to be ("how else could he play so well?," they reasoned). Sampras went on to beat Goran Ivanisevic in the semifinals and Michael Chang in the finals for his fourth U.S. Open title.

What Wimbledon finalist was **convicted of murder** and died in prison?

Vere Thomas St. Leger Goold reached the Wimbledon finals in 1879, losing to John Hartley. Goold and his French wife were convicted in French court of murdering Emma Levin. Goold was given a life sentence in prison, and he died two years later on Devil's Island in French Guiana.

What former number one male player **milked cows** as a child?

Roy Emerson, also known as "Emmo," who has won more combined Grand Slam titles than any other male player (28, with 12 singles titles and 16 doubles titles). Emerson grew up on a farm in Black Butt, Queensland, Australia, but eventually moved to Brisbane to take advantage of better tennis instruction and competition. As with most of the other great Australian male players of the 1950s, 1960s, and 1970s, Emerson was primarily a serve-and-volley player. He won six Australian singles titles—a record for male players—two French championships, two Wimbledons, and two U.S. championships. Emerson's best year was 1964, when he won three of the four major tournaments, narrowly missing a Grand Slam with a semifinal loss to Nicki Pietrangeli at the French. His three major titles that year were all at the expense of fellow Aussie Fred Stolle (who later became a broadcaster). Emerson played as an amateur during his hey-day of the 1960s, then turned pro in 1968. None of his 12 major singles championships, and only two of his 16 major doubles championships, came as a pro. He was elected to the International Tennis Hall of Fame in 1982.

WOMEN

Who was the **first female to win the Grand Slam**?

Maureen "Little Mo" Connolly flashed briefly but brilliantly on the tennis scene. Nicknamed "Little Mo" for her big-gunning, unerring ground strokes (it was an allusion to "Big Mo," the U.S. battleship Missouri), she was devastating from the baseline, and seldom needed to go to the net. She lost only one set en route to scoring her Grand Slam in 1953.

Whose **only loss in 1983** was to Kathy Horvath?

Martina Navratilova, during the fourth round of the French Open. Born in Czechoslovakia, Martina became a U.S. citizen in 1981, after defecting six years earlier. The left-hander is the game's most prolific winner of the open era.

How old was **Tracy Austin** when she made her first Wimbledon appearance?

Fourteen. One of the game's prodigies, Tracy Ann Austin was meteoric, an iron-willed girl whose blaze was glorious though fleeting. A variety of injuries cut short what had promised to be one of the great careers. She and her brother, John, won the Wimbledon mixed in 1980, the only brother-sister pairing to do so. She entered the Hall of Fame in 1992 and works frequently as a TV tennis commentator.

In the **rivalry between Chris Evert and Martina Navratilova**, which player won more head-to-head matches?

Martina Navratilova had the last laugh in one of the greatest sports rivalries of all time, holding a 43–37 edge in match victories over Evert. The rivalry began in 1973 at

Martina Navratilova, the most prolific winner of the open era, lost only once in 1983.

a tournament in Akron, Ohio; Evert won the match 7–6, 6–3, and for the next several years dominated Navratilova, eventually building a 21–4 lead in their rivalry. However, the tide began to turn in 1978, when Navratilova overcame Evert in three sets to win her first Wimbledon title. During the 1980s (and indeed for the remainder of their rivalry), it was Navratilova who was dominant. She eventually caught and passed Evert in head-to-head wins, and she bested her rival in several Grand Slam finals. Nonetheless, Evert often credited Navratilova with prolonging her career, noting that Navratilova's revolutionary fitness regime and dramatic improvement in the early 1980s forced Evert to improve her own fitness and game. With their contrasting styles and temperaments—the icy and reserved Evert held forth from the backcourt, while the openly emotional Navratilova charged the net at every opportunity—Evert and Navratilova made a uniquely compelling partnership.

What player has won the **most singles titles**?

Martina Navratilova won more singles titles than any player, male or female, triumphing in 167 events during her twenty-year career. Among her victories are 18 Grand Slam titles: three Australian Opens, two French Opens, four U.S. Opens, and a record nine Wimbledons. It's the latter tournament where Navratilova's skills were most apparent, namely her athletic, fearsome serve-and-volley game, featuring a great left-

Who is the only player to win at least one Grand Slam title for thirteen consecutive years?

This achievement belongs to Chris Evert, who won at least one major singles title—18 in all—every year from 1974 to 1986. Evert's total includes two Australian Open titles, seven French Open titles, three Wimbledon titles, and six U.S. Open titles. Evert's career was a model of consistency. She racked up a career winning percentage of nearly 90 percent; she was ranked in the top ten for seventeen years; she reached at least the semifinals of 53 of the 57 Grand Slam events she entered; and between 1973 and 1979, she did not lose a single match on clay, winning 125 straight matches on the surface before losing to Tracy Austin in a third-set tiebreak at the Italian Open. Known for her incredible mental toughness, controlled accuracy, two-handed backhand—which inspired a generation of youngsters to copy the shot—and superb court balance, Evert won 157 singles title as a professional, a number second only to her longtime rival, Martina Navratilova, who won 167 titles. Evert won nearly $9 million in prize money during her career.

handed serve and a net game unmatched by any other woman player of any era. During the early and middle 1980s, Navratilova dominated the women's game in a way that perhaps no previous player had. She reached the finals at Wimbledon every year between 1982 and 1990, winning seven of her nine titles during the decade. She also came very close to winning a Grand Slam in 1984, winning the first three Grand Slam events of the year and then rolling into the semifinals of the fourth, the Australian. However, she was beaten by Helena Sukova, snapping a streak of 74 consecutive wins, a streak matched by no other player, male or female. Born in Czechoslovakia, Navratilova defected to the U.S. in 1975 and later became a naturalized citizen.

During her career, Navratilova also teamed with Pam Shriver to form the best women's doubles team of all time. The pair won the Grand Slam in 1984 and piled up 20 total victories in Grand Slam events.

What is a **Saba-tweeny**?

It's a between-the-legs shot popularized by Gabriela Sabatini, also known as the "divine Argentine," the stylish beauty who won the U.S. Open in 1990. Typically, the shot is hit as a player races from the net to the baseline to retrieve a lob. With very few options other than to hit a lob in return, a player might opt to hit the Saba-tweeny—between the legs, facing away from the net. Although a low-percentage shot, it has the advantage of surprising one's opponent—and delighting the crowd. The name was

Chris Evert returns a shot en route to an easy 6-2, 6-0 win over Wendy Turnbull to win the 1979 French Open.

coined by TV commentator Mary Carillo. Gaby didn't invent the shot, however; numerous players, including Frenchman Yannick Noah, hit the shot previously.

Who is the only player to have **won a Grand Slam in both singles and doubles**?

Margaret Smith Court, who won a doubles Grand Slam in 1963 with Ken Fletcher and a singles Grand Slam in 1970. The tall Australian holds numerous records, among them the most Grand Slam singles titles by any player, male or female, with 24 titles, and the most combined Grand Slam titles (singles, doubles, and mixed doubles) with 62. Court was a classic serve-and-volley player, using her size and strength to dominate at the net. Among her most-important wins were her 1970 Wimbledon conquest of Billie Jean King, 14–12, 11–9, and her 1973 U.S. Open title, which she won after giving birth to her first child. (Fellow Aussie Evonne Goolagong would likewise win a major title—the 1980 Wimbledon crown—after having a baby.) Court's 1973 loss to Bobby Riggs in a televised challenge-of-the-sexes has been forgotten in light of Billie Jean King's landmark victory over Riggs in their famous duel, held later that year.

Who was the **first black woman to win Wimbledon**?

Althea Gibson, who remains the only black woman to win any of the major singles championships. Although born in South Carolina, Gibson grew up in New York City's Harlem neighborhood. As a young player, she was noticed by Walter Johnson, a Virginia physician prominent in black tennis circles who became Gibson's patron (he was also a patron for Arthur Ashe). He introduced Gibson into the USTA, which led to her invitation to play in amateur tournaments, including the 1950 U.S. Championships at Forest Hills, where she was the first black to play and where she nearly derailed Wimbledon champion Louise Brough in the second round. Gibson finally won her first U.S. Championship in 1957, a feat she repeated in 1958 (she swept Wimbledon in the same years). She also won the French Championship in 1956 as well as six major doubles championships during her career. Gibson turned pro in 1958, and later tried her hand at the women's professional golf tour as well. She became a member of the Hall of Fame in 1971.

Since Althea Gibson won the U.S. Open in 1957 and 1958, which black women have reached the **final of the U.S. Open**?

Only Venus Williams, who at 17, unseeded, and playing in just her third Grand Slam event, reached the U.S. Open final in 1997. She lost in straight sets to top-seeded Martina Hingis, but her showing in Flushing Meadow convinced the tennis establishment that she had finally arrived as a force in the women's game. Williams began attracting

459

Venus Williams is one of women's tennis brightest young stars.

attention from tennis observers before she was ten years old. After compiling a 63–0 record as a junior, she stopped competing in junior events to prepare for her eventual career as a professional. She finally turned pro at age 14, having already signed a multimillion-dollar endorsement contract with Reebok, but she played few tournaments for the next three years. Not until she was 17 did her father allow her to play a regular tour schedule. Once she began playing pro tournaments on a full-time basis, Williams made a rapid rise up the rankings. By May 1998, she had risen to number seven in the world and was clearly making an assault on the top spot, having beat the number one-ranked Hingis twice in early 1998. (Her younger sister, Serena, was likewise climbing the ranking ladder, moving from number 453 in October 1997 to number 27 in May 1998 and posting wins over several top players.)

Who was the first woman player to earn more than **$100,000 in a season**?

Billie Jean King, who was a great champion during the 1960s and 1970s as well as a passionate crusader and tireless builder of the women's professional circuit. King arrived on the tennis scene in 1960 as a seventeen-year-old, when she rose to number four among U.S. women. She won the first of her 12 major singles titles at Wimbledon in 1966, a title she won six times. Her cumulative Grand Slam titles (doubles and singles combined) are even more impressive: she won 39 major championships, including an astounding 11 Wimbledon doubles championships. Although she was one of the game's best players for more than 20 years, her legacy also rests on her achievements

What French tennis legend shocked the establishment when she played at Wimbledon with a dress cut above the calf?

Suzanne Lenglen, who won two French titles and six Wimbledons during her career and who was instrumental in raising the international popularity of the game. Lenglen's bold sartorial sense—lightweight fabrics that revealed not only bare legs but bare forearms as well—was in stark contrast to the standard court fashion of the day, which dictated long, heavy dresses that left almost no skin showing but which also restricted movement. The mercurial and athletic Lenglen was colorful in other respects as well. She was known to weep openly during her matches, and she often sipped a glass of brandy between sets. Lenglen died at the age of 39 in 1938.

in helping to start and build the women's pro circuit during the early 1970s, when the women pros split from the men to form a separate tour. Perhaps the crescendo of her popularizing role for women's tennis was her 1973 defeat of Bobby Riggs in the "Battle of the Sexes." Played at the Houston Astrodome before 30,000 spectators and on national TV before 50 million viewers, the heavily publicized match captured the attention of the country in a way that perhaps no other tennis match before or since has done. Riggs was 55 and called himself the "king of the chauvinist pigs," but King beat him easily, 6–4, 6–3, 6–3. After her playing career ended in the early 1980s, King remained active as a coach—often working with Martina Navratilova—and as a promoter of both professional team tennis and amateur programs of all kinds.

Who was involved in the **lace panties scandal** at Wimbledon in 1949?

Designer Ted Tinling and player Gertrude Moran, nicknamed "Gorgeous Gussy." Tinling had been part of the tennis establishment for many years, having umpired matches for the legendary Suzanne Lenglen. Fed up with the boring white blouse and skirt that women players were virtually mandated to play in, Tinling had begun designing tennis dresses with flashes of color in the late 1940s—to the chagrin of the Wimbledon organizers in particular, who decided to institute an "all-white" dress code for players in 1949.

Tinling could not be so easily outmaneuvered, though. After the fashionable Moran asked him to add some excitement to her attire, Tinling added one half inch of lace at the bottom of Moran's panties. The move shocked the staid Wimbledon crowds and organizers and caused front-page headlines around the world. Tinling went on to design dresses for many top players during the next three decades. Wimbledon,

Gertrude "Gorgeous Gussy" Moran in 1950 showing off another one of her daring fashing statements, which always got her in trouble at Wimbledon.

though, hasn't changed: it still has an all-white dress code for players, and on more than one occasion it has ordered non-compliant players to change their attire before entering the court to play a match.

Who was the first professional player from **China**?

Hu Na, who defected from China to the United States in 1982 and who became a U.S. citizen in 1989. She had a solid pro career, winning one doubles title and rising to number 58 in the women's rankings in 1987.

Who teamed with John McEnroe to win the **1977 French Open mixed doubles** title?

Mary Carillo, who later became a renowned tennis commentator. Carillo had a modest pro career of her own, but she won admiration and respect as a tennis journalist in the 1980s and 1990s with her refreshingly candid and humorous personality. Among other monikers, Carillo has coined such amusing phrases as the "Saba-tweenie"—a reference to a between-the-legs shot favored by Gabriela Sabatini—and "Big Babe Tennis"—the latter referring to the advent of statuesque big hitters in the women's game such as Mary Pierce and Lindsay Davenport. The 1977 French title was McEnroe's first Grand Slam title and prefigured his swift rise to the top of men's tennis—and the public's eye—that began a month later with his semifinal showing at Wimbledon.

Which women players have won more than **$20 million** in their careers?

Martina Navratilova ($20,344,000) and Steffi Graf ($20,130,000) are the only two players as of 1998 to win more than $20 million in a career. Although the overall prize money offered on the women's tour is somewhat less than that offered on the men's tour, top women players of the 1980s and 1990s often earn as much or more than their male counterparts. In 1997, Martina Hingis, who turned 17 late that year, became the first woman to earn more than $3 million in a single year. As with top male players, star women players are usually able to augment their prize money with huge earnings from exhibitions and endorsements.

Who are the only women to hold the **number one spot** in the rankings since the advent of the computerized ranking system in 1975?

The six are Chris Evert, Martina Navratilova, Tracy Austin, Steffi Graf, Monica Seles, Arantxa Sanchez Vicario, and Martina Hingis. As of 1998, Graf held the record for the most weeks at number one, with 374, followed by Navratilova with 331. Graf also held

463

the record for the most consecutive weeks at number one, with 186 weeks (between August 1987 and March 1991).

Who is the **youngest** person in the 20th century to win a Grand Slam singles title?

Martina Hingis, who was 16 years, three months, and 26 days old when she won the 1997 Australian Open, defeating Mary Pierce. Hingis followed her first Grand Slam event victory with wins at Wimbledon (over Jana Novotna) and the U.S. Open (over Venus Williams) in 1997; she missed winning the Grand Slam—winning all four majors in the same year—by one match, losing in the finals of the French Open to Iva Majoli. In January 1998, Hingis repeated as champion of the Australian Open, defeating Conchita Martinez. By that time, the Swiss teenager was clearly entrenched at the top of the women's game and had achieved a number of records: youngest player to earn $5 million in prize money (17 years, 4 months); first woman to win more than $3 million in a single year (1997); youngest player in the open era to win a singles title at Wimbledon (16 years, 9 months, 5 days); and youngest number one-ranked player since the advent of the computer rankings in 1975 (16 years, 6 months, 1 day). In contrast to the tall and powerful women who were her chief rivals, the smaller Hingis rose to the pinnacle of the game with an uncommon court strategy, a willingness to adapt her style to suit the occasion (and her opponent's game), and an ability to exploit all corners of the court with her beautifully controlled strokes.

Who was the first woman professional to have been **born a man**?

Renee Richards, who made worldwide headlines when she joined the women's circuit in 1976. Born Richard Raskind, Richards was a competent amateur player as a man who was good enough to play at Wimbledon and Forest Hills when those events were only open to amateurs. Richards underwent a sex-change operation in 1975 and moved from New York City to California to start a new life. In 1976, Richards entered a women's tournament in La Jolla, California, but her presence was noticed by a former acquaintance who alerted local media. Following the inevitable wave of publicity in which her true identity was revealed, the forty-one-year old Richards decided to abandon her successful ophthalmology practice and join the pro tour. The Women's Tennis Association (WTA) and the United States Tennis Association (USTA) initially sought to exclude Richards from the tour by instituting a chromosome test as a prerequisite to entering a tour event. Richards sued and won the right to compete in tour events. Richards played the tour for five years, winning one singles title and rising as high as number 22 in the rankings, but fears by the WTA and the USTA that she would enjoy an unfair advantage dissolved in the face of her less-than-spectacular results. In the early 1980s, Richards assisted Martina Navratilova with strategy as Navratilova began her dominance of the women's game.

What tennis player's last name means "tall tree by still waters" in an Aboriginal language?

Goolagong, the surname of Evonne Fay Goolagong Cawley. She is the only native Australian to become an international tennis player. As one of eight children of an itinerant sheep-shearer and his wife, she spent her formative years in the small country town of Barellan. Her parents were convinced by a tennis school proprietor in Sydney to allow Evonne (at age 13) to live in his household, where he could coach her. She won six Grand Slam events: four Australian Opens (1974–77), the French Open (1971), and Wimbledon (1971). Londoners called her Sunshine Supergirl.

How did **Guenter Parche** impact women's tennis?

Parche irrevocably altered the course of the women's game in April 1993, when he climbed onto the court during a routine quarterfinal match and stabbed Monica Seles in the back. At the time, 19-year-old Seles was the dominant woman player in the world, having won eight Grand Slam titles in three years. With her unusual two-handed strokes off both the forehand and backhand sides, her hard-hitting, go-for-broke baseline game, and her superior concentration and focus, Seles steamrolled opponents during her first few years on the circuit. Parche, a crazed fan of Steffi Graf, Seles's chief rival, walked on court during a changeover in Seles's match against Magdalena Maleeva and stabbed Seles just below the left shoulder as she sat; he used a nine-inch boning knife. Although Seles was not seriously injured, she didn't play another match for more than two years, finally returning to the women's tour in August 1995. After her return, Seles had much less success. As of May 1998, she had won only one additional Grand Slam title since her return. In court testimony, Parche admitted that he attacked Seles in the hopes that he could derail her career and thereby aid Graf's; incredibly, he was given a sentence of probation. During Seles's absence from the tour, Graf—who was horrified by Parche's actions—won 6 of the 10 Grand Slam events that were played.

VOLLEYBALL

ORIGINS AND RULES

Who came up with the idea for **volleyball**?

In 1895 a Holyoke, Massachusetts, YMCA director named William Morgan cobbled together a game he called Minonette, volleyball's earliest incarnation. A former student of William Naismith, who in 1891 had invented basketball, Morgan shared his professor's penchant for devising new games. But soon after assuming his YMCA post, Morgan realized that his clientele—primarily middle-aged businessmen of rotund dimensions—were ill-suited to Naismith's fast-paced game.

Morgan's new game was a more palatable alternative, although it was admittedly a sort of Frankenstein. Indeed, he grabbed elements from a wide range of other games to create his new diversion, sewing them together into a wholly new creature. For example, he used badminton's emphasis on keeping the ball in the air as a central component of his game. He also instituted a nine-inning rule that was akin to baseball's structure, and he borrowed the concept of dribbling from Naismith's game so that players could "set" themselves. The final result was a game unlike any that had been seen before.

In its earliest form, minonette was played with an inflated basketball bladder that was batted back and forth over a six feet, six inches-high rope. Each team crammed nine players onto their side of the court. But within a few years the name of the game had been changed to volleyball and the teams were reduced to six players a side. Other rules changed, too, as the current mode of play, with its emphasis on setting, passing, and spiking, began to take shape.

What drew **early players** to the game?

A Dayton, Ohio YMCA director named W. E. Day was a key figure in improving the sport and thus drawing new participants. In 1900 he introduced a number of innovations, such as raising the net and eliminating the dribble. Perhaps the most important change made by Day, however, was his decision to toss Morgan's nine-inning format in favor of a structure in which games were played until one team scored 21 points. By the early 1900s, Day's rule changes had transformed volleyball into a more exciting and challenging game, although it continued to be dogged by a "sissy" reputation for years. Another major innovator was Pop Idell, yet another in the line of YMCA directors who shaped the sport. From his position at a Philadelphia-area Y, he introduced six-women, mixed-doubles, and coed-sixes formats to the game.

Volleyball proponents also touted alleged medical benefits associated with playing the game.

"The game is valuable from a hygienic standpoint," claimed one early handbook, "as the chest is never in a contracted position." Another questionable assertion floated by supporters of the fledgling sport was that it helped young men afflicted with "round shoulders." But the fundamental attraction of volleyball, even at that early period of its development, was that it was fun to play. As the 1903 Volleyball Handbook stated, volleyball "cures the blues."

How did volleyball become such a popular sport in **other countries**?

The YMCA was integral to the development of interest in volleyball throughout Europe, Asia, and Latin America. In the early years of this century, the organization believed that sports was a potentially effective vehicle with which to introduce Christianity to other cultures. As part of this effort, the YMCA introduced volleyball to Canada in 1900, Cuba in 1905, the Philippines in 1910, and Mexico and Brazil in 1917. The sport benefited tremendously from its exposure to these nations. Filipino players, for instance, were the first to unleash the spike on unsuspecting opponents. Teams in the Philippines were also the first to introduce the three-hit rule, which stipulated that a team could hit the ball among themselves no more than three times before hitting it over the net to the other team. This latter innovation supposedly came about when one Filipino team that apparently had a lot of time on its hands hit it back and forth among themselves more than 50 times before hitting it over the net. The opposing team became so frustrated with this behavior that they threatened to quit.

Another important factor in the development of volleyball was the introduction of American troops to European soil during World War I. The YMCA had been charged by the U.S. military with the task of seeing to the recreational needs of its soldiers, and the organization soon had volleyballs bouncing through military bases across Europe. By the time the U.S. soldiers returned home, they had spread volleyball fever across

> ## When was the score necessary
> ## to achieve victory reduced from 21 to 15?
>
> This change took place in 1916, the same year that a number of other important changes to the rules were implemented. This was the year that representatives of the NCAA formed a committee to formally codify the rules of the game. The final result, which was produced in conjunction with George J. Fisher, the president of the Physical Directors' Society, laid the foundation for today's game. The committee raised the height of the net to eight feet, established the rotation of server rule, formally imposed the six-player-per-side limit, and introduced the concept wherein matches became best two out of three affairs.

much of the continent, and over the next few decades these European nations outpaced America in supporting competitive volleyball.

When did **blocking** emerge as a volleyball strategy?

In today's game, blocking is an integral element of both the indoor and outdoor versions of the game, as teams endeavor to neutralize the monster smashes of modern-day players. But back in the 1920s and early 1930s, blocking was regarded as a last-ditch sort of strategy. As Robert Laveaga, an early expert on the game, once pronounced, "in general, blocking is not worthwhile as an acceptable principle of play to be used consistently. There are times when it is advisable, but it is not considered effective as a general policy of play." But by the mid-1930s, teams were often employing walls of two or even three blockers to stop opposing spikers. Blocking maneuvers became so effective that a 1938 rule was passed that stipulated that teams could only use two blockers against a spike. This rule was later revoked, however, and in today's six-person competitions, all three members of the front line are permitted to block.

Can a **blocker hit the ball again** if his or her block puts the ball in play in the blocker's court?

Yes. Ideally, a block will plant a spiker's smash right back at his or her feet, but on many occasions the volleyball will ricochet off the block into the court of the blocking team. In such instances, the block does not count as the first contact for that team. The first contact *after* the block counts as the first of the team's three allotted hits, and the blocker has just as much of a right to initiate that first contact as anyone else on the team. This is the only circumstance in which a player is permitted to touch the ball twice consecutively (players are also permitted to touch the ball on the first and

Karch Kiraly, perhaps the best volleyball player ever, demonstrates the proper way to set a ball.

How high is the net in volleyball?

It depends. The official height of the net varies, depending on the identity of the players and the organization running the event. Most major volleyball organizations, including the FIVB (Federation Internationale de Volley-Ball), USA Volleyball, the CBVA (California Beach Volleyball Association), and the WPVA (Women's Professional Volleyball Association), are in agreement on net height. According to these organizations, the regulation height of the net for games played by men, co-ed mixed sixes, and outdoors is seven feet, eleven and 5/8 inches (2.43 meters). The regulation net height for women's play is seven feet, four and 1/8 inches (2.24 meters). The regulation height of the net for AVP (Association of Volleyball Professionals) play, however, is an even eight feet.

third hits of an offensive sequence). Front-line players should also remember that it is illegal to block serves.

What is a **joust**?

Joust is the highfalutin' term used to describe any confrontation between opposing players to contest the volleyball above the net.

What are the **dimensions of a volleyball court**?

In the early days of the sport, the court measured 50 feet by 25 feet in its entirety. This undersized court made collisions between teammates an all too common occurrence. In 1920 the rulemakers enlarged the court's dimensions to decrease congestion and encourage athletic play. Today, the dimensions of both indoor and outdoor volleyball courts are 60 feet by 30 feet. In indoor play, the court is surrounded by a "free zone" of at least six feet, 6 inches into which players can go to retrieve errant passes. This free zone is 10 feet wide on outdoor courts.

Under what circumstances is a **side-out** called?

A side-out is a play in which the serving team loses service to the opposing team, which then rotates its lineup and launches its own service. A side-out may be called for any number of reasons, including the following:

The ball touches the ground on the serving team's side, either because the receiving team successfully put the ball away or because the serving team committed an unforced error

A shot placed by the serving team hits the antennae or passes outside of the antennae

The serving team plays the ball more than three times in succession

The ball is played twice consecutively by one player on the serving team (an exception is made, however, if the first contact is a block)

The ball lands outside the boundary lines on the receiving team's side after being hit by a member of the serving team

A member of the service team commits a fault, such as touching the net, entering the other team's court underneath the net, or hitting the ball in illegal fashion

The server hits the ball out of bounds or so that it touches the net

The server crosses over the end line before serving the ball

Players carry out an individual or team screen during service

A member of the service team positions him or herself illegally, or rotates incorrectly

Illegal substitution

Interfering with the ball while it is in the opponents' half of the court; this includes attacks made while the ball is in the opponents' court

Player on the service team leaves the court without the permission of the referee

A back-line player on the service team attempts a spike from inside the 10-foot "attack" line of the court

Player on the service team receives a misconduct penalty

All of the above rules, with the exception of those that apply to the server, also apply to the receiving team. In instances wherein the team receiving serve commits a fault (for hitting the ball out of bounds, touching the net, committing an illegal hit, etc.), the serving team receives a point.

Are players allowed to **reach over the net**?

Activity at the net is often fast and furious, as the space above the net is volleyball's battleground. For both spikers and blockers, then, it's important that they know when it's permissible to have their hands over the net. It is legal for a spiker to pass his or her hand over the net as part of their follow-through, provided that the initial contact with the ball was made on their own side. Blockers may place both hands over the net to block the ball, provided that they don't touch the net or interfere with play on their opponents' side. A blocker who interferes with an opponent's set by touching the ball on their side of the net, for instance, would be whistled for an infraction.

TECHNIQUES AND TERMS

What are the **six basic skills** of volleyball?

Volleyball play is comprised of the following basic components: passing, setting, spiking, blocking, serving, and receiving serve.

1) Passing is the act of sending the volleyball to a setter so that he or she can, in turn, present the ball to the spiker for an attack. The two primary passing methods are the bump and the dig.

2) Setting the ball is a critical area of the overall offensive attack. If the set is poorly placed, it can dramatically lower the effectiveness of even versatile spikers, because it limits their hitting options and their likelihood of hitting a kill shot for a point or sideout. Conversely, a well-delivered set gives a hitter a much better chance to avoid blocks and direct the ball strategically.

3) Spiking is the act of driving the volleyball hard into an area of your opponent's court. The two basic power shots are the cross-court shot and the baseline shot. Once an opponent has developed a healthy respect for a team's spiking power, alternative offensive shots such as tips and dinks can be employed with greater effectiveness.

4) Blocking is the primary defensive skill used to neutralize strong spiking attacks. It involves using players' arms to form a wall in front of the spiker, thus making it more difficult for him or her to hit the ball into the opposite court. When properly executed, a good block can be an effective weapon in scoring points or securing sideouts. In high-level competition, teams commonly employ more than one blocker against good spikers.

5) Serving is a very important element of volleyball. A server who can serve the ball reliably and skillfully will help his or her team far more than will a player who, for instance, is inconsistent with their serving. There are a variety of serves that are employed in competitive volleyball, from "floaters" that seem to shimmy and shake on their way over the net to hard-driven jump serves.

6) Receiving the serve is vital to success for any team. Poor reception of service puts teams hoping to get a sideout at a huge disadvantage right from the beginning. If the person receiving the serve is unable to make a good pass to the setter, then the setter's task of setting a good ball to the spiker is made that much more difficult. Receiving the serve sets the tone, then, for the whole offensive sequence that follows.

Sinjin Smith demonstrates how to dive under a shot for a "dig."

What's the difference between a **bump and a dig**?

The bump is the primary passing method used in both beach and indoor volleyball. It's used to pass balls that are played below waist height, and is the usual method employed in receiving serve. Players employing the bump typically contact the ball with the undersides of their forearms, which are turned so they face upwards and placed so that they line up together. This passing method will only be effective, though, if the player keeps his or her arms together and straight. The idea is to hit the ball on your forearms midway between wrist and elbow, because a bumping stance, executed correctly, will form a flat surface there in which the force of the incoming ball can be absorbed and from which the player can make an accurate pass. Footwork is an important factor in effective passing as well. A player can have perfect form with his arms, but if he doesn't bend his knees before receiving the ball to get "under it," the player will find that most of his bumps will travel into the net or teammates' midsections rather than up in the air where their teammates can easily play it.

The term "dig," meanwhile, is a slang word that in recent years has become primarily associated with sequences in which a player saves a point or side-out by keeping a hard-driven spike by the other team in play. Such digs may be made via the two-forearm method described above, but players who are able to keep the ball in play through the use of only one hand, such as through one-armed saves performed with the back of the hand, are congratulated for their "dig" as well. The key to successful

What are the basic offensive schemes used by six-person teams?

Volleyball teams can employ a variety of offensive systems, depending on the talents of their players. Primary offensive schemes include the "5–1," in which the team uses only one setter, thus freeing all five teammates to serve as hitters; the "4–2," wherein the team always employs a setter that has rotated into the front row; and the "6–2," in which the team uses two setters, each of whom serves as the setter when he or she rotates into the back row.

defensive digging is preparation; in other words, a successful digger is a player who gets into the correct position before the ball is hit.

What is a **pancake**?

No, it's not Karch Kiraly's preferred pre-game meal. Rather, it's a one-handed defensive technique wherein a player extends his hand out and slides it along the floor, palm down, while diving or rolling, so that the ball bounces off the back of the hand and remains in play.

What are the names of the various **sets**?

Over a long period of time, volleyballers developed a system in which numbers were assigned to various kinds of sets. These assignments are somewhat subject to change over time, but the basic designations are as follows:

0—a high, wide set that carries to the sideline area

1—(also known as a quick set) a ball that's set right next to the setter so that the spiker can attack it on the way up rather than at the top or on the way down

2— a set about two feet above net height, sometimes right next to the setter

3—a set of medium height about midway between the setter and the attacker

4—(also sometimes called a shooter) is a low set directed to the sideline area

5—sometimes defined as a soft set directed back to the weak side

What is a **free ball**?

A "free ball" is a ball that will be returned over the net by a pass rather than an attack. In such instances, which arise when a team is unable to put together a bump-set-spike attack sequence, the team preparing to receive the free ball will place themselves in approximately the same court positions that it would if it were receiving serve.

What happens if a player **serves out of order**?

This rarely happens, but when it does it can have nasty consequences for the serving team. A player who serves out of rotation loses all points scored by the player on that serving sequence. In addition, the team must relinquish possession of the volleyball to their opponent. Finally, the team that messed up its rotation order must correct its order before play can resume.

TEAMS, CIRCUITS, AND LEAGUES

Who played in the first **beach doubles** volleyball game?

Beach volleyball was played as far back as the late 1920s out on the California coast, but these early contests featured six-person teams. In 1930, however, Paul Johnson, Charley Kahn, Johnny Allen, and Bill Brothers padded out to a stretch of California beach to play what is believed to be the first known game of sand doubles. The mid-week game was borne out of desperation rather than inspiration, for the foursome played only after they were unable to pry working players away from their offices. They initially limited the game to only a portion of the total court, but as the afternoon wore on they decided that the challenge of covering the full court with only two players a side was worth pursuing. Thus was sand doubles born. The game quickly gained favor with the young, athletic players who populated California's beach volleyball scene, and by the early 1940s a recognizable style could be seen.

Who played on the first **dominant women's doubles team**?

Jean Brunicardi and Jeannette Latreille cut a dominating swatch through the fledgling women's circuit of tournaments in the early and mid-1960s, a period when women's volleyball began to get some real respect for the first time. Prior to that, women players struggled against cultural stereotypes and ludicrous rules. Until 1958 women's indoor matches featured severely outdated rules that reflected the societal biases of previous generations. For example, women's volleyball featured eight players per side, two serves (presumably because of doubts about a woman's ability to get a serve over the net on the first try), and no limitation on the number of hits that one side could take before hitting the ball over. The women's regulations even called for a mandatory five-minute break every thirty minutes, a stipulation that was undoubtedly imposed to safeguard against overloads to their delicate constitutions.

But during the 1950s and early 1960s women like Brunicardi and Latreille left such myths in tatters and forced rulemakers to update the game. Brunicardi played a key role in organizing some of the first women's tournaments. In 1958, for instance, she helped launch the Women's Beach Doubles Open Tournament in Santa Monica, California. The success of that event encouraged the formation of other tournaments, and soon a circuit that included stops in Hermosa Beach, Mission Beach, Manhattan Beach, and Laguna Beach had formed. Brunicardi and Latreille routinely walked away with first place in these tournaments until the latter part of the '60s, when a new generation of players hit the sand.

Who were the **Shamrocks and the Renegades**?

For a number of years in the late 1950s and early 1960s, women's indoor volleyball was dominated by one team. In the 1950s that team was the Santa Monica Mariners, who won six national championships. By the early 1960s, however, the mantle had been passed on to the Shamrocks. Blessed with an abundance of talented players, including Jane Ward, Jeannie Gaertner, Johnette Latreille, Linda Murphy, and Mary Perry, the club had a stranglehold on the sport in 1962 and 1963. By 1964, however, the level of talent on the team had become so great that the squad threatened to burst at the seams. Playing time became an issue of considerable concern for many of the players, and finally a faction split off to form a new team, the Renegades. This new team was initially spearheaded by Gaertner and Perry, but it quickly added Mary Jo Peppler and Kathy Gregory, two young players who would cast a long and dominating shadow over women's volleyball for years to come. The two teams met in the finals of the 1964 championship tournament, and although the Shamrocks ultimately prevailed, it was clear that the split had added some needed vitality to the game.

What single tournament ranks as the most famous of the **pre-pro beach volleyball tournaments**?

Most volleyball aficionados point to the 1968 Manhattan Beach Open. By that time, Manhattan Beach was already firmly entrenched as the most prestigious sand tournament in the land. As the tournament unfolded, Lang and Von Hagan advanced to the finals, where they awaited the winner of the losers' bracket final between the team of Mike Bright and Butch May and the duo of Larry Rundle and Henry Bergmann, who over the course of the previous couple of years had emerged as the biggest threat to Lang and Von Hagan's status as kings of the beach.

In the middle of the match between Bright-May and Rundle-Bergmann, however, the action shifted to the sideline as a drunk shattered a beer bottle over the head of Steno Brunicardi, husband of the famous Jean Brunicardi, over a seating dispute. Rather than dispatching the imposing Brunicardi, however, the blow only enraged Steno, who chased his attacker out onto the court where May promptly tackled him.

When did mixed-doubles emerge as a viable beach volleyball game?

As far back as the 1950s, mixed doubles tournaments were played, with tandems like Edie Conrad and Mike O'Hara winning the lion's share of tourneys. But mixed doubles didn't really come into its own until the early 1970s, when a handful of new mixed double tourneys popped up. The most prestigious of the mixed doubles events was the Marine Street Mixed Tournament. This tournament was dominated throughout the 1970s by Butch May and Eileen Clancy (who first partnered up with May when she was 12 years old) and later, May and a national paddleball champion named Barbara Grubb, who he would eventually marry.

The scene dissolved into chaos as the players held back the berserk Brunicardi and the terrified drunk prayed for quick deliverance to the drunk tank.

When order was finally restored, Rundle and Bergmann prevailed. But tournament officials were mightily distressed, for the long semi-final match, coupled with the crazy mid-match disturbance, had pushed the tournament deep into the evening hours. A suggestion to call the tournament a draw was promptly rejected by both Rundle-Bergmann and Von Hagan-Lang, and the two teams marched out into the sand to play, even though the sun was already down. Lang and Von Hagan jumped out to an early lead, but by the midpoint of the game it was almost impossible for either the players or the referees to see the ball. After one point, a fan asked the referee, "Wasn't that a throw?" The ref responded, "I don't know. I can't see!" Fans turned on their car headlights to provide the players with some meager light, but the situation continued to deteriorate, and soon both teams were hitting the second ball over rather than chance making the extra pass. Rundle-Bergmann ultimately won the bizarre contest when Rundle thought of a way to make the darkness work to his advantage. When he stepped back to serve, he launched high skyballs that were lost in the darkness above the court. Lang and Von Hagan were helpless, as Rundle's serves plummeted down out of the darkness to land in the sand. Thus ended one of the most famous contests in beach volleyball history.

What professional volleyball team met its payroll obligations through illegal sales of **marijuana**?

In 1979 the financial underpinnings of the International Volleyball Association's Denver Comets were exposed to the public in spectacular fashion, thus hastening the demise of the struggling league.

During the 1970s the IVA signed many of the game's top young talents. This contributed to the evisceration of the U.S. men's national team during that time and helped draw many top women and men from international play over to America. But while the IVA offered some fine volleyball, it was in many respects a league that was ahead of its time. Back in the 1970s, volleyball didn't enjoy the level of popularity it currently maintains, and the league was forced to provide financial assistance to weaker franchises with distressing frequency. The league office found itself forever operating in the red, and in 1979 the plug was pulled on the league magazine.

Ironically, however, the death knell for the league may have been sounded when the true financial picture of one of its seemingly healthy franchises came to light. Unlike some of the league's other owners, the owners of the Denver Comets had always been able to pay their players on time. But it was eventually discovered that the team's operating expenses were paid for by proceeds from the sale of massive amounts of marijuana in Florida. As a result, the owners were arrested and hustled off to jail by Denver police officers sporting "Operation Spike" t-shirts during halftime of a 1979 game at Denver Coliseum. Later that evening, Denver-area television stations showed footage of the owners as they were handcuffed at the scorers' table and escorted out of the stadium. This unflattering incident did nothing to reverse the fortunes of the sputtering league, and a year later the IVA closed shop.

COLLEGE, NATIONAL, AND INTERNATIONAL COMPETITION

Who were the earliest powers in **college volleyball**?

As the 1960s wore on, a number of California's major universities (UCLA, USC, and Stanford, in particular) instituted volleyball programs that would become perennial powers. But at the beginning of that decade, the best team in the land may have been fielded by tiny Santa Monica City College. The key to SMCC's success was Colonel Burt DeGroot. A long-time volleyball coach who had retired from the game in 1960 to take a job as a counselor and professor at SMCC, he proved unable to resist the call of the sport. A mere month or so after retiring, he was approached by a group of young SMCC players who asked him to watch a few of their practices. Within a week or two he was hooked, and he subsequently guided the team to three consecutive collegiate championships. DeGroot's efforts in this regard were helped immeasurably by the eligibility parameters set out by SMCC. Players were eligible for the SMCC squad if they enrolled in 12 units of classes, which only cost about $10. The low expense of the

SMCC classes, coupled with the abundance of comely young women in and around the campus, attracted droves of young California talent to his program.

What U.S. Olympic Volleyball team was **defeated by a high school** team in a scrimmage?

In 1964 the United States sent a women's volleyball team to the Olympics for the first time. Unfazed by the circumstances under which they entered the competition—they replaced the Brazilian team after political turmoil forced them to drop out—the U.S. women were tremendously excited about the chance to represent their country in the world's preeminent athletic competition. But the players were nonplussed by the selection of Doc Burroughs, a longtime USVBA administrator, as their coach. An all-too-brief two-week training camp did nothing to dispel the players' growing unease about the squad's level of preparedness for international competition. "I remember two things said to me at that camp," recalled Mary Jo Peppler. "'Circle out!' which meant get in hitting position, and 'Bend your knees more, honey.'" Players bemoaned the lack of strategy and drilling during the camp, and their complaints intensified after the squad suffered a humiliating defeat at the hands of a high school team in a scrimmage. As the team traveled to Tokyo for the opening ceremonies, the demeanor of the players ranged from apprehension to outright dread. If they couldn't even beat a high school team, how could they possibly compete against the amazing squad that their Japanese hosts had put together? Sure enough, a few days later the Japanese team destroyed the Americans. The team ended up finishing fifth out of six teams in the competition.

How did the men's team do in their **first Olympics**?

The men's squad had a similarly frustrating experience in Tokyo. For years, America's volleyball rules had been diverging from those utilized in international play, and in the 1964 Olympics this difference had a devastating impact on the U.S. team. The international rule that had by far the biggest impact was the one that governed reception of serve. International teams had long since switched to rules that called for players to bump the ball on serve reception. The American rule makers, however, had stubbornly refused to follow suit. Instead, they continued to encourage overhand serve receptions, reasoning that since the game had been invented in the U.S., non-Americans couldn't possibly come up with an improved version of the game. Meanwhile, international teams embraced the change, and it became an established part of the game everywhere else.

When the U.S. men's team took the court in a scrimmage shortly after their arrival, they discovered to their horror that international officials were going to blow the whistle on those overhand serve receptions. American players, coaches, and officials joined in a chorus of outraged protestations, but to no avail. The men's squad was forced to change

> ## What was the youngest team ever to win a USVBA National Championship?
>
> In 1975 the Adidas girls team, comprised of high school girls, strolled into the USVBA Nationals and walked away with the championship. Led by Debbie Landreth, Debbie Green, Sue Woodstra, and Carolyn Becker, the Chuck Erbe-coached squad stunned the National Team (which didn't even make it to the finals) and the larger world of American volleyball with their disciplined play.

styles in mid-stream. Some of the players had middling experience with the bump, but others had never practiced it. Other problems hampered the team as well. Scouting reports on opposing teams were woefully incomplete, and it quickly became clear that the team didn't have enough setters with international experience. The men's squad, which had touched down in Tokyo confident of a medal, limped home with a ninth-place finish and a bitter realization that they had better start practicing bumping.

When did indoor volleyball become an **NCAA-sanctioned sport**?

In 1970 the college game came under the banner of the NCAA. Southern California squads quickly assumed positions of dominance, with UCLA winning the national championship eight out of the first ten years (San Diego State won the title in 1973 and Pepperdine took the crown in 1978).

Do the U.S. Men's and Women's **Indoor Teams** own the most world championship titles?

Hardly. In fact, historically the men's and women's teams have performed poorly in the world championships, which are held every four years. The lone championship garnered by the Americans in the men's competition, held since 1949, was won in 1986. In many other years, however, the men have posted abysmal results. From 1970 to 1982—a period in which the U.S. men's program was in considerable disarray—the team finished no better than 13th in the four championships held during that period (in 1978 the team finished 19th). The Soviets, on the other hand, have won six men's championships (1949, 1952, 1960, 1962, 1978, 1982).

The story is much the same on the women's side. The U.S. women have yet to win a world championship, although they have posted a number of second and third place finishes. As with the men's competition, the perennial titan of women's ball was the USSR. From 1952 to 1990, the Soviet women spiked their way to five titles (1952, 1956, 1960, 1970, 1990).

Which nation has historically **dominated the women's World Cup volleyball** competition?

Led by high-flying superstars such as Mireya Luis Hernandez, Cuba's national team has emerged as the team to beat in recent years. In 1973, the very first year of World Cup competition, it was the Soviets who prevailed. But in 1977 the Japanese team was victorious, and in both 1981 and 1985 the Chinese squad took the gold medal. The Asian stranglehold on the World Cup ended in 1989 with the ascension of the Cubans. Since then, the Cuban women have taken the gold in both the 1991 and 1995 competitions, making them the most successful team in World Cup history.

Which women's program has **won the most NCAA championships**?

In 1997 the Stanford Cardinal women's team won the championship for the fourth time. Their victory, which was their fourth championship in six years (their other titles came in 1992, 1994, and 1996) moved them ahead of UCLA and Hawaii, both of which have won three NCAA women's volleyball titles since 1981, when the championship was first instituted. Other programs that have won NCAA women's titles include USC (1981), UOP (1985, 1986), Texas (1988), Long Beach State (1989, 1993), and Nebraska (1995).

Who holds the NCAA tournament record for **most kills** in a match?

Penn State University's Chris Chase pummeled the University of Southern California for 49 kills in a May 1, 1987 match. Chase's amazing match against USC also vaulted him to the top spot in the NCAA recordbook for most kills in a tournament. In the same tournament in which he planted 49 kills against USC, he also smashed 24 kills against Ohio State, giving him a record 73 in one tournament.

Which **college coach** has guided his team to the most NCAA men's volleyball championships?

Al Scates has enjoyed a remarkable run as head coach of the UCLA Bruins men's program. In 1970 Scates' Bruins took three straight games from Long Beach State to win the first NCAA volleyball championship. Twenty-six years later, in 1996, a Scates-coached squad knocked off Hawaii in five hard-fought games to take its 16th championship title. A top-tier game coach who has helped shape the games of some of America's very best players, Scates is one of the most durable and important figures in U.S. volleyball history.

PLAYERS

Who were the **Joker and the Penguin**?

The nicknames were hung on Gene Selznick and Bernie Holtzman, sand partners who over the course of three years (1954–1956) only lost one beach tournament. Both players would be enduring presences on both indoor and sand courts for years to come.

What beach volleyball legend from the 1960s and 1970s was nicknamed "**Von Muscle**?"

In 1961 Ron Von Hagen emerged on the American sand volleyball scene, where he would remain a mainstay until the late 1970s. One of the original beach demi-gods, Von Hagan was equipped with an incredible body and a quiet demeanor that masked a tenacious desire to win. By 1966 he had succeeded Gene Selznick, one of volleyball's all-time giants both indoors and out, as Ronnie Lang's partner. The duo of Lang and Von Hagan dominated sand tournaments for the next several years.

Who was **America's best volleyball player** in the first half of the 20th century?

A number of top-notch players stalked American volleyball courts in the 1930s and 1940s, including Manny Saenz and Bernie Holtzman, who combined to form the sport's first great sand doubles team; Henry Valle, an athletic southpaw who was one of the game's most feared spikers; Whitey Wendt, who dominated opposing front-line players for a number of years; Jim Ward, one of the game's top setters; and Buddy and Jimmy Montague, brothers whose sand partnership ended prematurely with the death of Buddy in the Korean War. But it was Jimmy Wortham who was selected in 1954 by the Helms Foundation as the best player of the first 50 years of American volleyball.

Armed with a crushing spike and a fine all-around game, Wortham led the YMCA squads on which he played to a bundle of national championships during the 1930s. In 1931 and 1932, he led the San Antonio YMCA team to national championships. In 1933 another Lone Star State team reaped the benefits of having Wortham, as the tall hitter guided Houston to a national title. Over the next six years, from 1934 to 1939, Wortham led Houston to the national championship five times. The only year the Houston squad stumbled was 1937, when Wortham missed the championships because of illness.

How did the "**back-set**" originate?

Prior to 1947, six-person volleyball teams consisted of three pairs of players, with each pair composed of a setter and a hitter. The setter, or "henchman," as he was commonly

When did rivals Sinjin Smith and Karch Kiraly first compete against one another?

Two of the true giants of beach volleyball, Smith and Kiraly have a long and complex relationship that dates back to a 1977 AA tournament in Rosecrans, California, when they first faced off in the sand. Smith triumphed in that first encounter, but the two players eventually teamed up for several years. Indeed, Smith and Kiraly won two U.S. championships together, in 1979 and 1981, before parting ways. During the 1980s and early 1990s the two former teammates became big rivals, with both players routinely finishing at or near the top in tour victories and money earned.

referred to, typically set the ball straight up from his position along the front line and his hitter would then hit the ball. This state of affairs, in which a spiker on the front-line who wasn't paired with the setter was always ignored, made it easier for opposing defenses to block and/or prepare itself for the upcoming smash, since they always knew where the set pass would go. But despite the predictability of perpetual front setting, teams kept doing it until Dick "Cappy" Caplan joined Chicago's North Avenue Y team.

Cappy enjoyed playing for his new team, which boasted big spikers such as Whitey Wendt in its line-up. But as the season wore on he increasingly felt that Wendt was not being adequately used, since he never got an opportunity to hit when he was in the right front position. One night the star setter decided that he wanted to try "back setting" to Wendt. When he told his teammates about the idea in practice the next day, their reactions ranged from doubt to outright scoffing. But When Cappy and Wendt gave it a try and the big hitter decisively powered several sets into the far court, they were convinced. Buoyed by Cappy's back setting, the North Avenue Y team advanced to the National Championships, where they defeated a Pasadena squad for the title.

What **former NBA legend** spent several years playing professional volleyball?

In the mid-1970s former Los Angeles Laker great Wilt Chamberlain seemed to be a constant presence in the world of volleyball. A team owner and star player in the fledgling International Volleyball Association, a professional league that wheezed through several years of existence in the mid-1970s, Chamberlain was also named president of the league in its second year of existence. After quitting the IVA, he headed a barnstorming tour throughout the Midwest. Wilt's Big Dippers, as his team was called, fielded a four-man team that squared off against open or college teams. Some of his teammates during the tour included such legends as Gene Selznick, Keith Erickson, Larry Rundle, Kirk Kilgour, and Butch May.

Initially, some members of the volleyball world were skeptical of Chamberlain's place in the game. But Chamberlain silenced those whispers once and for all in 1978, when he dominated a nationally televised All-Star game that featured some of volleyball's biggest names. The seven foot, one inch giant peppered his opponents with a blizzard of withering spikes that earned him the game's MVP honors.

What was the biggest **men's beach rivalry** of the 1980s?

Throughout the 1980s, volleyball fans who tuned in to televised tournament finals were usually treated to the latest installment of the ongoing clash between Smith-Stoklos and Hovland-Dodd. Randy Stoklos and Sinjin Smith were gifted players who won about two tournaments for every one that the Hovland-Dodd duo garnered. But Tim Hovland and Mike Dodd became known as players who brought out their best games in the big tournaments. Indeed, Hovland-Dodd got the better of Smith-Stoklos in most of the marquee tournaments. They won five out of seven Manhattan open clashes, five out of six World Championship matchups, and two out of three U.S. Championship contests when pitted against Stoklos and Smith.

Which **television and film star** played on the Outrigger Canoe Club team that won the USVBA National Championship in the Master's Division?

Tom Selleck, star of the long-running television series "Magnum, P.I." and such films as "Lassiter" and "In and Out," grew up in volleyball-crazed California. He played on USC's highly regarded team in the pre-NCAA '60s before moving on to Hollywood. But his love for volleyball never left him, and when a Screen Actors Guild strike stopped production of the "Magnum" television series, he resumed playing the game that he had left a decade before.

From 1981 to 1985, Selleck played in four national championship games with the Outrigger Masters' Division team. His team rang up two championships during those years, and Selleck himself garnered a second-team All-American award one year. The actor stayed involved with the game throughout the 1980s. In addition to his play with Outrigger, he played in several fund-raising matches, and on one occasion he played in a pre-Olympic tune-up against the 1984 U.S. men's team. "[Selleck's teammates] started out kinda playing around him," recalled one observer. "Then he got a one-on-one stuff and things got more serious. He started banging away and balls were going down . . . consistently. He could deal!" Finally, Selleck proved to be a potent fundraising figure for U.S. volleyball. The actor appeared in two different volleyball posters that raised more than $100,000 for the men's program. In recognition of his contributions to the sport as both a supporter and player, Selleck was named honory captain of both the 1984 and 1988 men's Olympic teams.

Karolyn Kirby, shown here with Lisa Arce, was the first women's beach volleyball player to earn more than $200,000 in career earnings.

What famous volleyball player **died of a heart attack** in the middle of a match?

On January 24, 1986, American Flo Hyman was felled by a fatal heart attack in the middle of a match in Japan. It was later discovered that Hyman suffered from Marfan Syndrome, a connective tissue disorder that affects a person's bones, eyes, ligaments, heart, and lungs. In Hyman's case, the disease had taken its toll on one of the aortas in her heart.

The loss of Hyman stunned the entire volleyball world, and was a particular shock to women's ball. Hyman had been an idol to countless young women who entered the sport in the 1970s and 1980s. She was universally regarded as the top player on the women's national team for a number of years. Armed with a lethal spike and a firm command of all the game's many facets, Hyman was a key factor in the U.S. women's team's ascension into the upper echelons of the international game. Highlights of her career included a Silver Medal in the 1984 Olympics (the 1984 squad was the first women's team to medal in the Olympics), a fourth-place finish in the 1981 World Cup (Hyman was named to the All-World Cup Team), and numerous championships in U.S. competition.

Finally, Hyman was known for her efforts to encourage other women athletes, and for her lobbying efforts to gain passage of the Civil Rights Restoration Act. In recognition of her contributions both on and off the volleyball court, the Women's Sports Foundation annually bestows the Flo Hyman Memorial Award on woman athletes who show Hyman's "dignity, spirit, and commitment to excellence."

Who was the Midwesterner who beat out players from California and other international volleyball hotspots to be named best setter in the 1992 Olympics?

Lori Endicott Vandersnick was born in Kansas City, Missouri, and played college ball at the University of Kansas, far from America's historic volleyball meccas up and down the West Coast. Despite her Midwest roots, however, Vandersnick proved herself to be a top-notch setter in college, and she was instrumental in helping the women's team win a Bronze Medal at the 1992 Olympic Games. She helped set the U.S. women to a Silver Medal at the 1995 Pan American Games and a Gold Medal at the 1995 World Grand Prix.

Who was the first woman to make more than **$200,000 in career earnings** in beach volleyball?

Sand superstar Karolyn Kirby established herself as the top player on the women's circuit in the early 1990s, and as her tournament championships increased in number, so did her bank account.

Like most other beach players, Kirby first made a name for herself indoors. During the early 1980s she earned All-American recognition at both Utah State and the University of Kentucky, and secured a spot as an alternate setter on the 1984 Olympic team. In the mid-1980s, however, she joined the growing exodus of players to the sand, and although she initially struggled to adapt to the demands of the outdoor two-person game, by 1991 she and teammate Angela Rock were the team to beat. The duo won 12 of the 17 events they entered that year, earning a total of $135,000 for the season. In both 1991 and 1992 Kirby was named the Most Valuable Player of the Women's Professional Volleyball Association (WPVA).

Since then, Kirby has maintained her spot among the game's top players. In 1992 she won a beach volleyball world championship with Nancy Reno, and in 1994 she and Liz Masakayan brought home the gold medal in the Goodwill Games. As the decade draws to a close, Kirby continues to rank near the top in seasonal earnings.

Who were the top-ranked **women in doubles sand volleyball** in 1997?

Teammates Lisa Arce and Holly McPeak led the Women's Pro Beach Volleyball Association (WPVA) tour in 1997, posting an overall record of 61–10 on their way to seven first-place finishes in 12 events. Arce and McPeak also brought in the most bucks, with each player pulling in $55,300 in earnings (both players supplemented their income

487

Holly McPeak, shown here at the 1996 Olympics in Atlanta, teams with Lisa Arce to form the top women's sand volleyball team.

with lucrative endorsements as well). Other top players on the women's circuit in 1997 included Karolyn Kirby (three open titles, 53–17 record, $43,085 in earnings), former McPeak teammate Nancy Reno (three titles, 50–15 record, $41, 585), and the team of Barbra Fontana and Linda Hanley, who finished tied for fifth in the WPVA rankings even though they didn't win a tournament during the season. They did post a 47–23 record and four second place finishes, however, which earned them each $34,930 in prize money.

Who's the all-time leader in **money earned** in volleyball competition?

Several players have garnered $1 million or more in career prize money, as beach volleyball has benefited from the same factors (television exposure, sponsorships, etc.) that have boosted earnings in so many other sports. The all-time leader in career beach earnings is Karch Kiraly, who's raked in more than $2.3 million in prize money out on the sand. This is as it should be, for Kiraly is viewed by most volleyball observers as the top player of the past 20 years. "I've seen guys who are underachievers—physically limited—who compensate by hard work," said volleyball broadcaster Paul Sunderland. "But Karch had more physical ability than anyone in volleyball, and mentally as well. He has an incredible ability to focus and compete everyday. I've talked to Magic Johnson, to Barkley—the great ones are all the same. They've got the total package. So does Karch."

Indeed, Kiraly has been the game's most visible figure for nearly two decades. From 1979 to 1982 he anchored a UCLA team that won three national championships, winning tournament Most Outstanding Player recognition in both 1981 and 1982. In 1984 he was the youngest player on the American team that won Olympic Gold, but his steady passing and hard swinging made him a mainstay of that squad (he played in more games than any of his teammates). In the mid-1980s Kiraly led the U.S. National Team to Gold in a variety of international competitions, including the 1985 and 1986 World Cups. He was named Most Valuable Player of the former tournament, and after the 1986 competition, FIVB President Ruben Acosta named him the "World's Best Volleyball Player."

In 1988 Kiraly served as captain of the U.S. Olympic team that won Gold in Seoul, South Korea, picking up MVP honors along the way. But at the close of the decade, Kiraly left the indoor game for the beach, lured by the growing purses and the need to challenge himself. A long-time sand player who competed in his first beach tournament at age 11 with his father, Kiraly quickly established himself as the unquestioned "King of the Beach." He was voted AVP MVP in 1990, 1992, 1993, 1994, and 1995, adding to his list of major championships every year. In 1996 Kiraly won his third Olympic Gold Medal, as he and teammate Kent Steffes knocked off Mike Dodd and Mike Whitmarsh by 12–5 and 12–8 scores to secure a spot on top of the podium for the Olympics' first beach volleyball competition.

EXTREME SPORTS

GENERAL

Which world-class snowboarder **boycotted** the 1998 Winter Olympics?

Norway's Terje Haakonsen, who has been called the Michael Jordan of snowboarding, snubbed the Winter Games at Nagano, Japan. He claimed that the format and structure of the Olympics was conformist in nature and would negatively impact snowboarding's free-spirited ethos. "Snowboarding is about fresh tracks and carving powder and being yourself and not being judged by others," Haakonsen once said. "It's not about nationalism and politics and big money. . . Snowboarding is everything the Olympics isn't." Of course, plenty of other world-class snowboarders decided not to side with Haakonsen, and the snowboarding events at Nagano were a big success. In fact, the controversy over Canadian snowboarder Ross Rebagliati's temporary loss of a gold medal due to alleged marijuana use reassured the sport's rebellious followers that it would continue to enjoy outsider status even as it made its first official foray into the Games.

What is **street luge**?

One of the more popular of the ESPN X-Games, competitors in the street luge barrel down a winding asphalt course on a long piece of aluminum equipped with skateboard wheels. Reminiscent of the more established luge event of Winter Olympics fame, the street luge is essentially an urbanized version of its snowbound cousin.

Who were the winners of the **1997 ESPN Summer X Games**?

The '97 Games featured 11 different categories of competition and 27 events. Winners of the various events were as follows:

Terje Haakonsen boycotted the 1998 Olympics, saying they were too concerned with nationalism and money.

What is sky surfing?

Developed in the early 1990s, this extreme sport features two-person teams who dive out of airplanes together. One of the teammates is the "surfer," the person who, during a 60-second free fall, performs a variety of loops, spins, and other maneuvers with a five-foot-long board strapped to his feet. The surfer's partner, known as the "camera flyer," uses a helmet-cam to send a live-feed shot of his teammate's acrobatics to a panel of judges down on the ground, who score the surfer on artistic merit and technical ability. Participants note that while the surfer is the one who attracts all of the attention, the camera flyer has to be at the top of his game as well. Camera flyers have to be able to skillfully maneuver around their teammates so as to show off their abilities from the best angles. At the end of the 60-second period, both participants pull their parachutes and float to the ground to see their score.

In-Line Skating

Men's downhill: Derek Downing, United States
Women's downhill: Gypsy Tidwell, United States
Men's vertical: Tim Ward, Australia
Women's vertical: Fabiola da Silva, Brazil
Men's street: Aaron Feinberg, United States
Women's street: Sayaka Yabe, Japan

Waterskiing

Barefoot jumping: Peter Fleck, United States

Wakeboarding

Men: Jeremy Kovak, Canada
Women: Tara Hamilton, United States

Snowboarding

Men's big air: Peter Line, United States
Women's big air: Tina Dixon, United States

Bicycle Stunt

Street: Dave Mirra, United States
Flatland: Trevor Meyer, United States
Dirt Jumping: T.J. Lavin, United States
Vertical: Dave Mirra, United States

Skateboarding

Street: Chris Senn, United States
Vertical: Tony Hawk, United States
Vertical Doubles: Tony Hawk and Andy Macdonald, United States

Skysurfing

Troy Hartman and Vic Pappadato, United States

Sportclimbing

Men's difficulty: Francois Legrand, France
Women's difficulty: Katie Brown, United States
Men's speed: Hans Florine, United States
Women's speed: Elena Ovtchinnikova, Russia

Street Luge

Mass: Mike "Biker" Sherlock, United States
Super Mass: Chris Ponseti, United States
Dual: Mike "Biker" Sherlock, United States

X-Venture Race

Team Presidio (Ian Adamson, USA; John Howard, New Zealand; Andrea Spitzer, USA)

Who were the winners of the **1997 ESPN Winter X Games**?

The ESPN Winter X Games consisted of 18 events in five categories. Individual winners were as follows:

Crossover

Brian Patch, United States

Ice Climbing

Men's difficulty: **Jared Ogden, United States**
Women's difficulty: **Bird Lew, United States**
Men's speed: **Jared Ogden, United States**
Women's speed: **Bird Lew, United States**

Snowboarding

Men's half-pipe: **Todd Richards, United States**
Women's half-pipe: **Shannon Dunn, United States**
Men's boarder X: **Shaun Palmer, United States**
Women's boarder X: **Jennie Waara, Sweden**
Men's slopestyle: **Daniel Franck, Norway**
Women's slopestyle: **Barrett Christy, United States**
Men's big air: **Jimmy Halopoff, United States**
Women's big air: **Barrett Christy, United States**

Snow Mountain Bike Racing

Men's downhill: **Shaun Palmer, United States**
Women's downhill: **Missy Giove, United States**
Men's speed: **Phil Tintsman, United States**
Women's speed: **Cheri Elliott, United States**

Super-modified Shovel Racing

Don Adkins, United States

Which **mountain biking** champion set a new 24-hour off-road distance record, then tried to have it nullified?

In May 1995 endurance specialist John Stamstad—commonly known among the fat-tire crowd as "Stamina Man"— set a new 24-hour off-road distance record by riding 354.5 miles on loops in Maine's Acadia National Park. This distance broke his old record of 287 miles, which he had set on California's Mammoth Mountain. But by the time he got off his bike in Acadia, Stamstad had become so upset about the unchallenging course that he lobbied to have the new record thrown out. "The course required absolutely no skill whatsoever," he said. "The only thing challenging about [it] was overcoming boredom and dodging strollers and pets."

ENDURANCE COMPETITIONS

Which **international competition** has taken place in such remote locals as the deserts of Oman, the jagged mountains of Argentina, and the tropical rainforests of Costa Rica?

The Raid Gauloises is perhaps the most famous of the world's expedition competitions. The event, which was first held in 1989, pits mixed teams of five competitors (including at least one woman) and two assistants against one another in a race course that takes teams anywhere from eight to twelve days to complete. During that period, competing teams sneak nourishment and catnaps while pushing themselves through the course, which may stray through sweltering jungles, towering mountain passes, raging whitewater rivers, and scorching desert (sometimes all in one competition). In order to win, all five members of the team have to cross the finish line before the full contingent of any other team does so.

The Raid Gauloises competition, which is moved to a different spot on the globe by its organizers every year, typically includes healthy doses of orienteering, hiking, whitewater rafting, canoeing, and sea kayaking. Other disciplines that have made their way into one or more of the Raid Gauloises competitions include mountain biking, horse- and camel-riding, caving, skiing, skydiving, and hang gliding. Basically, the event orga- nizers can propose any discipline that's appropriate to the terrain being crossed.

Since the inaugural race was run in 1989 in New Zealand, the event has moved to the following sites: Costa Rica (1990), New Caledonia (1991), Oman (1992), Madagas- car (1993), Malaysia (1994), Argentina (1995), and South Africa (1997). The 1998 Raid Gauloises is scheduled to take place in Ecuador in September, and like its predeces- sors, is expected to draw participants from all around the world.

Has any one nation been particularly dominant in the **Raid Gauloises**?

French teams have dominated the event over the years, and the final results of the past few years indicate that this state of affairs won't change any time soon. In the 1995 competition, the French team Coflexip—one of 20 French teams in the Raid Gauloises—barreled to victory on the strength of top performances in the canoeing, horseback riding, and hiking legs of the journey.

Then in 1997, the French team Ertips took the title on a course through South Africa and Lesotho that many thought was the most difficult in the history of the event. The 450-mile course, which included a grueling 96-mile mountain biking seg- ment and a 37-mile rafting leg on the Class V Umkomaas River, vanquished several of the teams.

Who was the **first female participant** in the Hawaii Ironman?

Lyn Lemaire of Boston, Massachusetts, who finished in fifth place out of 15 competi- tors in the 1979 race. She finished the course in a time of 12 hours, 55 minutes, and 38 seconds.

Who has **won the most** Hawaii Ironman Triathlons?

Paula Newby-Fraser, who has taken the title eight times in her career. Born in Zim- babwe and raised in South Africa, she entered her first Ironman Triathlon in 1985, only eight weeks after purchasing her first bike. To her amazement, she finished third among the women participants. Her good showing convinced her to increase her training efforts, and in 1986 she won the first of her seven Hawaii Ironman championships when the initial winner, Patricia Puntous, was disqualified for draft- ing on her bike. Over the next several years, Newby-Fraser established a chokehold on the event, posting six more victories from 1988 to 1994. In recognition of her exploits, the Women's Sports Foundation named Newby-Fraser Professional Athlete of the Year in 1990. Prior to the 1995 Ironman competition, she announced that the

Who came up with the idea for the Hawaii Ironman Triathlon?

The Hawaii Ironman Triathlon was created in 1978 by Navy commander John Collins. His proposal to combine three established endurance events—the Waikiki Rough Water Swim (2.4 miles), the Around-Oahu Bike Race (112 miles), and the Honolulu Marathon (26.2 miles)—into one super-endurance event attracted 15 participants in the first year. The incredibly demanding event soon caught the attention of the media, and both negative and positive coverage followed. Sports Illustrated referred to it as a "lunatic" competition in 1979, but in 1980 ABC's Wide World of Sports provided televised coverage of the event, which featured 106 men and two women that year. By 1985 the Ironman Triathlon was firmly established as the world's premier event of its kind, and it attracted participants from 46 states and 34 countries. Today, it remains the top triathlon in the world, pulling in top-level athletes from all points of the globe.

event would be her last. She nearly managed yet another win, but she lost a substantial lead when she collapsed from exhaustion and dehydration only 200 feet from the finish line. By the time Newby-Fraser managed to drag herself over the line, she had dropped to fourth place (Karen Smyers won). Dissatisfied with her performance in the 1995 race, she changed her mind and entered the '96 Ironman. This time she won, beating all other women competitors in a time of 9 hours, six minutes, and 49 seconds.

Among men, the all-time leaders in Hawaii Ironman Triathlon victories are Dave Scott and Mark Allen, each of whom won six times. Scott won all six of his Ironman championships in the 1980s. He was succeeded by Allen, who established a similar record of dominance. Allen won the event five consecutive times from 1989 to 1993 and he retired in his prime, winning the Triathlon in his final appearance there (1995).

Who swept both of **ultramarathoning**'s most prestigious events in 1997?

Thirty-six-year-old Ann Trason won the women's division of both South Africa's 56-mile Comrades Marathon in South Africa and the Western States 100, which takes ultramarathoners through 100 miles of northern California. Remarkably, she won both events even though she had only 11 days rest in between the two races.

Paula Newby-Fraser (left) has the most victories in the Hawaii Ironman Triathlon, with eight.

ON WATER

Which **water sport championship** has been won by the same athlete for ten years in a row?

Boardsailor Bjorn Dunkerbeck has won the overall world title in windsurfing for an amazing ten consecutive years from 1988 to 1997. A native of Denmark, Dunkerbeck moved to the Canary Islands when he was a youngster, and it was in that locale that he developed his amazing windsurfing talent. Since knocking off the sport's previous king, Robbie Naish, in 1988 for the world title, Dunkerbeck has guarded his crown jealously, and as the decade draws to an end, the Dane is closing in on 100 career victories in individual events.

Which three canoe races are collectively known as the **Triple Crown of Paddling**?

The first jewel of the prestigious Triple Crown is the 70-mile General Clinton Canoe Regatta. The second is northern Michigan's 120-mile Au Sable Canoe Marathon. The last of the three races is the 140-mile Classique Internationale de Canots, which takes place in Quebec.

Which North American **kayaker** has made the biggest impact in international competition in the last 20 years?

Probably Michigan native Greg Barton, who's made his presence felt in a variety of kayaking disciplines over that span of time. He won a total of five Olympic medals—including two golds—in various flatwater kayaking events in the 1984, 1988, and 1992 games. Then, after retiring from Olympic competitions, Barton turned his attention to marathon kayaking. Within a matter of months he had established himself as one of the world's finest endurance kayakers by taking first place in the 1994 Finlandia Clean Water Challenge, an exhausting 765-mile stage race that takes paddlers from Chicago to New York City. He then proved that his victory in the Finlandia was no fluke by putting together an extended string of victories in marathon kayaking events around the world. Barton's feats ensure that his name will remain a prominent one in the world of competitive kayaking for years to come.

Who came out of nowhere to win the **1995 Finlandia Clean Water Challenge**?

South African Lee McGregor, at 34 the oldest of the 17 entrants in the 1995 race, shocked everyone with his victory in the 1995 Finlandia competition. A former world-class swimmer, McGregor was nonetheless completely unknown in kayaking circles.

Have women ever been allowed to compete in the famous Acapulco Cliff Diving Championships?

For many years, the all-male Acapulco Cliff Union refused to allow women to compete in the annual event, which is generally regarded as the most prestigious event in the world of cliff diving. But in 1996, concerns about slowly eroding coverage of the sport led them to give women the green light. Six women competed in the first women's cliff diving competition there, and when the day was through, American diver Heidi Pascoe had edged Canada's Adele Laurent for the first ever Acapulco Cliff Diving women's title.

Second-place finisher Greg Barton admitted after the race that he had never heard of the guy. But McGregor's performance put him on the paddling map in a hurry. He took the lead in the very first stage of the race and never relinquished it, finally finishing more than 30 minutes ahead of Barton and the rest of the field. McGregor's reward? A $25,000 purse, the largest in paddling history at the time.

Who has won the **Upper Youghiogheny River extreme whitewater race** 16 times in the past 17 years?

Roger Zbel is the owner of this remarkable record. Despite routinely facing elite paddlers from all over, such as world champion kayaker Jon Lugbill, Zbel won his 16th championship on the Upper Youghiogheny—a river known for throwing several miles of Class V+ rapids at paddlers—in August 1997.

Who was the first woman to complete a **solo east-to-west circumnavigation of the globe**?

On July 8, 1996, 29-year-old Samantha Brewster became the first woman (and the youngest person) to sail east to west around the world alone. Sailing east to west is regarded as a far greater challenge than sailing west to east, because of prevailing winds and currents. As Brewster's manager said, "sailing the wrong way is like walking up a mountain versus skiing down." But Brewster was determined, and in the fall of 1995 she set sail on the 67-foot Heath Insured. She had initially hoped to beat the record time of Mike Golding, who made the same solo trek in 161 days. But repairs slowed Brewster down, and she was at sea for a total of 247 days before she completed her voyage at the docks in Southhampton, England, becoming the third person in history to make the journey.

Who was the winner of the first-ever **BOC Challenge**, the 27,000-mile solo around-the-world sailing race?

The first BOC Challenge (now known as Around Alone) launched in August 1982 with 17 ships. Of the 10 vessels that completed the voyage, Frenchman Philippe Jeantot was the first. A year later, he successfully defended his BOC crown with another victory. Today, the Around Alone and the Vendee Globe sailing race, another solo around-the-world competition, stand as the world's two major transglobal sailing events.

ON SNOW

Who is widely regarded as the **inventor of snowboarding**?

Jake Burton, who founded his Burton Snowboards company in Burlington, Vermont, back in 1977, when nobody had ever heard of the sport. His inspiration for the snowboard was a toy called a Snurfer—essentially two skis that had been bolted together—that had been invented by Sherman Poppen in 1965 and licensed to the Brunswick Corp. After making 100 different prototype snowboards, Burton finally came up with one that pleased him. The first few years were a financial struggle for the company, but in the mid-1980s ski resorts finally began allowing snowboarders on their slopes. Today, Burton Snowboards stands as the leading manufacturer in the industry, which has experienced tremendous growth in recent years. Burton, meanwhile, is one of the more popular corporate presidents that you'll find; he runs a profitable but relaxed company that's been known to shut down for a staff snowboarding day when skiing conditions at the nearby Stowe resort are particularly good.

Which race is widely regarded as the **most demanding extreme-skiing event** in the world?

The 24 Hours of Aspen race, in which participants descend a total of more than 200,000 vertical feet at perilously high speeds.

Who was the first non-Alaskan to win the **Iditarod Trail Sled Dog Race**?

Montana native Doug Swingley became the first non-Alaskan to win North America's premier dogsledding race when he was the first to guide his team of huskies across the Nome finish line in 1995. Swingley didn't exactly hide his Montana roots at the finish

501

Jake Burton, inspired by a toy, practically invented the sport of snowboarding.

Who invented the modern ice climbing ax?

Yvon Chouinard, the mountaineering enthusiast who founded the internationally known Patagonia outdoor clothing and gear company. In addition to devising the modern ice climbing ax in the late 1960s, Chouinard also came up with better ice screws in the 1970s, as well as a number of other ice climbing innovations.

line, either. In fact, his wife and children greeted him by waving a huge Montana state flag through the streets of Nome.

Whose Iditarod victory prompted Alaskan vendors to start selling T-shirts reading "Alaska . . . Where men are men and **women win the Iditarod**."

In 1985 Libby Riddles became the first woman to win the Iditarod Trail sled dog race. Prior to her victory, she had never placed better than 18th in the competition, so it was a complete shock to everyone when she took the title. Riddles finished the race, which featured some of the event's all-time worst weather, in 18 days, 20 minutes, and 17 seconds, a full two hours before the second-place finisher. One year later, Susan Butcher became the second woman to win the Iditarod, and she went on to dominate the event for the next few years, taking first place in 1987, 1988, and 1990 as well.

SPORT CLIMBING

Which **sport climbing legend** retired after winning a fourth consecutive World Cup title?

American Robyn Erbesfield capped a tremendous sport climbing career in fitting style in December 1995, when she captured her fourth straight sport climbing title in dramatic fashion. As she entered the final event of the season, which was held in Aix-les-Bains, France, it appeared unlikely that she'd be able to overtake France's Laurence Guyon, who had a healthy lead in the season's standings. Erbesfield would have to win the event and hope that Guyon finished no better than fourth for the American to win the Cup. But the event unfolded in exactly that fashion. Erbesfield climbed superbly to take first place, and Guyon finished in fifth place. Erbesfield was thus able to retire as sport climbing's reigning champ. Since Erbesfield's departure from the sport, Guyon, **503**

Doug Swingley was the first non-Alaskan to win the Iditarod.

Libby Riddles was the first woman to win the Iditarod, in 1985.

American Katie Brown, and France's Liv Sansoz have battled for the top spot in the world of women's sport climbing.

Why was the **1995 Eco Challenge Adventure Race** so controversial?

The outdoor endurance race, which pits teams against one another in a seven-stage race through a remote high desert region of Utah, ended in somewhat bizarre fashion. During the final night of the race, which featured canyoneering, climbing and rappelling, and trekking components, the French Hewlett Packard team was clinging to a precarious lead over New Zealand's Team Southern Traverse.

As the New Zealand team crept ever closer, the HP squad resorted to a piece of subterfuge. Aware that their pursuers were tracking them by following the light of their headlamps, the French team deliberately struck out on a false path. Then, when they were sure that the New Zealand team was following them, they doused their headlamps and watched the New Zealand team march on past. Once their opponents had passed by their hiding place, the HP team backtracked to the correct trail and cruised on to victory.

After the race was concluded, some observers and competitors questioned the ethics of the HP ploy, but supporters of the French team pointed out that nobody had forced the New Zealand squad to follow the headlamps rather than use their own orienteering skills.

Who was the first woman to complete a **grade 5.14 climb**?

American rock climber Lynn Hill, who dominated women's climbing competitions through much of the 1980s, was the first woman to make such a difficult climb. She did it in Cimai, France, in 1990. Moreover, Hill remains the only climber—male or female—to free-climb the 3,000-foot Nose route on Yosemite's El Capitan in a single day.

MOUNTAIN CLIMBING

Who is the only climber in history to **scale every mountain on earth above 26,250 feet**?

Mountaineering legend Reinhold Messner is the only climber to have scaled all 14 mountains in the world with summits above 26,250 feet (8,000 meters). Moreover, in every instance Messner gained the summit without using bottled oxygen. This status, coupled with his pioneering routes on some of the mountaineering world's most fearsome prizes and his legendary 1980 solo ascent of Everest at the height of a terrifying storm, have made the climber the most famous mountaineer of modern times.

Who made the first successful ascent of **Mount McKinley** in midwinter?

In January 1998 a trio of Russian mountaineers—Artur Testov, Vladimir Ananich, and Alexandr Nikiforov—became the first climbers in history to successfully summit McKinley, North America's highest mountain, during its coldest month. The mountaineers used the West Buttress Route to tackle the peak, ignoring 100-mile-per-hour winds, -50 degree temperatures, and meager sunlight (in January the sun at McKinley peeks above the horizon for only about four hours a day).

OTHER
SPORTS

FOOTRACING

What is the **oldest regularly-contested foot race in the United States**?

The Boston Marathon was first run in 1897 and continues to be held annually on Patriot's Day in April. Since World War II the race has taken on a strong international flavor after being won by Americans and Canadians before then. Kenyans have won from 1991 through 1997. The last Americans to win were Greg Meyer in 1983 and Lisa Larsen Weidenbach in 1985. The first Boston Marathon run under 2 hours, 20 minutes occured in 1921. Bill Rodgers of Massachusetts was the first to break the 2 hour, 10 minute level (1979), and Cosmas Ndeti of Kenya set the all-time low of 2 hours, seven minutes, 15 seconds in 1994.

The Women's competition in the Boston Marathon began in 1972 with the winner's time over three hours. The 2 hour, 50 minute mark was broken in 1974, and the all-time best time occured in 1994 when Uta Pippig of Germany ran in 2 hours, 21 minutes, 45 seconds.

What famous incident of cheating occured at the **Boston Marathon**?

In 1980, the running world was stunned when an unknown named Rosie Ruiz came out of nowhere to win the women's division of the prestigious Boston Marathon. "How could she have done it?" people wondered. By cheating, turned out to be the answer. With only a little investigative work, it was discovered that Ruiz did not run the entire race, possibly taking the subway or a taxi to shorten the course. Once her sin was uncovered, she was stripped of first place and Canada's Jacqueline Garreau was declared the winner.

What race was **increased by 385 yards** so King Edward VII of Great Britain could see the finish line better?

At the 1908 Olympic Games in London, the marathon distance was increased slightly so the finishers would pass by British royalty.

What did **Forrest Smithson** carry for inspiration while running hurdles at the 1908 Olympics?

The Holy Bible. He set a world record in the 110 meter hurdles by running that race in 15 seconds. The current world record was set by Rod Milburn of the United States in 1972 at 13.24 seconds.

Can a pole vaulter who **knocks off the crossbar during a vault** still get credit for a successful vault?

He can by pushing the crossbar back onto the support poles before touching the ground.

ON THE WATER

What is the history of the **America's Cup** yacht races?

England's Royal Yacht Squadron organized a 60-mile regatta around the Isle of Wight in 1861 and offered a silver trophy—the Hundred Guinea Cup—to the winner. *America*, a 101-foot schooner from the New York Yacht Club, won the race and the trophy was deeded to the Club to defend it whenever challenged. Challenges have come in staggered time frames—from races held three consecutive years (1885-87) to having no competitions for seventeen (1903-20) and 21-year (1937-1958) periods.

From 1870-1937 the America's Cup was successfully defended 17 times in Schooners and J-Class boats; from 1958-1980, the America's Cup was successfully defended eight more times in 12-meter boats. *Australia II* broke American dominance in 1983 by winning four times in the best-of-seven format that had been in place since 1930. Four years later, *Stars & Stripes* of the San Diego Yacht Club won the trophy back, but they were immediately challenged the following year by Mercury Bay, a New Zealand crew.

New Zealand planned to race with a 133 ft. Monohull, and defending skipper Dennis Connor countered with a 60 ft. Catamaran. After the Catamaran easily won two

What are the different kinds of rowing competitions?

Regattas are competitions run in lanes where individual rowers and teams (referred to as shells) are eliminated over a series of races; Head Races are based on times, with boats going off at various intervals.

There are three kinds of Scull races—single scullers and double and quadruple teams; the scull is the type of boat and also refers to the oar, so in a Scull race scullers uses sculls to propel their sculls. Single sculls average about 27 feet in length, doubles about 34 feet in length, and quadruples about 44 feet in length.

In rowing contests the competitors use one oar, and a boat may or may not include a coxswain, or coach. Competitions include coxed and coxless pairs and fours and coxed eights. The coxless pair scull runs 34 feet in length, the coxed pair about 35 feet; the coxless four runs about 44 feet, the coxed four around 45; the coxed eight runs around 62 feet.

races, Mercury Bay protested use of the boat in court, leading to three years of legal wrangling. Since 1992, the America's Cup has been competed with 75-foot Monohulls with 110-foot masts. *America 3* won in 1992 and New Zealand's *Black Magic* won in 1995. Their defense is scheduled for the year 2000.

What is the history of the **America's Cup Trophy**?

The America's Cup trophy was originally called the Hundred Guinea's Cup when first contested for in 1851, but it was renamed to honor the first winner, the yacht *America*. It is 27 inches high and made of sterling silver and originally cost 100 guineas ($500); today it is valued at over $250,000. The trophy had to be restored after a Maori protester smashed it with a sledgehammer in 1997. The trophy is taken into possession by the winner of the America's Cup races who must defend the Cup when officially challenged.

What is the **oldest American college sport** still held today?

Rowing. Harvard and Yale held the first U.S. collegiate regatta in 1852.

Why might a **coxswain want his shell to lose a race** on the Amazon?

Traditionally, the winning team throws its coxswain overboard. Piranahs might make a meal of the winning coach in the Amazon.

What about **canoe** competitions?

Canoe and kayak sprint racing is held on 500 meter, 1000 meter and 10,000 meter courses for men, 500 meter and 5000 meter for women, in one-, two-, and four-person events. The paddler in a kayak sits with their legs outstretched before them in a decked or covered boat and uses a double-bladed paddle; canoeists paddle a singe-bladed oar from a kneeling position in an open boat.

The different races are distinguished by a K (denoting kayak) and C (denoting canoe) followed by the number of people in the boat. Men compete in K1 and K2 in the 500m 1000m and 10,000m events, but not in the 500m in K4. C1 and C2 are competed in each distance, but C4 competition does not include the 10,000m. Women compete only in Kayak competitions, but the women's K4 is not run at the 5000m distance.

Canoe slalom competiton contains a series of gates (at least 20) and various natural and artificial obstacles canoeists must negotiate. Men compete in K1, C1, and C2 events, women in K1. Each contestant is usually given one trial run on a course followed by one or two timed runs.

FREESTYLING:
GENERAL THINGS TO KNOW

What teams **can't you bet on in Vegas**?

You can't bet on Nevada college teams in Las Vegas or Reno.

What are the **most popular participatory sports** in the United States?

According to a 1997 survey by the National Sporting Goods Association, exercise walking is most popular with over 70 million participants. Swimming is second with just over 60 million participants and bicycle riding third at over 50 million.

Exercising with equipment ranked fourth (over 47 million) and aerobics 13th (over 24 million). Fishing ranked fifth (over 45 million), overnight camping sixth (over 44 million), hiking 11th (over 26 million), backpacking 25th (over 11 million), and mountain biking 27th (over 11 million). Bowling was seventh (over 42 million), pool/billiards eighth (over 34 million), basketball ninth (over 33 million), and power boating 10th (over 28 million).

Others not mentioned above include In-line skating (12th, over 25 million), golf (14th, over 23 million), running/jogging (15th, over 22 million), darts (16th, over 21

What is the Tour de France?

The Tour de France is an endurance bicycle race covering about 2,300 miles in France and neighboring countries held over three weeks in June-July. Four bikers have won the race on five times (Jacques Anquetil of France, Bernard Hinault of France, Miguel Indurain of Spain, and Eddie Merckx of Belgium). American Greg LeMond won the race three times. The Tour de France has been held annually since 1903.

million), softball (17th, just under 20 million), hunting with firearms (18th, over 19 million), volleyball (19th, 18 million), and target shooting (20th, over 15 million). Soccer ranked 23rd with just under 14 million participants and tennis tied for 25th with 11 million.

The survey involved Americans seven years of age and older.

What is the **top-grossing sports movie** of all-time?

Through October 1, 1997, Tom Cruise's *Jerry McGuire* was the box office champ, pulling in $153,620,822. Sylvester Stallone is probably the undisputed heavyweight champ of the silver screen, however, as his five *Rocky* movies have combined to earn more than $510 million. *Rocky 4, Rocky 3,* and the original *Rocky* finished 2nd, 3rd, and 4th behind *McGuire,* respectively. Two sports movies—the original *Rocky* in 1976 and *Chariots of Fire* in 1981, won the Oscar for Best Picture.

What is the **International Women's Sports Hall of Fame**, and how are athletes chosen for inclusion?

The International Women's Sports Hall of Fame was founded in 1980 by the Women's Sports Foundation of East Meadow, New York. That organization selects honorees whose achievements and contributions are internationally recognized. Honorees are divided into two categories, Pioneers (those whose accomplishments pre-date 1960) and Contemporary. Auto racer Janet Guthrie, basketball stars Ann Meyers and Cheryl Miller, figure skater Peggy Fleming, gymnast Mary Lou Retton, tennis stars Chris Evert and Billie Jean King, track star Wilma Rudolph, and eight prominent golfers are among the Americans represented.

What is the **Women's Global Challenge**?

The Woman's Global Challenge is a biannual event beginning in 1999 that matches the world's top amateur and professional female athletes and women's teams in such

What is the triathlon?

The triathlon, which will be an introduction sport at the 2000 Summer Olympic Games in Sydney, Australia, combines swimming, cycling, and running. For the 2000 Games, the longest Olympic swimming distance (1500 meters), cycling time trials (40 kilometers), and footrace (10,000 meters) will be used. The World Triathlon Championship, held annually since 1989, combines a 1.5 kilometer swim (.93 of a mile) a 40-kilometer bike (24.9 miles), and a 10-kilometer run (6.2 miles). Men have broken the 1 hour 40 minute mark for the competition, women the 1 hour 50 minute mark. The Ironman Triathlon Championship has been held since 1978 in Hawaii and features more grueling distances (2.4 mile swim, 112 mile bike, 26.2 mile run), with men challenging the 8-hour mark of total time, women challenging the 9-hour mark.

events as basketball, beach volleyball, diving, figure skating, gymnastics, soccer, swimming, and track and field. The top ten athletes in each sport and the top four to eight teams will be invited to compete. The Women's Global Challenge was conceived by the Women's Sports Foundation.

What are the teams of the **Japanese Baseball Leagues**?

There are six teams in each of two leagues: The Central League has the Chunichi Dragons, the Hanshin Tigers, the Hiroshima Carp, the Yakult Swallows, the Yokohama BayStars, and the Yomiuri Giants; the Pacific League has the Chiba Lotte Marines, the Fukuoka Daiei Hawks, the Kintesu Buffaloes, the Nippon Ham Fighters, the Orix Blue Wave, and the Seibu Lions.

Who was the first athlete whose **salary exceeded that of the President of the United States**?

Babe Ruth was the first athlete to have a contract with an annual salary higher than that of the president. When asked if he thought that was right, Ruth replied, "Yes. I had a better year."

Michael Jordan's 1997 salary was 16 1/2 times higher than President Clinton's.

Has anyone ever **bowled a perfect series** (900 over three games)?

The only sanctioned 900 series occurred in 1997, when Jeremy Sonnenfeld, a sophmore at Nebraska, rolled three perfect games in a row.

How did the **Ivy League** get its name?

Four schools—Harvard, Yale, Columbia, Princeton—formed an association called the League of IV; a sportswriter played with the name and turned it into the Ivy League.

How do **Canadian Football and Australian Rules football** differ from their American cousin?

The Canadian football field runs 110 yards and end zones are 25 yards deep (as opposed to 100 and 10 yards, respectively in American); there are 12 offensive and defensive players on the field (as opposed to eleven); a team gets three downs to make 10 yards (as opposed to four); and there is no fair catch in Canadian football, as players returning kicks are allowed a five-yard free zone to catch the ball and begin their run-back. In Canadian football, players in the backfield are free to move in any direction before the ball is snapped, while in American football only one player can go in motion before the snap and he has to run parallel to the line of scrimmage or away from it. Canadian football has a 25 yard penalty in addition to the 5-, 10-, and 15-yard penalty distances it has in common with American football. In addition to a touchdown (6 points), field goal (3), safety and conversion (2), and extra point (1), Canadian football features the single, or rouge, worth one point if a team cannot advance a kicked ball beyond its own end zone; unlike American football, kicked balls are not allowed to roll dead, so the receiving team must retrieve the ball or else lose possession. A player who cannot return a kick from the end zone will concede a single, rather than risk getting tackled for a two-point safety.

The field in Australian Rules Football is oval shaped, 110 to 155 meters wide, 135 to 185 meters long. Teams of 18 players advance the ball towards sets of goal posts on either end of the oval: kicking or punching the ball through the center posts is worth a goal (six points), while kicking or punching the ball within two outer posts are called "behinds" (one point). Players can advance the ball toward the goals by running, but they must bounce the ball or touch it on the ground every 10 meters; ball handlers can kick, hand off, or punch the ball to another player, but passes are not allowed.

Who are those **guys in raincoats and shorts who occasionally wave flags** at either end of the oval in Australian Rules Football?

They're not bookies. They are game officials who signal whether a ball has passed through the center posts (worth six points) or the outer points (worth one point).

Index

515

American Hockey Coaches Association (AHCA), 322

American Hockey League (AHL), 283, 291, 302

American League, 11-13, 33, 47-48, 50-51, 54, 56, 58, 60, 62, 66-67, 69-70, 76, 78, 83-84, 86-87, 130, 245, 302, 306, 311, 391, 397, 424, 482

American Professional Football Association (APFA), 186-187

American University, 434

American Women's College Hockey Alliance National Championship, 329

America's Cup, 254, 508-509

America's Cup Trophy, 509

"America's Team," 221

Amherst, 125

Amonte, Tony, 329

Anaheim Amigos, 110

Anaheim Angels, 41

Anaheim Mighty Ducks, 283

Ananich, Vladimir, 506

Andersen, Morten, 221

Anderson, Donny, 189-190

Anderson, Dick, 200

Anderson, Sparky, 69

Andretti, Aldo, 11

Andretti, Jeff, 11

Andretti, John, 15

Andretti, Mario, 7, 9, 11, 15, 22, 26-27

Andretti, Michael, 12

Anet, Bobby, 136

Angotti, Lou, 329

Anquetil, Jacques, 511

Anson, Cap, 33

Aochi, Seiji, 404

Aouita, Said, 381

The Apartment, 444

Apps, Syl, 291

Arbour, Al, 306, 311

Arcaro, Eddie, 338-339

Arce, Lisa, 486-488

Archbishop of Sanctandros, 252

Archbishop of York, 265

Archibald, Nate (Tiny), 98, 114

Arena Football League, 224

ArenaBowl, 224

Arguello, Alexis, 166

Aristides, 343

Arizin, Paul, 98

Arizona State University, 81, 242

Arizona Cardinals, 221

Arizona Diamondbacks, 41

Arlington International, 340

Armstrong, Gerry, 450

Armstrong, Hank, 163

"Arnie's Army", 269

Around Alone, 501

Around-Oahu Bike Race, 497

Arsenal, 429

Art Ross Trophy, 286, 289-291, 294

Arthur, Frederick, 306

Ashe, Arthur, 448-449, 459

Ashland Junior College, 128

Asian Cup, 424

Asinof, Eliot, 49

Assault, 344, 397, 410, 432, 460

Associated Press (AP), 228, 235, 340, 389

Association for Intercollegiate Athletics for Women (AIAW), 148

Association of Tennis Professionals (ATP), 438, 452, 454

Association of Volleyball Professionals (AVP), 471, 489

Astrodome, 41, 460

Atlanta Braves, 41, 62, 81

Atlanta Falcons, 87, 204, 216, 221

Atlanta Hawks, 97, 121

Atlanta Knights, 319

Atlanta Tip-Off Club, 149

Atlantic Coast Conference (ACC), 227

Au Sable Canoe Marathon, 499

Auerbach, Ann Hagedon, 337

Auerbach, Red, 100, 114, 120-121, 130, 337

Augusta National, 257, 261-262, 270, 274

Augustana College, 230

Austin, Tracy, 455, 457, 463

Australia II, 508

Australian Rules Football, 513

Australian Open, 444-45, 448-450, 454, 456, 458, 459, 464-465

Auto Racing, 1-5, 7, 9, 11-13, 15-17, 19, 21, 23, 25, 27, 29, 158

Automobile Club of America, 1

Avco Cup, 320

Avco Financial Services, 320

Axe, 247

Axel, 169, 407

Ayres, 347

Azinger, Paul, 267

Azteca Stadium, 418

B

back door play, 94

back-set, 483

backpacking, 510

backstroke, 369-370, 372

"Bad Boys," 119-120

Badminton, 357, 359-360, 467

Bagwell, Jeff, 64

Bailey, Donovan, 381

Bailey, Jerry, 333

Bailey, Robert, 222

Baja 500, 5

Baker, Buck, 22

Baker, Buddy, 22, 24

Baker, Frank "Home Run", 34, 78

Chase, Chris, 482

Cheeks, Maurice, 102

Cheevers, Gerry, 320

Chelios, Chris, 292, 329

Chen, T.C., 258

Chesbro, Jack, 51

chest protector, 40

Chevrolet Monte Carlo, 17

Chiba Lotte Marines, 512

Chicago Bears, 186-188, 199, 201-202, 204-205, 207, 210, 218, 221

Chicago Black Hawks, 276, 278, 290, 298, 305, 308

Chicago Bulls, 97-98, 103, 118, 120, 122

Chicago College All-Star Football Game, 69

Chicago Cubs, 36, 41, 49-50, 54, 60, 62, 66, 76

Chicago Golf Club, 254

Chicago Packers, 97

Chicago Stadium, 188

Chicago Tribune, 68

Chicago White Sox, 34, 41, 43, 48-49, 54, 58, 61, 72, 75-76, 82, 86, 99

chicane, 4

Chief Bromden, 103

Chilavert, Jose Luis, 429

Childress, Richard, 20

chole, 251

Chouinard, Yvon, 503

Christian, Frank, 24

Christian, Sarah, 24

Christy, Barrett, 494

Christy, Earl, 193

Chunichi Dragons, 512

Churchill Downs, 344-345

Cicotte, Eddie, 48

Cigar, 333-334

Cincinnati Bengals, 201-202

Cincinnati Cyclones, 319

Cincinnati Reds, 41, 46-49, 56, 60-61, 67, 74-75

Cincinnati Red Stockings, 32

Cincinnati Royals, 124

Cinergy Field, 41

Citation, 335, 338, 344

City College of New York, 96, 126

Civil Rights Movement, 204

Civil Rights Restoration Act, 486

Civil War, 32, 58, 341, 431

Claiborne Farm, 336-337

Clancy, Eileen, 478

Clancy, King, 287, 309

Clapper, Dit, 292

Clarence Campbell Conference, 315

Clark, Dwight, 195-197

Clarke, Bobby, 290, 316

Clarkson University, 323

Classique Internationale de Canots, 499

Cleary, Bill, 329

Clemens, Roger, 63

Clemente, Roberto, 59-60

Cleveland Browns, 186-187, 200-201, 215, 220-221, 223

Cleveland Cavaliers, 97

Cleveland, Grover, 87

Cleveland Indians, 41, 43, 47, 56-57, 60, 62, 70, 72, 74, 84

Cleveland Pipers, 104, 121

Cleveland Rams, 181, 189, 223

Clifton, Sweetwater, 91-92

Cline, Tim, 151

Clinton, Bill, 166, 512

clipping, 183, 236

closer, 35, 38-40, 48, 62, 414, 505

Clyde, David, 47

CNN-SI, 137

Coach of the Year, 121-122, 151

Cobb, Randall "Tex", 177

Cobb, Ty, 58, 66

Coca-Cola 600, 15-16

Cochet, Henre, 450

Cockell, Don, 167

Codex, 336-337

Coe College, 243

Coe, Sebastian, 381, 384, 387

Coffey, Joe, 248

Coffey, Paul, 291

Coflexip, 496

Cojocaru, Cristina, 388

Colgate Dinah Shore Tournament, 255

College Basketball, 93, 96, 112, 125-127, 130, 132-134, 137, 139-140, 144, 150-151, 154, 270

College Football, 215, 217, 224, 226-227, 231, 235, 237, 239, 241-248

College Football Hall of Fame, 248

College World Series, 80-81

Collins, Bud, 442

Collins, Eddie, 78, 173, 442, 497

Collins, John, 497

Collins, Mike, 173

collusion, 78

Colonel Bogey, 257

Colonial Affair, 338

color line, 47, 70-71, 73-74, 91

Colorado Avalanche, 294, 302

Colorado College, 323, 326-328

Colorado Rockies, 41, 64, 66

Columbia Auditorium, 163

Columbia Broadcasting System (CBS), 25, 191

Columbia Marching Band, 248

Columbia space shuttle, 317

Columbia University, 127, 163, 179-180, 225, 246, 248, 277, 317, 417, 513

Columbus Quest, 76, 82

Comaneci, Nadia, 374-378

Combined, 322, 399

Combs, Earl, 83

Comiskey, Charles, 41, 49, 68-69

Comiskey Park, 41, 68-69

E

Fittipaldi, Emerson, 9
Fitzsimmons, J.E., 334
fixed fights, 172
Flamingo, 425
Flanagan, John, 328, 392
Flanagan, Terry, 328
Flatwater Events, 364
Fleck, Peter, 493
Fleming, Peggy, 511
Flemington Racetrack, 343
Fletcher, Ken, 459
Flo Hyman Memorial Award, 486
Flock, Bob, 22, 24
Flock, Fonty, 22
Flock, Tim, 22
Flood, Curt, 76
Floor Exercise, 375-376, 378
Florence State University (Alabama), 136-137
Florida Marlins, 41, 57, 78
Florida Southern, 81
Florida State University, 143, 227-229, 233
Florine, Hans, 494
Fluminense, 425
Flushing Meadow, 449, 459
Flutie, Doug, 225
Flying Dutchman, 363
Flynn, William, 262
foal, 332, 337
foil, 360-361
Follis, Charles W., 208
Fontaine, Just, 421
Fontana, Barbra, 489
Foolish Pleasure, 343
Football, 69, 87, 116, 126, 157-158, 179-183, 185-189, 191-193, 195, 197, 199, 201, 203, 205-211, 213-227, 229-231, 233, 235, 237, 239-249, 252, 322, 326, 406, 413, 421-424, 426, 513
Football Writers Association of America, 231
Foote, Arthur, 321
Force, John, 28

force out, 50
Ford, Henry, 1-2, 297
Ford, Wanda, 154
Fordham University, 231
Foreman, George, 161-164, 166-167, 169, 175
Forest Hills, 448, 459, 464
forfeited game, 42-43
Forgan, Robert, 259
Formula Atlantic, 4
Formula Ford, 4
Formula One (F1), 3-4, 7-11, 13, 17, 19
Formula Renault, 4
Formula Three (F3), 3-4
Formula Two (F2), 3-4
Fort Sumter, 58
Fort Wayne Pistons, 98
forward pass, 180-181, 240
forward (soccer), 414, 417, 422, 426, 428
470 Class, 363
Fosbury, Dick, 390
Fosbury Flop, 390
Foster, Rube, 74
Foster, Willie, 74
Foudy, Julie, 430
fouls, 89-90, 93-95, 100, 102, 108, 119, 137, 156, 184, 413-414
Four Horsemen, 241
Fouts, Dan, 215
Fox, Billy, 173
Fox, Richard Kyle, 161
Foyt, A.J., 13, 26-27
France, Bill Sr., 16
Frances Pomeroy Naismith Award, 149
Francis, Clarence "Bevo", 127-128, 265
Franck, Daniel, 494
Frank J. Selke Trophy, 287
Frankenstein, 467
Frazee, Harry, 78
Frazier, Joe, 100, 102, 163-165, 167, 367

Frazier, Walt, 100, 102, 163-165, 167, 367
free agency, 76-78
free ball, 475
Free House, 345
free throw, 92, 94-95, 104, 110, 137
Freeman, Bruce, 234
freestyle, 369-373, 389, 399, 403-404
Freestyle Skiing, 399
"French Connection" Line, 298
French Open, 443-445, 455, 457-458, 463-465
Friedrich, Heike, 370
friendly, 416
fuel cell, 6
Fukuoka Daiei Hawks, 512
Fulks, Joe, 96
Funny Cars, 28
Fuqua, John, 195, 194-195
furlong, 332
Furman University, 128

G

Gabron-Brille, 1
Gaedel, Eddie, 46, 83
Gaertner, Jeannie, 477
Gage, Jody, 316
Gagnon, Marc, 412
Gainer, Jay, 68
Galarraga, Andres, 66
Gall, Dave, 340
Gallant Fox, 334, 344
Galvin, Pud, 61
Game Misconduct penalty, 325, 396
Gandil, Chick, 48
Garlits, Don, 29
Garreau, Jacqueline, 507
Gasiorek, Wieslaw, 446
Gate Dancer, 335
Gator Bowl, 238
Gatto, Vic, 234
Gebrselassie, Haile, 381

Groza, Alex, 139
Grubb, Barbara, 478
Gugelmin, Mauricio, 11
Guidolin, Armand, 305
Gulick, Luther, 89
Guseva, Klara, 412
Guthrie, Janet, 13-14, 24, 511
gutta-percha, 259
Guy, Ray, 204
Guyon, Laurence, 503
Gymnastics, 359, 373-378, 512

H

H-O-R-S-E, 118
Haakonsen, Terje, 491-492
Haase, Helga, 412
Habs, 284, 291, 310, 315-317
Hackensack High School, 127
Haddix, Harvey, 61
Hadl, John, 214
Hagen, Walter, 272, 483
Hagge, Marlene, 255
Hagler, Marvin, 166
Hainsworth, George, 292
hajme, 362
Halas, George, 87, 186, 188, 199, 204
half-pipe, 399-400, 494
Hall, Glenn, 290
Halopoff, Jimmy, 494
Ham, Jack, 202
Hambletonian, 347
Hamilton, Billy, 33
Hamilton, John, 252
Hamilton, Tara, 493
Hamilton Tigers, 300
Hamm, Mia, 429-431
Hammaker, Atlee, 69
hammer throw, 392
Hampden Park, 433
handicap, 256, 263-264, 332
"Hand of God" goal, 422
hands down, 331

"Handsome Eight," 450
hang time, 183
Hanley, Linda, 489
Hannah, John, 202
Hansel, 345
Hansen, Charlie, 173
Hanshin Tigers, 512
Hanson, Beverly, 243, 255
Hanson, Jason, 243
Harbaugh, Jack, 240
Harbaugh, Jim, 240
Harding, Tonya, 410
Harkes, John, 430, 433
Harkness, Jerry, 124
Harlem Globetrotters, 91-92, 150
Harlon Hill Awards Committee, 231
Harness Racing, 346-347
Harper, Derek, 122
Harris, Bucky, 56
Harris, Franco, 195
Harris, Lusia, 153
Hart, Cecil, 286
Hart, David A., 286
Hart Memorial Trophy, 286, 289, 300, 302, 305
Hartel, Lis, 364
Hartford Whalers, 32, 295, 304, 320
Hartley, John, 454
Hartman, Troy, 494
Hartung, Clint, 57
Harvard University, 40, 125, 179, 233-235, 323, 329, 509, 513
Harvey, Doug, 61, 208, 289, 297
Hase, Dagmar, 371
Hasek, Dominik, 398
Haskell Ball, 259
Haskell, Coburn, 259
Hatton, Charles, 344
Havlicek, John, 100, 114, 116, 122
Hawaii Ironman Triathlon, 497-498

Hawk, Tony, 494
Hawkins, Connie, 108, 110
Hayes, Elvin, 100, 238, 382
Hayes, John Joseph, 382
Hayes, Woody, 238
Haynes, Mike, 202
Haywood, Hurley, 3
Haywood, Spencer, 108
Head Races, 509
Heart Like a Wheel, 29
Heath Insured, 500
Hebner, Harry, 369
Heffelfinger, William "Pudge", 185
Heiden, Eric, 411-412
"Heidi" game, 192-193
Hein, Mel, 202
Heinsohn, Tommy, 114, 118
Heinz, Bob, 200
Heisman, John, 246
Heisman Trophy, 87, 209-210, 215, 225, 230-231, 233, 239, 241, 246-248
Heiss, Carol, 408
Held, Franklin, 393
helmet, 6, 181, 191, 206, 286
Helms Foundation, 483
Helsinki Stadium, 384
Henderson, Gerald, 116
Henderson, Paul, 314
Henderson, Rickey, 51
Hendrick, Rick, 19
Hendrick Motorsports, 19
Hendricks, Ted, 202
Hendrix, Johnny, 269
Henie, Sonja, 407-408, 410
Henry, Camille, 286
Henry VIII, 264
Henson, Drew, 87
heptathlon, 154
Herenandez, Willie, 36
Hermann Award, 430-431
Hernandez, Livan, 58
Hernandez, Mireya Luis, 482
Heroic style of design, 260-261
Hewitt, Foster, 277-278

539

University of Washington, 143

University of Wisconsin, 309, 326

University of Wisconsin-La Crosse, 230

Unocal, 17

Unseld, Wes, 100, 102, 105

Unser, Al, 3, 11-13

Unser, Al Jr., 11-12

up and down, 39, 256, 369, 487

Upper Youghiogheny River, 500

Upset, 169, 175, 192, 206, 241, 334, 419, 433, 495

Upshaw, Gene, 202

Uruguay Nacional, 425

USA Basketball, 148

USA Hockey, 398

USA Volleyball, 471

Utah Jazz, 97, 105, 104, 120

Utah Stars, 80, 102, 104, 121

Utah State University, 487

V

Valderrama, Carlos, 430

Valenzuela, Fernando, 83

Valle, Henry, 483

Van Alen, Jimmy, 446

Van Buren, Steve, 202

Van Dyken, Amy, 372, 374

Van Ranst, Cornelius, 341

van Schalkwyk, Theunis, 367

Vancouver Canucks, 298, 304, 316

Vancouver Grizzlies, 97, 123

Vander Meer, Johnny, 60

Vanderbilt Cup, 2

Vandersnick, Lori Endicott, 487

Vardon grip, 257

Vardon, Harry, 257, 265

Vasquez, Jacinto, 336

Vatican, 248

Vaughn, Mo, 74

Vault, 375, 378-379, 508

Veeck, Bill, 43, 46, 74, 82-83

Vendee Globe, 501

Veterans Committee, 59, 70

Veterans Stadium, 41

Vezina, Georges, 287

Vezina Trophy, 284, 286, 290-292, 298

Vicario, Arantxa Sanchez, 463

Victory Bell, 247

Victory Lane, 17

Vietnam, 164

Villanova, 98, 143, 275

Villeneuve, Jacques, 9

Vincent, Troy, 222

Vines, Ellsworth, 453

Virginia Wesleyan College, 181

Vogler, Matt, 242

volleyball, 154, 467-489, 511-512

Volleyball Handbook, 468

Von Hagen, Ron, 483

VRC Melboune Cup, 343

Vukovich, Bill, 13

W

Waara, Jennie, 494

Wade, Margaret, 149

Wade Trophy, 149

Wade, Virginia, 453

Wagner, Honus, 58, 80

Waikiki Rough Water Swim, 497

waiver, 183-184

wakeboarding, 493

Walcott, "Jersey" Joe, 167-168, 177

Waldo, Carolyn, 373

Walker, Chet, 116

Walker Cup, 265

Walker, Doak, 215

Walker, Hershel, 222-223

Walker, Larry, 64

Walker, Moses Fleetwood, 70

Walker, Welday, 70

Wallace, Kenny, 22

Wallace, Mike, 23

Wallace, Rusty, 17

Walter Kennedy Citizenship Award, 105

Walton, Bill, 105, 118, 139, 141

Waltrip, Darrell, 17, 20-22

Waltrip, Michael, 22

Wambsganss, Bill, 54

War Admiral, 335, 344

Ward, Arch, 68

Ward, Jane, 477

Ward, Jem, 173

Ward, Jim, 483

Ward, Tim, 493

Warfield, Paul, 200

Warner, Pop, 241

Washington & Jefferson, 229

Washington Bullets, 97-98

Washington Redskins, 181, 189, 199-202, 204-206, 211, 220-221, 223, 243

Washington Senators, 33, 56, 66, 81

Washington State University, 229, 243-244

Washington Wizards, 97

Waterfield, Bob, 189

waterskiing, 493

Watson, Robert, 265

Watson, Steve, 196

Weah, George, 429

Weatherspoon, Teresa, 151

Weaver, Buck, 48

Webb, Karrie, 266

Webb, Spud, 124

Webber, Chris, 134

Webster, Mike, 202

weight classes/divisions, 157-158, 161, 163

Weiler, William, 426

Weingartner, Hermann, 359

Weiskopf, Tom, 270

Weiss, Walt, 83

Weissmuller, Johnny, 372

Welch, Raquel, 207

World Cup, 391, 415, 417-426, 428-433, 482, 486, 503

World Hockey Association (WHA), 279, 289, 305, 320-321

World Series, 9, 12, 16, 24, 32, 34, 36-37, 40, 48-58, 72, 75, 80-81, 83-84, 87, 98, 103, 105, 114, 116, 124, 185-187, 191-192, 194, 235, 248, 278, 298, 303, 308, 311, 314, 320-321, 347, 349, 364, 375, 391, 397, 404, 406, 424-425, 446, 485, 509-510, 512

World Series of Profession Football, 185

World Triathlon Championship, 512

World War I, 34, 181, 265, 322, 351, 357, 468

World War II, 11, 36, 69, 140, 172, 177, 181, 223, 255, 281, 291, 314, 358, 431, 507

Worley, Al, 245

Wortham, Jimmy, 483

Worthy, James, 106, 116, 132, 144

Worthy, James, 106, 116, 132, 144

Wright, Mickey, 74, 255, 268-269, 335, 367

Wright, Wild Bill, 74

Wright, John, 367

Wright, Warren, 335

Wrigley Field, 33, 41, 186, 188

Wrigley, Philip K., 36

Wynalda, Eric, 426, 430

Y

Yakult Swallows, 512

Yakusha, Vasily, 363

Yale University, 125, 179, 185, 233-234, 321, 323, 509, 513

Yamaguchi, Kristi, 408-409

Yankee Stadium, 41, 51, 74, 86, 172

Yarborough, Cale, 16-17, 25-26

Yarborough, Lee Roy, 16-17, 25-26

Yardley, George, 120

Yashin, Lev, 428

Yastrzemski, Carl, 63, 87

Yates, Robert, 20

Yeager, Steve, 40

yellow card, 413-414

Yellow Sunday, 310

Yepremian, Garo, 194, 201

YMCA League, 91, 96

Yokahama BayStars, 512

Yomiuri Giants, 512

Yong, Zhuang, 370

Yonkers Trot, 347

Young, Cy, 58, 61

Young Men's Christian Association (YMCA), 89-91, 96, 185, 467-468, 483

Young, Steve, 210-211

Youngstown State, 230

Yount, Robin, 69

Z

Yugoslav Tennis Federation, 452

Yurchenko, 375

Zaharias, Babe, 255, 270

Zaharias, George, 270

Zale, Tony, 174, 177

Zamboni, Frank, 315

Zamboni machine, 315

Zanardi, Alex, 12

Zarate, Carlos, 166

Zbel, Roger, 500

Zegalo, Mario, 419

Zev, 345

Zheng, Haixia, 151

Zmuda, Wladyslaw, 421

zone commission, 96